PROCESS THEOLOGY

edited by
EWERT H. COUSINS

PROCESS THEOLOGY
basic writings

NEWMAN PRESS
New York   Paramus   Toronto

ACKNOWLEDGMENTS

Process Thought: A Contemporary Trend in Theology by W. Norman Pittenger: From "A Contemporary Trend in North American Theology: Process-Thought and Christian Faith," *The Expository Times,* 76 (1965), 268-273. Reprinted by permission of T. & T. Clark, Edinburgh.

Faith and the Formative Imagery of Our Time by Bernard E. Meland: From *The Realities of Faith: The Revolution in Cultural Forms* (New York: Oxford University Press, 1962, pp. 76-79; 85-87; 91-95. Reprinted by permission of the author.

The Development of Process Philosophy by Charles Hartshorne: From *Philosophers of Process,* Preface by Douglas Browning and Introduction by Charles Hartshorne. Copyright © 1965 by Random House, Inc. Reprinted by permission of publisher.

Whitehead's Method of Empirical Analysis by Bernard Loomer: From "The Theological Significance of the Method of Empirical Analysis in the Philosophy of A. N. Whitehead" (Ph.D. dissertation, Divinity School, The University of Chicago, 1942), pp. 369-387. Reprinted by permission.

God and the World by Alfred North Whitehead: Reprinted with permission of The Macmillan Company from *Process and Reality: An Essay in Cosmology* by Alfred North Whitehead. Copyright 1929 by The Macmillan Company, renewal 1957 by Evelyn Whitehead.

Philosophical and Religious Uses of 'God' by Charles Hartshorne: From *A Natural Theology of Our Time* (LaSalle, Ill.: The Open Court Publishing Co.), pp. 1-28. Reprinted by permission.

The Reality of God by Schubert M. Ogden: From *The Reality of God and Other Essays* (New York: Harper and Row, 1966), pp. 56-70. Copyright © 1966 by Schubert M. Ogden. Reprinted by permission of Harper & Row, Publishers, Inc.

The World and God by John B. Cobb, Jr.: From *God and the World* by John B. Cobb, Jr. Copyright © MCMLXIX, The Westminster Press. Used by permission.

God and Man by Daniel Day Williams: From *The Spirit and the Forms of Love* by Daniel Day Williams (New York: Harper & Row, 1968), pp. 130-141. Reprinted by permission of Harper & Row, Publishers, Inc.

The New Creation by Bernard E. Meland: From *The Realities of Faith: The Revolution in Culture Forms* (New York: Oxford University Press, 1962), pp. 256-266. Reprinted by permission of the author.

Bernard E. Meland, Process Thought and the Significance of Christ by W. Norman Pittenger: From *Religion in Life,* 37 (1968), 540-550. Reprinted by permission.

The Human Predicament by Henry Nelson Wieman: From *The Source of Human Good* by Henry N. Wieman. Copyright © 1946 by Southern Illinois University Press. Reprinted by permission of Southern Illinois University Press.

Teilhard de Chardin and the Orientation of Evolution: A Critical Essay by Theodosius Dobzhansky: From *Zygon, Journal of Religion and Science,* 3 (1968), 242-258. © 1968 by the University of Chicago. All rights reserved. Reprinted by permission.

My Universe by Pierre Teilhard de Chardin: From *Science and Christ* by Pierre Teilhard de Chardin (pp. 54-60), translated from the French by René Hague. Copyright © 1965 by Editions du Seuil. Copyright © 1968 in the English Translation by William Collins & Co., Ltd., London, and Harper & Row, Publishers, Inc., New York. Reprinted by permission of Harper & Row, Publishers, Inc.

The Cosmic Christ by Henri de Lubac: From *Teilhard Explained,* trans. Anthony Buono (New York: Paulist Press, 1968), pp. 14-21. Reprinted by permission.

Cosmology and Christology by N. M. Wildiers: From *An Introduction to Teilhard de Chardin* by N. M. Wildiers (pp 130-141). Copyright Translation © 1968 by William Collins & Sons Ltd., London. Reprinted by permission of Harper & Row, Publishers, Inc.

The Problem of Evil in Teilhard's Thought by Georges Crespy (pp. 96-113). Translated by George H. Shriver. English Translation Copyright © 1968 by Abingdon Press. Reprinted by permission.

Teilhard de Chardin and Christian Spirituality by Christopher F. Mooney: From *Thought* 42 (1967), 383-402. Reprinted by permission.

Teilhard's Process Metaphysics by Ian G. Barbour; From *The Journal of Religion* 49 (1969), 136-159. © 1969 by The University of Chicago. All rights reserved. Reprinted by permission.

Contents

v

PART FOUR

TEILHARD–EVOLUTION AND CHRISTIAN BELIEF

APPENDIX

TEILHARD AND WHITEHEAD

Preface

This volume is designed to orient the reader into a major movement in contemporary theology. The selections are chosen from American process theology, derived from Alfred North Whitehead, and from writings on the evolutionary world view of Pierre Teilhard de Chardin. Why these two schools of thought are brought together under the same cover and under the general title of Process Theology is explained in our introduction.

The book is planned with an eye to the needs of the college student interested in contemporary theology. Selections have been chosen which orient the reader into the central issues and the major thinkers of process theology. In general, the selections reflect an author's chief area of concern and his personal contribution. In addition to general orientation, the pieces contain explanations of many of the basic concepts of process thought. Both American process theology and Teilhardian thought have a highly technical side. This book is not designed to explore the technical dimensions directly, although they are touched frequently in the selections. After each piece, however, rather extensive readings are suggested in order to provide ample direction in both technical depth and broad scope in the area treated by the selection. It is hoped that these suggested readings and the bibliography at the end of the volume will adequately guide those who are engaged in research projects of a more specialized nature. Thus it is hoped that the book will be of value both to the beginner and to the advanced student in process thought.

As a practical aid, paperback editions have been noted in cases where they were listed in current catalogs of paperbacks in print. Where the volume appears only in paperback and is listed in current catalogs, this is indicated by the single term 'paperback' after the publishing data.

It is impossible to express my thanks to each person who helped in organizing this volume. Special gratitude is due to Daniel Day Williams and Bernard E. Meland for their extended discus-

1

sions of process theology and their specific suggestions on the volume. I am likewise indebted to Delwin Brown, Lewis Ford, and Robert Neville for detailed comments on the content and structure of the book; and to George Allan and the Society for the Study of Process Philosophies for assistance in obtaining valuable material.

Gratitude is due to my many friends in the American Teilhard de Chardin Association, especially to Theodosius Dobzhansky, Robert Francoeur, Father Romano Almagno, O.F.M., Mrs. Paul Cassard, Pieter de Jong, Jean Houston, Philip Hefner, Donald Gray, and Alfred Stiernotte. For discussion through the years and advice in the area of Teilhardian studies, I owe a special debt of gratitude to my former colleague and chairman at Fordham University, Father Christopher Mooney, S.J.

I am indebted to the graduate students of the Fordham Theology Department who assisted in many ways, particularly in compiling the bibliography: Christa Betty, Mary Rattigan, Stephen Greenfield, Joseph Hallman, and Father Robert Hale, O.S.B., Cam.

I would like to express my thanks to Father Kevin Lynch, C.S.P., and to the staff of the Paulist/Newman Press for their encouragement and assistance throughout the project.

Finally, I would like to express my gratitude to my wife for her work on the manuscript and for her patience and assistance in so many incalculable ways.

EWERT H. COUSINS
Fordham University

introduction | Process Models in Culture, Philosophy, and Theology

EWERT H. COUSINS

Modern man senses the dynamism of nature, the reality of time and the possibility of novelty. Out of this experience the process vision has emerged. It was nurtured by the revolution in the scientific world view: through Darwin's theory of evolution and Einstein's theory of relativity. It was formulated by philosophers in the nineteenth and twentieth centuries. Through Alfred North Whitehead and Pierre Teilhard de Chardin it is having an increasing influence on contemporary Christian theology. The selections in this volume present the vision of process theology as it articulates with new vigor and relevance the Christian doctrine of God's involvement in the world, the primacy of love and the relation of Christ to the universe.

In analyzing the impact of culture on theology, we could easily conclude that the two major forces shaping theology in the twentieth century have been war and science. The first World War shattered the optimism of the nineteenth century, with its faith in progress and in the inevitable moral improvement of mankind. The tragedy of four years of war created a mood of disillusionment, pessimism and despair. The world witnessed the dark side of human nature—with its hate and destructiveness—and experienced in a new way the absurdity of the human situation. Millions died in the meaningless impasse of trench warfare. Nations bogged down in attempts to extricate

3

themselves from the entanglements of war. Twentieth century man profoundly felt anxiety in the face of death and the futility of human endeavor. Out of this mood emerged the neo-orthodox theology of Karl Barth, Rudolf Bultmann, Paul Tillich, and others in the post-war era. Nourished by philosophical existentialism, neo-orthodoxy emphasized the sinfulness of man and the tragic character of human existence. The rise of Nazism and the second World War intensified the mood of anxiety and confirmed the position of neo-orthodoxy as the dominant movement in European and American theology in the first half of the twentieth century.

The second major force shaping twentieth century theology has been the revolution in the scientific world view. The revolution occurred in successive stages in two different scientific fields: in biology as a result of Darwin's theory of evolution and in physics as a result of Einstein's theory of relativity. The static world of fixed species was transformed by the notion of dynamically developing forms of life. One of the truly seminal ideas of modern times, the concept of evolution spread throughout the sciences to the realm of physics, chemistry, psychology, and the social sciences. A further change occurred in the early twentieth century when the mechanistic world view of Newtonian physics was transformed by Einstein's theory of relativity and the subsequent development of quantum mechanics and field theory. The Newtonian vision depicted the world as a machine, with discrete objects in abstract space interacting according to mechanical laws. Instead, the new physics looked upon the subatomic world as a flux of energy and a network of relations. In both Darwin's theory of evolution and Einstein's theory of relativity, time was taken seriously as a dimension of reality.

While the impact of the two World Wars was immediate, the influence of the scientific revolutions has been much slower to manifest itself in twentieth century theology. The notion of evolution had influenced the liberal theology of the late nineteenth century. Continuing into the twentieth century, this influence converged with that of the new physics and has gained considerable force in the last fifteen years, for example, in the process theology derived from the metaphysics of Alfred North Whitehead and in the theology formulated within the evolutionary vision of Pierre Teilhard de Chardin. Both Whitehead and Teilhard were scientists whose thought was nurtured by their scientific milieu, specifically by the revolutions in physics and biology. After a career as an eminent mathematician, Whitehead spent the last phase of his life elaborating a metaphysics that harmonized with the new science. It is this metaphysics that lies at the basis of American process theology. In another wing of the scientific community, Teilhard as a geologist spent much of his professional life on expeditions in search of man's prehistory. Deeply influenced by the notion of evolution in biology, Teilhard made it the basic model of his comprehensive vision, extending it to include the inorganic realm and the sphere of human culture. In terms of this evolutionary model he reinterpreted the basic tenets of Christian theology.

The shift in scientific models should be seen in the larger context of a shift in experience in our culture as a whole. The relation between scientific models, culture, and theology is a recurrent theme among process theologians. No one has explored this theme more consistently and in greater depth than Bernard E. Meland. In selecting material for this present volume, we have chosen a piece in which Meland gives a general statement of his position. In this selection, entitled "Faith and the Formative Imagery of Our Time," Meland claims that the thinking of a people moves within a set of images that illumine the meaning of terms and set limits to their understanding. This imagery is bound up with their life experience, the sensibilities of the age, and scientific constructs. Meland observes that we are in the midst of a change out of which new metaphors, peculiar to our time, are forming. In this process, not merely our imagery but our experience is undergoing change. He traces the shift in the scientific world view from Newtonian mechanism to twentieth century science and into the cultural ethos of the atom bomb and space travel. In a similar vein, throughout his writing Teilhard de Chardin traces the impact of cultural forces—of industrialization, technology, communications, and the expansion and convergence of world population—on the shaping of the consciousness of our time.

From this perspective, we can observe that the revolution in experience reflects the revolution in the scientific world view. The network of relations—depicted in the scientific models of the subatomic world—is now being experienced by mankind on the global and collective level. Industrialization and technology have produced a communications network that encircles the earth and now extends into outer space. Television makes us immediate participators in the most distant events. Electronic media bring diverse cultures—once alien and exotic—into our own life-world. Historical research has made the past, even primitive and prehistoric experience, part of our own continuous memory. Our environment is saturated with information, and computers are putting the most complex data at our fingertips. Although these forces often tend to depersonalization and although many feel a deep isolation and alienation in the contemporary world, others are aware of the emergence of a new sense of organic unity in mankind and nature: the sense of a single species living in a multi-dimensional environment. No longer does their collective experience mirror the atomistic model of radically separate units floating in the void and interacting only externally through mechanical forces. Instead, they feel a growing awareness of internally experienced relations which enhance their individuality while relating them to the whole.

In addition, there is a growing awareness of human energy and creativity. Through science man has entered into a deeper relation with nature, discovering not only the structures of the universe but ways of tapping its power—both creatively and destructively. In our age, we have witnessed a burst of creative energy in the explorations of space and in the advance in medicine. But we have been shocked by the destructiveness of the atom bomb and the pollution of our environment. The more deeply man penetrates nature, the more he realizes the ambiguity of nature's power and his own responsibility for himself and his future. He can no longer be a mere spectator of nature's processes, nor can he see nature merely as the stage on which he acts out his history. Nature itself has become part of the drama. The unfolding of the drama will be tragic or not in relation to man's ability to act intelligently with nature's energy. Since the human community is becoming organically interrelated, man must solve his problems as a single species and in the context of a total system. In this way, mankind's interrelatedness is bound up with the growing availability of energy and the possibilities of creativity.

Man's increasing involvement in nature and history has heightened his awareness of time, change, and the dynamic character of reality. To twentieth century man, the world is clearly not static. Movement and novelty are too intimately a part of his experience to be ignored or treated lightly. Having been plunged into the process, he senses its reality and searches for an understanding of its dynamics. For him time is not an illusion, but a reality; it is not merely the image of eternity, but has a value and consistency of its own. Change does not involve merely an eternal return of a pre-established pattern, but the emergence of genuine novelty.

In the more static cultures of the past, one could live his entire life without experiencing anything new which he had not learned from his past tradition. Of course, he would be aware of change, but only in the sense of recurrent patterns, such as the cycle of the seasons or of life and death. In such an environment, he could easily feel there is nothing new under the sun. At the most, he might look back to a golden age, to 'the good old days' when things were much better than at present, and decry the fact that the change which occurred before his time was indeed a change for the worse. In the twentieth century, however, change and novelty are part of the rhythm of life. Modern man has witnessed the proliferation of new tools and inventions that have transformed his experience and his life style; he has observed developments in culture that have no counterpart in the past; and he can look forward to a future which holds open the possibility of even more startling novelty. Whitehead has described the contemporary experience very graphically: "In the past human life was lived in a bullock cart; in the future it will be lived in an aeroplane; and the change of speed amounts to a difference in quality." [1]

This shift in experience coincides with the development of philosophies of process. Since the nineteenth century, philosophers have taken up with concerted seriousness the themes of becoming, relation, and novelty. In the present volume, Charles Hartshorne describes the nature of process philosophies and traces their history in the selection entitled "The Development of Process Philosophies." As he observes, philosophies of process—understood in a broad sense—are not new but existed in ancient times in both East and West. The Buddhist tradition, especially in its Theravada form, denied a static substance underlying the flux of experience and affirmed the primacy of becoming and interrelatedness. At

[1] Alfred North Whitehead, *Science and the Modern World* (New York: Macmillan, 1925), p. 142.

the dawn of Western philosophy, Heraclitus stated that all things are in flux and left in his fragments enigmatic statements of process themes. However, he was overshadowed by the mainstream of Greek philosophy, which since the time of Parmenides affirmed the primacy of being over becoming and of absoluteness over relativity. The tension between being and becoming has persisted throughout Western thought. Although the Christian doctrines of the Trinity and Incarnation favor the dynamic and relational view, they were often interpreted in static terms and subordinated to the notion of God as unmoved mover and timeless absolute.

Submerged throughout much of Western history, process themes surfaced in the nineteenth century with increasing sharpness and impact. Hegel elaborated a comprehensive vision of the dynamic unfolding of history, which Marx transformed into a dialectic materialism. In contrast to the rationalism of continental thought, Americans such as Charles Sanders Peirce, William James, and John Dewey developed process themes in the context of an experiential, empirical pragmatism. Alfred North Whitehead combined both rationalistic and empirical elements in his philosophy of organism. While Hartshorne's selection, mentioned above, presents the more rationalistic side of Whitehead's process philosophy, the empirical side is explored in the selection by Bernard M. Loomer on "Whitehead's Method of Empirical Analysis." Loomer concludes that Whitehead is a speculative or a rational empiricist. The dynamic evolutionary aspect of process thought was developed by Henri Bergson in France and by the emergent evolutionists Samuel Alexander and C. Lloyd Morgan in Britain. The model of evolution became the basis of the theologies of William Temple and Lionel Thornton, and more recently for the elaborated cosmological-theological vision of Teilhard de Chardin.

Taken in its broadest sense, the term 'process' can refer to all the thinkers and traditions listed above, from the Buddhists to Teilhard, even though there is considerable difference among them. At times the term is limited to the development in the nineteenth century from Hegel to the present. At other times it is restricted to the thinkers of the late nineteenth and the twentieth century: Peirce, James, Dewey, Whitehead, Bergson, and the emergent evolutionists. At other times it is applied exclusively to the thought of Alfred North Whitehead and the movement that has derived directly from him.

In using the term 'process' in the title of this volume, we intend it to convey three senses which can be looked upon as ever widening circles. First, the selections in Parts I-III reflect the most restricted sense of process: i.e., the tradition that takes its source in Whitehead. All of the authors here have been substantially influenced by Whitehead: Hartshorne, Meland, Loomer, Williams, Ogden, Cobb, Stokes, Pittenger, and Wieman. The position of Wieman, however, is complex. He was instrumental in bringing Whitehead's thought to the University of Chicago, where it took root; and he himself was under Whitehead's influence for a time. But he later rejected Whitehead's metaphysical superstructure, while remaining committed to process thought of a more Bergsonian than Whiteheadian character. The others show, in varying degrees, the continued influence of Whitehead and align themselves with the on-going theological movement derived from him.

The final section of the book, Part IV, implies a broader understanding of the term 'process' since it includes selections on Teilhard de Chardin, whose thought developed quite independently of Whitehead and American process theology. Yet Teilhard can be considered a process thinker both in terms of the content and the context of his thought. He emphasizes dynamism and becoming; he views the universe as an interrelated organism; and he looks towards the emergence of new possibilities. Since Teilhard's overarching model is that of evolution, he reflects the evolutionary wing of process thought, with antecedents in Morgan, Alexander, Bergson, and Hegel. Teilhard's evolutionary model marks what is perhaps his greatest divergence from Whitehead. For Whitehead the on-going process, which he calls the creative advance, moves through waxing and waning and in an unspecified variety of patterns—not in a cumulative evolution towards a climax. In contrast, Teilhard sees the process moving through successive evolutionary stages in a unilinear upwards development towards a culmination which he calls Omega. In an appendix to this volume, Ian Barbour studies in detail the similarities and differences between Whitehead and Teilhard. In this selection, entitled "Teilhard's Process Metaphysics," Barbour contends that Teilhard is a process thinker who shares many of the philosophical presuppositions of Whitehead, while at the same time differing from him on significant points.

The second and broader sense of process, then, encompasses both the Whiteheadian and Teilhardian traditions. The specific reason for including these two traditions under a single cover is their influence on theology. At the present time—certainly in America—they represent the major influence of process thought on contemporary Christian theology. Since the thirties a substantial body of literature has developed attempting to relate Whitehead's thought to Christian theology. The development of process theology was centered at the University of Chicago, where the work of Wieman, Hartshorne, Meland, Loomer, and Williams provided a solid base for expansion. Two younger theologians educated in this milieu, Cobb and Ogden, have made substantial contributions and have assured the continued development of the movement. More recently a number of younger men have written doctoral dissertations on Whitehead and his followers and have contributed to the growing technical literature in journals.[2] Selections of the literature—covering the earlier phase and more recent technical discussions—have been made available in an anthology of Whiteheadian process theology.[3] Interest has been sustained by the formation of the Society for the Study of Process Philosophies [4] and the founding, by John Cobb and Lewis Ford, of the journal *Process Studies,*[5] which in addition to original articles publishes abstracts of articles on process themes printed elsewhere. Although the movement has been confined chiefly to Protestant circles, there has been a growing interest on the part of Catholics, as is witnessed by the work of Walter Stokes, who before his premature death in 1969, had begun to explore the thought of Augustine and Thomas in the light of process themes. Geographically the movement has spread, with members of the original Chicago circle now teaching in New York, California, and Texas. After many years in New York, W. Norman

[2] Certain journals have recently devoted issues specially to process themes: cf. *The Christian Scholar,* 50/3 (Fall, 1967) and *Encounter,* 29/2 (Spring, 1968) on process theology; and *The Southern Journal of Philosophy,* 7/4 (Winter, 1969-1970) on Whitehead.

[3] Delwin Brown, Ralph E. James, Jr. and Gene Reeves (eds.), *Process Philosophy and Christian Thought* (Indianapolis: Bobbs-Merrill, 1971).

[4] Society for the Study of Process Philosophies, George Allan, Department of Philosophy, Dickinson College, Carlisle, Penna. 17013.

[5] *Process Studies,* Foothill Blvd. at College Ave., Claremont, Calif. 91711.

Pittenger moved to England, where his lecturing and writing stimulated interest in the movement. With a solid base and growing momentum, Whiteheadian process theology gives promise of continued development and influence.

The Teilhardian influence on theology is much more recent. Since Teilhard was prohibited from publishing anything but his strictly scientific treatises, his widespread influence has been delayed until after his death in 1955. A group of scientists and scholars formed a committee to publish his manuscripts in French. Translations followed, along with a steady stream of literature that has mounted to a rising tide—expositions, critical evaluations, polemical attacks and defenses, popular introductions, scientific analyses and doctoral dissertations. Throughout the world discussion groups have been formed and conferences held on the wide spectrum of his thought ranging from science to theology. In more than ten countries, associations have been organized to study his thought and its implications. The American Teilhard de Chardin Association has sponsored conferences, lectures, and study groups.[6] *The Teilhard Review,* published by the British organization, is one of several journals on Teilhard that are appearing in various countries.[7]

Teilhard's ideas have attracted the attention of both Catholic and Protestant theologians and have had an influence in technical theological circles. A number of specialists have studied his thought by analyzing its structure, situating it in history and evaluating it against theological norms. Others have expanded his ideas within the framework of his vision to areas he had not explored. Still others have used his thought as a point of departure for their original speculation. In the larger church community his influence is more difficult to assess. His ideas have filtered into the general religious ethos and have shaped the thinking of many churchmen and laymen on the relation of religion and culture, science and theology, Christ and the cosmos, human action and the Christian ideal. In a fashion impossible to chart with precision, Teilhard's thought played a role in the changes in the Catholic community surrounding and following Vatican II. His humanistic spirit can

---

[6] American Teilhard de Chardin Association, 157 E. 72nd St., New York, N.Y. 10021.

[7] *The Teilhard Review,* 3 Cromwell Place, London S.W. 7.

be discerned in the council documents on the Church and the world and in the ecumenical atmosphere engendered by the council. At a time when Catholics radically criticized their theological tradition and the neo-Thomism of the twentieth century, many found intellectual support in Teilhard's vision. On the broader scene, now that some of the initial enthusiasm and polemic have subsided and the body of technical-critical literature is increasing, there is reason to think that Teilhard's thought will have a sustained influence on theology.

The influence of Whitehead and Teilhard on contemporary theology leads us into the third and broadest sense of the term 'process.' One can look upon the visions of Whitehead and Teilhard as systems to be studied in their inner structure and coherence. Or one may look upon them as giving a specific expression at the present time of the broad process themes described above. Thus both Whitehead's and Teilhard's system would be seen, each in its own way, reflecting the larger process tradition. There is some concrete basis for this position, since there are clearly discernible and acknowledged interconnections between James and Whitehead, Bergson and Teilhard, and between Hegel and the entire evolutionary tradition. From this point of view, the title of this volume, *Process Theology,* along with its contents, would suggest that the Whiteheadian and Teilhardian traditions are channels through which the broader process themes are flowing into Christian theology at the present time.

What themes in Christian theology have come under the influence of process thought? Or from another point of view: What resources has process thought offered for a contemporary reformulation of the Christian message? In the first selection in this volume, entitled "Process Thought: A Contemporary Trend in Theology," W. Norman Pittenger sketches an overview of process theology and examines some of these themes and resources. He cites the theme of God as dynamic and intimately related to the world. The Christian God is the 'living God' who is related to every aspect of creaturely existence in nature and history. He is related by way of love, not omnipotence, to the on-going creative process of the universe. Jesus is not an intrusion from outside, not the supreme anomaly, but the decisive instance of God's creative, loving presence in the world. These themes, which form the core of the readings in this volume, are explored systematically by the White-headian thinkers in Parts II-III.

The central theme in American process theology is the doc-trine of God and his relation to the world. Because this theme is firmly rooted in Whitehead's doctrine of God, we have included as the first selection of Part II Whitehead's 'classic' presentation of his position. This piece, entitled "God and the World," is the final chapter of his major work *Process and Reality*. In it Whitehead criticizes three notions of God that have been dominant in the Christian tradition: the ruling monarch, in the likeness of Caesar; the ruthless moralist of the Hebrew prophets; and the unmoved mover of Aristotle. In what Whitehead calls the Galilean origins of Christianity, he finds another suggestion: the tender elements in the world which operate by love. Whitehead proceeds to examine the nature of God from the standpoint of metaphysical principles. "God is not to be treated," he says, "as an exception to all meta-physical principles, invoked to save their collapse. He is their chief exemplification." [8] This leads to Whitehead's dipolar conception of the divinity: God has a primordial and a consequent nature. As primordial God is the ground of actuality and "the lure for feeling, the eternal urge of desire." [9] The second aspect of God's nature is consequent upon the creative advance of the world. In the conse-quent nature the world reacts upon God. The world passes into the consequent nature where its values are made available for the on-going process. For Whitehead God "does not create the world, he saves it: or, more accurately, he is the poet of the world, with tender patience leading it by his vision of truth, beauty, and good-ness." [10] The love in the world passes into God and floods back into the world. God is thus "the great companion—the fellow-sufferer who understands." [11] With divine sympathy and redeeming love, God is in the process and the process is in God. According to Whitehead, neither God nor the world reaches static completion; they are both caught up in the creative advance into novelty.

Whitehead's doctrine of God has been explored and developed throughout the extensive writings of Charles Hartshorne. A severe

[8] Alfred North Whitehead, *Process and Reality* (New York: Macmillan, 1929), p. 521.
[9] *Ibid.*, p. 522.
[10] *Ibid.*, p. 526.
[11] *Ibid.*, p. 532.

critic of classical theism, Hartshorne proposes an alternate which he terms 'neo-classical' theism. Classical theism applied to God the Greek notion of perfection, claiming that God is absolutely perfect in all respects and in no way surpassable. In Hartshorne's view, God is perfect in love, in goodness, in the omnipresence and the omnicompetence of his sensitivity to the world. But his perfection must be defined in such a way that it includes the possibility of his self-surpassing experience of new value. This involves some limitations on classical doctrines of perfection, especially on omnipotence. Hartshorne develops a dipolar conception of God which is similar to Whitehead's notion of the primordial and consequent natures. God has an abstract, absolute aspect and a concrete, relative aspect. In the latter aspect God is self-surpassing creativity; he is also eminently social and relative. He is in the world and the world in him. This is conveyed by the term 'pan-en-theism' which expresses the interpenetration of God and the world while at the same time not identifying God with the world. These themes are reflected in Hartshorne's selection in Part II of this volume entitled "Religious and Philosophical Uses of 'God'."

In the selections that follow, the doctrine of God articulated by Whitehead and Hartshorne is explored further by Ogden, Stokes, and Cobb. Each examines human experience to throw light on the nature of God and his relation to the world. Ogden examines the human subject in his relatedness and temporality. As we are related to our bodies, God is related to the world. Stokes examines human freedom and interpersonal relations, and Cobb explores memory as an analogue for thinking of God. Cobb's selection is of special value to the beginning student in Whitehead since it contains a lucid explanation of Whitehead's notion of event, of the nature of sense knowledge, and of the immediate experience of process. While Ogden, Stokes, and Cobb use human experience to understand God, Daniel Williams' selection uses the process framework to understand the Christian doctrine of man. Beginning with the traditional concept of man as created in the image of God, Williams explores the distinctive dimensions that are added when man is considered to bear the image of God in temporality, for God also is temporal on one side of his nature.

Reflected throughout these selections is process theology's critique of the Christian theological tradition—especially Thomas

Aquinas—for separating God and the world. The problem lies in the Greek idea of perfection and in Aristotle's concept of relation. Aristotle views relation as involving change and dependence and hence imperfection. As a result, the Aristotelian-Thomistic school holds that the world can be related to God because it is dependent on him, but God cannot be really related to the world. If he were, then he would be dependent on creation and would not be the unmoved mover required by the Greek idea of perfection. This image of an aloof and distant deity, process thinkers maintain, is supported neither by the experience of human value nor by the testimony of Biblical revelation. These criticisms are expressed in the selections in Part II by Whitehead, Hartshorne, Ogden, and Stokes. However, Stokes takes a different tack from the others by searching out resources within the tradition—in Augustine's notion of freedom and in his Trinitarian theology—for articulating process themes.

Process theologians claim that their Whiteheadian doctrine of God reflects the God of Christian revelation. The process God, they maintain, is closer to the Christian experience and to the Biblical witness than is the timeless Absolute of Greek philosophy. For the Christian God is concerned with the world; he is involved in its suffering and its tragedy. The world, man, and human events make a difference to him. The deepest reality of God is seen not in his detachment or in his power, but in his love. In contrast with the static Absolute and the all-powerful monarch, the process God is the God of persuasive love revealed in Jesus Christ.

Their critics, however, assert that process theologians do not do justice to the transcendence of God, to his power and to his role as Lord of history. Although love is primary in the Christian message, it does not eliminate God's transcendence and power. Furthermore, the particular way in which process theology uses a secular philosophy to explicate the Christian message goes counter to the Christian tradition. Although in the past Augustine employed Platonism and Aquinas Aristotelianism to explore the Christian message, they were aware that Greek philosophy did not completely harmonize with the Christian vision. Hence in a case of conflict they opted for the Christian position and rejected the Greek alternative. The process theologians are accused of doing just the reverse: where Whitehead's philosophy does not coincide with the Christian tradition—as in the case of the transcendence of God—the process theologians follow Whitehead rather than the tradition.[12]

Section III is devoted to Christ and redemption within White-headian process theology. In the literature in this area, the doctrine of Christ has not been explored as thoroughly as the doctrine of God. Whitehead himself did not develop a Christology, but made only occasional observations on Christ. The same is true of Hartshorne. More extended and systematic statements of Christology have been worked out by Bernard E. Meland and Daniel Day Williams. A major development of Christology within process thought has been done by W. Norman Pittenger in his book *The Word Incarnate*, published in 1959, and in his subsequent writings. More recently younger Whiteheadians have published articles on process Christology, taking up special issues and problems, such as the finality of Christ. In the present volume we have included selections by Meland and Pittenger. After the Meland selection, we have added an extensive list of readings on Christology in process theology, covering both the major statements and the recent discussion in the journals. We have concluded the section with a piece by Henry Nelson Wieman dealing with the Christ event. Although Wieman moved away from his early contact with Whitehead, his thought reflects the process tradition, in a broad sense, especially in its empirical aspect.

While the doctrine of God is central in the Whiteheadian tradition and Christology is derivative, the reverse is true with Teilhard. His thought is emphatically Christo-centric. Around the focal point of Christ Teilhard unifies and clarifies all other theological themes. He does not direct his attention to the historical Jesus of Nazareth, but to the cosmic Christ, present in the universe from the least particle of matter to the farthest reach of the human spirit. This cosmic presence of Christ, however, is not static, merely an object of detached contemplation. On the contrary, the cosmic Christ is dynamic, drawing all individuals and the universe as a whole to a creative unity. It is here that Teilhard's vision reveals its distinctive features. He attempts to reformulate Christian belief within an evolving world. He was thoroughly convinced that this

[12] Cf. Langdon Gilkey's review of John Cobb's *A Christian Natural Theology* in *Theology Today*, 22 (1966), 530-545.

was the paramount theological task of our time. Already, he observed, the scientific community had accepted the evolutionary perspective, and men at large were beginning to feel the forces of evolution converging. A cosmic sense was developing spontaneously throughout the world, and the dynamism of evolution was becoming more and more conscious. What does faith mean in such a world? What is the significance of Christ? What task does the Christian have in building the universe and shaping the future? These were the questions Teilhard attempted to answer by developing a system that would integrate into one comprehensive vision the evolutionary perspective of science, the contemporary experience of dynamism and convergence, and faith in Christ.

At the core of Teilhard's vision is the concept of evolution. He extends the notion of biological evolution—derived from Darwin—into the subatomic world and into the sphere of culture and spirituality. He sees the entire universe evolving through successive stages, which he calls spheres: the geosphere, or the realm of inorganic matter; the biosphere, or the realm of life; and the noosphere, or the realm of mind. Evolution is continuing today and even accelerating, not primarily in the biosphere but in the sphere of consciousness. The forces that energized life to evolve into the sphere of consciousness are now drawing mankind together into a unified whole. Throughout the chain of evolution certain universal laws apply. From the subatomic realm to the human community, elements unite to form more complex units. The increase in complexity leads to an increase in interiority, which releases new energy for more complex unions. Subatomic particles unite to form atoms; atoms form molecules; molecules form cells and cells more complicated living organisms until in man consciousness appears. The greater the complexity the greater the consciousness; and the deeper the union, the more creative it is and the more it intensifies the uniqueness of each individual.

Human evolution is moving towards what Teilhard calls planetization. When the human species appeared, groups of men spread over the earth, moving farther apart and developing different cultures. In our time, however, the forces of expansion have taken a dramatic turn towards compression. Because the earth is a sphere, men cannot move endlessly apart. As population expands and communications increase, mankind must converge. A network of communications has encircled the earth. The forces of complexification are leading to an intensification of consciousness, bringing man to the threshold of a breakthrough unprecedented in history—into a new form of planetary consciousness. Since Teilhard's vision is intimately bound up with biological evolution, we have introduced Section IV, on Teilhard, with a selection by Theodosius Dobzhansky, the eminent genetist and theoretician of evolution. Like Teilhard, Dobzhansky has been concerned with the integration of biological evolution and humanistic values. In this piece he comments on Teilhard's notion of evolution both sympathetically and critically.

Evolution moves towards what Teilhard calls Omega, the goal of the process and the source of its energy. He identifies the Omega of evolution with the Christ of revelation, seeing Christ present throughout the cosmos, even in subatomic particles, energizing the process towards its goal of heightened consciousness. The notion of the cosmic Christ, who is also Christ the evolver, is Teilhard's central theological concept. To present this notion, we have chosen a group of texts, first from Teilhard and then from his commentators. In the selection from *My Universe,* Teilhard gives the New Testament basis for his notion of the cosmic Christ and explains his meaning of Christ's physical presence throughout the universe. In the next selection, Henri de Lubac, the historian of Christian doctrine, evaluates the similarities and differences between the Pauline and the Teilhardian concepts of the cosmic Christ. In a selection entitled "Cosmology and Christology," N. M. Wildiers traces the notion of the cosmic Christ in the Scotist school of medieval theology; he then discusses the role evolutionary cosmology plays in Teilhard's theology. Since many have found in Teilhard resources for a spirituality that is both Christian and contemporary, we have included a selection by Christopher Mooney analyzing the relevance of Teilhard's spirituality.

Teilhard's critics have attacked him for submerging the historical Jesus in the cosmic Christ, for subordinating the doctrine of creation to that of evolution and for swallowing up personal freedom in the collectivity. The most consistent critique—and perhaps the most penetrating—has been centered around his treatment of evil. Teilhard's vision has a tone of optimism that does not reflect certain strands of the Christian tradition, with their emphasis on sin, guilt, and the need for atonement. Hence, it is maintained, Teilhard fails to deal adequately with the reality of evil and the traditional doctrines of original sin and redemption. In a selection entitled "The Problem of Evil in Teilhard's Thought," Georges Crespy takes up these criticisms. While indicating inadequacies in Teilhard's treatment, Crespy points out the difficulties inherent in any theology of evil and discusses the specific contributions Teilhard has made in this problematic area.

The book concludes with an appendix by Ian Barbour on the similarities and differences between Teilhard and Whitehead. Both emphasize the process themes of temporality, relatedness, and novelty. Both affirm the involvement of God in the world, Whitehead through his doctrine of the consequent nature of God and Teilhard through his notion of the cosmic Christ. In keeping with the Biblical tradition, both see God active in history; but Whitehead limits God's power more than Teilhard, asserting more unequivocally the freedom of creatures. In line with traditional eschatology, Teilhard believes there will be a consummation of history, although he interprets this as being achieved through the evolutionary process. In contrast, Whitehead holds that time is infinite and there will be no single climax to the process. There may be various cosmic epochs, some with different types of order than we are familiar with.

Process theology, whether derived from Whitehead or Teilhard, offers the Christian fresh perspectives and new resources. It presents the Christian message in a way that harmonizes with contemporary experience and the twentieth century scientific world view. In the last decades much effort has been expended in demythologizing an outdated cosmology from the Biblical message. Rudolf Bultmann has accomplished this by shifting attention from cosmology to the existential subject. After Bultmann's clarification, the contemporary theologian can—by tapping the resources of process thought—once again situate the existential subject within a cosmological setting. Instead of the static cosmology of the past, process theology offers a world view that reflects the dynamic quality of contemporary experience. Furthermore, process theologians claim that this new perspective is more faithful to the content of Biblical revelation than has been the perspective of much of traditional theology. The dynamic, sympathetic God of Christian revelation, who reveals himself as love in the person of Jesus Christ, is less at home in a world of static substances than in the dynamic, related, and novel world of process thought.

.

PART ONE

PROCESS THOUGHT

W. Norman Pittenger
Bernard E. Meland
Charles Hartshorne
Bernard M. Loomer

1 Process Thought: A Contemporary Trend in Theology

W. NORMAN PITTENGER

In the following selection,* W. Norman Pittenger surveys the development of American process theology. After teaching for many years at General Theological Seminary in New York City, Pittenger became a senior resident member of King's College, Cambridge, and lectured widely in England. The present selection was originally delivered as a lecture before the University of Cambridge, November 6, 1964, and later printed in *The Expository Times.* For his British audience Pittenger discusses the leading American process theologians and the central themes of the movement: the nature of God as dynamic and related to the world, the primacy of love in the Christian world view, an integral Christology in which Jesus is seen as the supreme expression of God's presence and love throughout the universe. It is in this latter area that Pittenger has made his personal contribution to process theology, as is indicated in his selection on process Christology, printed below in Part III.

W hen the Faculty Board of Divinity kindly asked me to deliver a public lecture during my stay in Cambridge, I thought at once that my audience might be interested in hearing of current theological move-

* "A Contemporary Trend in North American Theology: Process-Thought and Christian Faith," *The Expository Times,* 76 (1965), 268-273. Reprinted with permission.

ments in the United States and Canada, since the lines of communication in Theology between you in Britain and us in North America are not always as open as they might be. And I was sufficiently immodest to think that the particular movement in which I myself am most involved might be of special interest to you, since very little is heard of it, so far as I can gather, on this side of the Atlantic. I refer to the group of theologians, of several denominational allegiances, who are concerned with what we in North America are now calling—for good or ill—'process-thought', in its relationship to Christian faith and especially in the re-conception of that faith in our own day.

Let me begin by mentioning some names and some books. Among those who in one way or another are associated with this rather loosely-connected group are several theologians whose names and whose books are doubtless familiar to you. First, Professor Daniel Day Williams of Union Seminary in New York, the successor of Paul Tillich in the Chair of Philosophical Theology in that college, and author of *God's Grace and Man's Hope* as well as the little book *Contemporary Theology*. Then, Professor Schubert Ogden of the Perkins School of Theology in Dallas, Texas, whose *Christ without Myth* and whose translations of Bultmann and whose many articles in religious journals, mostly on the German demythologizing controversy, have attracted wide attention. At the University of Chicago Divinity School, Bernard Meland and Bernard Loomer have written several books and essays which deal with the wider philosophical issues of process-thought and Christian faith. In the field of Biblical studies, Professor John Knox of Union Seminary is the leading name among those influenced by this movement, as his recent *Christ and the Reality of the Church* indicates. And if I may mention it, I myself have sought to use process-thought in three books, *Rethinking the Christian Message, The Word Incarnate,* and *The Christian Understanding of Human Nature,* attempts at re-statement of the Christian faith with special emphasis on the meaning of the Christian tradition, the doctrine of Christ, and the nature of man.

If one were looking for an ancestory to contemporary American process-thought, one would find it in the philosophers of emergent evolution in the first three decades of this century: in the work of such writers as C. Lloyd-Morgan, Samuel Alexander, and

Jan Smuts. But its American source is chiefly in Alfred North Whitehead, the Cambridge mathematician who in the mid-twenties, after several years in London, went to Harvard University as Professor of Philosophy to begin, as he put it, the third or philosophical phase of his career. Several of his books, written whilst at Harvard, have been enormously influential on the movement with which we are concerned. Three of them: *Science and the Modern World, Process and Reality,* and *Adventures of Ideas,* are large and original works; although I think that three smaller volumes, *Religion in the Making, Modes of Thought,* and *Symbolism,* may be said to sum up his thought and make it available in a way that only *Adventures of Ideas* can parallel. All of these are happily now reprinted in cheap paperbound editions. One of Whitehead's old students at Harvard, Professor Charles Hartshorne, is the American philosopher who has developed most fully his teacher's principles and in several books—chiefly *Beyond Humanism, The Vision of God, Reality as Social Process, The Logic of Perfection,* and a forthcoming *Philosophy of Religion*—has related Whitehead's process-thinking to Christian faith.

But you are not interested in lists of names. So let me give you, first, a sketch of the general line of thought upon which this group build their theology; and, second, some illustrations of ways in which theological re-conception has been developed by them.

The central conviction of American process-thought is that the evolutionary perspective must be taken with utmost seriousness. Here there is a resemblance to Teilhard de Chardin; and it is no wonder that the publication, posthumously, of Teilhard's work has been greeted with enthusiasm by the school. After a period in which theologians turned away from this perspective and gave their time largely to what some of us have called 'domestic housekeeping', there has been a new concern for the dynamics of physical nature and of human personality, the social nature of man and his organic relation to the universe in which he lives, and the interpenetration of mental and physical in human experience. Process-theologians are sure that modern man is right in seeing himself as part of a changing, moving, living, active world, in which we have to do not with inert substances but with dynamic processes, not so much with *things* as with *events.* Hence their conception of divine Reality —of what Tillich, who incidently has often said that he is in great sympathy, if not complete agreement, with Hartshorne and Williams and who in the third volume of his *Systematic Theology* has used much of their thought, not always with explicit acknowledgement, would call 'the ground of being'—is not that of an unmoved mover or changeless essence, but rather of a living, active, constantly creative, infinitely related, ceaselessly operative Reality; the universe at its core is movement, dynamism, activity, and not sheer and unrelated abstraction. Whitehead's view, that the cosmos is 'alive', is basic to the whole enterprise of process-thought; and this carries with it a conviction that the only reasonable explanation of the living cosmos is in fact 'the living God'.

Several writers have noted that this kind of thinking has appeared in a specifically Christian culture; Whitehead himself makes much of this in *Science and the Modern World*. I myself believe that its appearance in Christian culture is indeed not at all accidental; for the Biblical view of the world—by which I mean here the total *Weltanschauung*, as the Germans would say, and not *Weltbild*, or pre-scientific and mythological pictures in which it is stated—has a close affinity to the perspective associated with process-thought. The Bible speaks of the living God; it sees Him as intimately related to every aspect of creaturely existence both in Nature and history, and the world is 'open' to Him and patient of His activity upon it. Even though this is expressed in a science (if that word is at all appropriate to the scriptural way of picturing the physical world) and a mythology (a word surely well-known to-day!) neither of which we find acceptable, the obvious concern for the living God and for the dynamic quality both of nature and human experience has its relationship to the main stress in process-thought. It is true that some of the ways in which Whitehead, for example, has developed his metaphysics, especially with reference to the nature and activity of God, differ enormously from traditional Christian theology. But quite apart from the discontent which many feel to-day with the substance-philosophy of St. Thomas, it is at least an open possibility that a good deal of Christian writing has consisted in what Whitehead styled 'paying metaphysical compliments' to God, rather than in considering seriously enough the ways in which He has disclosed Himself in His world and the inductions which may properly be made from such disclosures. Many if not all the so-called metaphysical attributes of

God—infinity, omnipotence omniscience, omnipresence, and the like—are negative statements; they serve primarily as a refusal to limit God to the specifically human or creaturely categories of finitude, of reduced capacity to act, or inadequacy in knowledge or wisdom, and of confinement to specific temporal or spatial conditions. What they have to say positively is another matter. Here process-theology is prepared to undertake a considerable re-interpretation of the traditional ideas. Many follow Whitehead in insisting that God is *not* unlimited power, which indeed even St. Thomas would not allow; that His knowledge does not include the future save in the most general sense that He knows the purpose He entertains, the potentialities of the created order, and His own ability to over-rule evil for good; and that the concept of omnipresence needs to be stated in terms which guarantee that all things are present to Him precisely because all things occur 'within' Him—the panentheistic position, which of course needs to be distinguished very sharply from pantheism.

Some of us are sympathetic to Whitehead's explicit teaching about the nature of God Himself. The polar aspects of God as primordial and eternal and as consequent and everlasting; and the notion that divine activity consists in making concrete those possibilities contained, so to say, in His primordial aspect, which are in accord with His 'subjective aim', while God in His consequent aspect receives into Himself that which occurs in the world, so that it becomes the occasion for newer and richer, as well as better, concretions in the ongoing movement of divine activity: these have a considerable appeal to us. Professor Hartshorne in particular (who this autumn is lecturing at Union Seminary in New York on this very subject) has sought to work out along these lines a natural theology which will prepare for a statement of the significance of Jesus Christ that sees Him as the supreme, indeed in some sense unique, 'symbol' (a word which Professor Hartshorne takes with utmost seriousness) of what God is always up to in His world, rather than as an un-related and hence essentially meaningless intrusion into that world.

However this may be, it is the contention of process-theologians that despite the obvious fact that much of the world-picture in Scripture is impossible for us to accept, with the 'three-decker universe', the occasional divine 'interventions', un-natural wonders, and the like, and with a mythological manner of speaking about God and His self-disclosure, the basic view is surely that the deepest Reality is not static but dynamic, that God is both concerned with and related to the cosmos, and that as righteous and loving He is involved with and ceaselessly active in the whole creation as its source, its continuing ground, and its final end. God as active love, as loving Activity, has not always been central in Christian theology, but this Biblical view is taken by process-theologians as the distinctive point of the whole Christian faith.

Members of the process school are well aware of the impatience of many modern philosophers with the metaphysical aspect of their thought. But they think that the position they adopt is not so vulnerable to attack as the essentialist, substantialist, or idealistic metaphysic of other thinkers. As I have heard Professor Williams remark, in this kind of process-metaphysic we do have a referend, we do have the possibility of verification. For the world in which we live, so described, is no meaningless flight of fancy, no absurd leap out of common experience; and if we take seriously what evolutionary science has taught us, but take equally seriously what Whitehead calls the 'aesthetic'—the feeling-qualities, the apprehensions and intuitions, the poetic insight, the empathetic identity of man with his world—which springs out of the natural order and is both organic and continuous with it, we are led to take with the same seriousness the grounding of man in his world and the opening to him, in his experience, of the dynamic depths in that world: as Gerard Manley Hopkins put it, 'there lives the dearest freshness deep down things . . .'. Here is a connexion, a reference, and even in a certain sense a verification, of the religious interpretation, in 'the way things are', which may make sense to modern men and women who are impatient of an unrelated and abstract idealism or of a metaphysic of substance. But I am not expert in this matter and I can only refer you to Professor Hartshorne's discussion of them in his forthcoming book.

I have noted the ancestry of process-theology in emergent evolution; now I must go on to speak of three more contemporary movements which are also contributing to its development in North America. These are: (1) the existentialist analysis of subjective human experience; (2) the view that the meaning of history is found not so much in a catalogue of 'facts' (although these are essential) as in interpretation and living experience of facts in a community; and (3) the contribution of psychology, especially the 'depth-psychology' associated with Freud and Jung.

The existentialist, whatever his particular orientation, is the thinker who insists on the importance of decision, engagement, commitment, even surrender, as determinative of authenticity in human life. Whitehead spoke of the 'subjective aim', which unites the complex events of a given line of process; and he insisted that awareness of and dedication to that aim redeems existence from triviality and futility. So also the existentialist rejects the abstract, the un-related, the 'objective' in the sense of the 'unconcerned'; he speaks of belonging, the engaging of self, as the clue to whatever meaning life may hold for any one of us. When Marcel, for example, says that man is peculiarly to be characterized as 'one who makes promises', he is pointing towards a universe in which such promises can be made and kept—the structure of things and the dynamics of the cosmos give 'promise-making' a setting and even some sort of guarantee of viability. One of my colleagues has spoken of an ontology of gratitude, of trust, of hope, and of love. A world in which these qualities are found is a different world from one in which they might not be found; they tell us something about our human existence and they tell us something too about the living process in which that eventful existence, with its possibility of an all-embracing subjective aim, is known and experienced. In the very precariousness of existence, with its finitude and its vision, engagement is possible, indeed is necessary, for life which is to be more than 'useless passion'. I should refer you here to Professor Hartshorne's admirable essay on Berdyaev and Whitehead; it contains a sustained argument for the relation between existentialism and process-thought.

Again the notion of history as more than a cataloguing of the past is of use to the process-theologian. If history indeed demands such a knowledge of the past but essentially is a living-out of the past in the present; if historical enquiry is an account of 'how we got this way', as an old teacher of mine once put it; that is, if our social heritage, our present belonging to a community, our past-come-alive-in-the-now of our living tradition, all shape us and mould us and make us what we are—then man's memory is no longer a simple 'looking back'; it is a vital and dynamic awareness

of the past as it exists in and creates present communal existence
and prepares for our future. It is at this point that some of my
friends, who are Biblical scholars, like John Knox, find their point
of contact with process-thought; and I mention here particularly
Professor Knox's remarkable analysis, in the recent book to which
I have already referred, of the relation of the historical Jesus to
the Christ of the Church's present faith.

I have neither time nor requisite knowledge for discussion of
the influence of the newer psychology upon the process school.
Here Professor D. D. Williams has written extensively, especially
in a recently published volume treating of the meaning of the
ministry of word and sacrament in our time. But much of what
he has said and most of what my colleagues would wish to say
has also been said by Mr. Harry Williams in his chapter in *Soundings,*—although in North America to-day there is perhaps more
emphasis on *social* psychology. Especially I stress the use of 'acceptance' and its involvement with an 'awareness' both of the
depths of the self and the lives of others, and also of the strange
fact that in some fashion the universe itself, the Reality in which
we live and upon which we depend, seems to 'accept' us when we
accept others in love or self-giving, thus establishing an authenticity that is rooted in the nature of things. Here is a way of understanding how the dynamic, living God of love receives men and
expresses Himself through man. We may say, indeed, that reality
is such relationship, at both the divine and human levels.

The evolutionary perspective with its illumination of the
ground of the world as dynamic, relational, concerned; the existentialist emphasis on engagement and surrender; the significance
of history as the coming-alive, to a social group in the present,
of the past which has shaped it; the psychological insights which
teach us that in deep human interrelationship and in mutual acceptance lives are made whole:—these are the emphases which
determine the work of the North American process-theologian.

Now let me give examples of some ways in which this work
has been developed in recent years.

First, in respect to the nature of Christian faith itself. In such
a perspective Christianity is not a simple, fixed entity; it is itself
a living and developing process. To be committed to the Christian
faith is to be caught up into a community of life which does not

continue in one state but which goes on towards the future, incorporating in itself all sorts of novelty, changing whilst it remains ever the same in that its deepest engagement is with the movement of love, of relationship in love, of deepest concern, as these have been expressed in the life of Jesus and His saints. The *identity* of this on-going process which is the Christian tradition is precisely in the vision of the divine Activity in His continual interpenetration with the world and men, and in terms of which our understanding of our own existence as men-in-community, rooted in history and organic with the natural order, is enriched and deepened.

The Christian claim that in some profound sense the human life of Jesus is both expression and reflection of the depths of being, the ground, the divine Reality, or (as a process-theologian would prefer to say) the divine Activity which through the creative process is at work, is not only truth about that particular historical figure, although it *is* that; it is also truth about God, the world, and about every man. To put this in more theological language, the 'incarnation' of God in Jesus Christ is focally but not exclusively true of Him. He is indeed crucial and definitive, but what is seen there is pervasively true of the whole cosmos. It is all the sphere of the self-expressing activity, the incarnating work, of divine Love who Himself is indeed actual but whose self-expression is integral to His nature: God *is* self-giving love, who lives and moves and has His being not so much as First Mover, not at all as Sheer Omnipotence, but in relationship with that in and through which His love is working. This is why, for example, Schubert Ogden in *Christ without Myth* finds himself more in sympathy with Buri than with Bultmann; the 'excessive christo-centrism', to use von Hügel's phrase, of Bultmann and so much other modern theology is for Ogden and for all process-thinkers, not only a denial of the truth which the patristic *Logos*-theology sought in its own way to state, but is simply nonsense when one is confronted with what are plainly disclosures of Love in unconventional and non-ecclesiastical ways and places. Certainly Jesus is 'important', in Whitehead's sense of that word: He is the clue to the rest of God's working, and as such interprets the past and opens up new possibilities for the future, and yet is part of an on-going movement of God-man relationship. But Jesus is not an isolated 'entrance' or 'intervention' of God into a world which otherwise is without His presence and action. Rather He is, as a Man, a climactic and definitive point for God's presence and action among men in a world in which God is always present and ceaselessly active. Jesus is not the supreme anomaly; He is the classic instance. His uniqueness and such finality as may be claimed for Him are to be seen in this context, and only in this way can His 'importance' be preserved in a perspective such as the process-thinkers maintain is required in our time; the effort to save that 'importance' by the retention of more traditional categories is bound to be a failure.

Furthermore, because in Him the potential and partially actualized is found expressly realized—that is, vividly made real—and thus fulfilled, Jesus makes sense of and gives sense to the existence of any and every man. Not that we have here a matter of human achievement alone; on the contrary, this, like *all* fulfilment and actualization, is the re-action of man to the prior and incessant divine Action. In religious terms, God comes first, as He always does, for He is the creative Ground-Action upon which all else is dependent. The truth about man, and our awareness of it, is not the result of our 'unaided' human striving; it is by the divine Activity which sometimes in strange and unexpected ways (as Mr. Harry Williams has admirably illustrated for us) first awakens, then empowers, and finally completes and fulfils, the striving which is an indelible part of human existence.

I wish to say more about this, since it is exactly on this problem that process-theologians in North American circles have been hard at work. One of the facts which the neo-orthodox, Biblical-theological (call it what you will), reaction between 1930 and 1950 brought vividly before us was the sinfulness of man and the necessity for redemption. The cheerful picture of man as so good that he required nothing more than a bit of inspiration, coupled with a sufficient amount of information, to become quite perfect was destroyed once for all; and there can be no realistic Christian theology, nor indeed any intelligible understanding of man even on so-called 'secular' lines, which neglects the patent fact of his perversity. But this need not mean and should not mean an exaggerated portrayal of man's wickedness nor the narrowing of the conception of redemption to mean almost exclusively the extrication of man from his sinful condition for a life 'beyond the skies'. The process-theologians about whom we are speaking to-day do not commit this error. Precisely because they see the world and man within it as dynamic processes, driving towards fulfilment through increasing integration and by the mutual expression of love, they are enabled to see redemption in a much wider context, and to understand man's sinfulness more in terms of deviation of aim and failure of achievement—that is, in failure of love—than in terms of a radical evil, in the sense of rooted in man's very nature as such.

As Professor Daniel Williams and Professor Loomer have argued, human life requires for its authentic development the engagement of man by some cause or value, some over-arching purpose, which will bring about his increasing integration. Only so, in Sartrian language, can his *pour-soi,* or what Whitehead called his 'subjective aim', be delivered from loss in his *en-soi,* his sheer existence. Human life requires also a growing sense of belonging, of fulfilment of self in acceptance of and with acceptance by his fellows, and a deep participation in the historical existence of the race as this comes alive to him in his present social experience. And it requires some glimpse of a deeper, shall I say cosmic, acceptance, so that he can feel that his 'subjective aim' is identified with what a Christian would call the 'subjective aim' of Deity itself—the sense that the universe is 'on His side' because He has aligned Himself with the dynamic movement towards growth, towards enlargement, towards sharing in love. It is the conviction of Daniel Williams and Loomer—and it is my own view—that this fits in admirably with the Christian portrayal of human nature in its broad and central line. For by commitment to that One, who in being the expression of divine Activity is transparent to Deity, who is the classical instance, the focal revelation of the never-failing presence and action of supreme love, we are shown man as he is intended to be; and by such commitment true health, wholeness, right integration, genuine fulfilment, is made possible for men as they are identified with Jesus' loving activity. St. Augustine's words come to mind: 'Thou hast made us *ad te'*—'towards Thee', as a dynamic unfulfilled capacity for God; and 'our hearts are disquieted until they find their rest'—their intentional identification—in God who is Himself love seeking for love. We became true men—men 'in Christ' as St. Paul would put it—when our capacity and our urge are filled by and directed towards loving activity in and under and with the divine Activity who thus is the fulfilment of all in all. It is along lines such as these that the thinkers we are discussing would proceed as they attempt to state what 'atonement' is all about.

I should like to conclude by quoting some fine words of Whitehead, which seem to me to get to the root of the matter. 'The essence of Christianity is the appeal to the life of Christ as a revelation of the nature of God and of His agency in the world. The record is fragmentary, inconsistent, and uncertain . . . But there can be no doubt as to what elements in the record have evoked a response from all that is best in human nature. The Mother, the Child, and the bare manger: the lowly man, homeless and self-forgetful, with His message of peace, love, and sympathy; the suffering, the agony, the tender words as life ebbed, the final despair: and the whole with the authority of supreme victory.' It is exactly in this disclosure *in act* of what others, and chiefly for Whitehead Plato, have discerned *in theory,* that the distinctiveness of Christianity lies; so Whitehead himself concludes his discussion.

When these words are set in the context of process-thought with its insistence upon Deity as supremely related; as ultimate and perfect only because ultimately and perfectly Love; as dynamic, active, living, moving, energizing reality which grounds our own striving selves . . . then we can see how a 'new look', as we say in the United States, is given to the Christian faith. If this element could be stressed, and if we thought of Christianity as itself also a living process, the meaning of faith would be understood, not as assent to a set of propositions however true, but as commitment to an ongoing movement of love grounded in the universe and expressed in Jesus Christ; worship would be understood as intentional identification with that movement and the opening of self to its enabling power; Christian morality would be seen as the expression of love made possible by acceptance of love and the experience of being loved; and the Christian fellowship would be known as the knitting-together, in 'one bundle of life', of those who have been grasped by the Spirit of Christ who is Love embodied and made decisively visible and available. In any case, this is the direction in which the North American process-theologians are moving.

Suggested Readings

Surveys of Process Theology

Allan, George and Merle Allshouse. "Current Issues in Process Theology: Some Reflections," *The Christian Scholar,* 50 (1967), 167-175.

Arnold, Charles Harvey. *Near the Edge of Battle: A Short History of the Divinity School and the "Chicago School of Theology" 1866-1966.* Chicago: The Divinity School Association, The University of Chicago, 1966. Paperback.

Brown, Delwin. "Recent Process Theology," *Journal of the American Academy of Religion,* 35 (1967), 28-41.

Meland, Bernard E. "The Empirical Tradition in Theology at Chicago," *The Future of Empirical Theology.* Edited by Bernard E. Meland. Chicago: The University of Chicago Press, 1969, pp. 1-62.

Pittenger, W. Norman. *The Word Incarnate.* New York: Harper and Brothers, 1959, pp. 146-175.

————. *Process-Thought and Christian Faith.* New York: Macmillan, 1968, pp. 1-25.

Reeves, Gene and Delwin Brown. "The Development of Process Theology," *Process Philosophy and Christian Thought.* Edited by Delwin Brown, Ralph E. James, Jr., and Gene Reeves. Indianapolis: Bobbs-Merrill, 1971, pp. 21-64. Paperback—Indianapolis: Bobbs-Merrill.

Williams, Daniel Day. *What Present-Day Theologians Are Thinking.* 3rd edition, revised. New York: Harper and Row, 1967, pp. 72 ff. Paperback—New York: Harper and Row.

————. *The Spirit and the Forms of Love.* New York: Harper and Row, 1968, pp. 102-110.

2 Faith and the Formative Imagery of Our Time

BERNARD E. MELAND

Theology, philosophy, and science all coexist in a large cultural matrix. Their imagery, concepts, and models interact among themselves and shape our experience in a given period of history. In the selection below,* Bernard E. Meland analyzes the imagery that is molding our experience at the present time. He traces the shift from the Newtonian world view to that of twentieth century science and into the world of the atom bomb and moon rockets. Our experience itself is undergoing radical change. This broad cultural transformation forms the context for the development of process theology.

Bernard E. Meland studied at the University of Chicago, where he was Professor of Constructive Theology at the Divinity School for many years before his retirement in 1964. His primary concern has been with theology and culture and with the affective and aesthetic aspects of experience. Grounded in the tradition of empirical theology at the University of Chicago, Meland's thought has been influenced both by William James and Alfred North Whitehead.

The thinking of any people or generation within a historical culture moves within a circumscribing imagery that both illumines the meaning of terms and

* From *The Realities of Faith: The Revolution in Cultural Forms* (New York: Oxford University Press, 1962), pp. 76-79; 85-87; 91-95. Reprinted with permission.

limits the range of terms which can be used meaningfully. This is so because the creation of meaning occurs within an intelligible discourse which itself is organic, either to the living situation of a given period and place, or to experiences available within that situation. The vocabulary of a cultural group within a given period tends to form afresh around a certain set of experiences which have had decisive or dramatic consequences. In juxtaposition with these innovating terms, and somewhat related to them, one finds a cluster of words and phrases carrying into the period inherited meanings; these words and phrases simultaneously define and restrict the import of experiences which are being freshly described or reported. Thus first-century Christians, alive to the events centering around the Cross and the Resurrection, spoke in impassioned ways about recollections of these events and experiences—experiences that had been reported within their generation. Yet all of this was colored, too, by terms and phrases that recalled an earlier time and place, an earlier set of historical experiences: words such as "Messiah," "the Son of Man," and "the Suffering Servant." Past events and their terms, along with innovating experiences and the language they evoked, merged into a single discourse as a common witness. Similarly, Reformation voices rang out with the language of revolt and protest against abuses within the Church simultaneously with individual confessions of sin and the experience of forgiveness, bespeaking an imagery of an immediate encounter with the righteous God. "Direct access to the inward working of the Holy Spirit," as Calvin phrased it, opened up a wealth of imagery which had been virtually blotted out in medieval Christendom, except among the Piety groups, or except as it had been sublimated in the adoration of the Virgin Mary, who appears to have been the medieval counterpart of the Comforter. More of the medieval imagery of thought was retained in these impassioned declarations of Christian freedom than is often assumed; yet even more of an earlier imagery, recalling the vitality and zeal of that first eschatological community, was being repossessed and conveyed in this concern with "the direct access to the inward working of the Holy Spirit." Or again, the discovery of the individual person in the eighteenth century as a disclosure of the Infinite led to a fresh insistence upon individual freedom and liberation from social institutions as well as from the coercive control of nature, now viewed as a vast cosmic mechanism.

But even as eighteenth-century language gave vent to resentment and resistance against current forms of oppression in its stress upon individuality, it echoed forms of thought which had been reactivated in a Platonic renaissance in an effort to retain a sense of ultimate unity amidst this buzzing confusion of immediate diversities. Out of the interplay of innovating experience with inherited and disinherited notions, there was evoked a mind-set in which freedom and determination loomed as the defining antinomies.

We are in the process today of emerging from the shock of revolutionizing experiences out of which new metaphors, peculiar to our time, are forming; and we are on the brink of new ventures more radical in their degree of innovation than anything the human race has known in its history. For the range and character of experience itself is rapidly changing as the space in which these events and experiences occur expands beyond the scope of our imagination. Hence our imagery is in flux. Having already been jolted out of the formative notions of preatomic times, we are tentatively and hesitatingly groping our way in a discourse, the terms of which are but partially apprehended, and the directives only vaguely prescient of meaning.

Now it is generally true that innovating experiences create a break in established imageries, either by rendering certain notions obsolete and irrelevant, or by intruding swiftly and decisively a new fund of meanings expressive of these innovations. But there is an ordering of terms which seems to occur simultaneously with this inundation of fresh meaning. The structuring of language and discourse that follows such experience has the effect of establishing controlling ideas or concepts that seem to define the bounds of intelligible thought and discussion. Within the range of symbolism afforded by these ideas, this structuring of language tends to give a certain spread of meaning as well as a sense of direction to the course of intelligible inquiry. It is as if these controlling ideas formed a vast canopy over the minds of people within a given generation, or as if a low-hanging cloud enveloped them. . . .

II

The two most decisive sources of the present change in the imagery of thought are scientific exploration and the violence and suffering of a world at war. Each has had the effect of terminating one era of thought and its imagery and of evoking fresh imagery; in some instances the result is a reconception of terms long discarded or lying dormant for generations, and in other instances an introduction of radically new terms and determinations of thought.

Current scientific exploration in its total span, extending from the microscopic exploration of atomic structure to more recent ventures into outer space, constitutes in its way a counterpart of the discovery of new continents in the fifteenth century. In that earlier period of geographical extension by sea travel, the expansion of the horizons of thought among the European communities and, as a consequence, the intrusion of alien or at least of uncalculated realities into the cultural experience, brought a vivid sense of insecurity to the established ethos of thought and faith. In a similar way nuclear science and space exploration today have awakened vague and unanalyzed fears, along with specific misgivings concerning the continuing relevance of Christian faith. These premonitions are not wholly unfounded today any more than they were in the fifteenth century. Certainly the expansion of the European community beyond its historical shores brought immeasurable change in its mode of life, and along with this change, unmanageable responsibilities as Europe sought to capitalize upon its new opportunities. The sense of dread, however, was prescient of opportunity and promise as well as of hardship and dismay. And so may be the misgivings and anxiety of the present age in the face of nuclear experimentation and automation.

The one fear that was not wholly miscalculated in the fifteenth century was concern about the possible threat to the Christian ethos, resulting from the new conception of land and sea space and the mobility of life that could be expected to follow. Within a few generations the range of observation was to extend to stellar space as well, as Galileo's telescope surveyed the heavens and Newton's newly fashioned instruments of measurement could calculate the movement of the planets. Arnold Toynbee, as we have already noted, sees in this "secularizing" development "the discrediting of the West's Christian heritage," and the elevation of a technological civilization that has only tenuous connections at best with that heritage and ethos.[1] The assessment of what fol-

[1] Arnold Toynbee, *An Historian's Approach to Religion.* Oxford University Press, 1956, p. 184.

lowed between "the beginning of the eighteenth century and A.D. 1956," to use Toynbee's designation of time, will vary from scholar to scholar, and possibly from Christian to Christian. One thing is clear, however; the formative image of the world, and ultimately of man himself, that became a controlling factor in the thought of Western culture, followed in the wake of Newtonian science. It was to alter radically the vision of human resources and the capacity of Western man to apprehend realities beyond the scope of his own formulations. In a word, under the spell of the Newtonian image, the facilities for exact thought and prediction became so perfected that it became literally impossible for nineteenth-century man to distrust his human powers and ideals. Reality for Western man thus became the human equation writ large . . .

But now we need to speak more explicitly of that one aspect of our cultural experience which has contributed directly to a sharpened realism in our time. I refer to those agencies of thought which have brought forth a new image of man through a dissolution of the Newtonian image which so sorely distorted the estimate of our human powers.

It is one of the remarkable though ironical facts of modern history that the processes of scientific invention and discovery which led to the horrors of Hiroshima and Nagasaki, and to the explosive possibilities of the present cold war, also initiated the new era in science, and with it, an imagery of thought which has released Western thinking from its Newtonian captivity. The year of innovation was 1895, when Roentgen discovered the X-ray. The revolution in the conception of the atom occurred toward the end of the nineteenth century, about 1896, when Becquerel and the Curies discovered radioactive elements. Just after the turn of the century Rutherford discovered the proton and came upon the surprising disclosure that the atom is planetary in character, "a merry-go-round in miniature," as one physicist described it. This was the beginning of the shift from an atomistic conception of reality to the ontological notion of the individual in community, which is the basic formula in Whitehead's metaphysics. The break in imagery, separating the Newtonian-Cartesian age from that of the new vision of science, occurred as early as 1870. Yet as late as 1920 the new imagery of thought remained relatively unknown in many circles of theology and philosophy. Gestalt psychology was launched in 1925, and emergent philosophies began to appear about the same time. Suddenly scholars, insofar as they were susceptible to scientific influence, broke out with the markings of field theory and other holistic notions. Relativity was in all this, too. The theory had been set forth by Einstein in 1905, although it was not until Heisenberg announced the principle of indeterminacy in 1931 that these new theories in physics, relativity and quantum mechanics, assumed wide currency outside scientific discussions and highly technical philosophical speculations. Not until 1945, however, with the falling of atomic bombs on Hiroshima and Nagasaki, did all this revolution in imagery become a public fact. Thus the age of atomic power did not burst upon us out of the blue. Its antecedents can be fully studied. They had been widely known throughout scientific and industrial circles before the turn of the century. But to the man in the street they came as a gale in the night, bringing death and destruction.

What is now heralded as the new age of power is publicly acknowledged and acclaimed through the periodic launching of Sputniks, Vanguards, moon rockets, and man, into outer space. Beneath this visible physical display of scientific genius, however, there is a sobering human fact. It is that a radical reorientation of scientific thinking itself has occurred, affecting the way the scientist approaches natural events and the way he assesses his means of observing them. If the imagery of Newtonian science rejects any assumption that the realities of existence might elude the forms of human thought, the imagery of present-day physical science acknowledges the mystery and indeterminancy of events in certain respects. Unlike the Newtonian scientist of an earlier age, who could assume that his formula employing Euclidean geometry expressed a well-defined measure, the modern physicist knows he is using a tentative formulation of his own making, based on the geometrical theories of Gauss and Riemann rather than Euclid, thus explicitly acknowledging the experimental uncertainty of his effort. And he employs these geometrical equations as tentative models by which to test out certain possibilities and to verify theories or judgments to which his own reasoning from evidence has led him. What has disappeared from this mode of inquiry is the imagery of a mechanistic order in nature and the doctrinaire assumption of an absolute mathematical measure. In a word, the imagery and method of science, as these are presently understood and employed, compel recognition of some discontinuity between manageable and unmanageable aspects of events in existence. The very meaning of what in current terms has been called "the dimension of depth" is that the realities of any experience are to be accounted deeper than, or in some aspects resistant to, man's powers of observation and description. This is not to imply the rejection of reason and observation, either in science or in religious thought, but to acknowledge their limitations, and to recognize that the structures of reason which we are able to formulate and employ are but tentative ventures in apprehending the meaning of those realities. They may not be taken to be definitive and final descriptions of them in the sense of earlier mechanistic presuppositions.

Recognition of the dimension of depth has become commonplace in many of the disciplines of modern thought, including certain areas of the social sciences and psychology, as well as in modern physics, metaphysics, and theology. What is to be noted here is that depth has the connotation of complexity as well as discontinuity or indeterminacy. In this respect, field theory has as much, if not more, to do with intruding the notion as does quantum mechanics or the principle of indeterminacy. As employed in holistic thinking from James to Whitehead, such relational thinking resists the assumption that an examination of parts abstracted from its dynamic or living context can give full and adequate meaning to the reality of these parts in a relationship. Relationships thus provide a dimension of meaning and possibility of creativity which exceed the reality of parts taken as isolated data. It is this mystery of relationships, giving to events or phenomena their incalculable quality even as they yield to our apprehension of them, which contributes to a sense of depth in dealing with the living situation in any of its aspects.

Now within the ethos of thought in which these disciplines move, there is room for acknowledging or even pointing to imperceptible depths of meaning bearing upon observable events, made vivid intermittently by innovations, or by intimations of novel occurrences within the concrete events of history. In such an ethos of thought the doctrinaire dismissal of dimensions of reality which are unavailable to inquiry, or unresponsive to the logic we have been able to formulate, cannot be considered critical thought. One may choose not to concern himself with such dimensions, preferring to confine one's thought to manageable areas of experience; but the penumbra of possible meaning persists as a remainder of the unmanageable aspects of events which nevertheless attend one's thoughts, if only as a judgment upon one's formulations, and upon the clearly defined range of meaning one is able to establish within his norms of thought.

In such an ethos of thought, on the other hand, there is encouragement to be as attentive as we wish, to pursue the bearing of such dimensions of experience and their complexities upon the clearly formed judgments of thought. One is not justified by science or by critical theological opinion in simply affirming mystery and indeterminacy as controlling notions, as if critical and judicious inquiry made no claim upon the religious mind. But awareness of the dimension of depth, and a response to its judgment and to its extended range of possible meaning, appropriate to critical inquiry, is itself to be accounted the exercise of critical judgment in all inquiry.

Now it is in such an ethos of thought that the idea of "the mystery of the Kingdom" or "the New Creation" expressed by the notion of eschatology in theology and in New Testament research has again become relevant and intelligible. Intelligibility in this context is not the same as reasonableness. In the ethos of an earlier liberal thought that leaned heavily upon the imagery of the Enlightenment, reasonableness implied grasping realities "within the bounds of reason alone." Intelligibility as it may be employed in the present context implies no such domestication of the realities apprehended. Rather, it implies apprehending a margin of meaningful experience within an infinity of mystery which time and again, and for the most part, eludes our human measure. Intelligibility provides a basis for our human orientation toward what is more than human in the realities that hold us in existence.

Suggested Readings

Bernard E. Meland on Culture and Theology

Meland, Bernard E. *Faith and Culture.* New York: Oxford University Press, 1953.

————. *The Realities of Faith: The Revolution in Cultural Forms.* New York: Oxford University Press, 1962, pp. 109-169. Paperback— Chicago: Seminary Co-operative Bookstore.

————. "How is Culture a Source for Theology?" *Criterion,* 3 (1964), 10-21.

About Bernard E. Meland on Culture and Theology

Williams, Daniel Day. "Some Queries to Professor Meland on His Paper 'How Is Culture a Source of Theology?' " *Criterion,* 3 (1964), 28-33.

On Related Themes

Hamilton, Peter. *The Living God and the Modern World: Christian Theology Based on the Thought of A. N. Whitehead.* Philadelphia: United Church Press, 1967, pp. 38-72. Paperback.

Kuhn, Thomas. *The Structure of Scientific Revolutions.* Chicago: The University of Chicago Press, 1962. Paperback—Chicago: The University of Chicago Press.

Pittenger, W. Norman. *Rethinking the Christian Message.* Greenwich, Conn.: Seabury Press, 1956, pp. 13-34.

Whitehead, Alfred North. *Science and the Modern World.* New York: Macmillan, 1925. Paperback—New York: Free Press.

————. *Adventures of Ideas.* New York: Macmillan, 1933. Paperback —New York: Free Press.

3 The Development of Process Philosophy

CHARLES HARTSHORNE

Process philosophy is characterized by its emphasis on becoming and relation. As such, it stands in contrast to those philosophies that give primacy to being and absoluteness. In the following selection * Charles Hartshorne introduces the reader to some of the basic metaphysical notions of process philosophy, from the standpoint of becoming. While pointing to process themes in Buddhism, ancient Egyptian religion, and in certain isolated Western thinkers, he concentrates on the penetration and precision of the thought of Alfred North Whitehead.

Charles Hartshorne studied at Harvard University, where he was Whitehead's assistant. For many years he taught philosophy at the University of Chicago and established himself as a leading interpreter of Whitehead and an independent thinker in his own right. Although identified as a philosopher, he has had a major influence on the development of process theology. He is presently Ashbel Smith Professor of Philosophy at the University of Texas.

The term "process philosophy"—first used by I do not know whom, perhaps my friend Bernard Loomer—is one way of pointing to a profound change which has come over speculative philosophy or metaphysics in the modern period in Europe and America. I have myself often used the more noncommittal phrase "neoclassical metaphysics" for much

* From *Philosophers of Process,* edited by Douglas Browning (New York: Random House, 1965), v-xxii. Reprinted with permission.

the same purpose, since the emphasis upon process or becoming, though essential, is only one feature of this new way of viewing reality. Also characteristic is the emphasis upon relations and relativity. The Buddhistic phrase, "dependent origination," suggests the connection between the two points. What has an origin is relative to that origin; only what has always been as it is can be "absolute," wholly independent of other things. However, in this essay I shall deal chiefly with process, not relativity. It is not hard to translate talk about being and becoming into talk about absoluteness and relativity. But I shall not always attempt the translation in what follows.

Greek philosophy tended to depreciate becoming and exalt mere being, and—as was consistent—to depreciate relativity and exalt independence or absoluteness. Aristotle summed it up when he held that what was altogether immutable and hence immune to influence from others was superior to that which in any way changed or depended upon other things. Medieval natural theology never explicitly deviated from this attitude, though revealed doctrines of the trinity and the incarnation may have almost explicitly done so. (Did not the Son depend upon the Father without being inferior to Him?)

However, the harmony of some doctrines of the classical natural theology with the Greek attitude is extremely doubtful. Aristotle had denied God's knowledge of contingent and changing things, on the straightforward ground that knowing cannot be independent of what is known. Yet Christian and most Jewish and Mohammedan theists felt obliged, for religious reasons, to affirm God's knowledge of the contingent and changing world. Only a few Mohammedans dared even to hint that this must mean change in God. Christians and Jews would scarcely go so far. The result was a glaring inconsistency which troubled many. For precisely this reason Crescas, and later Spinoza, denied contingency (and by implication change) not only in God but in the world which God knows. For they saw that the known is in the knowing, and if there is contingency and change in the former then there is also in the latter. Thus in Spinoza the Greek bias came to its last great triumph in Western thought. Not only God, but the world, too, was to be made safe from accident or genuine alteration. And indeed, immutable omniscience, implying the immutability of all truth, consorts ill with the view that becoming is real. If there is novel reality, then to that extent the truth also must be novel. To say of future events that they "are going to be" is to imply that their entire character is a present fact, though a fact which, with our human limitations, we have not yet reached. But there the fact is, waiting for us to reach it, or there it is off-stage, waiting to come on. In this view, genuine becoming is missing. The truth, the reality, is eternally there, spread out to the divine gaze, though our present experience, being localized in the eternal panorama, cannot behold most of it. As St. Thomas put it, events in time are like travelers on a road who cannot see those far ahead of them though they can all be seen by one sufficiently high above the road looking down upon its entire length, i.e., by God in eternity. Bergson's phrase, "spatializing time," fits this view as a glove a hand. The theory entirely omits the aspect of creation involved in becoming. The entirety of creation cannot be viewed if there is no such totality. How can there be if the actual sum of events receives additions each moment? And what is becoming if not such perpetual adding of new realities? Thomas is assuming the falsity of a certain view of time; process philosophy adopts this view, and not without reason.

Since the eternalistic view reached explicit formulation in theological guise, it was fitting that the process doctrine should also emerge in a theological context. Philosophies of being, which treat becoming as secondary, have acquired powerful religious sanctions; it is therefore well that we should realize from the outset that process philosophy, in its origin at least, is a rival religious doctrine rather than an irreligious one. This is true in two important respects:

(1) The earliest great tradition which espoused a philosophy of becoming was Buddhism. Heracleitos, who said that things are new each moment, was isolated, and in addition obscure, for we have but fragmentary sayings. Only the followers of Buddha produced a great literature expressive of the doctrine that becoming is the universal form of reality. They carried this view through, in some respects, with admirable thoroughness, long before anything like it occurred in the West. Philosophies of being characteristically treat change either as "unreal" or as in principle but the substitution of one set of qualities for another in an abiding "sub-

stratum," "substance," or "subject of change." For them, reality consists essentially of beings, not happenings or events. If a being is not of the highest kind, it shows this deficiency by undergoing alterations. If it is of the highest kind, alteration could only be for the worse and hence could have no point. So the highest being is changeless, but the others, poor things, keep changing, apparently in the in principle vain effort to make up for their imperfection. This doctrine is Greek through and through, but, alas, the Church Fathers accepted it. True, the doctrine also arose long ago in the Orient. But there Buddhism came to challenge it, with a subtlety and persistence which had no counterpart in classical and medieval Europe. The Buddhists rejected "substance," including the "soul" as substance. The momentary experiences are the primary realities, and these do not change, they simply become, and what is called change is the successive becoming of events having certain relationships to their predecessors. The "soul" or the self-identical ego is merely the relatedness of experiences to their predecessors through memory and the persistence of various qualities or personality traits. The first great metaphysician in the West to hold this view clearly was Whitehead, in the present century. But we must not get ahead of our story, which is mainly that of the development of process philosophy in the West.

(2) The man who first squarely faced the conflict between the religious doctrine of an all-knowing God and Greek eternalism and decided against the latter was Fausto Socinus, whose sect was destroyed by persecution and whose bold theorizing has been ignored by historians of philosophy (not to their credit, I must add). Socinus rejected the immutability of God in order to be able consistently to affirm the reality of becoming. He did not quite put it in this way. What he said rather was that human freedom is incompatible with immutable divine knowledge of our free acts. However, our freedom is nothing but that case of becoming which we experience from the inside or by direct intuition, rather than infer from more or less indirect observation. We have to start with events we intimately know! A decision (and we make little ones each moment) is a settling of the otherwise unsettled; it occurs in time, not in eternity; to say that God eternally knows all decisions is to imply that the totality of decisions is a single all-inclusive eternally complete set of realities. But then there is nothing for

decisions to decide. We only imagine we are resolving a real indeterminacy when we make up our minds; in truth the resolution is eternal. But if eternal, it has no genuine becoming. We say that we "make" a decision; but religious philosophies of being tell us that God makes everything by a single eternal act. So then I make my decision now and God eternally makes it! But if God makes it, how is it my decision rather than His? Socinus in effect, perhaps without being fully explicit about it, was pointing to the paradox of the double determining of events to which Greek thought in its theological form had led. This brave and honest man had the courage to affirm that we really do make our decisions, and that in so far as we do God does not make them. We have here the idea of self-creation, which later in Lequier, the French philosopher of a century ago, and still later in William James, Dewey, Whitehead, Sartre, and others has been so often stressed. Note that it was a theological idea before it was an atheistic one (in Sartre). But if we, and not God, make our decisions, in what fashion can God know these decisions? He cannot decree them in eternity and, by knowing this decree, know what they are. Rather, He must perceive them as they occur, and then preserve them in memory. Events—at least those events which are free acts—come into being, are created, at a given time; to know them beforehand—even more, to know them eternally—is a logical absurdity, for it is not beforehand, much less eternally, that they exist to be known! Only as and after they occur are there any such entities to be known. Hence that God "fails" to know them eternally or beforehand is not properly a failure, for success here is mere nonsense, and where success is nonsense "failure" is inapplicable. Hence it is quibbling to call God "ignorant" because He does not know things which are not there to be known. This argument was hinted at much earlier (in Cicero, if not before him), but the Socinians were the first to make serious theological use of it. They courageously admitted real change in the divine knowledge, the becoming of new knowledge in God to harmonize with the becoming or creation of new things to be known. There is no total creation for God to know in one finally complete act of knowing. Rather, the totality of the real is enriched each moment by as many acts of freedom as occur in the world. With the growth of reality must come a growth of divine knowledge of reality. All this is somewhat further clarified by Lequier three centuries later, followed by Whitehead, who apparently knew little of his predecessors in this way of thinking.

It is notable that the earliest theist of all, Ikhnaton of Egypt, spoke of God "fashioning himself." Thus self-creation is an old religious idea. One can find it also in ancient India. Medieval anti-process theology may eventually be seen as but an interlude, a detour from which religious thought has happily returned to the main highway. And clearly, if Socinus allows man to determine part of the content of the divine knowledge by man's self-creation, he can hardly wish to deny self-creation to deity. For if God is to change, it surely should be in part voluntarily, and not solely as result of man's initiative. Besides, the self-creativity of man, like all his traits, can only be an imperfect image of what in God must be perfect. So there must be an "Eminent" or divine self-creation, of which ours is but a remote and inferior analogue. If, in making our decisions, we make something of ourselves, then analogously God in making His supreme decisions must in some supreme sense make Himself. Even Lequier seems not to see this implication of the process doctrine. Whitehead is our first great systematic philosopher to see it with any great clarity. But the German psychologist and religious thinker, Fechner, had said something like it in his *Zend-Avesta*.

One can, to be sure, read a sort of process philosophy into Hegel and Schelling. But in these writers there are so many concessions to, or echoes of, Greek thought that dispute concerning their classification is to my mind rather unrewarding. They are process philosophers perhaps—if they are anything clear and unambiguous. But what a big "if" this is! They doubtless helped to do away with the classical metaphysics of being; but that they constructed a viable alternative is much less clear.

Socinus and Lequier attacked the theological center of the philosophy of being and absoluteness and proposed a definite alternative. But they failed to generalize this alternative. Only man's freedom (and God's knowledge of man) was clearly taken out of the old context; the rest of nature could still be looked upon as unfree, and as subject to immutable divine knowledge. This is where Bergson and Whitehead, preceded at least vaguely by Fechner, come in. Bergson treats all life as to some extent free or creative, and definitely hints, in his later works, that all nature is to some extent free. In Whitehead this implication is made sharply explicit. Not only man is a "self-created creature" but every individual is, in some slight degree at least, self-creative, maker of its own decisions, and so of itself. Divinity is the Eminent or supreme form of self-creation, anything else is an inferior form. Whitehead combines this with the Socinian insight that a self-creative creature must also create something in God, for he who makes something in himself makes something in the knowledge of all those who know him, and so makes them to a certain extent. We make our friends and enemies just in so far as we are free and they know us. It could not be otherwise, given the essential meanings of "free" and "know." Since God knows all creatures, and a creature is merely an inferior case of what in God is supreme self-creativity, all creatures whatsoever are in part creators of (something in) God. And so Whitehead refers to God as Creature, or to the divine Consequent Nature—God as consequent upon or partly created by the world. This is how deity must be conceived in a consistent metaphysics of process.

Whitehead is not indulging in eccentricity at this point, he is merely following out the logic of the decision to make creative becoming the universal category. So when he tells us that creativity is the "category of the ultimate," the "universal of universals," he is summing up and crowning a long development. Freedom is now seen as the essence of reality, not a mere special case. To be is to create oneself and thereby to influence the self-creation of those by whom one is known, including God.

Process philosophy, fully thought out, is creationism! Multitudes have talked about God's "creating" of the world, but they usually had no philosophical category adequate to express this idea. All they could do was to say that God was "cause" and the world the effect. They were unable to show in our ordinary experiences of causation any unambiguously creative aspect. The potter shapes the clay, they said, but the supreme Potter, they also said, had shaped the lesser potter completely, and so the only genuine decision was the supreme Potter's. Thus free creation, genuine decision, is banished from the world. But how, from such a world, could we possibly form the conception of divine creation? I believe that three thousand years of speculation have led to this result, foreshadowed by Ikhnaton at the outset: Creativity, if real at all, must be universal, not limited to God alone, and it must be self-creativity as well as creative influencing of others. In the hymns of Ikhnaton there is nothing about mere causality, nothing about inexorable causal relationships, nothing (unless a vague hint or two) about God's determining the details of the creature's actions. The suggestion almost throughout is of free creatures responding to divine freedom, influencing God to delight in the spectacle they afford for Him, while they delight in His beneficent influence upon them. But it took three millennia to change this purely poetic and intuitive vision into a sharply defined philosophical doctrine. Many formidable obstacles had first to be overcome.

Let us look at some of these obstacles. There is the common-sense view, enshrined in European language (not in all languages), that the most concrete realities to which abstractions are to be applied, the real "subjects" which have "predicates" are things, individuals which change from one actual state to another—a person, a tree, a mountain, a star—not happenings. But there is something more concrete than an individual, and that is the actual history of the individual, the succession of "states," for instance, experiences, which constitute the reality of the individual through time. Is it not clear that the entire *actuality* of the individual is in his states, bodily and mental? True, his possibilities are not exhaustively realized by these states; he could have had other experiences; but we are not now asking what he potentially is, only what he actually has been up to now. The sole way to distinguish the individual from the happenings making up his history is in terms of possibility versus actuality, with the states constituting the *entire* actuality. Now I ask: Are not the actual and the concrete the same? Only in abstract terms can one speak of possible happenings; concrete happenings, knowable as such, and actual happenings are one and the same. Hence those who take individuals to be wholly concrete will, if they are clear-headed, be forced, with Leibniz, to identify the individual with the total succession of his states. But then we do not know who a man is until he is dead; we cannot speak of his capability of having done (or experienced) something else; for, as Leibniz said, it would not have been that individual but another who would have done it. The common-sense meaning of individual is destroyed if we simply identify an individual with an actual event-sequence. To save this meaning, and we need it for many purposes, we must admit, with the Buddhists and Whitehead, that individuality is somewhat abstract, compared to an actual event-sequence. It is the man now, his present actual state, which "has" the man as the same individual from birth to death, not the same individual which "has" the present actual state. We speak of someone's being "in a state" (not of the state as being in him). Whitehead can take this literally; substance philosophers cannot. The point is not that individual identity is an illusion, but that it is abstract. Concretely there is a new man each moment, "born anew" in religious language. But of course, in many important personality traits it may be the same man all the time. And each new state fits onto the one series which started with a certain embryo state in a certain mother. It is always, while the man lives, the same series, but the identity of such a series is somewhat abstract. To see the man as always the very same entity, we must abstract from what is new in him at each moment. Personal identity through experiences is a property of the experiences, they are not properties of the identity, or of the ego. If they were, to know an individual would mean knowing all his future. We should not really know which individual was John until John was dead. This is not how we use the idea of self-identity. It took European philosophy over two thousand years to think through this issue, which Buddhism thought through long ago. Contemporary physics, with its view of reality as consisting in events related in the four dimensions of space-time, helped Whitehead to see the point, but the Buddhists got there without his help.

The argument against the process view has been, "If there is change, something, X, must have changed from state A to state B." Very well, suppose the weather changes from wet to dry, does this mean there is an entity, the weather, as concrete as the wet and dry states? Are these "in" the weather? Surely the weather is in them. Suppose "public opinion" changes, or "the situation" changes—is it not obvious that the "subjects of change" here are relatively abstract entities? Process philosophy generalizes this insight. It treats change as the successive becoming of events related to one another, but also differing from one another in some more or less abstract respects which interest us. Change is the becoming of novelty, and process philosophy is all for that.

Another argument is: Memory shows us that we, the very same persons, were there in the past having certain experiences. But again, no one denies personal self-identity, provided its abstractness or partial nature is recognized. In the past that I recall, "I" was there, just in so far as what is important about "my" personal sequence of experiences was already in the earlier experiences. But why is it that we cannot remember our identical selves as small infants? Surely because in those early states what is now most important about us was not yet actual. To abstract from all that we have become since early infancy is more than we can do and still leave anything worth distinctly recalling as ourselves. But even in fairly early childhood important personality traits were already beginning to emerge, and so we can recall childhood experiences as making us already the "same" person we are now. Still, we certainly cannot ever remember that in the past we were concretely and precisely what we are now, for that we were not! The "self-same ego" is an abstraction from concrete realities, not itself a fully concrete reality. To see this is the beginning of wisdom in the theory of selfhood. The Buddhists saw it. (Did the Hindus? I am not convinced they did.)

One of the many signs of confusion in substance philosophy is the failure to deal with the obvious logical truth that identity is a symmetrical relation: if X is Y, then Y is X. Very well, if identity explains memory of the past, by the same token it does *not* explain the failure to "remember" the future. If memory is an entity being, or intuiting, that very same entity, then it ought to work equally in both directions. In spite of claims of some students of psychical research, the lack of real symmetry in this respect is too glaring to be ignored. We anticipate trends, extrapolate them into the future, but we remember not trends but particular incidents. Identity is not the logical structure to express this. And that substance philosophers rarely even mention this point is proof enough of how far they are from clarity as to the real problems. As Whitehead says, identity is "exactly the wrong answer" if the question is: How do we explain the creativity of process, its production of novelty? That it is the same entity does not imply that there are new states of the entity, still less that it is the previous states which are experienced, not the subsequent ones. In general, all attempts to explain becoming as a special case of being, novelty as a special case of permanence, have failed. Becoming is said to be a mixture of being and being-not-being is the whole mystery of becoming. A *fixed* mixture half-truth. Becoming is not simply a mixture of being and not-being, it is a mixture of which a *new* instance is *created* every moment, but in this moment-by-moment creation of *new* cases of being-not-being is the whole mystery of becoming. A *fixed* mixture of what is and what is not would still not be becoming, but at most only a deficient form of being. The *becoming* of new (allegedly) deficient forms of being is simply becoming, and no light is thrown on the *transition* to novelty by the talk about being and its negation. We shall see that, by contrast, being can very well be explicated as an aspect of novelty. The converse procedure has always failed, though men have often refused to take note of the failure. When they noted it, they excused themselves by declaring becoming "unreal." Its refusal to subordinate itself to being condemned it. But this is sheer question-begging. The necessity of the subordination having been assumed, of course it could also be deduced. But the validity of the assumption is not thereby confirmed; rather the resistance of becoming to the attempted subordination disconfirms the theory!

An important obstacle to the process view is the apparent continuity of becoming—for instance, of experiencing. It seems that experiencing is not a succession of distinct acts or happenings but just one perpetually changing act or happening, at least between waking and sleeping. Here some process philosophers have stopped short and never reached full clarity. This applies to Bergson and Dewey, for instance. And here again Whitehead, preceded by the Buddhists, and to his great credit by William James, carried the analysis through. Continuity is an abstract mathematical concept, not a given actuality. Half a continuum is itself a smaller continuum, but half a man is not a smaller man, nor is half a molecule just a smaller molecule. If happenings are actualities, and even more concrete than individuals, they must be like molecules or men, not like mathematical schema. If experiencing were continuous, then half of a half of a half . . . of an experience would also be an experience. However, though in a tenth of a second we can have an experience, in half of a half of a half of a tenth, it seems we cannot. Were we experiencing a continuum, indeed, we should have an infinite number of experiences between waking and having breakfast! This seems quite absurd. But the alternative is that we have a finite number of experiences, and no finite number can make a continuum. James said that each "specious present" was a new unit-happening which comes into actuality as a whole, not bit by bit. Whitehead accepts this, and generalizes it for other types of experiencing than the human, and ultimately for all happenings whatever. Reality consists of the becoming of unit-events, which he calls "actual entities," "actual occasions," "drops of experience." It is only with this doctrine that process philosophy can effectively compete with substance philosophies. For these had the advantage that individuals, at least individual animals, are units such that half a unit is not a unit in the same sense at all. In a room, the number of persons can be definite and finite; but in process philosophies which admit continuity, the number of happenings, even of a given kind, must be infinite in a single second. But then all definiteness is lost, and there are no objective units of reality. Giving up continuity —and here, too, Whitehead was helped by physics, with its quanta, while the Buddhists got there unaided—the difficulty is overcome. True, we cannot perhaps know what corresponds, in other animals and other types of process than human experiencing, to the human specious present of about .1 second. However, in some cases, e.g., birds, we can rather safely posit a greater number of experiences than ten while a clock ticks off one second. In any case this is a question of detail only.

Another difficulty which a process philosopher must deal with is the requirement that his view must *not* mean that literally "everything changes," or as the Buddhists put it, "everything is impermanent," passes away, from which they deduced the unimportance of ordinary human concerns. In meditation, in mysterious Nirvana, the Buddhists felt that they somehow transcended even impermanence, but only in nonrational fashion. It is necessary for a philosopher to have also a more theoretical escape. Buddha hinted once that there was something which does not pass away, but this was about as far as he would go. Here Bergson, along with Peirce, and then most explicitly and clearly Whitehead, has a great addition to make to the tradition of process philosophy. How do we even know that things *have* passed away, if not by preserving in memory at least something of what they have been? In memory, past happenings are still somehow with us. Moreover, in perception also past happenings in a fashion linger on in present experience. We now hear the explosion which in fact took place some seconds ago, we see a stellar explosion which took place years in the past. Memory and perception both somehow embrace the past and preserve something at least of its character. In human memory and perception this "immortality of the past" is faint and fragmentary; but then all human capacities are imperfect, limited. If we are to raise the question of deity at all, why not consider a perfect or divine memory, and a perfect or divine perception of happenings, once they have occurred? In such a perfect memory or perception the past might be literally immortal, adequately preserved in all its quality, all its beauty, forever.

Is this merely introducing God as a trick device to rid us of our difficulties? Yet what can any theory do but explain what otherwise remains inexplicable? And it is no merely emotional need that events should be preserved, that our lives should forever have some place or function in reality after they are over, or after, perhaps, all human life is ended. It is also a logical demand that after events have happened, it should always be true that they have. But if the Buddhists are right, what can make it true that things have happened just as they have? Truth must be true of reality. If the reality keeps fading out, so must truth. But what then would make it true that it had faded? Thus the literal immortality of the past, in principle accounted for by memory and perception, but adequately only in an adequate memory or perception, is required to explain what "truth" means.

One can justify introducing the idea of God into process philosophy in still other ways. I shall deal only with the following. If self-creativity is the universal principle, if all actualities are partly self-determined or free, what prevents indefinitely great confusion and conflict? Confusion and conflict are indeed real, but they are limited: The cosmos does go on in a reasonably foreseeable way, countless sorts of processes fit together into a varied and beautiful whole, and nobody thinks the universe is likely to blow up in universal conflict. The cosmic order can be viewed in one of two ways: (1) The many self-created creatures harmonize together sufficiently to constitute a cosmos, not thanks to any controlling influence or guidance, but purely spontaneously. Either by sheer luck or their own unimaginable wisdom and goodness, they co-operate to constitute and maintain a viable cosmos. (2) The many self-created creatures harmonize together to constitute a viable cosmos thanks to some controlling influence or guidance. This influence or guidance can, in a process philosophy, consist only in a supreme form of self-creative power, a supreme form of process which, because of its superiority, exerts an attraction upon all the others or, as Whitehead likes to put it, "persuades" or "lures" them to follow its directive. I believe a strong case indeed can be made for (2) as against (1). This is the "argument from design" or from order, as process philosophy conceives it.

You can read the great critics of the theistic proofs (say Hume and Kant), but you will not find that they have any clear conception of the argument in this form. For instance, they object that the order of the world, as we know it at least, is far from perfect. But process philosophy does not presume that there is an absolute order but only that, whatever disorder there may be in the cosmos, it *is* a thinkable cosmos, rather than an unthinkable chaos or confusion. And of course the order is not absolute if all creatures are partly self-determined. They respond to the universal lure or directive, but it is they who respond, and just *how* they respond is in some measure their own decision. Yet, though they can cause one another suffering by unfortunate responses, they cannot really disrupt the universe. Were there no universal directive, there seems no way to understand such an invulnerable integrity of the universe. And if it be said that we do not know this integrity to obtain, the reply is, it does not matter whether we know it or merely have faith in it, for to such faith there is no feasible alternative. Life itself is a venture of faith in the orderliness of reality. Only verbally can we renounce this faith. But some of us value, as a precious luxury if nothing more, the possibility of a rational theory of that orderliness. Theism alone can furnish such a theory. The rest is mystery pure and simple.

I wish to deal now with a central doctrine of Whitehead, that in the creative act which is reality itself "the many become one and are increased by one." To see what this means one may take one's own momentary experience as illustration. An experience is a unit-happening, and we have new ones about ten times a second, but they fit together so smoothly that we do not distinctly notice the transitions. In such a unit-experience there are memories of preceding experiences, especially those in the previous second or less, and there are various perceptions. But whatever is remembered and whatever is perceived also consists, from the most concrete point of view, in unit-happenings, analogous to single human experiences. The perceived or remembered happenings are the "many" referred to in the above quotation. That they "become one" is slightly elliptical, for "they are embraced together in a new unit-reality," the experience in question. But the multiplicity of events has thereby been "increased by one," as is obvious. And in the next moment this event, too, will be remembered or perceived, and so "become one" with various other events. Thus the process or experiencing is a perpetual unification of a pluralistic reality which, as fast as it gets unified, becomes pluralistic again, and so can never be finally unified. Process is creative synthesis, the many into a new one producing a new many—and so on forever. The synthesis is creative, for how could a plurality dictate its own increase? Determinism, if carried to the limit, is magic, not rationality. The causal conditions for each free act are previous acts of freedom; creativity feeds upon its own products and upon nothing else! (Whitehead's "eternal objects" may seem to contradict this; if they do, then I should myself reject them.) Because the previous products are retained in the new syntheses, there is (in spite of Buddhism) any amount of permanence in this philosophy. The products of creation are never destroyed by new creation, but always utilized and preserved forever, at least on the divine level.

What Whitehead calls the "principle of relativity" is the principle of creativity looked at in reverse, as it were. Whatever in any sense is, he says, furnishes a "potential" for all subsequent acts of synthesis. "Being" is here defined through becoming: That may be said to be which is available for memory or perception, for integration into ever new acts of synthesis, and in this sense is a potential for all future becoming. *To be is to be available* for all future actualities. This availability is the very meaning of present "reality." There are profound ethical and religious implications of this view which Buddhism (though without giving a clear rationale for them) appreciated, and Whitehead also emphasizes. I call the doctrine "contributionism." Individual existence is nothing more nor less than a contribution to the future world society, the entire life and value of which is destined to be appreciated and enjoyed forever by the Eminent or Divine creativity, this immortality in God being the creatures' only value in the long run. Egocentric motivations essentially consist in metaphysical confusion. And this is why a Buddhist termed the egocentric view "writhing in delusion." For it involves one in an utterly vain and painful attempt to make reality ultimately a contribution to oneself; whereas the final destiny and value of all nondivine life lies beyond the particular self.

It is to be noted that the foregoing doctrine literally defines "being," or permanent reality, in terms of becoming. Thus it is a misconception to suppose that process philosophy, siding with becoming, rejects being. Rather, it is a doctrine of being *in* becoming, permanence in the novel; by contrast, philosophies of being are doctrines of becoming in being, novelty in the permanent. The trouble is that to insinuate anything new into the permanent is to make it a new thing. The old with the least new factor is, as a whole, new. This is inherent in the meaning of "whole," that its parts contribute to it; and with new parts making new contributions there must to that extent be a new whole. Only abstractly, by disregarding the new, can we say that it is the very same whole. But then it becomes a relative and partly subjective matter how far the new is worthy of being disregarded in this fashion. And what is not relative or subjective is the logical necessity that in its concrete entirety the whole reality is always new, however unimportant the novel additions. The only clear alternative to this is Leibniz' denial that in reality anything new is ever added, since the individual contained all his adventures the moment he was born or created. It is a fine example of how little people want to speak precisely that nearly everyone in philosophy has thought he could reject Leibniz' proposal without going on to a philosophy of events and without giving up the meaning of individual needed in ordinary speech (that of an entity indentifiable in abstraction from many particular facts about it) and do all this without confusion or inconsistency. Leibniz saw with deadly accuracy the real issue: What does the concretely definite include in this definiteness? If the concretely definite is the individual as identical throughout his career, then at all times the individual's adventures, past and future, are parts of the individual. If the concretely definite is not the individual but the momentary states, then there can be a real distinction between present, past, and future, otherwise not. Leibniz never thought of taking this process view. But he did see once for all the impossibility of having it both ways, that is, taking the enduring individual as the definite or concrete entity and also supposing that the given individual might, as that same individual, take this course or that, make this decision or that, enjoy this experience or that. The common-sense meaning of individual as facing real alternatives is incompatible with the metaphysics which takes the most concrete units of reality to be enduring individuals; it is only consistent with a metaphysics which takes momentary states to be the concrete realities. That this is not a commonplace in philosophy is an illustration of cultural lag. Leibniz gave us our chance to be clear about the point; it is time we took advantage of his contribution.

So far from its being true that Whitehead, for instance, is denying our right to talk of persons as self-identical through change, he is rather protecting this right against the threat of a metaphysics which fails to harmonize with it except thanks to vagueness or ambiguity. There is a somewhat abstract identity of persons and enduring objects. This is just the point, that identity through change is abstractly real. And also, persons and things are *almost* concrete, they are concrete in comparison with obviously abstract entities such as "being human" or "triangle." Aristotelian substantialism was vaguely and roughly correct; Leibniz was precisely and with the clarity of genius wrong; Whitehead is as clear as Leibniz, but faithful to the indispensable elements of the notion of enduring individuality.

The reader may have been worried about the way in which we have taken human experience as the model of reality. Is this not suspiciously anthropomorphic? The answer is, we have taken human experience only as one end of an analogy which may be stretched as wide as one's imagination can stretch it. An amoeba can "learn" and make what look like "choices" or exhibit "strategy" toward a "desired" end. Of course its "experiences" or "feelings" are not much like ours. But to say that they are absolutely different, or (the same) that it has none, is merely to say that we cannot have the faintest idea of what it is like to be an amoeba, or that we can only know about an amoeba what it looks like to a human being observing it. Similarly, we can perhaps only know what a molecule is as a humanly-perceived phenomenon, but cannot know what it is to be a molecule. We can know it as an element in an event of human experience, but not as an event on its own. Whitehead does not deny that one may play safe in this way. But he thinks it is a sheer illusion to suppose that there is some *other* way to try to conceive what an amoeba or atom is in itself than to try to imagine how it feels. He finds no other way. And neither do I. A fair number of philosophers and scientists, from Leibniz down to our time, have agreed with us. The greatest process philosophers (Peirce also) have been universal *psychicalists,* seeing in mind or experience "the sole self-intelligible thing" (Peirce); in this, agreeing with the last great philosopher of being (Leibniz). They find no reasonable explanation of "matter," except as a form of manifestation of "mind." Metaphysics has always tended to reach this result. Northern Buddhism illustrates this, but so does Hinduism. It is only a little below the surface in Plato and Aristotle. The opponents of psychicalistic metaphysics are, whether they know it or not, opponents of all metaphysics. For no clear metaphysical alternative has ever been proposed. Dualism is a problem, not a solution. That experiences do occur cannot be denied; hence, the only open question is, does anything else occur? One may safely defy critics to prove the affirmative. Nonhuman experiences occur, no doubt, but that things constituted by no sort of experience, however different from ours, occur, this no science, no philosophy, can possibly establish. And an intelligible world-picture results from so modulating the idea of experience as such that it coincides with that of reality. At no lesser price can such a picture be had.

Neoclassical metaphysics is the fusion of the idealism or psychicalism which is implicit or explicit in all metaphysics with the full realization of the primacy of becoming as self-creativity or creative synthesis, feeding only upon its own products forever. This creativity may be conceived to have an eminent or divine form as well as lesser forms, and it perpetually immortalizes its products, literally so by virtue of the Eminent creativity. In no other philosophy, I believe, have so many theoretical and spiritual values been united with so much appearance of consistency and clarity. If this is not so, then I am indeed deluded.

SUGGESTED READINGS

On Process Philosophy and Theology

Brown, Delwin, Ralph E. James Jr., and Gene Reeves (eds.). *Process Philosophy and Christian Thought.* Indianapolis: Bobbs-Merrill, 1971. Paperback—Indianapolis: Bobbs-Merrill.

Cobb, John B., Jr. *A Christian Natural Theology: Based on the Thought of Alfred North Whitehead.* Philadelphia: Westminster Press, 1965.

Hartshorne, Charles. "Process Philosophy as a Resource for Christian Thought," *Philosophical Resources for Christian Thought.* Edited by Perry LeFevre. Nashville: Abingdon Press, 1968, pp. 44-66.

Loomer, Bernard M. "Christian Faith and Process Philosophy," *The Journal of Religion,* 29 (1949), 181-203. Reprinted in *Process Philosophy and Christian Thought,* pp. 70-98.

Peters, Eugene H. *The Creative Advance: An Introduction to Process Philosophy as a Context for Christian Faith.* St. Louis: Bethany Press, 1966. Paperback—St. Louis: Bethany Press.

See articles on this theme in *The Christian Scholar,* 50/3 (Fall, 1967).

Philosophers of Process

Alexander, Samuel. *Space, Time and Deity.* London: Macmillan, 1927. Paperback—New York: Dover.

Bergson, Henri. *Creative Evolution.* Translated by Arthur Mitchell. New York: Henry Holt, 1911.

Browning, Douglas, ed. *Philosophers of Process.* New York: Random House, 1965: an anthology containing selections from Henri Bergson, Charles Sanders Peirce, William James, Samuel Alexander, C. Lloyd Morgan, John Dewey, George Herbert Mead, and Alfred North Whitehead, with an introduction by Charles Hartshorne.

Morgan, C. Lloyd. *Emergent Evolution.* New York: Henry Holt, 1926.

Teilhard de Chardin, Pierre. *The Phenomenon of Man.* Revised English Edition. New York: Harper and Row, 1965. Paperback—New York: Harper Torchbook.

Whitehead, Alfred North. *Process and Reality.* New York: Macmillan, 1929. Paperback—New York: Free Press.

4 Whitehead's Method of Empirical Analysis

BERNARD M. LOOMER

Whitehead's process philosophy has both a rational and an empirical side. The rational and logical elements have been explored and developed at length in the writings of Charles Hartshorne. In the present selection,* Bernard M. Loomer examines the empirical side. This piece is the conclusion of Loomer's doctoral dissertation, which is one of the earliest efforts to use Whitehead's philosophy in formulating a theological method. Of this dissertation, Bernard E. Meland has written: "Even though this manuscript has not been published, it has wielded an influence comparable to that of a published work and remains one of the basic documents in process theology." [1] We are happy to be able to make the conclusion of this dissertation available in print. In the light of Whitehead's method of empirical analysis, Loomer explores the basic Whiteheadian notion of causal efficacy and the empirical dimension of Whitehead's doctrine of God.

For many years Bernard M. Loomer was Dean of the Divinity School and professor of philosophy of religion at the University of Chicago. He is presently professor of philosophical theology at the American Baptist Seminary of the West and in the Graduate Theological Union at Berkeley.

* From "The Theological Significance of the Method of Empirical Analysis in the Philosophy of A. N. Whitehead" (unpublished Ph.D. dissertation, Divinity School, The University of Chicago, 1942), pp. 369-387. Reprinted with permission.

[1] Bernard E. Meland, "The Empirical Tradition in Theology at Chicago," in *The Future of Empirial Theology*, edited by Bernard E. Meland (Chicago: The University of Chicago Press, 1969), p. 42.

Our inquiry has been concerned with (1) an analysis of Whitehead's methodology and the application of this method to (2) his epistemology and (3) his concept of God. Treating each of these three topics in turn, we can now state our findings in a summary fashion.

METHODOLOGY

The underlying principle of this thesis is the contention that Whitehead is a speculative or a rational empiricist. There are elements in his sytem which would seem to indicate an uncertainty or a wavering on his part, but essentially his methodology is truly empirical. A correlative contention is that Whitehead's method constitutes a novel contribution to the development of empirical philosophy.

These two theses are substantiated by an examination of Whitehead's basic methodology: what we have called "empirical analysis." The goal of philosophical inquiry is to discover and to designate as precisely as possible those factors which are to be found in all types of experiences. There are all kinds of elements or structures or forms to be found in our various types of experience. Some structures are found in some experiences, but not in others. Philosophy is concerned with those structures which are universal and which must be present if we are to have any experiences at all. Empirical analysis is the method which Whitehead uses in attempting to arrive at this goal. This method is not solely a logical procedure whereby one attempts to analyze propositions so as to elicit their most general forms; it is not merely logical analysis. Rather, and primarily, it is empirical analysis of non-linguistic structures that are exemplified in the events of our daily experiences. Of course, the analysis of logical constructions is a valuable tool which helps in this other type of analysis, but one is subordinate to the other.

Empirical analysis attempts to specify those elements which are necessary to any concreteness whatsoever in our experience. Concreteness (as opposed to abstractions) is attributable only to events, which are the individual, particular, organic, unified, wholistic occurrences which make up the life-stream of our experiences. They are individual totalities which are internally related to other totalities. Thus an event is mostly constituted by its relations to other events. When events interact with each other, structures are realized in the related events. And since the relations constituting an event are numerous, the total content of these contained structures is practically inexhaustible.

All inquiry is concerned with some of these realized forms or structures to the exclusion of others. With regard to certain purposes these excluded factors are irrelevant. Consequently all inquiries deal only with abstractions. Likewise philosophic categories are designative of abstractions because philosophy does not consist of an exhaustive inventory of all realized structures. But its categories, as contrasted with the categories of other disciplines, are necessary to concreteness in the sense that they refer to those structures which underlie all other structures. Therefore philosophy offers a critique of all abstractions which are of a lower order of generality than its own.

By means of empirical investigation, then, philosophy attempts to define the nature of the most general characters that pertain to all experience whatsoever. These most general and pervasive features of experience—the categories—are "necessary" in the sense that no experience is possible without their exemplification or ingression because all experiences testify to their presence.

This attempt to construct a system of general ideas which designate these most general structures of experience constitutes part of Whitehead's contribution to empirical philosophy. The other and correlative aspect of his contribution lies in his characterization of these empirical categories. His basic criticism of traditional empiricism is that it has not been sufficiently empirical: it has concerned itself with the "accidents" of experience and not with the necessities. Traditional empiricism has emphasized the trivial, superficial, and transient structures that occur in our experiences—the "manageable" aspects of events. It has assumed that those factors which are clear and distinct in our consciousness are important and basic in proportion to their clarity and distinctness. The vague and ill-defined factors have been interpreted in terms of these clearly and distinctly given elements. It has stressed too much those abstractions which are too far removed from the concreteness of inter-connected events.

Whitehead inverts this whole position. His primary concern is with those factors which are stable and universally recurring and therefore necessary. He tries to show how these necessities of experience underlie the accidents and how the latter presuppose the former. He stresses the "compulsions" of life, the elemental features of experience which make us what we are and which we cannot control. They are not manageable. For example, traditional empiricism has built its categories on the basis of our sense-experiences. But, says Whitehead, sense-experience is a manageable experience; we can control it at will. It is an accident of our relations with our environment because we can live without it. It is a necessary part of our humanity, but it does not cause us to exist in any elementary sense. Whitehead puts primary stress on "causal efficacy," a non-sensuous type of perception which underlies our sense-experiences and which is necessary for our continued existence. Similarly, he denies the notion that the clearly-given facts of life are important. It is an established principle in his methodology that the clear and distinct elements of experience are the variable facts, and the variable facts are superficial. They are surface phenomena. Whitehead's basic point is that the necessities of experience are, by their very nature, vaguely and obscurely given. This is the reason why the work of empirical analysis is so difficult. In our analysis of experience we must try to lay bare these most general and pervasive structures by figuratively casting aside those structures which are particular and transient.

The reasons for this vagueness and obscurity of these infallibly-given structures suggest themselves to us. In the first place, our habitual modes of attention point away from these general structures and our minds find it difficult to concentrate on them. We usually focus our attention on the passing, transient, novel, and superficial elements in our experience. We don't concentrate on or even notice those things which are always with us. We take them for granted and presuppose them. They are so permanent, stable, and recurring that they are part and parcel of our very existence. They are so close to us, so inextricably bound up with all that we are and do, that we cannot dissociate ourselves from them. We cannot get outside ourselves to look at them in any sustained manner. This situation is the context of Whitehead's common-sensism. Since these structures are so pervasive and so fundamental, they are presupposed in our every-day lives. And the common pre-suppositions of daily experience therefore furnish us with clues as to the nature of those structures. Philosophy thus becomes the rationalization of these basic common presuppositions, and failure to achieve this justification should make us sceptical of any dichotomous philosophy. For Whitehead, the ultimate court of appeal regarding evidence lies in the content of common-sense experience —but not in common-sense theories about this experience.

In the second place, our language leads us away from the concreteness of events. Whitehead urges us to be wary of the notion that language is adequate to designate clearly these underlying structures of all our experiences. Language presupposes but does not mention that which must be present. It usually specifies what might be absent. It is Whitehead's contention that most words have reference to those aspects of our experience which are sensational and arresting; they originated in practical contexts in order that people might share with others their superficial interactions with nature. For the most part language is concerned with the high abstractions of our communal life. Also erroneous viewpoints become embedded in language. We unconsciously inherit these misconceptions when we inherit a language, and language plays a dominant role in the construction of our mental functioning. It thereby becomes difficult for us to look at experience in ways other than those dictated by the construction of our language patterns. Many times we identify the structure of language with the structure of non-linguistic reality. Thus the task of empirical analysis is to probe beneath the apparent clarity of our everyday language and try to ascertain the nature of those structures which language enshrines but does not clearly designate.

One of the most important aids in the work of empirical analysis is the methodological principle of "descriptive generalization": the procedure of generalizing a description. The process consists of taking certain ideas which are actually descriptive of a certain area of experience and generalizing these ideas to see if they are applicable for all types of existence. One can start from any area of experience and use any ideas as a base—provided of course that the starting ideas are fairly general to begin with. We have found that Whitehead has generalized the concepts of relativity and quanta into metaphysical propositions. Similarly, some of his other basic principles consist of generalizations of certain fundamental aesthetic concepts. In other words this method is a generalized version of the scientific method, differing only in a degree of generality.

Admittedly, descriptive generalization is a speculative and imaginative adventure. It is the speculative aspect of speculative empiricism. But Whitehead defends speculative practices by all manner of beautiful and historical illustrations. Speculation is not antithetical to empiricism because speculation as such is not knowledge. All knowledge is empirically tested; but speculation is a necessary tool in the attainment of knowledge, and this for several reasons. In the first place, we usually don't find what we are not looking for. The speculative hypothesis of the scientist guides him in his investigations. Likewise in the case of the philosopher. It is an axiom with Whitehead that the development of abstract theories precedes our understanding of concrete facts. Speculative flights of the imagination may lead us astray; they often do. But even when they are wrong they have done us a service, for they have reduced the number of possible alternatives.

And, on the other hand, these speculative formulations of hypothetical connections open up new alternatives, new possibilities of interpretation. They furnish us with novel insights which tend to shake us out of our habitual modes of thought and observation. They compel us to return to those aspects of concrete events which have been overlooked and neglected; and all abstractions are neglective. And these novel ideas restimulate and recreate us in our very entertainment of them. They lift us out of the repetitious patterns of our usual experience which are deadening by virtue of their monotony. Progress in thought and action is dependent upon the novelty inherent in adventure.

Of course adventure has its dangers. And the imaginative construction of generalized hypotheses must be rigorously controlled by the demands of logical coherence and consistency. But Whitehead is an empiricist in an ultimate sense because the validity of a speculative scheme is derived from its conformity with observed facts. The scheme must be adequate on its descriptive side. The ideas will be applicable to some experience because they originated from selected fields of interest. But they must be adequate to all experience in order to be philosophic propositions.

There is another methodological principle which is important in the method of empirical analysis: what we have called the "monistic principle." This principle is used in science, but Whitehead again reverses the whole point. Physical science attempts to interpret living bodies in accordance with what it knows of other sections of the physical universe. Its cosmology has usually been that of a universalized physics. Whitehead attempts to construct, in a sense, a universalized psychology: the rest of the physical universe is to be interpreted in accordance with what we know of the human body. But there is this important qualification: this psychology must not be composed of those elements of our experience which are distinctively human. The projected interpretation should not be grounded upon the accidents of our humanity, but upon the necessary factors of our existence. The human body is selected as the basic course for our data because it is that part of our environment with which we most intimately react.

The alternative to the adoption of some such monistic principle is the frank acceptance of a dualistic world-view—which Whitehead just as frankly rejects.

EPISTEMOLOGY

One of the clearest and most fully developed illustrations of the method of empirical analysis and of Whitehead's methodological principles is to be found in his philosophical epistemology. Sense-perception, which heretofore has been accepted as the only means of obtaining and testing empirical knowledge, is found to be an element present in only a few types of experience. It is a manageable type of experience because we can control it: we can shut our eyes and blot out experiences of sight. It gives us elements which are clear and distinct, but these factors are not fundamental. It enhances the accuracy of our perceptual references and it makes science possible. It is necessary for our experiences as humans, but it leads us away from the concrete connections of experience. On the basis of sense-perception, our emotional reactions are only interpretations of our sensations, but they are not inherent in the sensation itself. By confining himself purely to the data derived from sense-experiences, Hume was not able to justify the ineradicable common-sense belief in the reality of causation. The notion of self-identity is also unintelligible on this theory. Similarly, the concept of power is purely an inference and an interpretation. Likewise the idea that we perceive actual, individual, concrete objects is ruled out.

Whitehead's primary emphasis is upon what he calls "causal efficacy"—a non-sensuous type of perception. It is a heavy, emotional and uncontrollable type of experience, wherein we feel ourselves driven by the efficient forces of our immediate past. It is a physical experience, not a conceptual interpretation, basically. The best and most conclusive illustration of the reality of this experience is to be found in our feeling of derivation from our immediately past self, that past self of a fifth of a second ago which is past and yet present. We feel ourselves to be almost identical with that past self because we feel ourselves conforming to it. It is a physical causal feeling. It is a vague feeling, and the factors are obscurely given; it almost eludes analysis. But it comes close to the concrete connections which form the basis of our on-going existence. We know that we were angry a quarter of a second ago because we now feel ourselves conforming to that anger. We remember it. But memory, for Whitehead, is a concept denoting the inherence of the past in the present. It is the causal efficaciousness of the past making the present conform to it. It is inheritance of the present from the past whereby the present reenacts the feelings of the immediate past. It is the physical feeling of power driving us on to further activity. And essentially it is an emotional feeling—a blind emotional reaction. Thus the fundamental and aboriginal type of perception is emotional.

Sense-perception, for Whitehead, confines us to the immediate present. From it we can gain no knowledge of the past or future. Knowledge of the past and the sense of projection into the future is wholly derived from causal efficacy. Since contemporary events are causally independent, we can learn nothing about present concrete occasions. Presentationally we see a color, but presentationally we cannot know whether it belongs to an external object or not. Sense-perception essentially is projection of our inherited bodily feelings, but causal efficacy is the inheritance. We conform to what we inherit, but we control what we project into the contemporaneous world about us.

Sense-perception is not an elemental structure in our experience because it is completely dependent upon and a derivation from causal efficacy. Sense-experience is wholly contingent upon the functioning of the body, what Whitehead calls "the witness of the body." For example, we say that we see with our eyes, hear with our ears, taste with our palate, etc. No one really doubts the reality of this experience and the validity of this description. But how do we know that we see with our eyes, etc.? It is not a question primarily as to which of our bodily organs function in a certain type of perception. That is, the fundamental question is not whether we see with our eyes or see with our ears. The primary question is how do we know that our bodies function in sense-perception anyway? This knowledge is not derived from sense-experience itself. Even if we were to look in a mirror, we would only see our eyes; we would not see our eyes functioning in sense-perception. The knowledge of the witness of our bodily organs in sense-perception is derived non-sensuously. Of course we can have an inferential type of knowledge on this point, but this is not what we mean ultimately. Whitehead's stress here is that the antecedent functioning of our bodies in sense-perception is derived from a causal physical feeling—vague to be sure but important. We inherit the data of our past bodily functionings and we conform to the type of feelings inherent in these functionings.

This is sense-experience in its dependence on causal efficacy. The dependence is grounded upon what Whitehead calls "physical feelings"—the feelings or prehensions of other actual concrete occasions of experience. They are causal in nature and compulsory in their import. They are emotional in regard to the transmission of their content. On the basis of Whitehead's monistic principle, they are interpreted as being fundamental to all types of experience, human and non-human. Whitehead accepts the empirical principle that all ideas or conceptual functionings—conceptual feelings—are derived from physical feelings. The derivation of sense-perception from non-sensuous perception is rooted in the theory that sense-perception is a product of the integration and reintegration of physical and conceptual feelings which take place in a relatively late stage in certain types of occasions of experience. These processes of integration and reintegration are always means of simplification. Thus sense-perception is a simplified and abstracted edition of the data we have non-sensuously inherited by means of causal physical feelings. If the simplification and abstraction did not take place, we would not be able to have the manageable experiences of sense-presentation. Sense-perception is more accurate in its references precisely because it is an abstracted view of reality.

This whole point can be seen more clearly by an examination of the role of sense-data or sensa. Sensa are the simplest type of what Whitehead calls "eternal objects." An eternal object is a form of definiteness, an element of determinateness which an actual occasion of experience must exemplify in order to be an actual, definite, and determined something. Its "ingression" into the actual course of events is the means whereby indeterminate creativity realizes itself in the form of actual, definite, and limited creatures. Eternal objects are the data of conceptual feelings, just as actual concrete occasions are the data of physical feelings. Each type of feeling has what is termed a "subjective form" which is that feeling as a definite, limited, specific feeling; it is a particularized "how" of feeling.

The usual epistemological theory of sensa (such as colors, sounds, smells, etc.) states that they are primarily perceived as colors, sounds, smells, etc., and that our emotional reactions are interpretations of these sensory experiences which in themselves are unrelated to our emotional feelings. It assumes that concrete actual objects are likewise inferences based upon our sensations of sensory qualities. Likewise our notions of causality are unjustifiable (in a rational sense) inferences. These experiences of sensa give us data which are clear and distinct, and we can find nothing more basic or fundamental in our perceptual experiences. The theory assumes that all more complex concepts are to be based on these primary sensations. The result is a Humian scepticism or Santayana's solipsism of the present moment.

Whitehead considers an experience of sensa, as sensa, to be a highly abstracted type of perception. For him, sensa are primarily felt emotionally as aspects of physical causal feelings. More specifically, they are basically apprehended as being qualifications of the subjective forms of physical feelings. In a later stage of an occasion of experience, conceptual feelings intervene and abstract the sensa from its physical and emotional content. The concept of bare sensa is a product of a process of abstraction and simplification due to conceptual functioning. That is, sensa are forms of emotional reactions; they are aspects of affective tones. They are qualifications of the "how" of specific physical feelings. For example, Whitehead says that we enjoy the green foliage of the trees in springtime greenly; we appreciate the beauties of a sunset with an emotional pattern including in its elements the colors and contrasts of the vision. That is, the basic non-sensuous experience consists of, say, a smelly feeling. By means of conceptual feelings, the intellect of man takes as a datum the feeling of that smell. But this datum is a derived abstraction minus the emotional context of the original situation. Thus sense-perception is a relatively rare phenomenon of planetary existence because it is dependent upon fairly complex conceptual functionings (mentality).

Sense-perception is not a fundamental structure of our experience for another reason. The data of sense-perception (i.e., sensa) are not primarily perceived as qualifications or attributes of regions external to the human body. They are basically felt as being qualitative aspects inherent in our antecedent bodily functions. Then they are abstracted and subsequently transmuted into the characters of external regions. They may or may not be objective qualities of external events. This depends upon the relations between our bodies and the larger and more distant environment. But the bodily organs inherit these eternal objects from the prior functionings of antecedent bodily organs and these latter organs inherit these sensa from the more distant environment. But this is wholly a non-sensuous perception. The geometrical references of our bodies in non-sensuous perception are very vague and indefinite. The increased precision of spatial reference in sense-perception is due to the simplification involved in transmutation. But the transmutation is dependent upon a relatively complex stage of conceptual functioning. The primary situation is the inheritance of emotional energy in the definite forms of sensa—an inheritance transmitted from bodily occasion to bodily occasion and finally "projected" onto an external region. It is therefore correct to say that sensa, such as colors, are both objective characters of external events and characters of our own subjective feelings.

Secondary qualities are as objective and as subjective as anything else in nature. The "projection" involved in sense-perception is not an arbitrary and fanciful affair. The sensa that are emotionally inherited (in non-sensuous perception) by our bodies are inherited with their integral geometrical relations. Sense-perception (as opposed to sense-reception) is a refinement of this cruder type of perception. Of course in cases of illusion and other distorted forms of perception, the sensa are mostly subjective in character. This is primarily the fault of our bodily reactions, and secondarily of our conceptual functionings. In the pure form of either causal efficacy or sense-perception, Whitehead claims that there is no error. Error arises from improper "symbolic reference" which is the fusion of the two pure modes. But it is through causal efficacy that we derive our data concerning other concrete actual entities. Sense-perception furnishes us with knowledge only about the present world expressed in terms of mathematical structures characterized by sense qualities. The actual entities that we causally feel are only past actual entities. Contemporaneous events are causally independent, and thus we can know them only indirectly through our knowledge of past events. But sense-experience in itself furnishes us with data which may or may not be characters of external events in their concrete particularity.

Events or occasions of experience are the final realities of the actual world. There is nothing more ultimate. The component parts of these actual entities are feelings or prehensions. By means of feelings, one actuality grasps or prehends aspects of other actualities. That is, actual entities are related to each other by means of their feelings. The actual occasions that are felt are always past occasions. Therefore it is Whitehead's position that the most elemental form of perception is emotional sympathy whereby one actual entity feels the feeling in a past actual entity and feels it conformally. The conformation is the sympathy.

But only a part of the past is felt in a sympathetic manner. The past is present only under an abstraction; that is, it exists in the present only in perspective and not in its totality. The reason for this abstraction from the totality of the past lies in the aesthetic natures of the occasions concerned. Each occasion is a process of becoming which is controlled by its own immanent ideals. The present occasion is a limited, finite, and definite something which prehends or feels some elements and excludes (negatively prehends) other elements. The exclusion or inclusion of the elements depends upon their compatibility or incompatibility with the ideal at which the occasion aims. Thus each occasion is an aesthetic achievement and an aesthetic synthesis of diverse elements (i.e., feelings) inherited from past actual occasions of experience. It is a debatable point in Whitehead's system as to whether each actual entity is a complete harmony, that is, without any discordant or incompatible elements. At least Whitehead is not clear on this point. But he is very definite on the point that the objectification of the past in the present is a reduction process: the past occasion is not felt in its complete concrete particularity and totality.

The dominant conclusion is that the most primitive form of perception is the transmission and conformal inheritance of emotional energy which is clothed in the specific forms provided by sensa. The inheritance consists of feeling-tones with evidence of their origin—that is, vector feeling-tones.

GOD

Whitehead's concept of God is another example of the functioning of empirical analysis. Some of his statements can be interpreted as being logical arguments for the existence of God, but fundamentally Whitehead's analysis aims at being descriptive. God is present in every type of experience, "experience drunk and experience sober," experience good and experience evil. God as primordial means that no matter when or where we examine experience, we always find this divine factor.

Whitehead's description is based on an analysis of "order," and order is essentially aesthetic in its designation. It has reference to the fact that an actual occasion of experience is an aesthetic achievement: it is a definite, limited, determined something. The fact of order in experience is necessary because pure creativity and pure potentiality in themselves are incapable of producing actual occasions. Of course we never experience either pure creativity or pure potentiality; but we are aware of our limitations, of our finiteness. We are conscious of this situation because we find ourselves surrounded by alternative possibilities. We exclude more than we include. How do we account for this fact of limitation?

Whitehead's answer is that the explanation of limitation lies in the ordered relevance of possibilities to actual occasions. Each possibility has a greater or less relevance to each actual occasion, and possibilities are graded in their relevance to each occasion. This gradation of relevance is the fact of order in experience. Some possibilities are contradictory in relation to some occasions, others are compatible, and still others are mutually supporting and vivifying. Possibilities are realized or not realized in events according to their degree of compatibility or incompatibility. The relevance of possibilities varies from occasion to occasion, but the structure of ordered relationship is inevitable.

Now this fact of order is a "divine" element in experience in the sense that this order is not man-made. We are more or less free to accept or reject certain possibilities as relevant for realization, but we do not create the fact or degree of relevance. Conceivably one could say that an individual could establish his own order of relevance, but this supposition does not explain the common relevance of a possibility for many individuals. It is true that we inherit from the past of our experience much of this ordered relevance, but this merely pushes the problem back through the past. At any rate the past alone does not account for the relevance of novel elements to already realized elements. Thus the relevance of possibilities to actual events is given as an integral aspect of our experience. The relevance of a possibility for an actual occasion constitutes the "lure" of that possibility (or eternal object). This is God functioning as a final cause, an objective "lure for feeling." This ordered relevance of all eternal objects is God conceived of as the principle of limitation or the principle of concretion. God is that ordering element whereby creativity assumes specific characters, and without which no actual occasions of experience are possible. God, in this function, is the infallibly-present ground of experience. God as primordial, as the principle of concretion, is the secularized version of the religious concept of "God as love." He is also the principle of value.

There is one God because the basic character of this ordering relationship remains unchanged. Every actual occasion (or, synonymously, every realization of value) is an aesthetic and harmonious fact. There must be some degree of compatible relationship between the diverse elements in order that there may be an actuality at all. The degree of harmony realized may vary from occasion to occasion, but complete chaos, complete mutual obstruction, can result in nothing actual. At least every experienced actuality exemplifies a harmonious pattern or structure to some extent. All instances of value exemplify the same basic structure, although there are variable or dimensional elements involved in the various particular illustrations of this generic structure. The relevance of possibilities varies from occasion to occasion precisely because of the identity of this structure which underlies all other relationships between possibilities. The same considerations apply to the concept of God conceived as the growth of value.

God is present, therefore, in every experience. But evil need not be. Most illustrations of value may exemplify elements which mitigate the harmony or good. But it is conceivable that certain types of perfection may be achieved. However, it is Whitehead's position that there is no final perfection—beyond which there is no greater possible perfection. There are grades and types of perfection. Thus ideals of perfection vary at different stages of our existence. Thus perfection is a relative term, at least as applied to actual achievement.

But God is not merely an abstract form or structure which is exemplified in every experience. In keeping with his ontological principle, Whitehead conceives of God as an actual concrete occasion. God is not only a structure, but He is also a process—a growth. This is God as "consequent." And in this aspect of his being, God is finite and therefore limited. Primordially, God is infinite in his conceptual ordering of all possibilities. As consequent, God is finite in his achievement of value, in the physical realization of his own conceptual nature. The consequent nature of God is composed of the world's reaction on God's primordial nature. Therefore God is physically limited by the realization of value in the world.

God as primordial seems to have a firm empirical rootage. But the concept of God as consequent has some difficulties, or at least ambiguities. In the first place, God as one event or occasion or experience cannot be considered as a present event because contemporaneous events are causally independent. He can only be a single individual in the immediate past. But, in the second place, if God is in our immediate past, why is he not an efficient cause as well as a final cause? Why doesn't he compel us to do certain things by virtue of our casual physical feelings of him? Whitehead's answer would probably be that our physical feeling of God is a "hybrid" physical feeling whereby we prehend him in terms of his conceptual feelings. But how then do we distinguish our physical feelings of God from our physical feelings of other past actual occasions? This position seems to come close to an ultimate monism with its denial of the ultimate plurality of individual events.

But, finally, God as "everlasting" seems to be a denial of Whitehead's basic naturalism. One of naturalism's chief tenets is that categories that apply to all events must likewise apply to God. God is not to be treated as an exception to metaphysical principles but rather as their chief exemplification. To hold otherwise is to deny that we can have any natural knowledge of God. One of Whitehead's basic points is that our prehension of past occasions always involves loss. But in God there is no loss when God physically prehends the world. This is his answer to what Whitehead feels is the deepest religious need, but the empirical grounds for this claim are not clear.

SUGGESTED READINGS

On the Empirical Aspect of Process Thought

See the following selections in *The Future of Empirical Theology,* edited by Bernard E. Meland (Chicago: The University of Chicago Press, 1969):

Cobb, John B., Jr. "What is Alive and What is Dead in Empirical Theology?" pp. 89-101.

Hefner, Philip J. "Towards a New Doctrine of Man: The Relationship of Man and Nature," pp. 235-266.

Loomer, Bernard M. "Empirical Theology within Process Thought," pp. 149-173.

Meland, Bernard E. "The Empirical Tradition in Theology at Chicago," pp. 1-62.

———. "Can Empirical Theology Learn Something from Phenomenology?" pp. 283-305.

Ogden, Schubert M. "Present Prospects for Empirical Theology," pp. 65-88.

Williams, Daniel Day. "Suffering and Being in Empirical Theology," pp. 175-194.

PART TWO

GOD AND THE WORLD

Alfred North Whitehead
Charles Hartshorne
Schubert M. Ogden
Walter E. Stokes
John B. Cobb, Jr.
Daniel Day Williams

5 God and the World

ALFRED NORTH WHITEHEAD

At the base of American process theology is White-head's doctrine of God. The following selection,* which is the final chapter of his major work *Process and Reality,* contains his most important statement of his position on God and the world. As the climax of an intricate philosophical work, the chapter builds upon categories and principles developed in the earlier part of the treatise. Yet even when read as an independent piece, it conveys the essential lines of his position. Whitehead criticizes the concepts of God as monarch, moralist, and unmoved mover; instead he proposes the notion of tender love operating in the world. In this context he develops his dipolar conception of the divinity, in which God is seen to have a primordial and a consequent nature. Through this conception he establishes the mutual involvement of God and the world in the creative advance.

After a distinguished career as a mathematician at the Universities of Cambridge and London, Whitehead accepted the position of Professor of Philosophy at Harvard University in 1924 at the age of sixty-three. Over the following years he developed the process metaphysics that has provided a foundation for the development of process theology. He died in 1947.

So long as the temporal world is conceived as a self-sufficient completion of the creative act, explicable by its derivation from an ultimate principle which is

---

* From *Process and Reality: An Essay in Cosmology* (New York: Macmillan, 1929), pp. 519-533. Reprinted with permission.

at once eminently real and the unmoved mover, from this conclusion there is no escape: the best that we can say of the turmoil is, 'For so he giveth his beloved—sleep.' This is the message of religions of the Buddhistic type, and in some sense it is true. In this final discussion we have to ask, whether metaphysical principles impose the belief that it is the whole truth. The complexity of the world must be reflected in the answer. It is childish to enter upon thought with the simple-minded question, What is the world made of? The task of reason is to fathom the deeper depths of the many-sidedness of things. We must not expect simple answers to far-reaching questions. However far our gaze penetrates, there are always heights beyond which block our vision.

The notion of God as the 'unmoved mover' is derived from Aristotle, at least so far as Western thought is concerned. The notion of God as 'eminently real' is a favourite doctrine of Christian theology. The combination of the two into the doctrine of an aboriginal, eminently real, transcendent creator, at whose fiat the world came into being, and whose imposed will it obeys, is the fallacy which has infused tragedy into the histories of Christianity and of Mahometanism.

When the Western world accepted Christianity, Caesar conquered; and the received text of Western theology was edited by his lawyers. The code of Justinian and the theology of Justinian are two volumes expressing one movement of the human spirit. The brief Galilean vision of humility flickered throughout the ages, uncertainly. In the official formulation of the religion it has assumed the trivial form of the mere attribution to the Jews that they cherished a misconception about their Messiah. But the deeper idolatry, of the fashioning of God in the image of the Egyptian, Persian, and Roman imperial rulers, was retained. The Church gave unto God the attributes which belonged exclusively to Caesar.

In the great formative period of theistic philosophy, which ended with the rise of Mahometanism, after a continuance coeval with civilization, three strains of thought emerge which, amid many variations in detail, respectively fashion God in the image of an imperial ruler, God in the image of a personification of moral energy, God in the image of an ultimate philosophical principle. Hume's *Dialogues* criticize unanswerably these modes of explaining the system of the world.

The three schools of thought can be associated respectively with the divine Caesars, the Hebrew prophets, and Aristotle. But Aristotle was antedated by Indian, and Buddhistic, thought; the Hebrew prophets can be paralleled in traces of earlier thought; Mahometanism and the divine Caesars merely represent the most natural, obvious, theistic idolatrous symbolism, at all epochs and places.

The history of theistic philosophy exhibits various stages of combination of these three diverse ways of entertaining the problem. There is, however, in the Galilean origin of Christianity yet another suggestion which does not fit very well with any of the three main strands of thought. It does not emphasize the ruling Caesar, or the ruthless moralist, or the unmoved mover. It dwells upon the tender elements in the world, which slowly and in quietness operate by love; and it finds purpose in the present immediacy of a kingdom not of this world. Love neither rules, nor is it unmoved; also it is a little oblivious as to morals. It does not look to the future; for it finds its own reward in the immediate present.

Section II

Apart from any reference to existing religions as they are, or as they ought to be, we must investigate dispassionately what the metaphysical principles, here developed, require on these points, as to the nature of God. There is nothing here in the nature of proof. There is merely the confrontation of the theoretic system with a certain rendering of the facts. But the unsystematized report upon the facts is itself highly controversial, and the system is confessedly inadequate. The deductions from it in this particular sphere of thought cannot be looked upon as more than suggestions as to how the problem is transformed in the light of that system. What follows is merely an attempt to add another speaker to that masterpiece, Hume's *Dialogues Concerning Natural Religion.* Any cogency of argument entirely depends upon elucidation of somewhat exceptional elements in our conscious experience—those elements which may roughly be classed together as religious and moral intuitions.

In the first place, God is not to be treated as an exception to all metaphysical principles, invoked to save their collapse. He is their chief exemplification.

Viewed as primordial, he is the unlimited conceptual realization of the absolute wealth of potentiality. In this aspect, he is not *before* all creation, but *with* all creation. But, as primordial, so far is he from 'eminent reality,' that in this abstraction he is 'deficiently actual'—and this in two ways. His feelings are only conceptual and so lack the fulness of actuality. Secondly, conceptual feelings, apart from complex integration with physical feelings, are devoid of consciousness in their subjective forms.

Thus, when we make a distinction of reason, and consider God in the abstraction of a primordial actuality, we must ascribe to him neither fulness of feeling, nor consciousness. He is the unconditioned actuality of conceptual feeling at the base of things; so that, by reason of this primordial actuality, there is an order in the relevance of eternal objects to the process of creation. His unity of conceptual operations is a free creative act, untrammelled by reference to any particular course of things. It is deflected neither by love, nor by hatred, for what in fact comes to pass. The *particularities* of the actual world presuppose *it;* while *it* merely presupposes the *general* metaphysical character of creative advance, of which it is the primordial exemplification. The primordial nature of God is the acquirement by creativity of a primordial character.

His conceptual actuality at once exemplifies and establishes the categoreal conditions. The conceptual feelings, which compose his primordial nature, exemplify in their subjective forms their mutual sensitivity and their subjective unity of subjective aim. These subjective forms are valuations determining the relative relevance of eternal objects for each occasion of actuality.

He is the lure for feeling, the eternal urge of desire. His particular relevance to each creative act as it arises from its own conditioned standpoint in the world, constitutes him the initial 'object of desire' establishing the initial phase of each subjective aim. A quotation from Aristotle's *Metaphysics* [1] expresses some analogies to, and some differences from, this line of thought: "And since that which is moved and mover is intermediate, there is a mover which moves without being moved, being eternal, substance, and actuality. And the object of desire and the object of

---

[1] Cf. *Metaphysics* 1072, trans. by Professor W. D. Ross. My attention was called to the appositeness of this particular quotation by Mr. F. J. Carson.

thought are the same. For the apparent good is the object of appetite, and the real good is the primary object of rational desire. But desire is consequent on opinion rather than opinion on desire; for the thinking is the starting point. And thought is moved by the object of thought, and one side of the list of opposites is in itself the object of thought; . . ." Aristotle had not made the distinction between conceptual feelings and the intellectual feelings which alone involve consciousness. But if 'conceptual feeling,' with its subjective form of valuation, be substituted for 'thought,' 'thinking,' and 'opinion,' in the above quotation, the agreement is exact.

SECTION III

There is another side to the nature of God which cannot be omitted. Throughout this exposition of the philosophy of organism we have been considering the primary action of God on the world. From this point of view, he is the principle of concretion—the principle whereby there is initiated a definite outcome from a situation otherwise riddled with ambiguity. Thus, so far, the primordial side of the nature of God has alone been relevant.

But God, as well as being primordial, is also consequent. He is the beginning and the end. He is not the beginning in the sense of being in the past of all members. He is the presupposed actuality of conceptual operation, in unison of becoming with every other creative act. Thus by reason of the relativity of all things, there is a reaction of the world on God. The completion of God's nature into a fulness of physical feeling is derived from the objectification of the world in God. He shares with every new creation its actual world; and the concrescent creature is objectified in God as a novel element in God's objectification of that actual world. This prehension into God of each creature is directed with the subjective aim, and clothed with the subjective form, wholly derivative from his all-inclusive primordial valuation. God's conceptual nature is unchanged, by reason of its final completeness. But his derivative nature is consequent upon the creative advance of the world.

Thus, analogously to all actual entities, the nature of God is dipolar. He has a primordial nature and a consequent nature. The consequent nature of God is conscious; and it is the realization of the actual world in the unity of his nature, and through the transformation of his wisdom. The primordial nature is conceptual, the consequent nature is the weaving of God's physical feelings upon his primordial concepts.

One side of God's nature is constituted by his conceptual experience. This experience is the primordial fact in the world, limited by no actuality which it presupposes. It is therefore infinite, devoid of all negative prehensions. This side of his nature is free, complete, primordial, eternal, actually deficient, and unconscious. The other side originates with physical experience derived from the temporal world, and then acquires integration with the primordial side. It is determined, incomplete, consequent, 'everlasting,' fully actual, and conscious. His necessary goodness expresses the determination of his consequent nature.

Conceptual experience can be infinite, but it belongs to the nature of physical experience that it is finite. An actual entity in the temporal world is to be conceived as originated by physical experience with its process of completion motivated by consequent, conceptual experience initially derived from God. God is to be conceived as originated by conceptual experience with his process of completion motivated by consequent, physical experience, initially derived from the temporal world.

SECTION IV

The perfection of God's subjective aim, derived from the completeness of his primordial nature, issues into the character of his consequent nature. In it there is no loss, no obstruction. The world is felt in a unison of immediacy. The property of combining creative advance with the retention of mutual immediacy is what in the previous section is meant by the term 'everlasting.'

The wisdom of subjective aim prehends every actuality for what it can be in such a perfected system—its sufferings, its sorrows, its failures, its triumphs, its immediacies of joy—woven by rightness of feeling into the harmony of the universal feeling, which is always immediate, always many, always one, always with novel advance, moving onward and never perishing. The revolts of destructive evil, purely self-regarding, are dismissed into their triviality of merely individual facts; and yet the good they did achieve in individual joy, in individual sorrow, in the introduction of needed contrast, is yet saved by its relation to the completed whole. The image—and it is but an image—the image under which this operative growth of God's nature is best conceived, is that of a tender care that nothing be lost.

The consequent nature of God is his judgment on the world. He saves the world as it passes into the immediacy of his own life. It is the judgment of a tenderness which loses nothing that can be saved. It is also the judgment of a wisdom which uses what in the temporal world is mere wreckage.

Another image which is also required to understand his consequent nature, is that of his infinite patience. The universe includes a threefold creative act composed of (i) the one infinite conceptual realization, (ii) the multiple solidarity of free physical realizations in the temporal world, (iii) the ultimate unity of the multiplicity of actual fact with the primordial conceptual fact. If we conceive the first term and the last term in their unity over against the intermediate multiple freedom of physical realizations in the temporal world, we conceive of the patience of God, tenderly saving the turmoil of the intermediate world by the completion of his own nature. The sheer force of things lies in the intermediate physical process: this is the energy of physical production. God's rôle is not the combat of productive force with productive force, of destructive force with destructive force; it lies in the patient operation of the overpowering rationality of his conceptual harmonization. He does not create the world, he saves it: or, more accurately, he is the poet of the world, with tender patience leading it by his vision of truth, beauty, and goodness.

SECTION V

The vicious separation of the flux from the permanence leads to the concept of an entirely static God, with eminent reality, in relation to an entirely fluent world, with deficient reality. But if the opposites, static and fluent, have once been so explained as separately to characterize diverse actualities, the interplay between the thing which is static and the things which are fluent involves contradiction at every step in its explanation. Such philosophies must include the notion of 'illusion' as a fundamental principle— the notion of 'mere appearance.' This is the final platonic problem.

Undoubtedly, the intuitions of Greek, Hebrew, and Christian thought have alike embodied the notions of a static God condescending to the world, and of a world *either* thoroughly fluent, *or* accidentally static, but finally fluent—'heaven and earth shall pass away.' In some schools of thought, the fluency of the world is mitigated by the assumption that selected components in the world are exempt from this final fluency, and achieve a static survival. Such components are not separated by any decisive line from analogous components for which the assumption is not made. Further, the survival is construed in terms of a final pair of opposites, happiness for some, torture for others.

Such systems have the common character of starting with a fundamental intuition which we do mean to express, and of entangling themselves in verbal expressions, which carry consequences at variance with the initial intuition of permanence in fluency and of fluency in permanence.

But civilized intuition has always, although obscurely, grasped the problem as double and not as single. There is not the mere problem of fluency *and* permanence. There is the double problem: actuality with permanence, requiring fluency as its completion; and actuality with fluency, requiring permanence as its completion. The first half of the problem concerns the completion of God's primordial nature by the derivation of his consequent nature from the temporal world. The second half of the problem concerns the completion of each fluent actual occasion by its function of objective immortality, devoid of 'perpetual perishing,' that is to say, 'everlasting.'

This double problem cannot be separated into two distinct problems. Either side can only be explained in terms of the other. The consequent nature of God is the fluent world become 'everlasting' by its objective immortality in God. Also the objective immortality of actual occasions requires the primordial permanence of God, whereby the creative advance ever re-establishes itself endowed with initial subjective aim derived from the relevance of God to the evolving world.

But objective immortality within the temporal world does not solve the problem set by the penetration of the finer religious intuition. 'Everlastingness' has been lost; and 'everlastingness' is the content of that vision upon which the finer religions are built— the 'many' absorbed everlastingly in the final unity. The problems of the fluency of God and of the everlastingness of passing experience are solved by the same factor in the universe. This factor is the temporal world perfected by its reception and its reformation, as a fulfilment of the primordial appetition which is the basis of all order. In this way God is completed by the individual, fluent satisfactions of finite fact, and the temporal occasions are completed by their everlasting union with their transformed selves, purged into conformation with the eternal order which is the final absolute 'wisdom.' The final summary can only be expressed in terms of a group of antitheses, whose apparent self-contradiction depends * on neglect of the diverse categories of existence. In each antithesis there is a shift of meaning which converts the opposition into a contrast.

It is as true to say that God is permanent and the World fluent, as that the World is permanent and God is fluent.

It is as true to say that God is one and the World many, as that the World is one and God many.

It is as true to say that, in comparison with the World, God is actual eminently, as that, in comparison with God, the World is actual eminently.

It is as true to say that the World is immanent in God, as that God is immanent in the World.

It is as true to say that God transcends the World, as that the World transcends God.

It is as true to say that God creates the World, as that the World creates God.

God and the World are the contrasted opposites in terms of which Creativity achieves its supreme task of transforming disjoined multiplicity, with its diversities in opposition, into concrescent unity, with its diversities in contrast. In each actuality there †️ are two concrescent poles of realization—'enjoyment' and 'appetition,' that is, the 'physical' and the 'conceptual.' For God the conceptual is prior to the physical, for the World the physical poles are prior to the conceptual poles.

A physical pole is in its own nature exclusive, bounded by contradiction: a conceptual pole is in its own nature all-embrac-

* [Editor's Note: The text has been emended to read "depends" rather than "depend"; cf. *Alfred North Whitehead: Essays on His Philosophy*, edited by George L. Kline (Englewood Cliffs, N.J.: Prentice Hall, 1963), p. 202.]

†️ [Editor's Note: The text has been emended to read "there" rather than "these"; cf. Kline, *op. cit.*, p. 202.]

ing, unbounded by contradiction. The former derives its share of infinity from the infinity of appetition; the latter derives its share of limitation from the exclusiveness of enjoyment. Thus, by reason of his priority of appetition, there can be but one primordial nature for God; and, by reason of their priority of enjoyment, there must be one history of many actualities in the physical world.

God and the World stand over against each other, expressing the final metaphysical truth that appetitive vision and physical enjoyment have equal claim to priority in creation. But no two actualities can be torn apart: each is all in all. Thus each temporal occasion embodies God, and is embodied in God. In God's nature, permanence is primordial and flux is derivative from the World: in the World's nature, flux is primordial and permanence is derivative from God. Also the World's nature is a primordial datum for God; and God's nature is a primordial datum for the World. Creation achieves the reconciliation of permanence and flux when it has reached its final term which is everlastingness—the Apotheosis of the World.

Opposed elements stand to each other in mutual requirement. In their unity, they inhibit or contrast. God and the World stand to each other in this opposed requirement. God is the infinite ground of all mentality, the unity of vision seeking physical multiplicity. The World is the multiplicity of finites, actualities seeking a perfected unity. Neither God, nor the World, reaches static completion. Both are in the grip of the ultimate metaphysical ground, the creative advance into novelty. Either of them, God and the World, is the instrument of novelty for the other.

In every respect God and the World move conversely to each other in respect to their process. God is primordially one, namely, he is the primordial unity of relevance of the many potential forms: in the process he acquires a consequent multiplicity, which the primordial character absorbs into its own unity. The World is primordially many, namely, the many actual occasions with their physical finitude; in the process it acquires a consequent unity, which is a novel occasion and is absorbed into the multiplicity of the primordial character. Thus God is to be conceived as one and as many in the converse sense in which the World is to be conceived as many and as one. The theme of Cosmology, which is the basis of all religions, is the story of the dynamic effort of the World passing into everlasting unity, and of the static majesty of God's vision, accomplishing its purpose of completion by absorption of the World's multiplicity of effort.

SECTION VI

The consequent nature of God is the fulfilment of his experience by his reception of the multiple freedom of actuality into the harmony of his own actualization. It is God as really actual, completing the deficiency of his mere conceptual actuality.

Every categoreal type of existence in the world presupposes the other types in terms of which it is explained. Thus the many eternal objects conceived in their bare isolated multiplicity lack any existent character. They require the transition to the conception of them as efficaciously existent by reason of God's conceptual realization of them.

But God's conceptual realization is nonsense if thought of under the guise of a barren, eternal hypothesis. It is God's conceptual realization performing an efficacious rôle in multiple unifications of the universe, which are free creations of actualities arising out of decided situations. Again this discordant multiplicity of actual things, requiring each other and neglecting each other, utilizing and discarding, perishing and yet claiming life as obstinate matter of fact, requires an enlargement of the understanding to the comprehension of another phase in the nature of things. In this later phase, the many actualities are one actuality, and the one actuality is many actualities. Each actuality has its present life and its immediate passage into novelty; but its passage is not its death. This final phase of passage in God's nature is ever enlarging itself. In it the complete adjustment of the immediacy of joy and suffering reaches the final end of creation. This end is existence in the perfect unity of adjustment as means, and in the perfect multiplicity of the attainment of individual types of self-existence. The function of being a means is not disjoined from the function of being an end. The sense of worth beyond itself is immediately enjoyed as an overpowering element in the individual self-attainment. It is in this way that the immediacy of sorrow and pain is transformed into an element of triumph. This is the notion of redemption

through suffering, which haunts the world. It is the generalization
of its very minor exemplification as the aesthetic value of discords
in art.

Thus the universe is to be conceived as attaining the active
self-expression of its own variety of opposites—of its own freedom
and its own necessity, of its own multiplicity and its own unity, of
its own imperfection and its own perfection. All the 'opposites'
are elements in the nature of things, and are incorrigibly there.
The concept of 'God' is the way in which we understand this incredible fact—that what cannot be, yet is.

SECTION VII

Thus the consequent nature of God is composed of a multiplicity of elements with individual self-realization. It is just as much
a multiplicity as it is a unity; it is just as much one immediate fact
as it is an unresting advance beyond itself. Thus the actuality of
God must also be understood as a multiplicity of actual components in process of creation. This is God in his function of the
kingdom of heaven.

Each actuality in the temporal world has its reception into
God's nature. The corresponding element in God's nature is not
temporal actuality, but is the transmutation of that temporal actuality into a living, ever-present fact. An enduring personality in the
temporal world is a route of occasions in which the successors with
some peculiar completeness sum up their predecessors. The correlate fact in God's nature is an even more complete unity of life in a
chain of elements for which succession does not mean loss of
immediate unison. This element in God's nature inherits from the
temporal counterpart according to the same principle as in the
temporal world the future inherits from the past. Thus in the sense
in which the present occasion is the person now, and yet with his
own past, so the counterpart in God is that person in God.

But the principle of universal relativity is not to be stopped
at the consequent nature of God. This nature itself passes into the
temporal world according to its gradation of relevance to the various concrescent occasions. There are thus four creative phases in
which the universe accomplishes its actuality. There is first the
phase of conceptual origination, deficient in actuality, but infinite
in its adjustment of valuation. Secondly, there is the temporal

phase of physical origination, with its multiplicity of actualities. In this phase full actuality is attained; but there is deficiency in the solidarity of individuals with each other. This phase derives its determinate conditions from the first phase. Thirdly, there is the phase of perfected actuality, in which the many are one everlastingly, without the qualification of any loss either of individual identity or of completeness of unity. In everlastingness, immediacy is reconciled with objective immortality. This phase derives the conditions of its being from the two antecedent phases. In the fourth phase, the creative action completes itself. For the perfected actuality passes back into the temporal world, and qualifies this world so that each temporal actuality includes it as an immediate fact of relevant experience. For the kingdom of heaven is with us today. The action of the fourth phase is the love of God for the world. It is the particular providence for particular occasions. What is done in the world is transformed into a reality in heaven, and the reality in heaven passes back into the world. By reason of this reciprocal relation, the love in the world passes into the love in heaven, and floods back again into the world. In this sense, God is the great companion—the fellow-sufferer who understands.

We find here the final application of the doctrine of objective immortality. Throughout the perishing occasions in the life of each temporal Creature, the inward source of distaste or of refreshment, the judge arising out of the very nature of things, redeemer or goddess of mischief, is the transformation of Itself, everlasting in the Being of God. In this way, the insistent craving is justified—the insistent craving that zest for existence be refreshed by the ever-present, unfading importance of our immediate actions, which perish and yet live for evermore.

SUGGESTED READINGS

Alfred North Whitehead on God

Whitehead, Alfred North. *Science and the Modern World.* New York: Macmillan, 1925, Chapter XI, pp. 249-258. Paperback—New York: Free Press.

————. *Religion in the Making.* New York: Macmillan, 1926, Chapter II-IV, pp. 47-160. Paperback—New York: Meridian Books.

On Alfred North Whitehead's Doctrine of God

Cobb, John B., Jr. *A Christian Natural Theology: Based on the Thought of Alfred North Whitehead.* Philadelphia: Westminster Press, 1965, pp. 135-251. Pp. 176-214 reprinted in *Process Philosophy and Christian Thought.* Edited by Delwin Brown, Ralph E. James, Jr., and Gene Reeves. Indianapolis: Bobbs-Merrill, 1971, pp. 215-243. Paperback—Indianapolis: Bobbs-Merrill.

Ely, Stephen. *The Religious Availability of Whitehead's God: A Critical Analysis.* Madison, Wisc.: The University of Wisconsin Press, 1942.

Ford, Lewis S. "Divine Persuasion and the Triumph of Good," *The Christian Scholar,* 50 (1967), 235-250. Reprinted in *Process Philosophy and Christian Thought,* pp. 287-304.

Hartshorne, Charles. "Whitehead's Idea of God," *The Philosophy of Alfred North Whitehead.* Edited by Paul A. Schilpp. Evanston and Chicago: Northwestern University, 1941, pp. 513-559.

————. "Is Whitehead's God the God of Religion?" *Ethics,* 53 (1943), 219-227.

Loomer, Bernard M. "Ely on Whitehead's God," *The Journal of Religion,* 24 (1944), 162-179. Reprinted in *Process Philosophy and Christian Thought,* pp. 264-286.

Sherburne, Donald W. "Whitehead Without God," *The Christian Scholar,* 50 (1967), 251-272. Reprinted, in revised form, in *Process Philosophy and Christian Thought,* pp. 305-328.

Williams, Daniel Day. "Deity, Monarchy, and Metaphysics: Whitehead's Critique of the Theological Tradition," *The Relevance of Whitehead.* Edited by Ivor Leclerc. New York: Macmillan, 1961, pp. 353-372.

On Alfred North Whitehead's Philosophy

Christian, William A. *An Interpretation of Whitehead's Metaphysics.* New Haven: Yale University Press, 1959. Paperback—New Haven: Yale University Press.

Emmet, Dorothy M. *Whitehead's Philosophy of Organism.* London: Macmillan, 1932. Paperback—New York: St. Martin's.

Leclerc, Ivor. *Whitehead's Metaphysics: An Introductory Exposition.* New York: Macmillan, 1958.

Lowe, Victor. *Understanding Whitehead.* Baltimore: The Johns Hopkins Press, 1962. Paperback—Baltimore: The Johns Hopkins Press.

Sherburne, Donald W. *A Key to Whitehead's Process and Reality.* New York: Macmillan, 1966.

6 Philosophical and Religious Uses of 'God'

CHARLES HARTSHORNE

In the development of process theology the most influential interpreter of Whitehead's doctrine of God has been Charles Hartshorne. In line with Whitehead's notion of God's primordial and consequent natures, he has elaborated a dipolar conception of divinity in which the abstract, absolute dimension of God is balanced by a concrete, relative dimension. In addition, Hartshorne has made extensive studies of the logic of theism, defending Anselm's ontological argument while reinterpreting his conception of God. In the following selection,* Hartshorne presents some of his major themes from the standpoint of worship. The creative relation of God and the world is illustrated through the analogy of the teacher who is enriched by his sympathetic involvement in the pupil's learning experience. Hartshorne deals briefly with Anselm's ontological argument and his own critique of the Greek notion of perfection. He closes with an analysis of the kind of philosophy with which the religious idea of God is most at home. It is a philosophy that affirms becoming, novelty, creativity, and internal relations.

Charles Hartshorne has taught at the University of Chicago, Emory University, and presently at the University of Texas. During his many years of teaching philosophy at the University of Chicago, he had a major influence in shaping the intellectual milieu out of which process theology developed.

* From *A Natural Theology for Our Time* (LaSalle, Ill.: Open Court, 1967), pp. 1-28. Reprinted with permission.

W hat is a philosopher to mean by 'God'—
assuming he uses the word? There are
three ways of reaching an answer to this question. One is to ask theologians. But there are important disagreements among theologians
as to the connotations of the central religious term, and these disagreements have if anything increased during the past century or
two. Thus we cannot find an answer to the terminological
question in this way. A second approach is the following. If the
philosopher's system or method leads him to formulate a conception having at least some analogy with the central operative idea
in the practices, not simply in the theological theories, of one or
more of the high religions, he may call his conception by the religious name. If the analogy is weak he may with some justice be
accused of misusing the word. Spinoza has been called "God-
intoxicated" and also "atheist." There is a fairly strong case for
both descriptions. But this, in my view, constitutes an objection of
some force to Spinoza's system. It seems odd to think that an idea
so essentially religious should be so mistakenly conceived by all
the great religions concerned with it as the religious idea must be
if Spinoza is correct. Contrariwise, it is an argument in favor of a
philosophy if it can make more religious sense out of the theistic
view than other philosophies have been able to do.

A further consideration is the following. Basic ideas derive
somehow from direct experience or intuition, life as concretely
lived. Moreover, it is demonstrable from almost any classical conception of God that he cannot be known in any merely indirect
way, by inference only, but must somehow be present in all experience. No theist can without qualification deny the universal
'immanence' of God. Even Aquinas did not do this. And if God
is in all things, he is in our experiences and also in what we experience, and thus is in some fashion a universal datum of experience.
But then it seems reasonable to suppose that religion, whatever else
it may be, is the cultivation of this aspect of experience. Hence
what it says about 'God' deserves to be taken seriously, at least so
far as the meaning of the term is concerned. The burden of
justification is upon those who would use the word in a drastically
nonreligious sense. So our first question is, what is the religious
sense?

In theistic religions God is the One Who is Worshipped. This is in some sort a definition. We have, therefore, only to find out what worship is to know the proper use of the name 'God'. This is the third approach to the definitional problem. But here, too, a difficulty arises. Are there not many sorts of worship—noble, ignoble, primitive, sophisticated, superstitious, relatively enlightened, idolatrous . . . what you will? And does not divinity take on a different apparent character with each form of worship? Spinoza claimed to have the noblest and most enlightened form of worship, the "intellectual love of God"; hence to require him to refrain from using the word because other, perhaps less enlightened, people worship differently may be to rule against enlightenment and in favor of vulgar superstition. Moreover, the mere fact that many, or even most, people (at least in certain cultures) have worshipped God in a certain way is nothing but a contingent empirical fact. Should we allow our view concerning the essential nature of the eternal deity to depend upon any such facts? All classical meanings treat God as in some sense eternal. How can there be valid inference from a mere temporal fact to truth about eternal things? Much less could counting noses determine such truth.

If worship is to be definitive of deity, it must be worship as more than a mere fact of terrestrial human culture. The definitional problem has a clear solution only if there is a rationale, an inner logic, to the *idea* of worship such that inferior forms violate or fail adequately to express this logic. And it cannot be a rationale of worship as a mere terrestrial phenomenon, but must concern an a priori possibility for rational animals generally, on no matter what planet, and even in no matter what possible world. Indeed, we do not have to say 'animal', for there is a sense in which God can worship, that is, worship himself. But only God can in the full sense *be* worshipped.

To obtain a broad perspective we may remind ourselves that subrational animals, below the level of language, can scarcely be thought to worship, unless in some radically deficient sense. Only man, among this earth's inhabitants, is a 'religious animal'. This suggests that consciousness, in the sense requiring language (or else, if God is conscious, something superior to language), is part of the definition of worship. To worship is to do something consciously. To do what? That which all sentient individuals must do, at least unconsciously, so far as they are sane and not in at least a mild neurosis or psychosis. Worship is the *integrating* of all one's thoughts and purposes, all valuations and meanings, all perceptions and conceptions. A sentient creature feels and acts as one, its sensations and strivings are all *its* sensations and strivings. So are its thoughts, if it has them. Thus one element of worship is present without worship, unity of response. The added element is consciousness: worship is a consciously unitary response to life. It lifts to the level of explicit awareness the integrity of an individual responding to reality. Or, worship is individual wholeness flooded with consciousness. This is the ideal toward which actual worship may tend.

If this account is correct, worship is in principle the opposite of a primitive phenomenon. The more consciousness, the more completely the ideal of worship can be realized. Those who pride themselves on transcending worship may only be falling back to a more primitive level. Of course, as many are fond of reminding us, one can live without worship. Why not, since the lower animals do so? And we are all animals; the animal way is partly open to us still.

However, there are two possible theories of worship, the theistic and the nontheistic. According to the former, the conscious wholeness of the individual is correlative to an inclusive wholeness in the world of which the individual is aware, and this wholeness is deity. According to the nontheistic view, either there is no inclusive wholeness, or if there is one, it is not what religions have meant by deity. Perhaps it is just The Unknown, or Nature as a Great Mystery, not to be thought of as conscious, or as an individual in principle superior to all others. Perhaps it is even Humanity. Or (more reasonably) it is all sentient creatures.

My view I shall put bluntly. It is the lower animals for whom the Whole must be simply Unknown, sheer Mystery, and their own species practically all that has value. The difference between agnostics (or 'humanists') and the nonspeaking creatures is that, whereas the mere animal simply *has* integrity, the agnostic feels the need and possibility of raising integrity to the conscious level, but does not quite know how to do so. Thus he is in some degree in conflict with himself. However, animal innocence is there to fall back upon.

God is the wholeness of the world, correlative to the wholeness of every sound individual dealing with the world. Note that this has no peculiar connection with the human race, 'father-images', the parental function, or anything of the sort. Any sentient individual in any world experiences and acts as one: the question is if its total environment is not therewith experienced as, in some profoundly analogous sense, one. An individual (other than God) is only a fragment of reality, not the whole; but is *all* individuality (in other than the trivial sense in which a junk pile, say, is an 'individual' junk pile) similarly fragmentary? Or is the cosmic or all-inclusive whole also an integrated individual, the sole non-fragmentary individual?

Note, too, that our question is definitely not the question, 'Are all wholes or individuals "finite", "limited"?' For it is at best a leap in the dark to assert the nonfinitude of our *total* environment (or "all with which we have to do"—as W. E. Hocking puts it). This totality is vastly more than, and includes, ourselves; but it may for all that be finite in certain respects. Indeed, it must be so! Fragmentariness, not finitude, sets the problem of worship. Here countless theologians long ago made an initial mistake for which the full price has yet to be paid: they began the idolatrous worship of 'the infinite'. Cosmic wholeness, not infinity, is the essential concept. Infinity comes in if and only if—or in whatever sense and only that sense—we should view the whole as infinite. And this is to be determined by inquiry, not taken for granted.

The reader may feel that we have not followed our own injunction to look to the religions for the meaning of 'God'. Is 'cosmic wholeness' a religious conception? My reply is, by fairly clear and direct implication, yes, it is such a conception. I shall now try to show this. Three religions, if no more, Judaism, Christianity, and Islam would, I think, agree with the conception of worship embodied in: "Thou shalt love the Lord thy God with all thy heart and with all thy mind and with all thy soul and with all thy strength." I ask, how more plainly could the idea of wholeness of individual response be stated in simple, generally intelligible language? The word 'all' reiterated four times in one sentence means,

I take it, what it says. It does not mean, *nearly* all—or, all *important*—responses, or aspects of personality. Simply every response, every aspect, must be a way of loving God. That the God correlative to this integrity of response is Himself 'One' or individual is also a Jewish-Christian-Islamic tenet, at least apart from the subtleties of the Trinity, which are surely not *intended* to contradict the divine wholeness or integrity.

But, perhaps you say, the God of the religions mentioned is not the cosmic *whole:* he is only the cosmic creator. This 'only' suggests that there could be more than God! Or is God more than the all-inclusive reality? Yet this is nonsense. Thus we seem to have a severe paradox or dilemma. Are the basic religious writings responsible for this paradox? True, the Bible, for instance, nowhere says in so many words that God is the whole of things, but no more does it say that he is not the whole. The 'pantheistic' issue had not arisen, and so the wrong solution could not yet be given. (We so easily forget that our sophistication is a danger as well as an opportunity.) Of course "no graven image" of God was permitted, but what sculptor knows how to image the whole of things? What is there in the Bible to show that the word 'God' refers to less than, or even other than, the all-inclusive reality—except a few passages which would discomfort traditional theists as much as they would any pantheist, e.g., "God walked in the garden." And Paul says that we live, move, and have our being "in" God. Precisely.

Ah, you say, but the religious God is creator, and 'X creates Y' contradicts 'Y is in X'. Does it indeed? In that case no man can create his own thoughts, and a poet does not create the verbal images which constitute lines of his poem before he writes them down. And if you say, but of course divine creating has nothing in common with human creating, then I ask how the word 'create' can be a human word? Or, if you say, but God creates free, self-active individuals other than himself, and this the human thinker or poet does not do, I am still not greatly impressed. For one thing, a human child grows new nerve or brain cells for a time after birth, and even an adult perpetually grows new cells of many kinds; and these cells are living individuals which remain in the child or adult. (That they have some slight freedom of action I cannot empirically prove and the reader cannot disprove.) For another thing, either a poet does ultimately create something in other individuals, or he writes in vain. Still more obviously, a teacher, parent, or friend creates important elements in the personalities of pupils, children, or friends. Is there an absolute difference between this and divine creating? If you say that God—and he alone—creates the entire personality of a man, you seem to leave nothing for the man to create in himself, and then when we say, as it is good idiom to say, that a man 'makes' a decision or an effort, we do not know what we are talking about. Not much is left of personality if we abstract from all the past decisions and efforts which the individual has himself made. Sartre's phrase for man, *causa sui*, needs qualification, but is not wholly wrong. And, once more, if no human making has relevance to God's making of the world, the latter phrase is mere equivocation, indeed gibberish.

But now probably you are about to overwhelm me with an inconsistency. For what the poet, teacher, parent, or friend makes in another human being does not become a constitutive element within the first human being, the maker. And I have been saying that what God makes in us does become a constitutive element in him. My defense, however, is not so difficult. For is it absolutely, or only relatively, true that what we make in others fails to become part of our own reality? If only relatively true, then it is not absolutely false to say that it becomes such a part. And then the corresponding affirmation need not be false at all of God.

Let us consider this further. If a pupil listens in silence to a teacher, absorbing valuable ideas but never communicating the changes in himself to the teacher, who never learns the results of his teaching, then indeed it seems that what is created in the pupil remains outside the teacher. But suppose the latter intimately follows the pupil's mental growth and personality changes. Can we then say that these, his own creations in the pupil's mind, in no degree become constitutive of the teacher's mind? For instance, the teacher shares sympathetically in the pupil's excitement over ideas new to him, enjoys the nuances of his emotional and intellectual responses to the ideas. Is not his own life thereby enriched? Consider also that when we speak of the teacher's "following with sympathetic understanding" the pupil's responses we are talking about fallible human operations. The teacher does not entirely understand or altogether sympathetically follow. By contrast, if God knows the results in us of his creative actions upon us, he knows and shares them with a completeness, an intimacy, compared to which our knowledge is always partial and external. The pupil remains indeed outside the human teacher, and by the same token much in the pupil remains hidden from the teacher. It even remains more or less hidden from the pupil, much of whose reality can be said to be outside his own clearly conscious experience. Omniscience, if the term is to have human meaning, must not be absolutely different from our knowing; but still, it must somehow differ in principle from ours. The clue to this likeness and this difference is in our hands: God is the all-inclusive reality; his knowing, accordingly, must likewise be all-inclusive; ours, by contrast, is fragmentary, as our whole being is fragmentary; much remains outside us as knowers. Strange that men should think to exalt God by putting everything outside him as knower. Almost everything is outside us and our knowledge; that is why we are not God! But nothing can be outside God, in his total reality. Thus when God creates, he creates additional contents of his own awareness, enriches the panorama of existence as his to enjoy.

The idea that worship is love with the whole of one's being is correlated, in many high religions, with the idea that what we thus wholly love is itself also love, the divine love for all creatures, and for God himself as including all. And this in my opinion is not simply a pretty sentiment but is, in cold logic, the most rational way to view the matter. Two reasons among many for this belief:

(1) It seems impossible to love an unloving being with all one's own being. For instance, if we cannot entirely avoid self-love (and we cannot), then in loving the object of all our love must we not somehow be loving ourselves? The same is true of love for our friend or neighbor. But how can these loves be elements in our love for God? Only if the inclusive referent of our concern Himself cherishes all creatures, only if he loves all-inclusively, is the puzzle solved. Only supreme love can be supremely lovable.

(2) What is concrete knowledge, knowledge inclusive of the actual concrete feeling of creatures, if not some kind of sympathetic participation or love? Must not God, as the well-integrated whole of things, have such knowledge? Mere intellect cannot know

concrete qualities of feeling, for they are not concepts, abstract forms or patterns, and no mere form or pattern can contain them in their fullness. If God knows but does not love, this means either that he is indifferent to, or that he hates, what he knows. But the first is an impossible psychology. One knows only that in which one takes some sort of interest; we, for instance, know the actual feelings of others because we have at least an unconscious, or even instinctive and animal, sympathy with these feelings. What reason is there to suppose that to speak of purely nonemotional knowledge of particular emotions in their concrete uniqueness is anything but gibberish or contradiction? One may classify emotions relatively unemotionally, but classification is precisely not knowing the concrete in its concreteness. And only those who feel some emotions can even classify them and know what they are doing.

If God cannot be indifferent to creaturely feelings, he also cannot hate them. For God is inclusive and hate is exclusive. It is saved from complete blindness only because there is, as subtle psychologists have long known, an element of love in it. There is also an element of self-conflict in hate which would contradict any classical religious idea of God.

If I am right, is it not odd that the Greeks were so nearly unable to conceive love as a divine quality? Plato almost managed to do it, in saying that God created because he was not jealous or stingy, and was willing to have others enjoy the blessings of existence. But he put it strangely negatively. Why? Apparently because he was partly trapped (as Aristotle was wholly trapped) in the verbal confusion: God is worshipped because he is complete, perfect, free of any defect, hence he is immutable and incapable of wishing for any good not already possessed; 'love', on the contrary, means desire for the not yet attained. Hence, Plato thought —and a fortiori Aristotle thought—the ultimate object of love must be quite other than love. It must be absolute beauty, sheer excellence, stilling all longing for anything further. But neither Plato nor anyone else has been able to show us how there can be a beauty or excellence inclusive of all value whatever, unless it be the beauty of a love which cherishes all valuable, beautiful, or loving creatures. Beauty as a value is actualized only in experience. However, the concrete beauty of the cosmos—and a mere abstraction cannot be the inclusive object of interest—could not be adequately appreciated by our fragmentary kind of perception and thought. There can then be an all-inclusive beauty only if there be an all-inclusive appreciation of beauty, and what would that be if not a cosmic sympathy? Cosmic beauty as a value must be actualized in cosmic experience, and this, as we have shown, can only be a cosmic love.

If such a love must in some sense be incomplete and mutable, so much the worse for the identification of the One Worshipped with the complete or immutable. Our love for God is not immutably complete and should not be; for it includes new responses to neighborly needs which are changing from moment to moment. Also our total environment, that with which we have to deal, is mutable. It is complete, finished once for all, only if it be correct to view future events as no less determinate than past events—a view which is at best paradoxical. Should religion be saddled from the outset and by definition with this paradox? I think not. The idea of worship as conscious integrity, achieved through an inclusive integral object of love, does not of itself commit us to the immutable completeness of the One Who is Inclusively Loved. If anything, it conflicts with this idea, for who knows what love could be, combined with immutability? Were the Greeks not right as to that?

Not completeness, but all-inclusiveness, is what is required. And here nontheistic theories of worship fail. 'Humanity' leaves a vast world outside. Consider for example, the quintillions of singing birds which have lived and died where no man heard them sing, or the other habitable planets, the nonexistence of which we have no right to assume. If God, or the One Worshipped, does not include these, then in being even slightly interested in them we are doing something besides loving God.

It is not enough to say, "But we thank God for creating them." God, qua creator-of-X, either does or does not include X. If he does, my point is granted. If he does not, then in thinking this very thought I have gone beyond loving God to loving (or being mildly interested in) certain individuals outside him. But then my total interest is not in God, but only a part of my interest.

I conclude that the wholeness view of worship and of the divine correlate of worship makes good religious sense and is more obviously relevant to the religious documents than the identification of deity with the infinite, absolute, unconditioned (*pace* Tillich), immutable, uncaused, cause, most real being, or kindred philosophical objects. If Spinoza had asserted only that all things are in and constitutive of deity, he would not have been an 'atheist' at all. But he also asserted the absolute infinity, impassibility, and noncontingency of deity, and these ideas (not merely these terms) are not religious. He identified the all-inclusive divineness with sheer infinity, necessity, or nonreceptivity, and this, so far as religion is concerned, is at best a leap in the dark.

There is another way, besides using the ideas of all-inclusiveness and universal love, to define the One Who is Worshipped. This third way was Anselm's discovery (though Philo and others almost anticipated him)—a stroke of genius even apart from its use in the ontological argument. God is the not conceivably surpassable being. For, if God could be surpassed by a greater or better, should we not worship the one who would surpass him— even were this but a conceivable not an actual being? Also, in merely thinking about the better possible being our interest would go beyond God to something else, and we should not be able to obey the Great Commandment of total devotion to the One Being.

But Anselm spoiled his formula by his way of construing it. He supposed that it was equivalent to the standard definition in terms of immutable perfection. It is indeed so equivalent if, but only if, we take 'unsurpassable' to mean 'by and being, even the being itself'. For there are two ways of being surpassed: by another, and by self. An individual can be or become superior to itself, without—so far as anyone has shown—this necessarily entailing, even as a possibility, that another than itself should surpass it. Anselm's mind, however, was full of the Greek glorification of the immutable; he accepted the Platonic-Aristotelian argument that what is worshipful must be self-sufficient and perfect in the sense of complete, and that what is complete cannot change—obviously not for the better, and surely not for the worse. Change is a sign of weakness, it was thought, and its only value must be to remedy a prior defect. But there is nothing in the religions (unless in Hinduism or Buddhism) to indicate that change simply as such is a weakness; and the only sense in which 'perfection' is used biblically is the ethical sense. "Be ye perfect" does not mean, 'be ye immutable'! Nor is any immutability attributed to deity in the Scriptures save what the context implies is purely ethical. A fixity of ethical principles is one thing, a fixity of a being's whole perceptive-conscious reality is another, and worlds apart from the first. I hope this seems as clear to the reader as it does to me, that is to say, very clear indeed.

Perfection taken as an absolute maximum does exclude change, as well as any possibility of being surpassed by another. But the converse deduction, of the absolute maximum from unsurpassability by another, succeeds only if we assume that what is unsurpassable by another must be unsurpassable by self as well. And this assumption is not self-evident; if anything, it is clearly false, as we shall see. Granted that what can be surpassed, even if only by self, is not an absolute maximum of value or reality. Granted further that *if* such a maximum is conceivable, then any self-surpassing being must fall short of this maximum, and so it could be surpassed by a being which possessed the maximum. On that basis the self-surpassing must also be conceivably surpassable by another. But is an absolute maximum conceivable? The truth is that our ancestors had not yet learned our hard modern lessons concerning the ease with which grammatically smooth expressions—class of all classes, for example—can fall into implicit contradiction or nonsense. 'Greatest possible number' is grammatical, but it is sheer nonsense if it means 'greatest finite number'; it is also, according to some mathematicians, nonsense if it means 'greatest infinite number'; and it is at best problematic, according to any mathematician. Why then should 'greatest possible value' be regarded as safe? It is vaguer, but perhaps only because it has no definite meaning at all.

Since it is at best doubtful that 'X is in all respects maximal' expresses a coherent idea, we cannot infer 'surpassable by another' from 'surpassable by self'. Moreover, our idea of wholeness throws a clear light on how 'self-surpassing' can be combined with 'unsurpassability by another'. For, if a being is in principle, or without possible failure, all-inclusive, then any possible rival could only be one of its own possible constituents, and so not a rival after all. For this to hold, God must be viewed as *necessarily* all-inclusive, incapable of a genuinely 'external' environment. Anselm, rightly, I hold, argued that the very existence of the unsurpassable being must be necessary.

A being necessarily all-inclusive must be one whose potentiality for change is coextensive with the logically possible. I call this property 'modal coincidence'. All actual things must be actual in God, they must be constituents of his actuality, and all possible things must be potentially his constituents. He is the Whole in every categorial sense, all actuality in one individual actuality, and all possibility in one individual potentiality. This relatively simple idea was apparently too complex for most of our ancestors to hit upon. They did not reject it, they failed so much as to formulate it. (Exceptions are relatively little-known figures in the history of philosophy and theology, and even they were not too explicit about it. Plato, with his World Soul doctrine, is the nearest to an illustrious exception.)

Modal coincidence implies that the traditional identification of deity with infinity was a half truth. All-possibility—which is indeed infinite if anything is—coincides with divine potentiality. Thus, God is infinite in what he could be, not in what he is; he is infinitely capable of actuality, rather than infinitely actual. Not that he thus lacks an infinity which some conceivable being might have, but that an 'absolutely infinite or unsurpassable maximum of actuality' makes no sense. Possibility is in principle inexhaustible; it could not be fully actualized. Actuality and finitude belong together, possibility and infinity belong together. (This may not be quite all that needs to be said about their relations, but it is a good part of what needs to be said.)

We have so far justified our explication of 'God' or 'deity' with reference to religions other than those of East Indian origin. Is not Buddhism atheistic, and yet a way of reaching individual wholeness? And does not Hinduism admit God only as an inferior manifestation of the mysterious Ultimate? These are subtle questions. There is no doubt that Buddhism, at least in the Northern form, aims at and claims to reach an experience of oneness with all things. How close this comes to theism varies in different sects. Suzuki once said that it comes very close in Zen. My contention is simply this: Buddhism does not offer an explicit alternative to the theistic version of the all-inclusive reality; rather the

Buddhist refuses to rationalize what is given in 'satori' or salvation. His doctrine is an intuitionism, not a speculative account of the Whole. (To identify this intuitionism with Western 'scientific naturalism' is, I should think, arbitrary in the extreme.) Buddhism is rather a renunciation of theorizing than a theoretical rival to theism. (And it certainly is not natural science. Supernatural overtones are pervasive in Buddhist writings, even though one cannot readily articulate them conceptually.) Metaphysics, being an attempt to theorize about first principles, does not face a choice between theism and Buddhistic nontheism. The only clear-cut metaphysical theory in Buddhism is its analysis of 'substance' into unit-events or momentary states. This analysis Western metaphysics may well take seriously and even in large part accept. But the question of deity is not thereby answered. Whitehead, granted a rather simple correction of his analysis, has shown how God can be conceived in these terms.

As for Hinduism, it tends, like Buddhism, "when the chips are down" to renounce theory for sheer intuition. The contrast between Maya, correlative to ignorance, and Reality, correlative to true knowledge, resists conceptual analysis. Is Maya a form of being (and what form?), a form of nonbeing, a mixture of being and nonbeing, neither being nor nonbeing? The question is put, but orthodox exponents are coy with the answer. The analogies, such as the rope seeming to be a snake, are not concepts but extremely vague suggestions. We are told that, as a dream is cancelled by waking and finding it was but a dream, so Maya is cancelled by waking to True Reality. But in sober truth dreams, like ropes, are not cancelled. They remain just as real events as waking experiences. True, what they seemed to reveal concerning the rest of the world may have been largely (though never, as could be shown, wholly) mistaken, but if so the mistakes were really made. It will never be true that they were not made. And the rope was also really there. Press any statement by the followers of Sankara and you find, I am convinced, that the semblance of conceptual definiteness and logical structure is itself Maya. Or, if there is an intellectual doctrine other than the renunciation of intellect, it is the familiar Western doctrine (as in Plotinus) of 'the absolute', the formless 'infinite', viewed as superior to, but manifested in, all definite, finite actuality, even divine actuality. This doctrine I hold is an intellectual as well as religious mistake. Only potentiality can be strictly infinite, nonrelative, and immutable; actuality, which is richer than potentiality, is finite, relative, and in process of creation. God as actual is more than the absolute (which indeed is a mere abstraction), not less.

I am open to conviction in these matters, but my trouble can hardly be a result of not having read enough Hindu philosophy. For there have been and are learned thinkers in India who have said much the same thing as I have just done. Eventually we may all, in East and West, hope to reach better understanding concerning the role of logic in religious thought. Intuition is valuable, and indeed indispensable; but I have a certain faith in the rights and duties of rational metaphysical inquiry, and I shall give up this faith only when the inevitable failure of rational metaphysics has been shown in some more conclusive way than by arguing ad nauseam from the difficulties of certain traditional forms of metaphysics whose failure I admit from the outset.

In what kind of philosophy is the religious idea of God most at home?

(1) It must be a philosophy in which becoming is not considered inferior to being. For the self-surpassing divinity is in process of surpassing itself, and if the supreme reality is thus a supreme process, lesser individual realities will be instances of an inferior form of process. Being can then be no more than an abstraction from becoming.

(2) It must be a philosophy which avoids declaring all individual existence to be contingent. For God, to be unsurpassable by others, must exist necessarily. Yet at the same time all actuality must indeed be contingent, even divine actuality, for the latter includes all contingent things. It follows that we need a philosophy which distinguishes between the bare or abstract truth that an individual exists and the how or actual concrete state in which it exists. Individual self-identity must be granted a certain independence from concrete actuality. Philosophies which clearly provide for this are of the Buddhist-Whiteheadian type, according to which the most concrete mode of reality is not existing substance, thing, or person, but actually occurring event, state, or experience.

(3) A theistic philosophy must be in some sense indeterministic. It must admit (as Hume and Kant would not) that process is creative of novelty that is not definitely implicit in the antecedent situation. For otherwise only ignorance would make self-surpassing seem real; while for God past, present, and future would form but a single perpetually complete reality. And this, we have seen, is not the religious view. Also a deterministic theory of temporal process implies theologically either a denial of all contingency, as in Spinoza, or an absolutely mysterious nontemporal freedom (at least for God), as in Kant.

(4) A theistic philosophy must take 'create' or 'creator' as a universal category, rather than as applicable to God alone. It must distinguish supreme creativity from lesser forms and attribute some degree of creativity to all actuality. It must make of creativity a 'transcendental', the very essence of reality as self-surpassing process. This is precisely what Whitehead does in his "category of the ultimate" (Chapter 2 of *Process and Reality*).

(5) A theistic philosophy must have a theory of internal relations and also a theory of external relations. Of internal relations, for a whole logically requires its constituents and God in his concrete actuality being the inclusive whole requires all things; moreover, the creatures require God as the correlate of their own integrity. In some deficient sense the creatures include God, as well as God the creatures. Finally, any creative act requires its antecedent data. Of external relations, for though God in his particular or contingent actuality includes all actuality, yet in his bare individual existence as the divine being and no other he—and he alone—is necessary, and what is necessary cannot include, or be constituted by, relation to anything contingent. Only the contingent can be relative. Hence the abstract necessary aspect of God does not include the actual world, and is not relative to it. (In addition, the antecedent data of a creative synthesis are independent of the synthesis.) Both types of relations are provided for by Whitehead's theory of 'prehensions' and the two 'natures' of God.

With these requirements in mind I ask you, Was it any such doctrine as this 'neoclassical theism' (as I call it) which Hume and Kant evaluated in their alleged refutations of all natural theology? Or were they—and especially, perhaps, Kant—as unaware as any child that such a doctrine could be formulated and seriously defended? I confess I find the latter view to fit the known facts. Kant, at least, did not so much as dream of neoclassical theism, or the metaphysics which can adequately express it. If then he refuted the doctrine, this was indeed a stupendous achievement, an amazing piece of luck or feat of divination. But did he refute it? I fail altogether to see that he did.

Perhaps there is one qualification: the first Antinomy might be thought to be such a refutation, provided one accepts the finitistic trend in mathematics as authoritative. In the present work this matter must remain unfinished business.

There seems to be no equally clear religious alternative to theistic metaphysics, defined as belief in the modally all-inclusive or nonfragmentary being, surpassable only by Himself. These characterizations spring much more directly from the ideal of worship than terms like 'absolute', 'infinite', 'immutable', 'unconditioned', and similar legacies from Aristotle, Philo, Plotinus, or Plato badly understood. How different intellectual history might have been had we not been saddled so long with these pseudo-platonic simplifications! However, as a politician once remarked, "the future is before us."

SUGGESTED READINGS

Charles Hartshorne on God

Hartshorne, Charles. *Man's Vision of God and the Logic of Theism.* Chicago: Willett, Clark, 1941; Hamden, Conn.: Archon Books, 1964.

———. *The Divine Relativity: A Social Conception of God.* New Haven: Yale University Press, 1948. Paperback—New Haven: Yale University Press.

———. (With William L. Reese) *Philosophers Speak of God.* Chicago: The University of Chicago Press, 1953, especially pp. 1-25. Paperback—Chicago: The University of Chicago Press.

———. *A Natural Theology for Our Time.* LaSalle, Ill.: Open Court, 1967. Paperback—LaSalle, Ill.: Open Court.

———. *Creative Synthesis and Philosophic Method.* LaSalle, Ill.: Open Court, 1970, especially pp. 261-297.

On Charles Hartshorne's Doctrine of God

James, Ralph E., Jr. *The Concrete God: A New Beginning for Theology—The Thought of Charles Hartshorne.* Indianapolis: Bobbs-Merrill, 1967.

Ogden, Schubert M. "Bultmann's Demythologizing and Hartshorne's Dipolar Theism," *Process and Divinity: The Hartshorne Festschrift.* Edited by William L. Reese and Eugene Freeman. LaSalle, Ill.: Open Court, 1964, pp. 579-591.

Peters, Eugene H. *The Creative Advance: An Introduction to Process Philosophy as a Context for Christian Faith.* St. Louis: Bethany Press, 1966, pp. 77-104. Paperback—St. Louis: Bethany Press.

On Related Themes

See the listings after the selection by Schubert M. Ogden, pp. 134-135.

7 The Reality of God

SCHUBERT M. OGDEN

A former student of Hartshorne at the University of Chicago, Schubert Ogden made a vigorous statement of the process doctrine of God in his book *The Reality of God*. The following selection,* taken from the initial essay of the book, presents the essence of Ogden's position. Using Whitehead's reformed subjectivist principle, Ogden analyzes human subjectivity to understand God. I observe that, as a self, I am related to my body and to an encompassing society of beings and that I am essentially temporal. By analogy God must be conceived as genuinely temporal and social, hence radically different from the timeless and unrelated Absolute of classical theism. This neo-classical notion of God avoids the dilemma of the wholly external God of Aquinas and the immanent God of Spinoza who would make the world wholly necessary. Furthermore, it is immeasurably more appropriate to the Scriptural witness, while at the same time understandable to secular man.

Schubert M. Ogden taught at the Perkins School of Theology before returning to the University of Chicago, where he is presently University Professor of Theology in the Divinity School.

Among the most significant intellectual achievements of the twentieth century has been the creation at last of a neoclassical alternative to the metaphysics and philosophical theology of our classical tradition. Espe-

* From *The Reality of God and Other Essays* (New York: Harper and Row, 1966), pp. 56-70. Reprinted with permission.

120   SCHUBERT M. OGDEN

cially through the work of Alfred North Whitehead and, in the area usually designated "natural theology," or Charles Hartshorne, the ancient problems of philosophy have received a new, thoroughly modern treatment, which in its scope and depth easily rivals the so-called *philosophia perennis*.[1] It is my belief that the conceptuality provided by this new philosophy enables us so to conceive the reality of God that we may respect all that is legitimate in modern secularity, while also fully respecting the distinctive claims of Christian faith itself. In the rest of the essay, I shall try to give the reasons for this belief.

The starting-point for a genuinely new theistic conception is what Whitehead speaks of as "the reformed subjectivist principle."[2] According to this principle, we can be given an adequate answer to the metaphysical question of the meaning of "reality" only by imaginatively generalizing "elements disclosed in the analysis of the experiences of subjects." In other words, the principle requires that we take as the experiential basis of all our most fundamental concepts the primal phenomenon of our own existence as experiencing subjects or selves.

To adhere to this requirement is to be led ineluctably to a distinctly different kind of metaphysics and philosophical theology from those of the classical tradition. As not only Whitehead, but also Heidegger and others have made clear, the characteristics of classical philosophy all derive from its virtually exclusive orientation away from the primal phenomenon of selfhood toward the secondary phenomenon of the world constituted by the experience of our senses. It assumes that the paradigmatic cases of reality are

[1] The most complete and technical formulation of Whitehead's metaphysics is given in *Process and Reality: An Essay in Cosmology*, New York: The Macmillan Co., 1929. The others of his many writings of greatest relevance for the problem of this essay are *Religion in the Making*, New York: The Macmillan Co., 1926; *Adventures of Ideas*, New York: The Macmillan Co., 1933, especially Part III; and *Modes of Thought*, New York: The Macmillan Co., 1938. In addition to the works of Hartshorne already referred to, see especially *Beyond Humanism: Essays in the New Philosophy of Nature*, Chicago: Willett, Clark & Co., 1937; *The Divine Relativity: A Social Conception of God*, New Haven: Yale University Press, 1948; and *Reality as Social Process: Studies in Metaphysics and Religion*, Glencoe, Ill.: The Free Press, 1953. For a discussion of the contribution of Martin Heidegger's *Sein und Zeit*, Halle: Max Niemeyer Verlag, 1927, to the same end, see below, pp. 144-63.
[2] *Process and Reality*, pp. 252 f.

the objects of ordinary perception—such things as tables and chairs, and persons as we may know them by observing their behavior—and from these objects it constructs its fundamental concepts or categories of interpretation. The chief of these categories is that of "substance" or "being," understood as that which is essentially nontemporal and lacking in real internal relations to anything beyond itself. Insofar as the self is focused by classical philosophy, it, too, is interpreted in these categories and thus conceived as a special kind of substance. As soon, however, as we orient our metaphysical reflection to the self as we actually experience it, as itself the primal ground of our world of perceived objects, this whole classical approach is, in the Heideggerian sense of the word, "dismantled" (*destruiert*). Whatever else the self is, it is hardly a substance which, in Descartes' phrase, "requires nothing but itself in order to exist," [3] nor is it altogether without intrinsic temporal structure. To the contrary, the very being of the self is relational or social; and it is nothing if not a process of change involving the distinct modes of present, past, and future.

To exist as a self, as each of us does, is always to be related, first of all, to the intimate world constituted by one's own body. What I think and feel has its most direct effects on my own brain cells and central nervous system, and thence on the rest of the organism in which I as a self am incarnate. Likewise, what most directly affects me as a conscious subject is just the incredibly complex state of that same organism in which I as a self participate by immediate sympathetic feeling. By means of my body, then, I am also affected by, and in turn affect, the larger whole of things beyond myself. But, whether directly or indirectly, I am really related to an encompassing society of other beings and am a self at all only by reason of that real relatedness. No less constitutive of my selfhood is its essential temporality. I know myself most immediately only as an ever-changing sequence of occasions of experience, each of which is the present integration of remembered past and anticipated future into a new whole of significance. My life history continually leads through moments of decision in which I must somehow determine what both I and those with whom I am

[3] *The Philosophical Works of Descartes*, Vol. I, trans. E. S. Haldane and G. R. T. Ross, Cambridge: Cambridge University Press, 1911, p. 239 (*Principles of Philosophy*, LI).

related are to be. Selecting from the heritage of the already actual and the wealth of possibility awaiting realization, I freely fashion myself in creative interaction with a universe of others who also are not dead but alive.

If we begin by taking the self as thus experienced as paradigmatic for reality as such, the result is a complete revolution of classical metaphysics. It thereupon becomes clear that real internal relation to others and intrinsic temporality are not "mixed perfections" peculiar to finite beings such as ourselves, but "simple perfections" inherent in the meaning of "reality" in the most fundamental use of the word. In consequence, the chief category for finally interpreting anything real can no longer be "substance" or "being" (as traditionally understood), but must be "process" or "creative becoming," construed as that which is in principle social and temporal. Whatever is, is to be conceived, in the last analysis, either as an instance of, or an element in, such creative becoming and thus as somehow analogous to our own existence as selves.

By *this* "analogy of being," however, God, too, must be conceived as a genuinely temporal and social reality, and therefore as radically different from the wholly timeless and unrelated Absolute of traditional theism. This is not to say that God is to be thought of as only one more instance of creative becoming alongside all the others. As we saw earlier (Section 2), the idea of God cannot be thought at all unless that to which it refers is in all ways truly supreme, a unique reality qualitatively different from everything else. But this may all be granted, indeed, insisted upon, even though one still maintains that God must be conceived in strict analogy with ourselves. The whole point of any *analogia entis* is to enable one to think and speak of God in meaningful concepts, while yet acknowledging that those concepts apply to him only in an eminent sense, which is in principle different from that intended in their other uses. All that a valid method of analogy requires is that the eminence attributed to God really follow from, rather than contradict, the positive meaning of our fundamental concepts as given them by experience. Just this, of course, as we saw from Aquinas' interpretation of the divine knowledge, the classical practice of analogy is unable to do. Because it rests on the premise that God can be in no sense really relative or temporal, it can say that he "knows" or "loves" only by contradicting the meaning of those words as we otherwise use them.

On neoclassical premises, this difficulty, along with innumerable others, is at last removed. God is now conceived as precisely the unique or in all ways perfect instance of creative becoming, and so as the one reality which is eminently social and temporal. Instead of being merely the barren Absolute, which by definition can be really related to nothing, God is in truth related to everything, and that through an immediate sympathetic participation of which our own relation to our bodies is but an image. Similarly, God is no longer thought of as utterly unchangeable and empty of all temporal distinctions. Rather, he, too, is understood to be continually in process of self-creation, synthesizing in each new moment of his experience the whole of achieved actuality with the plenitude of possibility as yet unrealized.

This implies, naturally, that God is by analogy a living and even growing God and that he is related to the universe of other beings somewhat as the human self is related to its body. And yet, just as surely implied is that God is even in these respects the truly eminent or perfect reality, whose unsurpassability by others is a matter of principle, not simply of fact.[4] If God is the

----

[4] This is commonly overlooked by critics of neoclassical theism. Thus, for instance, John Macquarrie (*Twentieth Century Religious Thought: The Frontiers of Philosophy and Theology, 1900-1960*, New York: Harper & Row, 1963, p. 277) questions whether a conception of God such as Whitehead's and Hartshorne's is "satisfying *religiously*," since God "becomes to some extent a God who is 'on his way,' so to speak, a God who in one way or another is not yet complete in his perfection, a natural God rather than a supernatural God." Macquarrie's question, like the vagueness of his language ("to some extent," "so to speak," "in one way or another"), betrays that he has missed the point of the neoclassical view of God. That point is not that God is growing and therefore is "a God who is not or who is not yet completely perfect," but that "growing" is itself a wholly positive conception, of which, as of *all* positive conceptions, God is the eminent or perfect exemplification. In other words, the new theism asserts that God *is* "completely perfect" *in whatever sense these words have any coherent meaning* and then questions whether the old use of the words is not, in part, meaningless. It asks, for example, whether the very idea of *actus purus,* of the simultaneous actualization of *all* (even incompossible) possibilities of being and value, is not an incoherent idea, given what we mean by "actuality" and "possibility." If its answer to this question is correct, then a God who is, in the right sense, "on his way" could not be less, but only

eminently temporal and changing One, to whose time and change there can be neither beginning nor end, then he must be just as surely the One who is also eternal and unchangeable. *That* he is ever-changing is itself the product or effect of no change whatever, but is in the strictest sense changeless, the immutable ground of change as such, both his own and all others. Likewise, the notion that God is not utterly immaterial or bodiless ("without body, parts, or passions"), but, on the contrary, is the *eminently* incarnate One establishes a qualitative difference between his being and everything else. The human self, as we noted, is incarnate in the world only in a radically inferior fashion. It directly interacts with little more than its own brain cells, and so is always a localized self, limited by an encompassing external environment. As the eminent Self, by radical contrast, God's sphere of interaction or body is the whole universe of nondivine beings, with each one of which his relation is unsurpassably immediate and direct. His only environment is wholly internal, which means that he can never be localized in any particular space and time but is omnipresent. Hence, just because God is the *eminently* relative One, there is also a sense in which he is strictly absolute. His being related to all others is itself relative to nothing, but is the absolute ground of any and all real relationships, whether his own or those of his creatures.

In its way, therefore, a neoclassical conception of God's reality incorporates all the "metaphysical attributes" on which classical theists alone insist. For it, too, God is in a literal sense "eternal," "immutable," "impassive," "immaterial"—in brief, the metaphysical Absolute. The difference, however—and it is radical—is that God is now conceived not as simply identical with the Absolute, but

infinitely more perfect than a God who is "pure actuality," since the latter could be at most merely nonsense. In fairness to Macquarrie and others, however, it must be admitted that even the most careful neoclassical theists have sometimes made their point in a misleading way—as when they have said that God "is perfect and complete in some respects, but not in all" (Charles Hartshorne, *Reality as Social Process,* p. 155). Although, in context, the meaning of such a statement ought to be clear, it nevertheless reinforces a classical conception (and, by the new theist's lights, a total misconception) of what "perfection" alone can properly mean. This is hardly the first case, however, where an attempt to make a radically new philosophical point has been in part betrayed by the very conceptions it wishes to overcome.

as the supremely relative Self or Thou who includes the Absolute as the abstract principle of his own concrete identity. In other words, the traditional attributes of God are all reconceived on the analogical basis provided by our own existence as selves. Just as in our case, our defining characteristics are but abstract elements in our concrete experiences, so in the case of God, his attributes are really only abstractions. As such, they define that sense of his eminence or perfection which is indeed statically complete, an absolute maximum. But, because they are in themselves nothing more than abstractions, they are far from constituting the whole of his perfection. That, to the contrary, is nothing merely abstract, but something unimaginably concrete: the ever new synthesis into his own everlasting and all-embracing life of all that has been or ever shall be.

Such, in its main outlines, is the new theism I am proposing. From a classical standpoint, the principal objection to it is almost certain to be that it is not really theism at all, but simply another form of an untenable pantheism. After all, it even goes so far as to conceive God as having a body and as therefore necessarily dependent on a world of other beings.

To this objection, I reply that if the view I have outlined is to be called "pantheism," it is nevertheless at one point significantly different from the views of Spinoza, Hegel, Schleiermacher, Royce, and others, which have also been called by that name. The conventional assumption that the pantheism of these thinkers and the old theism are logically contradictory of one another obscures the fact that both conceptions rest on the same metaphysical premises. They share, namely, a common monopolar denial that God can be in any way conceived as genuinely temporal or related to others.[5] Given this denial, one is unavoidably faced with two choices, of which the positions of Aquinas and Spinoza respectively may be taken to be representative. Either one must conceive God with Aquinas as wholly external to the world, something merely alongside it, and so but part of a whole somehow including God and the world together; or else one must say with Spinoza that it is God who includes the world, but only so as to make the world itself wholly necessary and our experience of its contingency and

[5] Cf. the development of this point by Hartshorne and Reese in *Philosophers Speak of God*, pp. 1 ff.

dependence an illusion. When faced with this dilemma, classical theists typically treat the absurdities of their own position as "mystery" and exploit those of the pantheists as doing at least as much violence to our actual experience. Thus Frederick C. Copleston, in discussing this very issue, assures us that "Obviously, we are here in the region of mystery; in the region of contradiction, some would say," and then goes on to conclude: "Pantheism does nothing to diminish the difficulties which may be thought to accompany theism. It involves one in denying or explaining away or in falsifying the foundation from which all our metaphysical reflections must start, namely, the real multiplicity of distinct finite things with which we are acquainted in experience." [6] The truth, however, is that neither of the traditional choices offers the least hope of permitting us to solve what another Roman Catholic theologian has recently called "the central problem of Christian philosophy—the problem of the coexistence and coagency of the infinite and the finite, the necessary and the contingent, the eternal and the temporal, the absolute and the relative." [7]

But, on the dipolar view of God outlined here, this "problem of synthesis" seems at last to have found a solution—and that in a way which is as far removed from classical pantheism as from its traditional theistic alternative. By conceiving God as infinite personal existence or creative becoming, one can assert God's independence of the actual world (in his abstract identity) without saying he is wholly external to it, and one can affirm his inclusion of the actual world (in his concrete existence) without denying that the world as actual is completely contingent and radically dependent on him as its sole necessary ground. This is to say that, on the new conception, the real motive of the traditional doctrine of *creatio ex nihilo a deo*, which is the theological point at issue in any warranted rejection of pantheism, can be fully expressed. What is at stake in that doctrine (as even Aquinas in a way saw) is not the claim that God once existed in lonely isolation, as the Creator of no actual world of creatures. Its point, rather, is to deny, against all forms of metaphysical dualism, that there is any being or principle save God alone which is the necessary ground of whatever exists or is even possible. This denial, however, is an essential

[6] *Aquinas,* Harmondsworth: Penguin Books Ltd., 1955, pp. 139, 141.
[7] John Courtney Murray, *op. cit.,* p. 92.

implication of the new theism, as surely as it ever was of the old. Although, for the new view, one cannot meaningfully claim that God was ever without *some* actual world of creatures, any such world was itself created "out of nothing," in the sense that there once was when it was not. Its real potentiality, of course, lay in the conjoint actuality of God and of the creatures constituting the precedent actual world (or worlds). But to suppose that this in any way denies *creatio ex nihilo* can appeal to no valid theological warrant and runs the risk of involving obvious absurdity besides. After all, children do have parents; and classical theism itself has always been insistent (however incoherently) on the real agency of "secondary causes." Furthermore—and this is the essential point—no actual world with which God ever co-operates in creating a new world is in any sense necessary or eternal. It, too, was once his completely free contingent creation, so that his prerogatives of strict necessity and eternity of existence are shared by him with no one, but belong to him alone.[8]

In sum, the point at which the new theism most obviously differs from the old is the very point at which it is also utterly different from what is properly called "pantheism"—namely, its insistence that reality as such and, to an eminent degree, God are by their very natures temporal and social. Because of this insistence, the new view discloses the older conceptions to be related logically not as contradictories, but as mere contraries, to which it is in each case the real contradictory or alternative.

There is ample reason, therefore, to dismiss the charge of pantheism and to claim that the new conception is in its way genuinely theistic. But just as evident and, to my mind, considera-

---

[8] Since the new theism has sometimes been designated, especially by Hartshorne, as "panentheism," it is of interest to note what is said of this term in Karl Rahner and Herbert Vorgrimler, *Kleines theologisches Wörterbuch*, Freiburg: Herder Verlag, 1961, p. 275: "This form of pantheism does not intend simply to identify the world and God monistically (God = the 'all'), but intends, instead, to conceive the 'all' of the world 'in' God as his inner modification and appearance, even if God is not exhausted by the 'all.' The doctrine of such a 'being-in' of the world in God is false and heretical when (and *only* when) it denies the creation and the distinction of the world from God (not only of God from the world). . . . Otherwise it is a challenge to ontology to think the relation between absolute and finite being both more exactly and more deeply, (i.e., by grasping the reciprocal relation between unity and difference which increase in the same degree)."

bly more important is that it is a way of conceiving God's reality which is able to do justice to modern secularity. Indeed, the preceding exposition should have made clear that this form of theism offers a full reflective explication of the understanding of God which is present at least implicitly in any serious affirmation of the secular. We saw that, although such an affirmation necessarily rests on an equally emphatic affirmation of God's reality, the only God it thus affirms is the dipolar ground of the ultimate significance of our life in the world. It is just such a God, however, whom the premises of a neoclassical metaphysics enable and even require us to conceive. Given these premises, God both may and must be thought of as the eminently relative One who makes possible "a general confidence about the future," an assurance of the final worth of our life which will not be disappointed.

Thus we may at last render really intelligible our deep conviction as modern men that it is our own secular decisions and finite processes of creative becoming which are the very stuff of the "really real" and so themselves somehow of permanent significance. Because God himself is most immediately affected by all that we are and do, the future for which we ultimately live our lives is neither merely our own nor that of others as limited as ourselves, but also the unending future of God's own creative becoming, in which we are each given to share. It is his self-creation that is the ultimate cause advanced or retarded by all our lesser causes and their issues; and the motive finally inspiring our own decisions as men, in relation to one another and to all our fellow creatures, is so to maximize the being and joy of the world as to increase as fully as we can the concrete perfection of his everlasting life. So, too, are our sufferings at last conceivable as having the nature and importance our secularity prompts us to claim for them. No longer must they be thought of as ultimately indifferent, as secularism and supernaturalism alike imply; nor need we heed the pantheist's discouraging word that they are the wholly necessary parts of what James once described, characteristically, as "one vast instantaneous co-implicated completeness." [9] Rather, our sufferings also may be conceived as of a piece with a reality which is through-and-through temporal and social. They are the partly avoidable, partly unavoidable, products of finite-free choices

[9] *A Pluralistic Universe*, p. 322.

and, like everything else, are redolent of eternal significance. Because they, too, occur only within the horizon of God's all-encompassing sympathy, they are the very opposite of the merely indifferent. When they can be prevented, the responsibility for their prevention may now be realized in all its infinite importance; and, when they must be borne with, even that may be understood to have the consolation which alone enables any of us to bear them.

Only slightly less important is that the new theism is also free of the incoherence, of the antinomies and contradictions, that make the old supernaturalism incredible to the modern mind. As we saw, the reason for this incoherence is the classical metaphysical denial that God can be in any sense temporal and relative, which stands in stark contradiction to Scripture's representation of God as the eminent Self or Thou. But, with the new metaphysical premises, by contrast, there is no longer any basis for such a contradiction. While the new theism does indeed conceive God as both absolute and relative, it so understands these two aspects of his nature that they may be seen to be complementary, instead of contradictory. By completely reversing the classical procedure and thinking of God as, first of all, the eminently relative One, the new view construes God's absoluteness as simply the abstract structure or identifying principle of his eminent relativity. It is thereby able to show what could never be shown by classical theism, how the Thou with the greatest conceivable degree of real relatedness to others—namely, relatedness to all others—is for that very reason the most truly absolute Thou any mind can conceive. It can similarly show how maximum temporality entails strict eternity; maximum capacity for change, unsurpassable immutability; and maximum passivity to the actions of others, the greatest possible activity in all their numberless processes of self-creation.

I cannot develop the details of this demonstration, to make clear how with this, so to speak, great reversal, the main antinomies of traditional theism—including the allegedly insoluble problem of evil—are all capable of resolution. But I trust it is clear at least in principle why the new theism can overcome the theoretical incoherence which also precludes supernaturalism as a live option for secular man.

There remains the question, crucial for Protestant theology, whether this new view can also do justice to the faith in God's reality decisively re-presented in Jesus Christ. Granted that it is a form of theism which seems possible for secular man, does it also make possible, as I believe, a distinctively *Christian* theism?

Let us be clear from the outset that no answer to this question can ever be completely convincing. What we are given to understand of Christ is always dependent in part on our own concepts, so any attempt to justify those concepts always tends to be circular. We may simply read out of revelation a warrant for the conceptions we first had to read into it in order to understand it at all. Nevertheless, in this, as in any other process of interpretation, it is possible to reach judgments that are at least relatively sure. Some conceptualities clearly seem more appropriate than others to the witness to God in Christ which is given in Holy Scripture.

If the argument of this essay is correct, the concepts taken over by Christian theologians from classical metaphysics can only be pronounced inadequate when judged by *this* criterion of appropriateness. From the standpoint of theology's total concern and task, the objection to supernaturalism is not simply that it is an impossible conception for contemporary men, but that it also makes impossible an appropriate theological witness to the God of Jesus Christ. By conceiving God as, first of all, the metaphysical Absolute, traditional theists completely reverse the priority of Scripture, thereby creating a totally different theological problem. Now the question becomes the one endlessly discussed in the tradition, "How can the Absolute somehow be understood as personal?" instead of "How can the eminently personal One be appropriately conceived in his absoluteness?" [10] By the same criterion, however, the new theism proposed here seems immeasurably more adequate. For it, just as for Scripture, the first (and last!) thing to be said about God is that he is the supreme Self or Thou, whose absolute relativity or all-embracing love is the beginning and end of

---

[10] Cf., e.g., Anselm's question in *Proslogium*, VIII: "But how art thou compassionate, and, at the same time, passionless? For if thou art passionless, thou dost not feel sympathy; and if thou dost not feel sympathy, thy heart is not wretched from sympathy for the wretched; but this it is to be compassionate. . . . How, then, art thou compassionate and not compassionate, O Lord, unless because [and this, incredibly enough, is Anselm's answer to his question] thou art compassionate in terms of our experience, and not compassionate in terms of thy being?" (*St. Anselm: Proslogium; Monologium; etc.*, trans. S. N. Deane, La Salle, Ill.: Open Court Publishing Co., 1903, p. 13).

man and, indeed, of the whole creation (cf. Romans 8). Is it really too much to say, then, that this form of theism is the expression in abstract philosophical concepts of the same understanding of God represented more concretely in the mythologoumena of Holy Scripture? Is one unreasonable in claiming that it is the "theory" for which the scriptural myths provide the "model" —and that theory and model together effect *one* disclosure of the encompassing mystery of our existence? [11]

The only way to answer these questions, so far as they can be answered at all, is to make use of the new conceptuality in the actual hermeneutical process, continually testing it against the designations of God in the texts of Scripture.[12] But, if the answer should prove to be the one I am implying, it would be hard to exaggerate the importance of the new theism to Protestant theology. The whole task of this theology, finally, is to provide a critical, constructive interpretation of the understanding of faith in God to which witness is borne in Holy Scripture. To accomplish

[11] See Ian T. Ramsey, *Models and Mystery*, London: Oxford University Press, 1964; also Frederick Ferré, "Mapping the Logic of Models in Science and Theology," *Christian Scholar*, Spring, 1963, pp. 9-39.

[12] Thus one should even ask, for example, whether the new theism enables us so to conceive God that we may meaningfully pray to him as Scripture plainly enjoins us to do. Of course, those who regard this as *the* test question often betray an understanding of prayer that is not only superstitious from the standpoint of secularity, but also sub-Christian by the criterion of faith itself. Where man's prayers have been subjected to the "permanent revolution" effected by the Christian witness, they are invariably defined by two characteristics: first, they are always addressed to the One whom Jesus calls Father (in accordance with the old maxim, *oratio semper dirigatur ad Patrem*); and, second, they are for that reason always offered "through" or "in the name of" Jesus Christ our Lord. But this means that, whatever else Christian prayers are, they can never be a matter either of informing God as to what he otherwise would not know or of importuning him to do what, but for our prayers, he is unwilling to do. If we are Christians, we pray, as Luther suggests, not to instruct God, but to instruct ourselves. Our "praying teaches us to recognize who we are and who God is, and to learn what we need and where we are to look for it and find it" (*Luther's Works*, Vol. XXI, ed. Jaroslav Pelikan, St. Louis: Concordia Publishing House, 1956, p. 145; cf. pp. 143 f.). But, even on this understanding, prayer has no sense, unless God himself is genuinely affected by all that we say and do. The minimal condition of our praying, as of our life generally, is that it have an ultimate significance, that it be "heard" by God. This condition the new theism clearly seems able to meet in a way that the old view, in principle, never could.

this task, however, requires a fully developed conceptuality which is understandable in the present situation *and* appropriate to the essential claims of the scriptural witness. My suggestion is that the new theism is adequate by the second criterion as well as the first —or at least is sufficiently superior by this standard to the other available options to deserve the most serious testing.

This suggestion is further supported when one considers the new theism in relation to the response to the scriptural witness historically represented by Protestant Christianity. As often noted, Protestantism's most distinctive claims all share a certain paradoxical or dialectical character. Beginning with its central doctrine of justification by grace and faith alone, all its main teachings seem either to affirm or to imply what Kierkegaard spoke of as "the infinite qualitative difference" between God and the world. On the one hand, God is said to be "wholly other" than the world, and the world by itself utterly secular or profane; on the other hand, the very otherness of God is understood as his being for the world, not against it, so that the world in itself is affirmed to be of ultimate significance. This genuinely dialectical vision of God's relation to the world has always been the despair of Catholic interpreters of our common Christian heritage; and it is evident that even Protestant theologians have only seldom caught a glimpse of its full implications. Too often, it has seemed to combine, as it were, the worst of both worlds, what with an extreme otherworldliness, which is alleged to destroy nature instead of perfecting it, and an extreme this-worldliness, which its critics claim dulls man's sense for his final supernatural end. Yet it is clear, I think, that, if anything is to be called "the spirit of Protestantism," it is just this dialectical vision of God and the world and the total style of Christian life to which it gives rise. And equally clear is the reason why Protestants tend to share this vision almost as if by instinct: from the beginning, their chief inspiration has not been the spirit which informs the rich culture of classical antiquity, but the quite different Spirit who moves over the pages of Holy Scripture, witnessing simply that "God is love." It is precisely and only eminent love, in the distinctively scriptural sense of pure personal relationship, that could relate God to his world by such a profound dialectic of difference and identity. But the question the Protestant theologian must ask is how this eminent love is to be clarified *conceptually,* if not by means of something like the new theism. Is it not evident, in fact, that this dipolar theism is an analysis in the general terms of philosophy of just that love and its dialectic?

Throughout its history, Protestant theology has rarely succeeded in bringing together fidelity to the scriptural witness, to the word of God's "pure unbounded love," and constructive formulations of undoubted conceptual power. When it has been most systematic, its concepts have usually been determined in one way or another by classical metaphysics and so have tended to obscure its evangelical inspiration. In other cases, when it has remained truest to that inspiration, its conceptual structure has often been unclear and uncertain, thus making it seem outside of, or even opposed to, the rest of our reflective life. But, with the resources provided by the new theism and, more generally, by a neoclassical metaphysics, there is every reason why this fateful divorce should no longer be necessary. Now, at last, we can develop a comprehensive philosophical outlook for which the words "God is love" are no longer foolishness, but the very sum of wisdom. In its terms, therefore, it should prove possible to bear witness not only through preaching and worship, but through theological formulations as well, to the peculiar paradox of Protestant Christianity —that God is radically other than the world and never to be confused with it, but that, *just for this reason,* the world itself has an unconditioned worth and significance.

It may appear strange and even suspicious that a form of theism which seems genuinely possible for secular man should turn out to be thus conformable to Christian faith. But such strangeness should be dispelled as soon as it is recalled that neither secularity itself nor the new metaphysics in which it is most completely expressed is without a history. The evidence is clear that both phenomena trace their origin to the distinctively Christian understanding of existence, especially in its Protestant form. Thus, as many others have pointed out, even the ethos of modern science must be understood against the background of the Christian doctrine of creation, with its claim that the world is utterly secular and therefore open to the most probing inquiry, and yet is also sufficiently significant to be worthy of our most careful attention.[13] And so, too, with our modern moral attitude, our insistence, in

[13] See, e.g., H. Richard Niebuhr, *op. cit.,* especially pp. 78-89, 127-41.

the words of a contemporary philosopher, that "Morality is made for man, not man for morality." [14] As is clear even from the allusion of this statement, our secular emphasis on man's full autonomy as moral agent and on the surpassing importance of his present decisions is a principal part of our Christian inheritance.

Consequently, there is nothing strange, much less contradictory, about the notion of a "secular Christianity." Rightly understood, Christianity has always been secular, because in its essence, in the presence in our human history of Jesus Christ, it is simply the representation to man and the world of their ultimate significance within the encompassing mystery of God's love.[15] But it is also only to be expected that neoclassical theism should prove peculiarly transparent to Christian claims. As with the secularity of which it is the integral expression, its roots reach down deep within the soil of Christianity, and it is not to be explained historically except as "secularized" Christian theology.

Yet, strange or not, the fact seems to be that here is a form of theism that not only is understandable to secular men, but is also appropriate to Christian faith. One can only hope, therefore, that the significance of this fact will not be lost on the Protestant theology of our time. By making resolute use of this "system of thought," theology today should be able, in considerable measure, to accomplish its proper task: to bear witness in the most adequate conceptual form now possible to the reality of God which is represented to us all in Jesus Christ.

SUGGESTED READINGS

Schubert M. Ogden on God

Ogden, Schubert M. "Bultmann's Demythologizing and Hartshorne's Dipolar Theism," *Process and Divinity: The Hartshorne Festschrift.*

[14] William K. Frankena, *Ethics,* Englewood Cliffs, N.J.: Prentice-Hall, Inc., 1963, p. 98.
[15] Cf. the parallel development and defense of this judgment in Ronald Gregor Smith, *Secular Christianity,* New York: Harper & Row, 1966, which I have been privileged to read in proof only after these pages were on the press.

Edited by William L. Reese and Eugene Freeman. LaSalle, Ill.: Open Court, 1964, pp. 579-591. Paperback—LaSalle, Ill.: Open Court.

————. *The Reality of God and Other Essays.* New York: Harper and Row, 1966.

————. "Toward a New Theism," *Process Philosophy and Christian Thought.* Edited by Delwin Brown, Ralph E. James, Jr., and Gene Reeves. Indianapolis: Bobbs-Merrill, 1971, pp. 173-187. Paperback—Indianapolis: Bobbs-Merrill.

On Schubert M. Ogden's Doctrine of God

Gilkey, Langdon. "A Theology in Process: Schubert Ogden's Developing Theology," *Interpretation,* 21 (1967), 447-459.

Kelly, Anthony. "God: How Near a Relation?" *The Thomist,* 34 (1970), 191-229.

Neville, Robert. "Neoclassical Metaphysics and Christianity: A Critical Study of Ogden's *Reality of God,*" *International Philosophical Quarterly,* 9 (1969), 605-624.

Robertson, John C., Jr. "Rahner and Ogden: Man's Knowledge of God," *Harvard Theological Review,* 63 (1970), 377-407.

On Related Themes

See the listings after the selection by Charles Hartshorne, pp. 117-118.

8 A Whiteheadian Reflection on God's Relation to the World

WALTER E. STOKES

A recurrent theme in process theology is a critique of Thomas Aquinas and the classical theism he represents. Process thinkers charge him with developing a doctrine of God as changeless Absolute wholly unrelated to the world. According to the Aristotelian-Thomistic notion of relation, the world is really related to God, but God is related to the world only with a relation of reason. In the following selection,* Walter Stokes indicates how Thomas' thought can be enriched by viewing issues from a Whiteheadian perspective. At the same time he challenges the critique of the tradition. By tapping Augustine's notion of freedom and his theology of the Trinity, Stokes points to more compatibility between process thought and the Christian tradition than critics tend to acknowledge.

A Jesuit priest, Walter E. Stokes received his doctorate from St. Louis University, where he wrote his dissertation on Whitehead's notion of creativity. He did post-doctoral study at Cambridge University and taught philosophy at the Jesuit seminary at Shrub Oak, New York, and at Fordham University. At the time of his death in 1969, at the age of forty-five, he

* This was originally delivered as a paper at a meeting of the Society for the Study of Process Philosophies held in conjunction with a Fellows Meeting of the Society for Religion in Higher Education at Oberlin College, August, 1967. Sections of this paper have appeared in "Freedom as Perfection: Whitehead, Thomas and Augustine," *Proceedings of the American Catholic Philosophical Association,* 36 (1962), 140-142; and in "Is God Really Related to This World?" *Proceedings of the American Catholic Philosophical Association,* 39 (1965), 145-151. Reprinted with permission.

137

*was the leading Catholic contributor to the White-
headian process movement.*

The problem of God's relation to the world
is receiving more attention at present than
heretofore both in theology and philosophy. For me the question
becomes acute when I reflect on the present-day awareness that
love is a free interchange of gifts. Love is a dynamic relation
whereby the lover places himself in the state of a gift, and this
relation finds full maturity in the free responses of the one loved.
Outgoing self-relating in mutual self-giving has been given classical
expression in St. Ignatius' *Contemplatio ad Amorem* as "a mutual
sharing of goods, for example, the lover gives and shares with
the beloved what he possesses, or something of that which he has
or is able to give; and vice versa, the beloved shares with the
lover".[1] Now, the question is: Can God's love for this world be
more adequately expressed than it has been in the traditional
theistic position which holds that God's knowledge and love of
this world involves in Him nothing more than a rational relation?
Perhaps new dimensions in the doctrine of relation can provide a
perspective for articulating a real relation of God to the world.
Since the meaning and value of history are at stake, these dimensions may well be worth exploring. If God's relation to the
world were to be only a relation of reason, in what sense does
this world matter? If this relation to it in knowledge and love is
not a real relation, do time and history really count? If God is just
as He is whether or not He loves this world or no world at all, do
man's free acts in time make a difference?

The Problem

The philosophical problem of God's relation to the world
has been raised sharply by Charles Hartshorne. Perhaps he has
done more than any other philosopher to make us aware of the
difficulties built into the traditional theistic view of this relation.

[1] Ignatius of Loyola, *The Spiritual Exercises of St. Ignatius,* trans. by
Louis J. Puhl, S.J. (Westminster, Md., 1951), p. 101.

His criticism of this view is that it regards God as somehow indifferent to persons and to the interrelations of things; it regards God as being what He is eternally, whether He creates this world or no world at all; it regards Him, not as a subject or person, but as a thing, not conceived at all with relations to persons. Yet religious intuition tells us that God loves all beings and is related to them by a sympathetic union surpassing any human sympathy. And all our experience supports the view that knowing and loving are constitutive of the knower or lover, rather than of the known or loved. But to this rule, according to the traditional view, God's knowledge and love of this world are an enormous exception. For divine knowledge and love make a real difference in the creature, but not at all in God Himself. This, in spite of the fact that real relations, even in the teaching of St. Thomas, are normally associated with the more perfect and more conscious beings.

The standard doctrine is illustrated by the following: if an animal stands to the left of a pillar, it is really related to the pillar, but the pillar is not related to the animal. What makes the animal at least more conspicuously relative than the pillar is its superiority as a being. In fact, apart from God, it is the knower who is really related to the known, not the known to the knower. As one ascends the scale of increasing complexity and consciousness, the capacity to place oneself in relation increases. Nevertheless, God is not really related to this world in knowledge and love, and so ". . . it follows that God does not know or love or will us, His creatures. At most, we can say only that we are known, loved and willed by Him." [2] In the traditional doctrines of creation and conservation there is, of course, much to blunt the fierceness of Hartshorne's attack. Indeed, the depth of creation as the key to the intelligibility of creatures has been well brought out by Josef Pieper: ". . . things in so far as they are creatively thought by God possess these two properties: on the one hand their ontological clarity and self-revelation and, on the other hand, their inexhaustibleness; their knowability as well as their unknowability." [3] And Hartshorne's own absolute-relative doctrine of divine relativity is not without

[2] C. Hartshorne, *The Divine Relativity*, 2nd ed. (New Haven, 1964), p. 16. The question is discussed thoroughly, *ibid.*, pp. 1-59.
[3] J. Pieper, *The Silence of St. Thomas* (New York, 1957), p. 69.

serious difficulties in its own right.[4] Still the question remains: Has the traditional position adequately conceived and satisfactorily articulated God's relation to the world? In a discussion of Paul Weiss' Whiteheadian approach to God's relation to the world, Kenneth L. Schmitz [5] rightly sees that in this matter "relation" is the central philosophical question: ". . . the modal philosophy sees the margin of being of Actualities to be in their standing over against an imperfect God, whereas the philosophy of creative act sees the margin of being of creatures to lie within their being a non-reciprocal relation to a perfect God. The philosophical issue, then, is between differing conceptions of relation." [6] However, a development of new dimensions of the philosophy of relation with the philosophy of creative act would enable us to move in between the alternatives which are delineated so well by Schmitz.

Classical Formulation of Traditional Position

With his usual succinctness, St. Thomas states the traditional view clearly enough: "God's temporal relations to creatures are in Him only because of our way of thinking of Him; but the opposite relation of creatures to Him are realities in creatures." [7] And St. Thomas' reasoning is equally clear and sound.[8] God's real relation to the world can be neither a predicamental relation nor a transcendental relation. Not the former, because it would mean that God acquired a new accidental relation; [9] nor the latter, because it would mean that God was dependent on creatures. Rejection of accidental perfection is deeply rooted in St. Thomas' metaphysics of God as *esse subsistens* and offers no path to a new perspective from which to reconsider His relation to the world. Certain aspects, however, of St. Thomas' argument for rejecting a real transcendental relation of God to the world suggests that not

---

[4] See J. Wild, *Review of Metaphysics*, 1 (1948), 65-77; C. Hartshorne, *ibid.*, 3 (1950), 31-60, and J. Wild, *ibid.*, 61-84, for discussion that brings out some of the basic issues between theism and Hartshorne's divine relativity.

[5] K. Schmitz, "Weiss and Creation," *Review of Metaphysics*, 18 (1964) 147-69.

[6] *Ibid.*, 162.

[7] *S.T.*, I. 13, 7 ad 4. Also see *S.C.G.*, 11, chs. 11-14; *DePot.*, q. 7, art. 8-11.

[8] The basic argument is given in *S.C.G.*, 11, 12.

[9] *S.C.G.*, 1, 23; *S.T.*, 1, 3, 6 resp.

all perspectives and possibilities have been considered. The key to St. Thomas' view is that, whatever by its very nature is referred to something else, depends on it at least as a condition of its being, since without it this being can neither be nor be thought of. Accordingly, God could not be transcendentally related to creatures in or by a real relationship without being dependent on this world. In such a case, His nature could neither be nor be thought of apart from this world. But such dependence would make of Him a radically contingent being and would be contrary to St. Thomas' conclusion, which he judges he has well established, that God is a necessary being.[10] On these grounds, a real transcendental relation is impossible. The constant appeal to nature, however, and to the consequences which follow if God in His nature were to be essentially ordered to this world, suggests that personal relation and a doctrine of relation proper to person may not have been adequately considered in the traditional scheme.

Towards a New Perspective

The possibility of such a new perspective is indicated by Metz's [11] thesis that St. Thomas' basic understanding of reality is Christian rather than Greek. Even though St. Thomas still works in the Greek categories of nature, substance and matter, he no longer values nature over person, the universal over the individual. This means that man, open to God through the created world of time and history, is the true focal point of St. Thomas' thought. For this reason, then, the use of Greek categories may create a definite tension within the articulation of the Christian experience. It seems to me that St. Thomas' doctrine of relation may be a prime instance of this. The Greek conceptual tools used in St. Thomas' doctrine of relation were forged exclusively in the Greek world of necessary natures. Thus a tension is inevitably set up between such tools and the inner spirit of St. Thomas' Christian thought. There is room, then, for a doctrine of personal relation which may be a more adequate instrument for expressing the Christian experience. This Christian perspective is more adequately assimilated by a properly Whiteheadian reflection on God's relation to the world.

[10] *S.C.G.*, I, 13.
[11] J. Metz, *Chrisliche Anthropozentrik* (Munich, 1962).

Starting Point

The meaning one gives to the word "God" depends on one's approach to the problem of God. It seems characteristic of a Whiteheadian approach to stress an experiential grounding for the notion of God. In this way, God is not "a-god-of-the-gods," a metaphysical *deus ex machina* called in to shore up tottering metaphysical structures by supplying a desperately needed explanation. Instead, God is a factor in properly human experience and is found at work within the world.

The experience central to the human situation is value-affirmation. For man knows himself as situated in the world confronted by a variety of values-to-be-realized. He recognizes that some values are real possibilities for him and others are not. He also realizes that some values are compatible with his historical situation and some are not, some are compatible with each other and others are not. In the project of self-creation throughout his life, man must strive to bring these values into aesthetic harmony aiming at intensity of feeling both in its subjective immediacy and in the relevant occasions beyond itself.[12]

At any moment of his life-project a man can know that he must choose those values that aim at intensity of feeling. He must choose because not to choose would itself be activity. To achieve some of these values, one can freely enter into communities of knowledge and love. In fact, it can be apparent that communal activity may be the only way some of these values can be realized.

In entering such a community, a man implicity affirms that he knows and loves something. In this way, man affirms that he knows and loves something as true, or as good, or as beautiful, and also knows and loves truth, goodness and beauty yet to be realized. What is actually known and loved is limited and recognized as limited compared to what is as yet unrealized and remains to be realized. Furthermore, the drive for truth, goodness and beauty which led to joining the community can be recognized to be beyond the goals already achieved. This means that there is a dynamism in the valuing process that cannot be satisfied with any succession of temporal values or any intensification of these temporal values. For man discovers within his life-process a non-

[12] Alfred North Whitehead, *Process and Reality* (New York, 1929), p. 41.

temporal factor which transcends all temporal realization and yet is immanent to each temporal process. For example, a man's drive for truth can be satisfied by no limited truth whatsoever. To recognize limited truth as limited is to be already beyond limited truth in one's dynamism of knowledge and love for unlimited truth. Each new discovery of truth is recognized for what it is—limited truth unable to stifle man's drive for unlimited truth. This recognition of truth as limited implies that the drive for truth transcends its temporal embodiment. Moreover, no temporal truth added to temporal truth could satisfy this drive. Furthermore, no intensification of temporal truths could satisfy this drive. In fact, man is a valuing-process which is a drive for an unconditioned nontemporal source of value which man can value without reservation or qualification. This answers to man's finer religious instincts and can be called God, the source of all value in the temporal world.

Language analysis has taught us that God is not an object of knowledge the way "tables and chairs" can be objects of knowledge. And God here can be known as the term of man's dynamism not to be reduced to any object of knowledge and desire to be adequately and properly conceptualized by man. Knowledge of God is directional not directly conceptual. We can know that God transcends the limits of any proper concept so that God is truth itself without limitation, the term of the dynamism for truth itself. Death of God philosophers have taught us not to accept as God a being who is totally other and totally transcendent. But God can be known as at once immanent within man's life-process and yet necessarily transcending it. Marxism has taught us to recognize the dynamism which constitutes man's inner life. That very dynamism can be seen to manifest God's activity as final cause in the world. But the problem remains as to how to articulate God's relation to the world so as to preserve both God's immanence and his transcendence. Up to now, theists have tended to preserve God's transcendence by denying that God is really related to this world and panentheists have tended to preserve God's immanence in insisting that God is really related to this world.

Freedom as Perfection

Still the lure remains in Whitehead's notion that God enjoys maximum freedom. In the views of God often advanced by followers of Aquinas, Whitehead sees a totally static God with eminent reality set over against a fluent world with deficient reality. From Whitehead's viewpoint, the notion that God is only free with regard to beings other than Himself is scandalous. To meet this challenge and to bring out the richness of the Thomistic notion of God, it may be useful to revive and give renewed stress to the Augustinian notion of freedom. It seems to me that these notions need each other. Both together present a balance of emphasis sorely needed in a consideration of the freedom of God. Both together clear Thomism of the charge that its notion of God is that of a static, eminent reality. I suggest a doctrine of complementarity of the traditional scholastic notion of freedom and the Augustinian notion of freedom.

The Augustinian discussion of freedom adds another perspective to the problem. Since Augustine conceives freedom by analogy with the freedom from the legal bond of slavery, freedom does not refer directly to the power to act or not act. Freedom is not freedom from necessity, but freedom from coercion. In slavery, a man was the property of another man so that his very life was ordered to the good of another. By analogy, a being is not free only if it is coerced by forces other than itself; a being is free if it acts for its own proper good, not coerced by forces other than itself. The only necessity that this freedom is opposed to is the necessity "by which one is forced against his will." [13] As far as this notion of freedom is concerned, it does not matter whether or not a being has the power to act or not act, the power of free choice may or may not be present.

In his proof that man is free, Augustine shows only that the human will cannot be forced to act by forces from without. So that the will of man is free because its activity is in the power of the will. At its lowest grade the freedom common to all men is that whereby their voluntary acts flow from their desire for perfect happiness: "That freedom of the will is . . . unchangeable by

[13] *Op. imp. contra Jul.,* 122, *PL* XIV, 1299. Although the Augustinian notion of freedom does imply "liberty of indifference," this scholastic notion of freedom is not explicitly and clearly discussed by Augustine. For a valuable discussion of the historical development of the notion of liberty from Augustine to St. Thomas see Vitus de Broglie, S.J., *De Fine Ultimo Humanae Vitae* (Paris, 1948).

which we all wish to be happy and are unable not to so wish." [14]
At its highest, freedom for man is the immediate and immutable
possession of man's final goal. Not only does the necessity of this
state not lessen man's freedom, it is the hallmark of the highest
grade of freedom: "For choice will indeed be more free because
it can in no way submit to sin." [15] In this perspective, free choice
is only the means whereby man is able to attain the highest grade
of freedom. And God is free not only with regard to creatures,
but also in His love of Himself. In fact, the power of self-determination without coercion is realized perfectly in God's love of His
infinite Goodness. From this vantage point, the liberty of indifference of the Thomistic tradition is seen to be a means to an end,
not an end in itself. But the freedom of the Augustinian tradition
is explicitly applied to what perfectly and adequately satisfies the
drive of the will. No account of freedom can be complete without
a consideration of liberty of indifference, but that account is misleading if it does not consider the freedom involved in the possession of the goal that gives value to the means themselves.

Possibly if the complementarity of these diverse notions were
given sufficient emphasis, a more balanced view of God's freedom
may be attained. The only innovation would be on the stress and
the development of their interdependence. For example, writing
of God's love of His own Goodness: ". . . the divine will has
necessity, not indeed of coercion but of the order of nature, which
does not contradict liberty, according to Augustine in *De Civitate
Dei*, V." [16] But generally this has not been noticed by the followers
of Aquinas. If it were stressed more, perhaps the impression that
for Thomists God is a sterile, metaphysical counter might be dispelled. For if God is by His nature absolute freedom, the continuity between the permanent world of transcendent reality and
the fluent world of contingency might be more manifest. Then the
creative activity of God with its effects in time might be seen to
flow from the spontaneity that is *Esse Subsistens*. The central
truth about God's freedom would not be that God is free in the
act of creation because of the defect on the part of the object,
but that God's creative activity is but a manifestation of His

---

[14] *Ibid.*, 1524.
[15] *Ench. de Fide, Spe, Caritate*, CV, PL XI, 281.
[16] *De Veritate*, a. 4, c.

absolute freedom. Then natural theology would be seen to terminate, not in a lifeless, metaphysical stop-gap, but in Absolute Freedom that is immanent in this world. Also, the power of free choice that man experiences would be valued for what it is, a means whereby man can attain freedom in the possession of his final goal. No longer could the philosopher be tempted to glory in the power of free choice as an end in itself. And finally, man could then appreciate the fact that God enjoys maximum freedom.

Indeed, St. Thomas was not unaware of the Augustinian notion of liberty which is based on an analogy of person rather than on a contrast between liberty of indifference and determined inanimate natures.[17] The Augustinian notion of liberty is conceived by contrasting the personal autonomy of the free man with the bondage of a slave. What it excludes is not necessity but coercion from outside. A being who enjoys this liberty acts for its own good without being coerced. This contrasts the unique personal value of an individual's power of self-determination or auto-finality whereby he has dominion over himself with the slave who is merely a means for obtaining goals set by others. It is in this sense that God, although He loves Himself necessarily, loves Himself freely. In this sense, too, if God wills to extend His love to creatures, in doing so He is free. From this perspective, in His creation of the world, liberty of indifference is necessarily involved. But the more significant aspect is the personal dimension: God in self-giving, in self-relating to the world places Himself in a state of gift.

Personal Relation

Admittedly, it was concern with the category of nature that led St. Thomas to stress God's liberty of indifference in creating this world. This concern led in turn to an emphasis rather upon God's perfection as an incommunicable supposit than upon His perfection as person in outgoing self-relation. In fact, St. Thomas leans heavily on St. Augustine's theology of the Trinity. It is this doctrine which has enabled modern philosophy to appreciate the need of conceiving person not only as incommunicable but also as

[17] *De Ver.* q. 23, a. 4 resp. See W. Stokes, "Freedom as Perfection: Whitehead, Thomas and Augustine," *Proceedings of American Catholic Philosophical Association*, 36 (1962), 134-42.

communicable.[18] For Augustine, person is at once absolute and essentially related to another, and this in such a way that its very relativity defines it.

In order to obtain some understanding of the Persons in the Trinity, Augustine, instead of the analogy of the cosmos, used the analogy of man, mind and soul. Memory, intellection and that love of self which is identical with the ecstatic love of God—man seen as related to God, proceeding from God, and constituted in his personality by a pre-awareness of God as the source of his being—such is the analogy that enables Augustine to develop his theology of the Trinity. St. Thomas, similarly, in his theology of the Trinity insists that within the Trinitarian life of God, into the very notion of person, there enters the idea of relation: the Persons are subsistent relations. Within the Trinity the persons are constituted distinct subsistent relations: subsistent because of their identity with God's absolute essence, and distinct because of their relative opposition.

It seems to me that now we have the elements for a reconsideration of God's relation to the world. First of all, God's freedom may be understood as self-determination, self-relation or self-giving without coercion from without. And this may extend itself to self-giving in creation. Secondly, person may be understood to have two aspects, that of the incommunicability of a rational supposit and that of the communicability of that relativity which constitutes persons. Both together provide a new dimension to the doctrine of relations—a dynamic, self-relating outgoing personal relation. And this St. Thomas did not consider in his own explicit doctrine.

A Reconsideration

From this new perspective of analogy of person it is possible to conceive of God's relation to the world as real without thereby attributing any imperfection to Him. If He is a personal, self-relating being, He can in part be understood to be what He is by an eternal, free decision to create this universe. It goes without saying that His nature and personal being as infinite actuality also determine Him to be what He is. But creation reveals that in part

[18] For an excellent summary of this point, see P. Henry, *St. Augustine on Personality* (New York, 1960).

He is what He is eternally also by a free decision to create the world. Now by His decision to create, God becomes a distinct, subsistent being in a new way which could not be realized apart from that historical situation with its relation of opposition. By reason of this new relation of opposition, in part, God is what He is eternally. Nor does this new relation imply imperfection in Him any more than do the relations of opposition in His trinitarian life. Since this opposition is real, God's relation to the world is real. This real relation is identified with His personal being as He freely chooses time, history and human freedom. God's free self-giving, or self-relating, adds no perfection to Him; rather it gives rise to a real distinction based on the reality of a new relation of opposition. In this way, the mystery of God's creation is placed, not in the immutability of His nature, but in His personal activity.

According to the Aristotelian categories of relation, the real relation of God to the world would surely entail His acquiring at least new accidental perfections. For from Aristotle's perspective, a real relation presupposes its terminus as constituted in reality even when the relation is conceived as distinct from it. But, if relation can be active-self-relating, it can be identical with directing one's powers in love. Such a relation based on the relative opposition of God and this world can be His actuality directed in creative activity loving *this* world rather than another or no world at all. Nor need this involve the acquisition of new accidental perfection by God, since the essence of love is the sharing of gifts possessed. Therefore, God's love can be directed to this world as other without His acquiring anything.

Since by reason of this relation of opposition God is really related to this world, He is in history. Through this relation He reveals Himself to us through time and history as other than He could have been. This might seem at first to be opposed to His immutability, and therefore to be incompatible with His infinite perfection. But the only perfection it destroys, I think, is that conceived in the Greek world wherein a being is more perfect if it is what it is by necessity than by any kind of spontaneity. This Greek notion of the perfection of necessity seems to have its roots in accepting the human mind as the measure of intelligibility. Undoubtedly, the mind associates intelligibility with necessity. But once the supreme reality is known to be a personal being, the human mind, with its imperious demand for the intelligible to be the one same thing, finds itself no longer able to measure what is ultimately real and valuable.

We know the gift by reading God's self-revelation in time and history. The evolving universe gives testimony to the totality of that gift. That that gift may achieve its full maturity in the response of free beings who are themselves capable of placing themselves in return in state of gift, the universe is ordered in time and history to become a universe-with-man. To bring about a universe in which God's love can attain its fullness in man's free response, all the forces of nature interact. Time, history and freedom make a difference because through them God reveals Himself as waiting for man's free return of self. They have a meaning because God wills to be a lover waiting upon man's free return of love. God wills to be what He is eternally in part by reason of man's free response to His call to place himself in state of gift. The paradox is that the autonomy of man's free response is nothing but God's gift of Self to man. And that gift increases as man's return gift of self increases, for man's life is a project to be achieved in time through history. In this way, God through His own act of self-giving constitutes man whose genuine free response completes God's gift. Freedom, in the Augustinian sense of self-relating without coercion, is the necessary condition of God's gift. Without freedom, man could not place self in state of gift in return and God's love of the world would be without the fullness that freedom makes possible. And in community, man can strive for those social conditions which can make possible man's free response to God. Aware of God's call to a share in His creative activity, man grows in the consciousness of his responsibility to make that response possible. Since God wills to give Himself in personal love, risk becomes a necessary element in creation, for only free self-giving creatures can give personal love in return. Were there no creatures to return personal love, God's personal love would terminate within His own life.

To be capable of response, man had to be spirit—matter is capable only of being related, never of self-relating. When we look more closely at the highest moment that we know of God's gift in men, we see that this spirit is essentially ordered to fulfilling its destiny in time. *To be* a man is *to be becoming* one through personal history. Since man is spirit in flesh, it is a spirit that must live in the world of matter and time to become what by nature and destiny it is. For man as spirit-ordered-to-time—time becomes a necessity for placing self in state of gift in return of God's love. Time does make a difference, for it is only in time that man completes God's love. In choosing to give self in love to a spirit-in-flesh, God makes time necessary and valuable.

Creation

Whitehead himself insists that God has priority in ontological status over the world but no temporal priority so that God is not before all creation but with all creation. This seems to leave open whether or not God is the Creator of the world since the notion of creation is not tied to the notion of the world having a beginning in time.

Certainly, the traditional phrase "creation out of nothing" seems to imply that the created world has a beginning in time. But the phrase "out of nothing" means only that the creator makes the world neither from pre-existing material nor from his own being. Therefore, in itself the notion of creation is indifferent to the world being eternal or having a beginning in time. Creation means that God has a radical and fundamental initiative in the coming-to-be of each temporal process.

Once the analogy of person rather than the analogy of "thing" is used to consider the relation between Creator and creature this radical initiative need not be considered as a threat to the autonomy of the creature. In fact, in interpersonal relations the causal activity of one person or another not only need not diminish one's freedom and autonomy but can actually enhance it. One person can act on another without constructing the other because the final causality is a call to another to be himself fully. On this analogy one can see that God's initiative can be a call to man to create himself freely and not at all a threat to man's autonomy. Of course, this supposes that God also freely chooses as He does to wait upon man's decisions. From this viewpoint, there is nothing about man or any other creature that does not radically depend on God's initial causal activity, but also there is nothing about man or any other creature that does not depend on their own active response. There is lawfulness because each creature receives God's call proper to itself; there is room for spontaneity because each creature freely responds to God's call. Each actual occasion is created by God because it receives its subjective view from God and it creates itself because that subjective aim is a call to self-creation. Once this creative activity is thought of in the analogy of person rather than the analogy of things, it is possible to understand that God's creative activity is a call to the creature to create itself. Since this involves interpersonal activity, the intensity of God's activity does not diminish but enhances the autonomy of the creature. Certainly it is true that the increase of activity of a mechanical force acting on a thing which is responding in a purely mechanical way diminishes the autonomy of the thing acted upon, but a person acting on another need not lessen the freedom of the person acted upon but can even intensify the freedom of the person to be himself fully. Furthermore, since the creature depends totally on the creator for its creative aim, the creature's autonomy may be in direct not inverse proportion to God's creative activity.

Consequences

From this vantage point, time and history do make a difference. Man's free decisions are seen to share truly in God's creative activity and produce real novelty that really matters. Further developments of the implications of this view suggest themselves, such as God's really waiting upon man's free decisions; His concurrence with man's self-creativity and with the real novelty in man's free decisions; a doctrine of Soul conceived in terms of "self-relating" rather than "unmoved mover" or "self-moving mover"; a morality built around man's call to responsible creative activity. But these must wait for another time and another place. Moreover, God's real relation to the world seems most compatible with developments in theology, especially in that of the Incarnation and of the indwelling of the Holy Spirit. For these reasons a recasting of the traditional view is worth exploring. Between a philosophy of creative act which excludes the possibility of the real relation of God to the world and a modal philosophy which demands reciprocal relations between God and the world, it is possible to posit a "third position": a philosophy of creative act with really asymmetrical relations between God and the world.

SUGGESTED READINGS

Walter E. Stokes on God and the World

Stokes, Walter E., S.J. "Freedom as Perfection: Whitehead, Thomas and Augustine," *Proceedings of the American Catholic Philosophical Association,* 36 (1962), 134-142.

————. "Whitehead's Challenge to Theistic Realism," *The New Scholasticism,* 38 (1964), 1-21.

————. "God for Today and Tomorrow," *The New Scholasticism,* 43 (1969), 351-378. Reprinted in *Process Philosophy and Christian Thought.* Edited by Delwin Brown, Ralph E. James, Jr., and Gene Reeves. Indianapolis: Bobbs-Merrill, 1971, pp. 244-263. Paperback.—Indianapolis: Bobbs-Merrill.

About Walter E. Stokes on God and the World

Azar, Larry. "Whitehead: Challenging a Challenge," *The Thomist,* 30 (1966), 80-87.

On Related Themes

Cousins, Ewert. "Truth in St. Bonaventure," *Proceedings of the American Catholic Philosophical Association,* 43 (1969), 204-210.

Henry, Paul, S.J. *St. Augustine on Personality.* New York: Macmillan, 1960.

Kelly, Anthony. "God: How Near a Relation?" *The Thomist,* 34 (1970), 191-229.

————. "Trinity and Process: Relevance of the Basic Christian Confession of God," *Theological Studies,* 31 (1970), 393-414.

Ogden, Schubert. "The Challenge to Protestant Thought," *Continuum,* 6 (1968), 236-240.

9 The World and God

JOHN B. COBB, JR.

The impact of the new science is visible in John Cobb's analysis of the physical as an energy-event. We naively consider the physical to be what our senses convey, e.g., a stone, with its massive endurance and passivity. Yet the electron can be understood only as a succession of events. The notion of energy-event can be applied to mind and also to God. In exploring God's relation to space, Cobb explicates the doctrine of "pan-en-theism," a term used to situate process theology between supernaturalism and pantheism. God is related to creaturely events as the One Who Calls us to what we might be. Finally Cobb discusses how the world affects God in his consequent nature. Throughout the entire selection,* Cobb is deeply indebted to the thought of Whitehead.

Born in Kobe, Japan, John B. Cobb, Jr., received his doctorate from the University of Chicago. He is presently Ingraham Professor of Theology at the School of Theology at Claremont, California. One of the leading contributors to the process movement, he has made an extended application of Whitehead's metaphysics to theology in his major work A Christian Natural Theology.

In the preceding chapter an approach to affirming God as the One Who Calls us forward was developed in three stages. First, features of our ex-

* From *God and the World* (Philadelphia: Westminster Press, 1969), pp. 67-86. Reprinted with permission.

perience which are oriented to the ideal and the possible were highlighted in distinction from the causal influence of the past. Second, the need to ascribe some objectivity to ideal possibilities was urged. Third, it was proposed that this objectivity is best understood when the effective presentation of ideal possibilities is attributed to God. When God is viewed in this way, he ceases to function as the sanction for established rules and achieved goods and is rather the call to go beyond them, whatever their merits may be. God does not hold us back from taking full responsibility for ourselves and our world, but rather calls us to precisely that responsibility. He does not oppose our quest to become more fully human, but is rather the ground of that quest.

This way of thinking of God has much to commend it. It stands with rather than against the restless search of our day. It is more faithful to what is revealed to us in Jesus Christ. It allows for rational treatment of the problem of evil. It liberates man from repression and channels his energies into a creative future.

But there are reasons for rejecting talk of God to which all of this is irrelevant. There are those who deny that such talk is meaningful or true because they cannot conceive of a reality other than the empirically given plurality of physical things. Whatever else is thinkable is for them abstract, and an abstract God is no God at all. There are others who would be able to think of another kind of reality alongside all of these physical things but can see no *place* for such a reality in their world. There is no longer any "up there" or "out there" where God could be. There are still others for whom the chief problem is that they can see no way in which God, supposing he exists, can be effective or relevant in the world. They may hold, for example, that all experience arises in sense experience and that God can at best be an inference from such experience. If he occurs in experience only as an inference, how can he function as the forward call or in any other way?

This chapter will deal briefly with these three topics: the mode of reality to be attributed to God, his relation to space, and the nature of the divine influence on the world. What is here proposed is developed with greater philosophical precision in *A Christian Natural Theology*. As in that book, the ideas expressed in this chapter are heavily dependent on the philosophy of Alfred

North Whitehead. The chapter concludes with a brief discussion of what Whitehead called "the consequent nature of God" and some quotations on the peace which he believed is possible for man only in his experience of God in this form.

The first question is the ontological one. Is there any other kind of reality besides the physical one? If not, God must be either physical or unreal. Since we cannot assert in the ordinary sense that God is physical, the believer in God must affirm some order of reality different from what common sense means by physical.

There are two ways in which we could proceed. We could accept the commonsense understanding of the physical and then show that such realities as thought cannot be understood as physical in this sense. We could then argue that alongside the physical world there is a mental one.

This procedure has a certain merit. All too many textbooks are written as if all reality could be reduced to a naïvely conceived form of physicality. It cannot. The human mind is capable of functions no machine will ever be able to perform, and in our day it is important to make this point again and again.

However, the addition to a naïve notion of the physical of an equally naïve notion of the mental leads to numerous problems which have made themselves apparent frequently in the history of philosophy. Although thought cannot be reduced to physical activities, it is intimately interrelated with them, and this relation is unintelligible if we adopt an ontological dualism which treats mind and matter as two completely different types of reality. Furthermore, if thought is viewed as the characteristic function of mind and sensory extension as that of the physical, the experience of the physical through the senses is neither clearly mental nor clearly physical. Emotion likewise falls under neither heading. For these and other reasons, ontological dualism is profoundly unsatisfactory and cannot be used as a way of understanding God's relation to the physical world, except very provisionally.

A better approach is through a critique of the notion of the physical. This critique was carried out in a purely philosophical way in the eighteenth century by such men as Berkeley and Hume, who demonstrated that we could form no clear notion of what common sense understood by physicality. It seemed to be reduced to sensory impressions alongside an unintelligible intuition that something external to the sensing organism caused these impressions. More recently the physical sciences have supplemented this philosophical critique with an equally devastating one. The apparently solid, inert objects which give rise to our naïve notion of the physical turn out to be composed exhaustively of subatomic entities whose nature is to act and react. These entities *can*, of course, be termed physical, but they cannot be understood as like the bodies we normally call physical only smaller. Hardly any of the characteristics we commonly attribute to a stone—such as its massive endurance and self-identity through time, its passivity, its impermeability—apply to an electron. The electron can only be understood as a *succession of events* or happenings. These events can be viewed as transmissions of energy from past events to future ones. If we ask what they are in themselves, the only answer possible to the physicist is energy. The building blocks of the universe, the things of which everything else is composed, are energy-events.

The dissolution of the physical into energy-events does not solve the question as to how we should think of God, but it should at least cause us to give up the still widely held notion that only what is physical in the naïve sense is real. It would be truer to say that what is physical in the naïve sense is the by-product of the interaction of energy-events outside the body with those that constitute the sense organs. That God is not physical in this way by no means reduces his actuality.

When we conceive the physical as composed of certain types or aspects of energy-events rather than in the naïve way, the question of its relation to the mental is placed in a quite different context. A thought cannot be understood as a physical activity in the old sense, but it can be understood as an energy-event. My act of thinking receives energy from past occurrences in my body and transmits that energy, appropriately modified, to subsequent events. It thus functions in a way similar to the functioning of an electronic event. The older question of the relation of mind to matter becomes the question of the relation of that energy-event which is conscious and in which thinking takes place to those much more elementary ones where there is neither consciousness nor thought. The former cannot be reduced to the latter or regarded as a mere by-product of them, for the event of conscious thinking has its own unity and creativity. But it need not be regarded as belonging to a completely different order of being.

If the general notion of energy-event is flexible enough to include both unconscious electronic events and activities of human thinking, then it might be extended to include God as well. The believer cannot think of God as physical in the old sense, but when we have probed behind the physical to the kind of reality which gives rise to it, we have stripped the physical of most of those properties which once caused us to contrast God's spirituality with it. For example, the individual energy-event is invisible and, in general, not to be apprehended by the senses. (Only where large numbers of these events occur together are human sense organs activated.) The individual event is active, rather than simply passive; it is a subject rather than just an object.

Just as there are specific differences between those energy-events we call electronic and those we call human, so there must be vast differences between human energy-events and the divine. But the problem posed by such differences is quite other than that which is generated when one supposes he has a more or less adequate notion of the physical and that whatever does not conform to that notion must be to that extent abstract. We now see that the physical in that sense is a secondary product of more fundamental processes, and that when we identify these processes, we have arrived at the kind of reality which can include also what we usually call mental and spiritual phenomena. If what is most real are energy-events, and if these are highly diverse in character, then God can be conceived as a very special kind of energy-event.

One thing that all such events have in common is that they transmit energy from preceding events to following ones. In some instances, that which is inherited by the successors is virtually unaltered in the event; in other instances, it is considerably modified. In the former instance we have to do with phenomena which we commonly call inorganic, in the latter with life and mentality. In both instances there is reception from the past, fresh embodiment, and then a completion which gives rise to a new reception in successors. The difference lies rather in the variety of data from the past which can be taken into account, in the complexity in which the diverse data are integrated and reintegrated in the fresh embodiment, and in the element of novelty that sometimes appears in this process.

The term "energy-event" is a quite neutral one. When we think of an electronic event, we imagine it from the outside. We try to conceive visually or otherwise how such a burst of energy might appear to an observer, even though we know it cannot be observed. When we think of a moment of human experience as an energy-event, on the other hand, we think of it from the inside as it feels to itself, for we are thinking of those events which constitute our own existence. If we thought of God as an energy-event in the former sense only, as if his reality consisted solely in his appearance to others, we would be far removed from the Christian God of whom the earlier chapters spoke. But if we think of God as an event in the latter sense, as an occurrence of thinking, willing, feeling, and loving, then we are close to the heart of Biblical faith. Is there any justification for thinking of a divine energy-event as a subject like ourselves rather than in the external way in which we try to think of an electronic event?

I believe there is. Indeed the problem is not that it is improper to think of energy-events as subjects but how we could think of them in any other way. Consider again the electronic event. When we do so, we suppose that its occurrence is something other than our imaginative entertainment of the idea. We want to conform our idea in some manner to what occurs. Our first instinct, to think of it as somehow visible or tangible, we know to be erroneous. What other means have we of conceiving it objectively? We can conceive of it as it impinges upon its successor in the chain of energy-events which we call the electron. But how can we think of that unless we can conceive of the successor in its act of receiving? And if we do that, then we are thinking of the successor as a subject receiving the earlier event as its object. In that case we must recognize that the only way in which we can think of such events at all is as subjects which become objects for successor events. The alternative is simply not to conceive of them at all, and I mean *at all*. We cannot think of "something, I know not what" unless we have some notion of what "something" means. We can continue to play extraordinary games with symbols and deduce predictions about instrumental readings, but we must then regard the word "electron" as having no referent in the real world. We can avoid this strange result and overcome the remaining perplexing dualism of subjects and objects if we recognize that every individual event or entity is, in its moment of immediacy, a subject, usually an unconscious one, which then passes into objectivity in the sense of becoming a datum for new subjects. These data when grouped in certain large societies impinge upon our sense organs in such a way as to give rise in our simplified consciousness to the naïve notion of the physical. Under these circumstances, whatever subtle difficulties may arise, there is no fundamental reason to hesitate to ascribe subjectivity to God as well.

If the foregoing is sound, then the closest analogue for thinking of God is our own immediate experience. Of course, this cannot be a very close analogue. For example, our subjective experience is heavily dependent upon the contribution of the senses, whereas there is no reason to suppose that God experiences in that way. If, as some philosophers have supposed, all human subjectivity arises out of sense experience, then, after all, we have no clue whatsoever to the divine experience, and even our ascription of subjectivity to God is virtually empty of meaning.

The foregoing point can also be made with respect to the attribution of subjectivity to electronic events. If subjectivity as we know it is vision, audition, touch, and so forth, and if electrons have none of these sensory experiences, then it is quite meaningless to declare that they enjoy a moment of subjectivity, however helpful that might be in solving other difficulties.

But in fact human experience is not fundamentally sensory. Just as it is necessary to go behind what we naïvely call the physical, so also it is necessary to go behind what we naïvely regard as the fundamental givens of human experience. These givens, whether we call them sense data or objects of perception, have been shown by physiology not to be the primitive givens at all; rather, they are highly organized products of the psyche's life arising from its immediate apprehension of quite another order of data.

Let me explain. One of the most widely held assumptions of physicists is that there is no physical action at a distance. But if a particular chair as a complex of sense data or as a perceived object were understood as *immediately* given to me, that would violate this principle in a most remarkable way. Actually there is no evidence whatever for such a violation. The energy-event in which the chair image arises is a mental one occurring somewhere in the region of the brain. It inherits most immediately from cellular or subcellular events in the brain which in turn have inherited from others in the chain that leads to the eye and finally through intervening space to the chair. The chair *image* may be regarded as immediate, but as such it is effect and not cause of the primarily mental energy-event in which it arose. The chair as a *given*, on the contrary, is very complexly mediated and very indirectly determinative of the event.

This means that the fundamental data for the human mind or subject are not physical objects outside the body, but energy-events within the body. The events that we call mental get their content mostly from events in the brain that we usually call physical. No sense organs are involved here; so this experience is not sensory. There is, therefore, in our own experience a basis for conceiving what nonsensory experience is.

One might object that although we can infer the priority of the nonsensory, all of our experience of the external world is at the level of the sensory. This is almost true, since clear conscious experience is overwhelmingly sensory. But even at this level we find adequate evidence of the importance of nonsensory experience.

Consider, for example, the belief in any given moment that there were preceding moments and that there will be future ones. It is doubtful that anyone can ever succeed in radically doubting the reality of past and future. Yet sense experience as such provides absolutely no evidence for either. It is in any moment simply what it is, wholly silent with respect to antecedents or consequents. One may object that he remembers a past and anticipates a future, and that both the past he remembers and the future he anticipates are sensory in character. But even if that were so, it would not alter the point I am making. Neither memory nor anticipation is a sensory relation. If one remembers a past visual experience, the visual qualities may be faintly present to him. If so, he may include them in his present sensory experience. But if he regards them as stemming from a past experience, then he is introducing an element into their interpretation that he cannot derive from present sensory experience, i.e., an awareness of the past as distinct from the present.

Not only our awareness of our past and future, but also our conviction that there is a real world which exists quite independently of our experience of it witnesses to the presence of nonsensory experience. Sense experience as such can give us nothing but sensa or sense-data, and these are given as parts of the present experience. Either we are to regard our indubitable conviction that we are in a real world transcending our experience as an inference for which there is no evidence, or else we must acknowledge that we are bound to that world in nonsensory experience.

Nonsensory experience occasionally manifests itself in striking fashion in what is called extrasensory perception. Extrasensory perception is by no means the basic evidence for nonsensory perception, but it is a peculiarly vivid expression of it. The prejudice against accepting its reality has been great, but the evidence of its occurrence is greater still, and the time has come for us to try to understand it rather than simply to prove or disprove its existence. Recognition of the primacy of the nonsensory elements in all experience provides the context for interpreting this special form.

Nonsensory elements in human experience are usually on or beyond the boundary line of consciousness. Analysis of conscious experience shows their presence, but it is extremely difficult to focus on them in sharp attention. Most of them are submerged far below the level of consciousness, and it is in this unconscious nonsensory experience that we have our only clue to the subjectivity of such energy-events as electrons.

But when we think of God it would be disappointing, not to say blasphemous, to take such low-level experience as the clue. God, like electrons, must experience in a nonsensory way, but we would not suppose, therefore, unconsciously. Rather, we must suppose that the immediate nonsensory experience, which in man is overlaid and obscured by the vivid consciousness of mediated ones, is for God fully conscious. The best analogy in human experience for reflection on the divine is to be found in memory.

Consider, for example, a vivid recollection of a past experience. That past experience is present in consciousness now almost as if it were reoccurring. Here there is immediate experience of one occasion by another occasion which is grasped in a non-sensory way. Of course, the earlier experience is usually dominated by sensory elements, but that is no hindrance to the analogy. Although we do not think of God as having eyes, there is no reason to deny him the power to enjoy our visual experiences with us.

Let us suppose, then, that it makes sense to think of a divine energy-event which is a conscious subject sharing immediately in human as well as subhuman experiences. We are now ready for the second major topic of this chapter: Where can this energy-event be? Neither the old imagery of "up there" and "out there" nor the new imagery of "in there" and "down there" is of much use to us, insofar as it is allowed the spatial connotations which lie upon the surface. We may, of course, use these prepositions without spatial connotations. That God is "up there" can mean that he is incomparably greater than we are. That he is "out there" may mean that we experience him at times in his remoteness. That he is "within" may mean that our relation to him is a profoundly intimate one. That he is "in the depths of things" may mean that we find him more really as we go "deeper" into our own souls. But none of this helps the questioner who wants to know where, in spatial terms, he can think of God as being.

To such a question there are just two possible answers, answers which are not as different from each other as they seem. One may say, first, that God is nowhere. The primary import of this is to deny that God has a place alongside other places such that one could be closer to him by moving from one place to another. In this view space is understood essentially in terms of external relations, whereas God is related to us internally. Or space is a function of the kind of extension which physical bodies have, and God is not extended. God as Spirit, it is said, transcends radically our categories of space and time which derive from sensory experience of a physical world.

There is no religious objection to this understanding of God as nonspatial, and it is probable that Whitehead himself held it, but I find it more intelligible to say that God is everywhere. In the first instance this means, what adherents of the other view also hold, that God is immediately related to every place, that there is nowhere one can flee from him. Certainly it agrees with the first view in the insistence that God is no more at one place than another and that, when space is conceived visually, it fails to apply to God. But the visual understanding of space has been overcome also in physics without the abandonment of the idea of space in general.

In modern thought space or space-time is not to be thought of as a fixed receptacle which preexists events. Rather, energy-events themselves are the ultimate reality. But these events have patterns of relations with each other which can only be described as extensive. These extensive patterns include successiveness and contemporaneity. They can be analyzed into temporal and spatial relations, but in the last resort even this distinction is secondary. Each energy-event is indissolubly spatiotemporal.

Since each event is both a subject for itself and an object for its successors, we may consider how space or space-time functions in these two dimensions. Physics deals with it in terms of the objectification of events in their spatiotemporal connectedness, but the primary reality is the becoming of new events in their subjectivity. For them space-time is important in that each receives the world from a particular standpoint. That standpoint determines the spatiotemporal system in terms of which it experiences past and present and the relative movements of other bodies.

Both those who assert that God is nowhere and those who assert that he is everywhere deny that God is bound to any limited standpoint within the whole of space-time. Those who assert that he is nowhere argue that God in this respect differs from all other energy-events. Whereas all others must occupy particular standpoints within the whole, God occupies none whatsoever and is thus wholly impartial with respect to all. The alternative is the view that God's impartiality toward all is a function of his omni-spatial or all-inclusive standpoint.

The chief objection to this latter view is that it implies that the same region of space-time that is occupied by an electron or a human experience is simultaneously occupied by God. That goes against the widely held view that two entities cannot occupy the same space at the same time.

This doctrine has prima facie merit at the level of what we naïvely regard as physical objects. One book cannot occupy the same space as another, and the same holds true of two molecules. If the space occupied by one entity is included in that occupied by another, we speak of the first as a part of the second, as a page is a part of a book, or a molecule a part of a page. But in this case the whole is simply the sum of its parts. If we think of God as related to us in this way, then either God is everything and we are simply parts and pieces, or else we are everything and "God" is simply another name for the sum total of all the parts. In neither case have we a model by which we can think of both man and God.

But all of this presupposes that the entities of which we speak are objects. If we think of subjects, and especially of the one subject we know immediately, the situation changes. My subjective experience has its own spatiotemporal standpoint. In one sense it extends out over the room and through the past as it brings a new synthesis out of the data it inherits. But it inherits these data from a particular spatiotemporal locus. Spatially, this locus seems to include much if not all the brain. There is no reason to exclude this possibility on the grounds that the presence of my subjective experience would exclude that of the electrons or vice versa. The electrons can enjoy their subjectivity from their very limited standpoints within the brain while I am enjoying mine from the more inclusive one. Each has its self-identity independent of the other. As each passes into objectivity it influences the other. The electronic events in my brain influence my human thought and feeling. My human thought and feeling influence some of the energy-events in my brain in ways that lead to specific bodily functioning obedient to my conscious intentions. Thus the events occupying the inclusive space and those occupying the included space act upon each other in complex ways, but they have also their distinct individuality and autonomy. They are independent as well as interdependent.

I have developed this at some length since I believe it offers us our best analogy for thinking of the spatial relation of God and the world. God's standpoint is all-inclusive, and so, in a sense, we are parts of God. But we are not parts of God in the sense that God is simply the sum total of the parts or that the parts are lacking in independence and self-determination. God and the creatures interact as separate entities, while God includes the standpoints of all of them in his omnispatial standpoint. In this sense God is everywhere, but he is not everything. The world does not exist outside God or apart from God, but the world is not God or simply part of God. The character of the world is influenced by God, but it is not determined by him, and the world in its turn contributes novelty and richness to the divine experience.

The doctrine that I am developing here is a form of "pan-en-theism." It is, in my understanding, a type of theism. But it differs from much traditional theism insofar as the latter stressed the mutual externality of God and the world, with God conceived as occupying another, supernatural, sphere. It differs from pantheism when pantheism is understood to be the identification of God and the world.

Yet, in reality, panentheism is the synthesis of the central concerns of traditional theism and pantheism, and it distinguishes itself from both only in ways that are secondary. The central concern of traditional theism as against pantheism is not spatial separateness of God and the world, and indeed such spatial separateness has been qualified or denied by many who are recognized as theists. The central concern is that God and man be each understood as having integrity in himself. Theism denies both that God is the impersonal whole and that man is a subordinated part. The central concern of pantheism is to reject an external creator outside of and over against the world who manipulates or controls from without and to assert that God pervades the world and is manifest in all its parts. To both of these central concerns panentheism says Yes, while providing a way conceptually to hold them together.

The third question to be treated in this chapter is that of how God is related to creaturely events and especially to occasions of human experience. Specifically, how does God function as the One Who Calls us to turn from what we have achieved to a new and greater possibility that lies before us?

The answer is that by the way God constitutes himself he calls us to be what we can be and are not. He constitutes himself so as to provide each occasion with an ideal for its self-actualization, and it is in relation to that ideal that each human energy-event forms itself. In Whitehead's technical terminology, in its initial phase every becoming occasion derives its initial aim from God. I shall try to make some sense of what this means in less technical language.

Every occasion of human experience begins with a given past. The past includes energy-events in the brain, as well as past occasions of that person's experience. The new experience must take some account of all of these events, which means that all of them affect or influence the new occasion. How they function in this influence depends on what they are, that is, on how they have constituted themselves. If in the past moment I constituted myself as angry at my friend, in this moment I enter into a situation in which that anger is part of the given. I cannot constitute myself in this moment without reference to that anger. Furthermore, there is a strong tendency for that anger to be reenacted in the new moment. Yet there is no strict inevitability as to the fullness of its reenactments. I may, for example, become suddenly ashamed of that anger, and although that does not cause it at once to disappear, it alters its force. Or I may feed the anger by meditating on past grievances. Whatever I do, I am profoundly affected by the way the past occasions constituted themselves, but what I now become is not strictly determined by that.

What I do with the anger is partly determined by the purpose I entertain. If my purpose is to win my friend's support for a project, I will try to swallow the anger. If I have resolved to do him some injury, I may try to intensify it to assuage or overcome the guilt that accompanies my resolution. My purpose, like the feeling of anger, is largely inherited from the previous occasion, but it is not strictly bound by it. The anger may alter the previous purpose. The previous purpose will not lose all effectiveness at once, for the tendency to reenact is too strong for that, but it can be subordinated, even quite suddenly, to another purpose.

The total reality out of which each human occasion arises includes not only the adjacent events in the brain and the past human experiences but also God. Like other events, God influences the becoming occasion by being what he is. He entertains a purpose for the new occasion, differing from that entertained by the previous human experience. He seeks to lure the new occasion beyond the mere repetition of past purposes and past feelings or new combinations among them. God is thus at once the source of novelty and the lure to finer and richer actualizations embodying that novelty. Thus God is the One Who Calls us beyond all that we have become to what we might be.

Clearly, we are not to understand every event as simply the embodiment of the ideal that is offered to it. The power of our own past over us in each new present is immense, not only as mere data to be accounted for but also as ground of our new purposes and projects. It is easier to ignore the lure of God than to overcome the weight of that past; hence the appalling slowness of our progress toward full humanity and the ever-impending possibility that we turn away from it catastrophically. Yet over the longer period we can see that even beyond the willing cooperation of his creatures, God has brought us a long way. And in men of peculiar sensitivity and openness we can catch some glimpse of that finer life toward which God calls us.

At this point I have completed the central course of the argument. In the preceding chapters I displayed a consensus of contemporary theology that God must be reconceived in a way more faithful to Jesus Christ. This way points to God's presence as coming to us from the open future rather than from the settled past. We do find in our experience a call forward into this future. That call can be most adequately viewed as coming from something which offers us in each moment a new possibility for our existence. Reflection shows that this is best understood as God. In *this* chapter I have shown that the affirmation of God which grew out of the previous considerations is more compatible than many suppose with reflection upon reality as it is known in contemporary science and philosophy. I do not suppose that in all this I have *proved* the existence of the Christian God, but I do hope to have shown that the Christian can affirm God in a way that is purified and strengthened by the recent attacks on theism and that is at the same time fully responsible philosophically. The believer has no reason to ask more.

Throughout these chapters, and especially in the present one, I have been heavily dependent on the thought of Whitehead. The mode of relation to God which has been in the center of attention is, in Whitehead's terminology, the derivation by every occasion of experience of its initial aim from God. Whitehead speaks of that in God which is the source of this aim as his primordial nature. But he argues that in God there is also a consequent nature. Just as with every occasion of experience there is not only an influence upon the subsequent world, but also, in its own becoming, the influence of the prior world upon it, so also in God. Not only does God influence every occasion of experience, but also, he is in turn affected by each. He takes up into himself the whole richness of each experience, synthesizing its values with all the rest and preserving them everlastingly in the immediacy of his own life. Even the miseries and failures of life are so transmuted in the divine experience as to redeem all that can be redeemed.

The Christian not only understands his faith as a continual challenge to do and dare, to take responsibility upon himself, and to venture out beyond the limits laid down by the past; he also finds in his faith the grounds for confidence that what happens matters. Regardless of how ephemeral the joys and sorrows of life, his own and those of others, they are not trivial or insignificant. Even if man destroys his planet in the near future, our efforts now to preserve it are not worthless. Because what we are and do matters to God, our lives are meaningful even when we recognize that in the course of history our accomplishments may soon be swept away.

Schubert Ogden in *The Reality of God* builds his case on the deep, underlying confidence that life is meaningful, a confidence he finds also among those who consciously and explicitly deny the existence of God. This confidence bears witness to a relatedness to God, because it cannot be grounded in the merely phenomenal or empirical flux of experience. What happens *really* matters only if it matters everlastingly. What happens can matter everlastingly only if it matters to him who is everlasting. Hence, seriousness about life implicitly involves faith in God.

Whether or not this is to be regarded as in any sense an argument for the existence of God, it does effectively and realistically point up the alternative to Christian faith in God as being, not optimistic secular humanism, but genuine nihilism. The sense of meaning which Western man now struggles desperately to retain has its historic ground in faith in God. For some generations, perhaps, it can survive that faith, but not forever. Whitehead provides us with an adequate reflective grounding for the meaningfulness of life.

Whitehead himself does not speak characteristically of meaning but rather of peace. The last two chapters of *Adventures of Ideas* are entitled "Adventure" and "Peace." In these chapters he rarely uses the word "God," but he is nevertheless speaking of that reality which he elsewhere calls God. The primordial nature of God is here pictured as the love that lures man to adventure. This aspect of God and his relation to the world has been the focus of these chapters. But Whitehead rightly feels that something more is needed for human existence, needed even to sustain the adventure itself, and it is this something else which he calls "peace." It derives from man's dim intuition of the reality of God's consequent nature. Nowhere else in all his writings does he recognize so clearly that what he strives to express stands at the very limits of the expressible. The attempt to translate his tentative expression into my own language would only serve to obscure it. Hence I close with an extended quotation from this moving chapter.

The Peace that is here meant is not the negative conception of anaesthesia. It is a positive feeling which crowns the "life and motion" of the soul. It is hard to define and difficult to speak of. It is not a hope for the future, nor is it an interest in present details. It is a broadening of feeling due to the emergence of some deep metaphysical insight, unverbalized and yet momentous in its coördination of values. Its first effect is the removal of the stress of acquisitive feeling arising from the soul's preoccupation with itself. Thus Peace carries with it a surpassing of personality. There is an inversion of relative values. It is primarily a trust in the efficacy of Beauty. It is a sense that fineness of achievement is as it were a key unlocking treasures that the narrow nature of things would keep remote. There is thus involved a grasp of infinitude, an appeal beyond boundaries. Its emotional effect is the subsidence of turbulence which inhibits. More accurately, it preserves the springs of energy, and at the same time masters them for the avoidance of paralyzing distractions. The trust in the self-justification of Beauty introduces faith, where reason fails to reveal the details.

The experience of Peace is largely beyond the control of purpose. It comes as a gift. The deliberate aim at Peace very easily passes into its bastard substitute, Anaesthesia. In other words, in the place of a quality of "life and motion," there is substituted their destruction. Thus Peace is the removal of inhibition and not its introduction. It results in a wider sweep of conscious interest. It enlarges the field of attention. Thus Peace is self-control at its widest, —at the width where the "self" has been lost, and interest has been transferred to coördinations wider than personality. (Pp. 367-368.)

At the heart of the nature of things, there are always the dream of youth and the harvest of tragedy. The Adventure of the Universe starts with the dream and reaps tragic Beauty. This is the secret of the union of Zest with Peace:—That the suffering attains its end in a Harmony of Harmonies. The immediate experience of this Final Fact, with its union of Youth and Tragedy, is the sense of Peace. (P. 381.)

SUGGESTED READINGS

John B. Cobb on God and the World

Cobb, John B., Jr. *A Christian Natural Theology: Based on the Thought of Alfred North Whitehead.* Philadelphia: Westminster Press, 1965.

————. *God and the World.* Philadelphia: Westminster Press, 1969. Paperback—Philadelphia: Westminster Press.

On John B. Cobb's Doctrine of God

Gilkey, Langdon. Review of *A Christian Natural Theology, Theology Today,* 22 (1966), 530-545. Reply by Cobb: "Can Natural Theology be Christian?" *Theology Today,* 23 (1966), 140-142.

Guy, Fritz. "Comments on a Recent Whiteheadian Doctrine of God," *Andrews University Seminary Studies,* 4 (1966), 107-134.

Ross, James F. "God and the World," *Journal of the American Academy of Religion,* 38 (1970), 310-315.

On Related Themes

Ford, Lewis S. "Divine Persuasion and the Triumph of Good," *The Christian Scholar,* 50 (1967), 235-250. Reprinted in *Process Philosophy and Christian Thought.* Edited by Delwin Brown, Ralph E.

James, Jr., and Gene Reeves. Indianapolis: Bobbs-Merrill, 1971, pp. 287-304. Paperback—Indianapolis: Bobbs-Merrill.

————. "Whitehead's Conception of Divine Spatiality," *The Southern Journal of Philosophy*, 6 (1968), 1-23.

10 God and Man

Process thought holds rich resources for developing a contemporary Christian doctrine of man. One of the most penetrating and systematic uses of these resources has been by Daniel Day Williams in his book *The Spirit and the Forms of Love*. The following selection,* taken from the book, explores the notion of man as image of God. In keeping with the trend of contemporary theology, Williams interprets the image in dynamic terms, but adds a process dimension. Love is disclosed in history where the spirit of God creates new forms. Man is an image of God also in his temporality. Love is in process. This has implications for understanding God's love as creative power, our love of creatures in God, and our awesome power at the present time. In an unprecedented way, man can reshape his world or destroy it. Love as creative power must do its work.

A member of the Chicago process circle, Daniel Day Williams studied and taught at the University of Chicago. He is presently Roosevelt Professor of Systematic Theology in Union Theological Seminary, New York. An author of many books and articles, he has explored the social, psychological, and metaphysical implications of process thought for Christian theology.

In his great essay, *The Fire Next Time,* James Baldwin describes his youth in New York City's Harlem:

* From *The Spirit and the Forms of Love* (New York: Harper and Row, 1968), pp. 130-141. Reprinted with permission.

Yes, it does indeed mean something—something unspeakable—to be born, in a white country, an Anglo-Teutonic, anti-sexual country, black. You very soon, without knowing it, give up all hope of communion. Black people, mainly, look down or look up but do not look at each other, not at you, and white people, mainly, look away. . . . The universe which is not merely the stars and the moon and the planets, flowers, grass, and trees, but *other people*, has evolved no terms for your existence, has made no room for you, and if love will not swing wide the gates no other power will or can.[1]

The situation Baldwin describes has its specific context in the racial problem, but within it he has discovered the crux of the human situation. Communion is another word for love. Man is created for communion but he loses it and he loses the power to recover it. If we believe that in spite of man's failure love can be recovered we have the triple theme of the Christian Gospel. Man bears the image of God who is love. Man's love falls into disorder; but there is a work of God which restores man's integrity and his power to enter into communion. Every Christian theology is an elaboration of this theme. Man is a battlefield upon which many loves clash. His self-love may become so powerful that it can over-rule every other force. Man is the source of love's perversion, the speaker of the kindly word which covers the vicious evil, the wearer of the mask of pride. Man falls into unlove, and experiences the boredom and horror of life without meaning. Man is captured by some loves to the exclusion of others. He is the sensualist for whom the flesh becomes God, or the moral idealist for whom 'love of mankind' is drained of all emotion and there is neither concern nor pity for real human beings. Yet man must find love in and with others for it is the only fulfilment life offers. He is the being whom no earthly love satisfies, until it becomes a way to the love of God. When man's love fails or becomes distorted, the final resource in the love of God is a creative act of healing. Love is disclosed as grace. In this and the two succeeding chapters we examine these major assertions of Christian faith in the light of our interpretation of love as spirit at work in history.

---

[1] James Baldwin, *The Fire Next Time* (New York: Dial Press, 1963, p. 44; London: Michael Joseph, 1963).

(1)

LOVE AND THE IMAGE OF GOD IN MAN

In the biblical faith man's greatness is understood in the light of the image of God which he bears. If God is love the image of God in man defines the forms of love in human existence. Yet the image is defaced, distorted, 'ruined', so the Reformers said, by man's wilful self-separation from God. Can we get light on the nature of the divine love from man's distorted experience of love? This question of what happens to the image of God through sin underlies some of the most critical issues in the Christian interpretation of love and it will be worthwhile to give some attention to the history of this theme and its development in contemporary theology.

The traditional Roman Catholic doctrine is derived from Irenaeus, who noted that two words, *tselem* and *demuth* are used in Genesis I to assert that God has created man in his image. Irenaeus therefore made a distinction between the *image* of God which is man's distinctive endowment of reason, his dominion over nature, and his creaturely dignity; and the *similitude* to God which is faith, hope and love, that is, the full and righteous relation which man is supposed to enjoy as God's creature. For Irenaeus it is this *similitude* which is lost in the fall but the image remains relatively intact. This has formed the ground plan of all subsequent Catholic theology with its formula of 'grace completing nature' as the pattern of redemption. The *similitude* must be restored to the *imago*. There are, of course, many qualifications to be made of this brief characterization, but it is essentially the traditional Catholic position.[2]

The Protestant Reformers attacked this structure. They said that not only is the similitude lost in the fall, but the whole image of God is left in 'ruins'. Nothing in human nature is left intact after sin. The reformers wanted to show that the corruption of the fall extends to the whole man. They believed that the Catholic pattern leads to an unjustified confidence in human reason which is subject to pride and demonry. They saw the image of God as

[2] Full critical discussion of the history of the doctrine of the *imago dei* in Emil Brunner, *Man in Revolt* (London: Lutterworth Press, 1939; New York: Charles Scribner's Sons, 1939), Appendix 1. David Cairns, *The Image of God in Man* (New York: Philosophical Library, 1953).

constituted by the 'original righteousness' with which God endowed Adam. They said this righteousness, which is man's right relation to God, has been lost almost completely. We say 'almost' because Luther and Calvin had to make some qualification concerning the effects of the fall. Neither they nor their followers in Protestant orthodoxy believed that man has lost all sense of God or of moral obligation. Something constructive must be left in human reason and conscience if man is to have a basis for a collective life with a measure of justice and sanity. Thus Calvin asserts that the capacity for 'civic righteousness' remains in fallen man.[3]

Whichever of these traditional positions we take, we see that our view of the place of love in human existence is at stake. The Catholic doctrine makes the love of God one of the three supernatural virtues, and says that in the fall faith, hope and love are lost. But can the love of God be lost without profound effect upon the whole of man's life? When St. Augustine says that without faith and love the reason cannot be rightly ordered in the world or rightly directed toward God he seems closer to the Reformers than to St. Thomas. On the other hand, the Catholic tradition contends for a truth which must not be surrendered, that there are in fallen man capacities for reason, conscience, and creativity which are not wholly destroyed by sin.

Theology in the twentieth century has been interpreting the *imago dei* in a way which expresses the personal and historical nature of the relation between God and man. Thus the foundation is laid for a theology which understands love as the centre of human existence. Since it is the Christian faith that God is love, it is curious that theology has been so late in taking love as the key to the Christian doctrine of man. Let us see what this new direction involves for an understanding of human love and the divine love.

In a well-known controversy Karl Barth and Emil Brunner debated Brunner's thesis that the *imago dei* remains in fallen man *formally,* but that it is lost *materially.* To this Karl Barth replied, 'Nein'.[4] Subsequently both Barth and Brunner explicated their

[3] Calvin, *Institutes,* Bk. II, 2, xiii.
[4] Eng. Tr. of the debate in *Natural Theology,* a translation by Peter Fraenkel of the principal texts (London: G. Bles, 1946).

positions in ways which not only brought their views closer together, but which may avoid the compromise of the reformers
with the 'relic' of the imago, and the dubious simplicity of the
Catholic view that sin leaves the *humanum* relatively intact.

Karl Barth now speaks of the *imago dei* as the distinctive
form of human existence, that is, life in community. Following a
suggestion made by Dietrich Bonhoeffer, Barth says that the connection in Genesis between the *imago dei* and the creation 'male
and female' is not incidental, but that this primary form of human
community indicates the meaning of the image of God in man.
Barth analyses man's life in community in four 'categories of
the distinctively human'. These are:

(1) Being in encounter is a being in which one man looks another
    in the eye.
(2) There is mutual speaking and hearing.
(3) We render mutual assistance in the act of being.
(4) All the occurrence so far described as the basic form of hu-
    manity stands under the sign that it is done on both sides with
    gladness.[5]

In this structure of community Barth sees a reflection of the
divine community, the Trinity. Barth reminds us that God says,
'Let *us* make man in *our* image'. Barth thus gives his own version of St. Augustine's bold suggestion that in the being of man
there is a reflection of the holy Trinity, God's being as Creator,
the Father; the knowledge of his being, the Logos; and the rejoicing in that knowledge, the Spirit. Barth here continues the
tradition of 'metaphysical' theology except for one very important
difference. Barth says this 'image of God' does not give man any
knowledge of God whatever. Man does not know God. His human existence does not point him toward God. All man's religion
is false and idolatrous. Thus Barth seems in the end to maintain
the position he asserted against Brunner: there is nothing in man
as he actually is which in any way discloses his origin in God.

It is hard to see how Barth's ambivalent position here can
be defended. If the form of man's life in community is derived
from the being of God, then there is something in man which
does point toward the true God, however obscurely it may be

[5] Karl Barth, *Church Dogmatics*, III/2, No. 45, 2.

known. Process theologians make this criticism of Barth. They believe man has an awareness of his God-relationship, however confused it becomes.

Apart from the special issue concerning Barth's doctrine of sexuality as the key to the *imago dei,* there is something like a consensus in contemporary theology concerning the theme of the *imago dei.* What we are coming to see is that it is a mistake to define the *imago dei* as any set of attributes or qualities which man may possess. The *imago dei* needs to be conceived in dynamic terms as the relatedness which God has established between himself and man and to which man can respond. Karl Barth sees the *imago* in the forms of human interaction, the life of personal communication in sharing and rejoicing. Emil Brunner stresses the theme of responsibility.[6] Man is the being who can respond to the claim of the other, and give himself to the other. James Muilenburg interprets the Genesis in similar terms:

This is characteristic of Old Testament thought, everywhere; divine revelation is revelation which places man before a choice, a decision which must be made. The highest purpose of man—his supreme task and function—is to do the will of God. It is not coincidence that Christian faith sees the Son of God wrestling in the torment of decision before he goes to the cross. . . . It is the image of God in man which makes him a decision-making person. His ability to choose, the freedom implied in his choice, his sense of difference and value, these surely are aspects of what is divine in him.[7]

All these converge on the view that the *imago dei* should not be conceived as a special quality, but as the relationship for which man is created with his neighbour before God. The image of God is reflected in every aspect of man's being, not as a special entity but as the meaning of the life of man in its essential integrity. But surely this can be most clearly grasped if we say that love is the meaning of the *imago dei.* In this way we can recognize in man that which underlies his special capacities such as reason, moral judgment, artistic creativity, and religious awareness. All these find their meaning in life which is created for communion,

---

[6] Emil Brunner, *Man in Revolt, passim.*

[7] James Muilenburg, unpublished paper, *The Doctrine of Man in the Image of God,* p. 6.

that is personal existence in community with others. This is the universal fact of facts, deeper than reason and the integrating reality in life.

This thesis that the *imago dei* is the form of creation for life fulfilled in love gives us our basis for the interpretation of sin. The root of sin is failure to realize life in love. The cleft in man which results from sin is more than the loss of a supernatural endowment. It is disorder in the roots of his being. It is the disaster resulting from twisted, impotent or perverted love. Sin infects the whole man. It does not at once destroy the reasoning powers, though in extremity it may do even that. It does not completely take away conscience, though the loss of love may finally result in the disappearance of conscience. It does not eliminate creativity from man's life, though it may turn that creativity into demonic self-destructiveness. It does not leave man without any sense of God or knowledge of the holy, though it may distort this sense, turning man's worship into idolatry and leaving him without hope and seemingly without God.

If this analysis be correct all human loves have something in them which pulls them on a tangent toward the love of God. They reflect their origin in God. A doctrine of man following this clue will search in the human loves, even in their incredible distortions, for that which reveals man's relationship to the loving God who is his Creator. The love of God can be present whether it is overtly recognized or not.

In this way contemporary theology has moved to a dynamic interpretation of the image of God, its loss and restoration. The process theology which informs our interpretation of Christian faith agrees wholeheartedly with this view of the image of God in man; but it proposes a distinctive addition to the doctrine, for process theology sees love disclosed in a history in which the spirit of God creates new forms. In this history God is involved with the world both as its eternal ground and as the supreme participant in the suffering which his creativity involves. In process theology therefore the 'analogy of being' which holds between God and the creatures must be related to a fully historical conception of what being is. Man bears the image of God in his temporality as well as his participation in eternity, in suffering as well as in peace. His loves are in process. There are three implications of this way of understanding the image of God in man, which have important consequences for our understanding of man's estrangement from God and the consequent disorder in his existence.

(2)

GOD'S CREATIVITY AND MAN'S

God's love is creative power bringing the worlds into being, and working with them for the fulfilment of an ever new creative order of life. The Kingdom of God is the goal of his creation, but we need not conceive the Kingdom as a fixed 'state of being' toward which things tend. The Kingdom of God is the fulfilment of God's being in relation to every creature, and if being is love, then the Kingdom must be an infinite realm of creative life.

Man's creation in the image of God is his call to participate in creativity, in its splendour and its suffering. Creativity is at work in all things, and certainly in what we call the secular orders. To love is to become responsible for doing what needs to be done to make the world a more tolerable place which reflects more fully the glory of its origin. When we love God we love the infinite creature source of being. God's work is everywhere and needs no state of completion for its meaning is endless creative life. To love God is to love the one who sets the ultimate boundaries to life, boundaries which are not defined by a final state of affairs, but by ever new possibilities of growth.

The second implication of this doctrine has to do with the metaphysical truth that to be is to respond. We have seen that passivity to the other, setting the other free, and the will to have one's own existence shaped by the other as well as to give oneself creatively constitutes one of the categorial conditions of love. If then life in communion is the essential nature of man, this includes transformation by participation with the other, and the acceptance of suffering with and for the other. It is not the essence of man to try to make himself invulnerable. That is sin. It is the essence of man to find the meaning of his life in a community of mutual responsiveness and sharing.

This doctrine exactly reverses Jean-Paul Sartre's view that what marks human existence is the impossibility of breaking through to the other or being reached by the other. The tragedy is indeed where Sartre sees it, in the way we do become 'walled off' from one another. But this is tragic because it contradicts man's essential being, which is his will to communion.

We also find here a resolution of the problem which D'Arcy has posed in the tension between the two loves of self-affirmation and self-giving. Something has to link these two loves, and in D'Arcy's structure as we saw it there would have to be still a third love. But in the process view there is no need for that complication. Both self-affirmation and self-giving are aspects of the essential love which is the will to communion. Self-affirmation without response is deadly. That is why egoism so often becomes desperate. Self-giving without self-affirmation is meaningless. That is why much of what appears to be self-giving love is really self-destruction. What we need to see is that self-affirmation and self-giving are united in the essence of love which is communion. Tensions are present indeed, and the failure to reconcile them constitutes the dark side of the human condition, but there is no contradiction in the essential pattern of love.

We are speaking of the *imago dei,* and this means that the love which God gives to man and which man may return to God bears some analogy to the human will to participation. God makes himself vulnerable to receive into his being what the world does in its freedom, and to respond to the world's action. We acknowledge always a drastic limitation in speaking of the being of God and his love. What it means for God to love the world, to suffer, to give freedom to the creatures and to will communion with them is the very mystery of existence. We must not equate our being with God's and say that love, suffering, freedom, and creativity mean for him precisely what they mean for us. What we can do, however, within the perspective of Christian faith, is to give an account of the love of God which does not make nonsense out of the profoundest aspects of love in human experience. If we say that the *imago dei* in man is his creation for communion with God and the creatures, we mean that God wills communion on terms of man's real freedom and responsiveness. It is to know that the love God offers is responsive love, in which he takes into himself the consequences of human actions, bears with the world, and urges all things toward a society of real freedom in communion.

This doctrine in no way negates the great assurance of the New Testament of the steadfastness and the inexorableness of the love of God. Paul's hymn at the close of Romans 8 expresses the ground of Christian faith:

I am persuaded . . . that nothing can separate us from the love of God.

So also does his assertion that love never passes away (I Corinthians 13). What God gives is his absolute faithfulness, his everlastingness in unceasing love. The meaning of existence lies in the possibility of communion in freedom; this is what is assured to faith.

The power of God, however, is not that of absolute omnipotence to do anything. It is the power to do everything that the loving ground of all being can do to express and to communicate and fulfil the society of loving beings. God's power expresses his love, it does not violate it. Therefore it is the kind of power which holds the world together in one society, setting limits to the freedom of the creatures without destroying that freedom. Whitehead remarks, 'The power of God is the worship He inspires'.[8]

If this view of the relation of love and power be accepted the book of Job must be read as a half-way point on the way to clarification of the meaning of God's power. To be stunned into silence before the sheer might of God's creativity is indeed one dimension of man's discovery of his place in things. The power of God stretches beyond all imagination and description. We cannot solve the riddle of why things are as they are. But the biblical doctrine of God does not remain with man abased before omnipotence. It asserts that man is given knowledge of God by the way God gives himself in his encounter with the world's evil. He persuades the world by an act of suffering love with the kind of power which leaves its object free to respond in humility and love.

Love does not put everything at rest; it puts everything in motion. Love does not end all risk; it accepts every risk which is necessary for its work. Love does not resolve every conflict; it accepts conflict as the arena in which the work of love is to be done. Love does not neatly separate the good people from the bad, bestowing endless bliss on one, and endless torment on the other.

[8] A. N. Whitehead, *Science and the Modern World* (New York: Macmillan, 1927, p. 276; Cambridge University Press, 1936).

Love seeks the reconciliation of every life so that it may share with all the others. If a man or a culture is finally lost, it is not because love wills that lostness, but because we have condemned ourselves to separation and refuse reconciliation. We make our hells and we cling to them in our lovelessness.

Much conventional religiousness, born of a mixture of piety and anxiety, conceives love as a special power which will bring every problem to resolution and every life to completion. There is, however, a subtle error in the view that love's goal is to bring life to rest. In the name of love it deifies the power of absolute disposal. It makes the goal the peace of completion rather than the peace of openness to new experience in a shared community. It makes love a special kind of power which renders all others impotent, whereas love is just the power of being, using, shaping, eliciting, and reconciling all the special powers in the creative movement of life. Many distortions of religious devotion and ethical life come from a too simple view of what the love of God is, and from the use of love as escape from the risks of life, rather than as the will and power to accept them.

Here, then, is the first consequence of the doctrine of God's being as love in process. Man, created in God's image, is created for participation in the infinite life of communion within the everlasting creativity of God.

(3)

The Love of God and the Love of His Creatures

A second consequence of the process doctrine of God is that while the distinction is preserved between man's love for God and man's love for the neighbour, this is not the distinction between love for what is merely temporal and love for what is eternal. We can distinguish between love for the eternal source of creativity which works in the temporal world, and love for the creatures whose being involves their participation both in God's eternal structure and in his temporal creativity. This point is worth our especial attention. Much confusion about love results from the supposition that what is in time and unfinished cannot be loved as fully as that which is complete.

We have seen how St. Augustine, in spite of his clear teaching of the goodness of the creation, asserted the superiority of loving

God to loving the world because God is eternal and the world is temporal.[9] This devaluation of the temporal world is a remnant of platonism. Our present doctrine seeks to counteract it.

We say that God has both an eternal and temporal dimension in his being. To love eternal being as a different kind of being is to miss the real point about God's love, that it is manifest not only in his eternity, but in his temporality. It is the essence of God to move the world toward new possibilities, and his being is 'complete' only as an infinite series of creative acts, each of which enriches, modifies, and shapes the whole society of being.

God's being abides. This is the supreme contrast between his mode of being and ours. Augustine is so far right. God is not at the mercy of time. His love remains constant in its intention. He does not pass away. All times are in his hands. There is indeed a dimension in the love of God which differs from human love, and the platonists and many mystics have seen it. To discover or be discovered by the love of God is in one sense to find the unchanging, perfect and final meaning of all things. This is that aspect of rest in love which finds its completion only in the love of God. But that is only one side of the truth. The other side is that the love of God not only creates the temporal world, but shares in its temporality and its becoming.

The true contrast between God and the world is not that between timeless eternity and the temporality of the creatures. It is the contrast between the supremely creative temporal life of God and the fragmentary, limited creativity of the creatures. To love God, then, is to set the highest value on temporality as well as on eternality, for in this view temporality is a dimension of all value.

It is this explicit evaluation of temporality which is the critical point. The creatures are not to be contrasted with perfection because they are temporal; but only because their creativity is fragmented, distorted and partial. To love God is to do more than love the creatures, but it is not to turn away from the creatures. It is to rejoice as fully in temporality as in eternality. The Kingdom of God is not a static state, but an everlastingly rich process of becoming.

In this view we can still accept St. Augustine's doctrine that we love others in God. Nothing has its being solely in itself. To

[9] *Supra,* chapter 5.

love another is to seek that person as he is, in all the dimensions of his life, and in all that makes him a person. It is to love the bond which makes us one with him, that is to love God. The Christian doctrine here presents a sharp contrast to all humanism. If Christianity is true, there is no such thing as loving another only for himself, for every person is a participant in the society of being. He bears the image of God and he is loved as one who belongs in communion with God and with his fellows.

This doctrine that we love others 'in God' has been criticized as leading to depersonalizing of love. To love another 'in God' seems to suggest that the other is devalued. He is merely an illustration of being so it is not really the person that we love, but God.

We have seen this danger in St. Augustine's version of the doctrine; but the danger lies in Augustine's presupposition about the contrast between God's being and the being of the creatures. To love another in God does depersonalize, *if we make God's eternity the key to his perfection in contrast to the creatures.* Then another person can only be a pointer toward the eternal which is superior to all temporality. But in process doctrine the meaning of God's being is his creative communion with the creatures. God values each person in himself, and as a participant in the creative history of the world. Thus to love another in God is to acknowledge in the divine love that which affirms the unique value of the person. Once we break through the traditional deification of timelessness for its own sake, the meaning of the *imago dei* takes on a new dimension.

(4)

HUMAN CREATIVITY

The third important consequence of this doctrine is the affirmation of human creativity as implicit in the *imago dei.* Man bears power and responsibility to reconstruct his world, reshape his life, and create new value.

This theme, to be sure, is not altogether absent from the traditional doctrines of the *imago dei.* Christian theology has always asserted some margin for man's creative self-expression. The *imago dei* includes reason, and the power of reason to grasp meaning involves creative expression of that meaning. Aesthetic creativity is shown in the uniqueness and greatness of human culture. As C. N. Cochrane says in his *Christianity and Classical Culture*, the Christian faith discovered a depth in human personality which classical culture had not envisaged.[10]

In the modern period the potential creativity of man has been disclosed in ways beyond the imagination of every previous culture. Man can reshape the conditions of his life, change the face of nature, eliminate killing diseases, reconstruct the human body, control the growth of population in ways beyond anything remotely conceivable before the twentieth century. Natural disasters are still present in flood and earthquake, yet to an increasing degree man changes the conditions of the earth, his homeland. Now he begins to explore the far universe, lengthen his life span, discover unlimited sources of energies in the atom, and crack the genetic code.

Creativity can be demonic as well as productive. The new powers of man bring possibilities of total self-destruction. Man can end his existence on this planet. He can dehumanize as well as create. All this means that the significance of the *imago dei* must be reassessed. God sets limits to life, but those limits include much wider possibilities than we have known. Man's cultural development produces a raging despair as he contemplates the possibilities for self-destruction, and also the megalomania of complete self-confidence compounded by the fanaticisms of groups and national passions. In this new historical situation love has to do its work.

SUGGESTED READINGS

Daniel Day Williams on Man

Williams, Daniel Day. *God's Grace and Man's Hope.* New York: Harper and Brothers, 1949.

————. *The Minister and the Care of Souls.* New York: Harper and Brothers, 1961.

[10] Charles N. Cochrane, *Christianity and Classical Culture* (Oxford University Press, 1940).

—————. *The Spirit and the Forms of Love.* New York: Harper and Row, 1968.

On Daniel Day Williams on Love

Cobb, John B., Jr. "A Process Systematic Theology" [Review of *The Spirit and the Forms of Love*], *The Journal of Religion,* 50 (1970), 199-206.

On Related Themes

Browning, Don S. *Atonement and Psychotherapy.* Philadelphia: Westminster Press, 1966.

Cobb, John B., Jr. "Whitehead's Philosophy and a Christian Doctrine of Man," *The Journal of Bible and Religion,* 32 (1964), 209-220.

—————. *A Christian Natural Theology: Based on the Thought of Alfred North Whitehead.* Philadelphia: Westminster Press, 1965, pp. 47-134.

PART THREE

CHRIST AND REDEMPTION

Bernard E. Meland
W. Norman Pittenger
Henry Nelson Wieman

11 The New Creation

BERNARD E. MELAND

What is the meaning of Christ in a process universe?
If we view the world as an on-going process issuing
in novelty, then the New Creation in Christ takes on
added significance. In the selection below,* Bernard
E. Meland traces the emergence of Christ out of his
cultural past, but highlights the genuine novelty of
the New Creation. In Christ a new level of consciousness of spirit broke upon the structures of history. A new social energy was released—a love that
freed men from guilt, anxiety, and despair. Process
theology is especially rich in the area of the redemption. This richness is revealed in Meland's treatment
of the Suffering Servant and God's sympathetic involvement in the suffering of the world.

*Before his retirement in 1964, Bernard E. Meland
was Professor of Constructive Theology at the Divinity School of the University of Chicago. In his
extensive writings he has explored Christology and
other theological themes within the framework of
culture and the transformation of human experience.*

M any currents of thought in our day have
converged to enable us to recover genuine
awareness of this deeper meaning of the Christ as the New Creation.
This has come about, not just through the study of the theological
concern in Christology, but through a re-examination of the meaning of nature and of history as they apply to all scholarly disciplines.

* From *The Realities of Faith: The Revolution in Culture Forms* (New
York: Oxford University Press, 1962), pp. 256-266. Reprinted with permission.

No area of thought has been more revealing here than that of the new physics and the various metaphysical efforts in process thought to extend this revolutionary inquiry into problems of space-time to the larger issues of historical existence. Serious work in the philosophical analysis of this problem has been progressing under other auspices as well, notably in Existentialist philosophy such as that of Heidegger, Jaspers, and Berdyaev. Theologians have availed themselves of several of these strands of current inquiry, and at the same time have given serious attention to studies in New Testament scholarship bearing upon the nature of the *kerygma,* that core of primal witness to faith in the New Testament which appears to be our nearest approach to the human response to these signal events comprising the New Creation in Christ. With these resources at hand, there has been every reason to suppose that modern theologians might accomplish what theologians historically have, for various reasons, evaded, or failed to accomplish, namely, to express the full Christian evangel within the contemporary idiom. My purpose in this chapter is to contribute further toward that end. And I shall begin that task by enumerating some observations which could lead to that accomplishment.

An important corrective to make of liberal interpretations of the Gospel story, beyond the ones dictated by New Testament criticism, is in this sphere of understanding natural and historical events. Neither Newtonian physics nor Kantian Idealism was able to do justice to the subtle and organic happenings of concrete events. Nor could Darwinian evolution, or any sociological variation of this theory, do justice to events of novelty or mystery, or to any sensitive occurrence in structures in which transcendence and immanent happening intermingle. All that I have been trying to convey in the preceding pages bearing on an ontology of spirit, which is based upon a knowledge of the development of structures through what has lately been called field theory, the dynamic interplay of relations in a situation of emergence, throws a flood of light upon these events of history which the theologian may not ignore.

1. The first point to make, then, in moving toward an explanation of what happened in the situation reported by the Gospel story is that real novelty, real mystery, was encountered in the historical process.

2. The nature of that novelty is in part illumined by its antecedents. That is, the events surrounding the Christ stand in a relation to redemptive and prophetic events in Hebraic history in a way that compares with the relation between any novel event and its antecedent structure. That is to say, they are similar, but not identical. The earlier anticipates the later, but in the context in which the earlier events appeared, one could not make the judgments and declarations that were evoked by the later, more decisive event of emergence.

3. The ground of sensitivity, from which the Gospel events flared forth, was equally present in the earlier events of Hebrew history, but the structures differed. The time was not at hand. There is a ripeness of time and events when energies of the spirit break forth with novelty, just as surely as there is a ripeness of time and events when physical energies can be released into the actual processes of history.

I would insist that the Christ event was a revelatory moment in history, summoning the motives, the intellectual vision, and imagination of men to a new center of focus as truly as the heralding of atomic energy was a radical disclosure of a new level of physical powers, altering materially the structured experiences of men. We are dealing here with the dynamics of relations. In the one instance, physical structures were altered by man's inventiveness to release into history a power hitherto unknown, except faintly through scientific intuition and imagination, anticipating it as possibility. In the other instance, human structures, already impregnated with the seeds of Redemption through antecedent events, became articulate and responsive with a sensitivity and perceptiveness that literally thrust upon the social community a new level of consciousness, a new center of consciousness and concern. One may speak of this new level of consciousness, in which love (agape) became regulative as the appreciative consciousness, in contrast to the levels of conscious decision characteristic of the human structure of experience, namely, the rational consciousness and the moral consciousness. I think anyone who has the patience and perceptiveness to observe the contrasts noted in the Gospel witness between the appeals to love as over against the law, faith as over against reason, will be moved to ponder this suggestion.

The orders of justice and reason were not set aside. They

were the antecedent structures in which the new emergence, agape, appeared in the relations of men who had become responsive to the Christ. The initiating vehicle of agape, releasing the matrix of sensitivity or creative ground of spirit into full actuality as a historical being, was the person of Jesus. All one can say is that this structure of consciousness became the bearer of sensitivity in which this love was dominant.

Here was a new center of consciousness in which spirit appeared, not as a margin of sensitivity, characteristic of the human structure, but as a full release of the sensitivity of grace which is of God. What may be called the second level of freedom, freedom of the spirit, was in dominance, and thus wholly responsive to the sensitive internal relations uniting this individuated experience with the lives of other men and with God. In the language of the *Imago Dei,* this was the image of God unbroken, the new life in God.

I would not wish to have these remarks on Christ as a new center of consciousness interpreted to mean a nonhistorical or superhistorical occurrence. What occurred took place within the conflict of two social orders in which the tenuous but creative forces of the new Israel, working through the Christ, engaged in deadly battle with the vested interests of a receding Jewish order. Amos Wilder's depiction of this setting in his *Eschatology and the Ethics of Jesus* seems to me to be highly relevant. In a later volume, *Otherworldliness and the New Testament,* he writes, "Jesus' message was both political and religious at the same time: a call to repentance, a challenge to corrupt institutions and authorities, and a compassionate action directed toward the neglected and the victimized of his day. He was indeed concerned with the eschatological new age to come, but in his context this meant no lack of realism as regards the actual historical situation of his people." [1]

All this I would agree to; only I would insist that this very revolution within the culture of Israel in which Jesus played the crucial role is not wholly understandable within the methodology of the sociohistorical analysis. The mystery of the Kingdom must be taken seriously as a work of spirit issuing from a new center of consciousness, providing a "new center of history," to use Tillich's phrase, a new level of creation.

[1] Amos Wilder, *Otherworldliness and the New Testament.* Harper, 1954.

In speaking this way of the new center of consciousness in Jesus I am overreaching a bit. I am speaking as if we had access to the historical Jesus for direct inquiry. On the contrary, I am persuaded by the judgments of New Testament scholars who say we cannot go back of the picture which the Gospel witness presents to us. Yet the reality of this historical life is acknowledged, in Bultmann's words, as a presupposition of the *kergyma*. I have simply brought to bear upon this presupposition the light of a contemporary imagery and orientation of thought which seems to offer intelligibility to this event of novelty, this revelation of grace and spirit, without detracting from the mystery that attends it.

The historical datum that we have is a vivid account of the transformation of human lives, individually and corporately, in response to this new life in Christ. And this, we are earnestly advised by New Testament scholars, we must take seriously as being of a piece with the reality that was in Christ. This is the leaven of spirit at work in history as a communal event. This is "new being" assuming structured form. This is the meaning of Christ, agape embodied in the structures of human experience as redemptive energy, the work of grace reconciling the world to Him in whose infinite judgment and grace we have our ultimate ground.

Jesus Christ, then, as an innovation of sensitivity in human form, appears as the summit of a working of grace within a Middle Eastern culture. This antecedent aspect of the revelatory event should never be minimized. But to treat it simply as a cultural evolution is to miss the radical and revolutionary character of this innovation of spirit. The Christian assertion in speaking of Christ that "this is very God" points up the objective fact that a new level of conscious spirit had broken upon the structures of history. This is the force of the Pauline assertion that Christ is the New Creation, the New Man, who, in the familiar language of Christianity, is the God-Man. Present-day theology is at pains to reassert this transcendent truth of the Incarnation, yet to see it in juxtaposition with the dynamic events of a cultural history. Thus if we speak of this event as a new emergence, we point up the radical innovation of spirit within the structures of man. When we speak of this event as the New Creation, we point up the work of God in history as grace transcending the moral and rational consciousness, as love transcending the law.

Important as the person of Jesus Christ is in the story of the Gospel, the magnitude of the event of revelation is obscured if one does not see that a significant dimension of that event was the energy of spirit that broke afresh from the community of people into which this new life had come. They were transformed, the Gospels say—yes, but not just individually; relationally as well. Centers of an innovating righteousness appeared within the culture, in which the New Creation became flesh again and again. The Christian witness becomes vivid and impressive when it is seen in its corporate context. The new life becomes a cultural force. It becomes an enduring depth of grace within the relationships that body forth the living Christ and his reconciling Word, in the decisions, acts, negotiations, and responses of men and women working at pertinent issues in society. Here we see the goodness of grace assuming the force of a new level of social energy. Here we have the seminal beginnings of the Church as a witnessing community becoming the body of Christ.

But what was the nature of this new social energy? This is another way of pressing for an understanding of the nature of the New Creation which proved redemptive again and again. We have already intimated that it was a decisive expression of mind and of personal response that stood in judgment of the rigid structures of law and rational decisions. It was not amoral, or irrational; yet it transcended these codes and categories in a way that brought greater vision to each critical human situation. Moral law and reason were not routed, but summoned up to a higher order of goodness and righteousness. God's love as a judging yet redemptive power was made manifest to the dismay of legalist and rationalist. Love, issuing in justice, bearing grace and forgiveness, triumphed as a saving and healing force amidst the brokenness of men and women. This new kind of goodness, or you might say this new kind of justice motivated by love and forgiveness, releasing men and women from guilt and failure, from despair and anxiety, from the unrelenting actualities of history, opened up the life of hope in the face of defeat. This was the new life that looked to the future, leaving the dead to bury their dead, the antiquarian to cherish his tradition, the rigid moralist to nurture his offended sensibilities.

In recent writings in Christology it has become common

to employ the symbol of the Suffering Servant as being expressive of the quality of new life disclosed in this work of grace, a quality of life that stands in sharp contrast to the strutting power structures of modern life. The force of this symbol is to say that this new life of God released into history as a work of grace and Redemption is no easy way out for whosoever might try to possess it. The love of God incarnate in Jesus Christ is a suffering love. And this is the heart of the matter.

Enough attention has not been paid to the symbol of the Suffering Servant which runs through the whole of the Biblical story, coming to a climax in the Cross and the Resurrection. Yet the clue to God's nature as seen in Jesus Christ is given here. It acknowledges that the way of love and forgiveness is at a price—to one who loves and who forgives, whether God or man; yet that suffering, when it is incurred through acts of love and forgiveness, is the way to a significance which transcends all other forms of satisfaction or good, both in the common events of history and in the life of the spirit as an ultimate goal.

Let us see how significance in this new form follows from a life that is free to have relationships, that is free to love, to forgive, and thereby to accept the role of the Suffering Servant. Concern with the security of the self turns life in an opposite direction. The aversion to suffering, or the fear of it, will lead in the direction of disciplines that still the sensibilities, that restrain relationships, that hold in check the flow of fellow feeling; for in these investments of self, the risks of well-being, to serenity of mind and spirit, are great. One may not necessarily come to the conclusion, as did the Buddha, that all existence is suffering, and thereby seek to insulate the self from the actualities of human existence, through a studied practice of world denial. He may, instead, rear a citadel of selfhood that remains impregnable in the face of life's demands and responsibilities. In one's self-assurance, bolstered by indifference to humankind, and by a studied effort not to become involved in their sensibilities and needs, one may escape the anguish of relationships, though one will hardly escape the hell of isolation and of alienation, for these are of a piece with the life of security in its egoistic extremes.

Egoism, or hedonism, which is the denial of relationships, and a clinging to the sensibilities of the self, must mean the forfeiting of the goodness of life that can come through relationships and through the New Creation of spirit that is made manifest in such relationships. Asceticism, whether it takes a middle path, as in Buddhism, or a more extreme form of denial, forfeits the significance of the New Creation as a final goal as well as a present reality in its quest for equanimity which must eventuate in the dissolution of consciousness. These are choices which hedonistic egoism and asceticism make respectively, setting them apart from the Christian path of grace and forgiveness which steadily sets its face toward Jerusalem.

Now it must be recognized that, indispensable as the concerns for the moral and reasonable life are in themselves, their bent of interest, when exclusively pursued, tends to magnify the will to security at the expense of the life of the spirit. This is no easy problem, and we should not deal lightly with it. But there were ample grounds for Jesus' impatience with the Pharisees; and they are the same grounds that make it imperative that we do not allow Christian faith to lapse into an ethical legalism or a rigid moralism. The work of the spirit is a creative movement of life beyond these fixities; and in the end, it must triumph over them, else an inversion of good must follow.

Lest we lose sight of the essential thrust of the symbol of the Suffering Servant as it is being employed in modern Christological thinking we would do well at this point to state its meaning more explicitly. Professor Daniel Day Williams's words will help us here. He writes:

We miss what is involved in the question about God's suffering if we think primarily of physical pain, mental torment, or death. These are forms of human suffering, to be sure. In Christ, God has in some way experienced them. But "suffering" has a broader meaning. It signifies to undergo, to be acted upon, to live in a give and take with others. To say that God suffers means that he is actively engaged in dealing with a history which is real to him. What happens makes a difference to him. He wins an actual victory over the world through a love which endures and forgives. It means that the world's sorrow and agony are real to God, indeed in one way more real to him than to us, for only an infinite love can enter completely into sympathetic union with all life.[2]

[2] Daniel D. Williams, *What Present-Day Theologians Are Thinking.* Harper, 1952.

In pointing up this symbol of the Suffering Servant as meaning a God who participates in His world in the relationships that form it, modern Christology parts company with that kind of thinking about God with makes of Him an impassive sovereign or the Absolute, devoid of relationships. The essence of God's meaning, and this is the essence of the meaning of Christ as a revelation of God, is that God is related to men, that He is concerned, that He is involved in the travail of our critical circumstances. This is not to say that He is involved as we are in the turmoil and indecision of this troubled existence; but He is intimately concerned. In our agony, our arrogance, our stupidity, our willfulness, our blindness, God suffers, as He suffered in Jesus Christ who died on the Cross.

To say that God suffers, then, is to assert the ultimacy of relationships, and to affirm their significance, both as the bearers of good and as the creative ground of the new life which spirit alone can generate. There is a way by which a goodness in life beyond all cherished goods may be apprehended, known, and enjoyed. It is participation in the New Creation, which is to live in Christ.

I am troubled a bit about what may seem to be implied in what I have said in this analysis, namely, that the Christian life must emulate the divine life of suffering. In a sense this is what must be affirmed; but it must be affirmed with a realistic recognition of our human limits and frailties. We are human beings, not God. We may participate in the New Creation and be judged by it; we may not hope to be Christ himself.

One of the most persisting obstacles to understanding the force of the Christian interpretation of life is the perfectionism which assumes that we have only to define the nature of God and Christ, and thereby live out that divine nature. This is clearly to think more highly of ourselves than we ought to think. The life of the spirit is strong medicine when it is taken seriously. It may not be undertaken as a romantic venture. In our human and finite existence we could not bear the life of the Cross in its fullness as a daily demand. We participate in the New Creation that is born of the life of the Cross. As human beings, seeking to do the will of God, our human spirits will be bent toward this ultimate demand. But our lives are ambiguous. Our dedications are ambiguous. Though our faces are turned toward the light, we of necessity grope through the darkness of daily events. We participate in the demands of self-experience, even as we participate in the New Creation. We cannot escape this ambiguity of human existence, so long as we are in existence, though we may rise to moments of genuine encounter with the life of spirit. To be self-accepting, yet fully aware that we are under the judgment of the love that is in Christ, is to assure, not only our sanity, but our capacity to receive the grace that is given, which can do exceedingly abundantly above all that we can ask or think.

The symbol of the Suffering Servant points to the way of the Cross as the life of significance beyond every other good. It is, however, a way, not the goal nor the end of the Christian life. For the Christian faith points beyond tragedy to a life of triumph, even in defeat; to hope, even as we despair; to a capacity for joy, even in days of sorrow; to life, even in death. Thus in the last analysis the New Creation, which is a dimension of spirit beyond every structure of existence, is a resurrection experience which comes to us again and again, bringing perennial renewal amidst moments of decay and defeat. To know this is to know the depths of our existence when we say that our life is in God.

Suggested Readings

On Christ in Process Thought

Barnhart, J. E. "Incarnation and Process Philosophy," *Religious Studies,* 2 (1967), 225-232.

Browning, Don S. *Atonement and Psychotherapy.* Philadelphia: Westminster Press, 1966.

Clarke, Bowman L. "Whitehead's Cosmology and the Christian Drama," *The Journal of Religion,* 39 (1959), 162-169.

Cobb, John B., Jr. "Some Thoughts on the Meaning of Christ's Death," *Religion in Life,* 28 (1959), 212-222.

——. "The Finality of Christ in a Whiteheadian Perspective," *The Finality of Christ.* Edited by Dow Kirkpatrick. Nashville: Abingdon Press, 1966, pp. 122-154.

——. *The Structure of Christian Existence*. Philadelphia: Westminster Press, 1967, pp. 108-124; 137-150.

——. "A Whiteheadian Christology," *Process Philosophy and Christian Thought*. Edited by Delwin Brown, Ralph E. James, Jr., and Gene Reeves. Indianapolis: Bobbs-Merrill, 1971, pp. 382-398. Paperback—Indianapolis: Bobbs-Merrill.

Griffin, David. "Schubert Ogden's Christology and the Possibilities of Process Philosophy," *The Christian Scholar*, 50 (1967), 290-303. Reprinted in *Process Philosophy and Christian Thought*, pp. 347-361.

Hamilton, Peter. *The Living God and the Modern World: Christian Theology Based on the Thought of A. N. Whitehead*. Philadelphia: United Church Press, 1967, pp. 180-234. Paperback.

——. "Some Proposals for a Modern Christology," *Christ for Us Today*. Edited by W. Norman Pittenger. London: SCM Press, 1968, pp. 154-175. Reprinted in *Process Philosophy and Christian Thought*, pp. 362-381.

Hartshorne, Charles. *Reality as Social Process: Studies in Metaphysics and Religion*. Glencoe, Ill.: The Free Press and Boston: Beacon Press, 1953, pp. 145-154.

James, Ralph E., Jr. *The Concrete God: A New Beginning for Theology —The Thought of Charles Hartshorne*. Indianapolis: Bobbs-Merrill, 1967, pp. 127-148.

——. "A Theology of Acceptance," *The Journal of Religion*, 49 (1969), 376-387.

——. "Process Cosmology and Theological Particularity," *Process Philosophy and Christian Thought*. Edited by Delwin Brown, Ralph E. James, Jr., and Gene Reeves. Indianapolis: Bobbs-Merrill, 1971, pp. 399-407. Paperback—Indianapolis: Bobbs-Merrill.

Loomer, Bernard M. "Christian Faith and Process Philosophy," *The Journal of Religion*, 29 (1949), 190-198. Reprinted in *Process Philosophy and Christian Thought*, pp. 81-91.

——. "Empirical Theology within Process Thought," *The Future of Empirical Theology*. Edited by Bernard E. Meland. Chicago: The University of Chicago Press, 1969, pp. 159-164.

Meland, Bernard E. *Faith and Culture*. New York: Oxford University Press, 1953, pp. 190-223.

————. *The Realities of Faith: The Revolution in Cultural Forms.* New York: Oxford University Press, 1962, pp. 248-324.

Ogden, Schubert M. *Christ Without Myth: A Study Based on the Theology of Rudolf Bultmann.* New York: Harper and Brothers, 1961.

————. *The Reality of God and Other Essays.* New York: Harper and Row, 1966, pp. 188-205.

Ogletree, Thomas. "A Christological Assessment of Dipolar Theism," *The Journal of Religion,* 47 (1967), 87-99. Reprinted in *Process Philosophy and Christian Thought,* pp. 331-346.

Pailin, David A. "The Incarnation as a Continuing Reality," *Religious Studies,* 6 (1970), 303-327.

Peters, Eugene. *The Creative Advance: An Introduction to Process Philosophy as a Context for Christian Faith.* St. Louis: Bethany Press, 1966, pp. 111-117. Paperback—St. Louis: Bethany Press.

Pittenger, W. Norman. See the listings below on pp. 215-216.

Reeves, Gene and Delwin Brown. "The Development of Process Theology," *Process Philosophy and Christian Thought.* Edited by Delwin Brown, Ralph E. James, Jr., and Gene Reeves. Indianapolis: Bobbs-Merrill, 1971, pp. 58-62. Paperback—Indianapolis: Bobbs-Merrill.

Teilhard de Chardin, Pierre. See below, Part IV.

Whitehead, Alfred North. *Religion in the Making.* New York: Macmillan, 1926, Chapter II, Section I, pp. 47-57. Paperback—New York: Meridian.
————. *Adventures of Ideas.* New York: Macmillan, 1933, Part Two, 10, pp. 205-221. Paperback—New York: Free Press.

Wieman, Henry Nelson. See the listings below on p. 226.

Williams, Daniel Day. Comment on "Theological Reflections on the Accounts of Jesus' Death and Resurrection," by Hans W. Frei, *The Christian Scholar,* 49 (1966), 310-312.

————. *The Spirit and the Forms of Love.* New York: Harper and Row, 1968, pp. 155-172.

Williams, Ronald L. "The Two Types of Christology: A Neoclassical Analysis," *The Journal of Religion,* 49 (1969), 18-40.

12 Bernard E. Meland, Process Thought and the Significance of Christ

W. NORMAN PITTENGER

The classical Christological formulations were worked out within a world view that is foreign to our age. In the selection below,* W. Norman Pittenger sketches the outlines of a reconstruction of Christology within a process world view. He claims that Jesus must be seen as genuinely *in* and *of* this world, not as an intruder from another realm. Jesus is the coinciding of God's action and man's responsive action. Following the patristic tradition, Pittenger sees the creative Word present and active throughout the universe and history. In Jesus the Word is "enfleshed" and is most dynamically operative. In him we see the expression in human terms of the love which is God himself. In this context Pittenger discusses the question of the uniqueness and finality of Christ.

W. Norman Pittenger's chief contribution to process theology lies in the area of Christology. His book The Word Incarnate, *published in 1959 while he was teaching at General Theological Seminary in New York City, presented one of the most extensive and systematic restatements of Christology with a process orientation. In 1970 he reviewed his current position in the book* Christology Reconsidered.

This essay is an attempt in constructive theology; it is appropriate that a piece of writing in honor of Bernard Meland should be such, since for many years

* From *Religion in Life*, 37 (1968), 540-550. Reprinted with permission.

he was the distinguished occupant of the chair called by that name at the Divinity School of the University of Chicago. And the special area with which we shall be concerned is the significance of Christ in the light of process thought; it is appropriate that such a subject should be discussed, not only because Professor Meland has himself regularly used the insights of process thought in his own books but also because he has been kind enough to speak approvingly of this writer's earlier Christological studies in which the meaning of Jesus has been interpreted through those insights. Especially in two recent books, *Faith and Culture* and *The Realities of Faith,* we find Professor Meland developing constructively the way in which a basic process metaphysic, implemented by other important modern insights (such as the importance of myth), can provide a ground for a new statement of basic Christian faith. Along with Schubert Ogden and John Cobb, of the younger generation of theologians, and Bernard Loomer and Daniel Day Williams, of an older generation, Meland has been working toward "a Christian natural theology" (to employ the title of Cobb's fascinating book) but also intimating the results in Christian reconception in respect to beliefs and actions which are historically part of the ongoing Christian tradition of faith and life.

The person and achievement of Jesus Christ has a central place in that tradition. A theological construction in which Jesus is not central can hardly be called Christian at all, but this does not mean that we must rest content with older formulations, especially when they seem to make little or no contact with the patterns of thought which are taken to be true by our contemporaries. It is Jesus himself, both in his proper person and in his achievement, that must be central, not the conventional theories about him. It is the perennial Christian experience that in some fashion he illuminates what Whitehead called "the nature of God and his agency in the world," while at the same time he illuminates the nature of man and his dynamic becoming in manhood. That is central; the ways in which it is interpreted cannot claim the same abiding importance.

In this essay we shall interest ourselves in four main topics: (1) process thought and the various contemporary emphases which implement it for Christian theological purposes; (2) the place of Jesus in a processive world; (3) how the significance of

Jesus may be given appropriate statement in such a context; (4) some related questions, namely the continuing Christian sense that Jesus is "unique," "final," and the "source of new life." Each of these topics has its relationship to Professor Meland's own writing, but in this essay we shall attempt to work them out independently and without reliance on his, or any other, theological construction in our time.

I

Process thought is the name usually given to that view of the world which takes with utmost seriousness the dynamic, living, evolutionary quality of our existence and of the world in which we live. Ours is not a world of unchanging substances, of fixed entities, of permanently located "nows" and "thens"; it is a world in change, in which we have to do not so much with being as with becoming, and in which we find ourselves caught up in processive movements rather than imprisoned in fixed habitations. From its lowest components—societal energies at the subatomic level—up to the highest grades known to us, we see this same energizing, dynamic quality. Furthermore, the story of the world is to be told in an account of increasingly complicated organic structures, forming social patterns of greater or less intensity, until in human life itself we know an interrelated, interpenetrating sort of integration which is remarkably full and rich, bringing into some degree of unity the various "systems" of which physiologically and psychologically—not to say physically and chemically—we are made up; and all of this in community with others to create a society of persons whose existence is known in intercommunication and participation, one in and with others.

The principle of explanation for such a world must in some genuine fashion be *like* that world; as Whitehead remarked, God cannot, in such a world, be the exception to the metaphysical principles required to understand the world, but must be the chief exemplification of those principles. God is living, dynamic, energizing. He is also *related*. The perfection which can be claimed for him is not that proper to some unmoved mover or absolute essence; it is the perfection of his own identity as being himself, but that perfection subsists in his identity in and with relationships. He is the One who is sufficient to remain himself even while he continually surpasses himself in his expression and activity. What happens in the world contributes to his satisfaction, enriches his possibilities in further self-expression, and provides ever new opportunities for his loving care. Indeed, he may best be defined as perfect love or the perfect lover, working ceaselessly to express his love and to establish communities of love.

I find the concept of God which follows from taking process with utmost seriousness best worked out in the writings of Charles Hartshorne, but Hartshorne himself would acknowledge that most of his thought on these and related matters is, so to say, a series of footnotes on the work of Alfred North Whitehead. There have been other exponents of this view; in England during the first three decades of this century C. Lloyd-Morgan was the chief representative, while later Canon Charles Raven undertook the theological development of the view. Recently the work of Teilhard de Chardin has been made available to us; here, too, one finds essentially the same position. The interpretation of the world and the reading of the nature of the divine Reality in process terms is basic to the modern enterprise of theological reconstruction; it is much more satisfactory than the alternatives available today, such as existentialism, taken as a philosophy, or the revived idealism of Tillich, and certainly much more useful than the kind of biblical theology which has assumed that the arrangement of biblical motifs and themes (without restatement but simply in their precise biblical form) provides all that we need for the task.

On the other hand, the basic process approach requires supplementation. I have argued that there are three or four significant contemporary emphases which not only provide this supplementation but have the special appeal (for process thinkers) of fitting in admirably with the general processive view. Since the argument has been presented elsewhere,[1] it will suffice to mention these emphases very briefly.

First, there is the existentialist analysis of human experience in its most deeply felt levels, with the recognition that man's integration depends upon his being "engaged" or "committed." Existentialism as a philosophy (which seems indeed to be a contradiction in terms!) is truncated and inadequate; but the existen-

[1] *Process Thought and Christian Faith* (New York: Macmillan, 1968).

tialist study of what it means to be a man, thrust into the world with other men, with a dynamic drive that temporally speaking is "toward death," yet with the provision of purpose if one is enabled to engage himself in a compelling aim, has about it the ring of truth. It speaks directly to our own inner experience of being human. But coupled with this there is the contemporary emphasis on man's societal nature, his "social mind," his life in community, his awareness of "belonging." This recognition that we are "knit together in a bundle of life" (as the Old Testament puts it), with the implications of such a social existence for our grasp not only of thought but also of activity, provides the complement to the existentialist penetration into the personal depths of human experience. From these two together—existentialist analysis and recognition of our social experience—comes still another contemporary insistence, which has to do with the meaning of history. On such a view, history is not to be seen simply as chronology or the annals of the past. Rather, history is the communal participation in the events which have made us what we are; it is the coming-alive in our present of all that the past has been and done. And in this connection it is the entering into the *important* moments which have been signally instrumental in shaping us in our society. This concept of *importance,* which was stressed by Whitehead in *Modes of Thought* and elsewhere, and which is significant in our historical existence and its interpretation, will play an important part in the next section of this essay.

Finally, there is the enormous contribution made to our understanding of ourselves, of the dynamics of our personality, of the motivations in and behind our actions, provided by the various depth psychologies which have become so important a factor in contemporary thinking. Freud and Jung, Adler and Reik, Fromm and Horney—and many others, differing among themselves in many respects—have opened to us a new field of inquiry. But above all, they have made it possible for us to penetrate much more profoundly into ourselves. And the new psychology, like existentialism, social thought, and the changed idea of history, stresses the dynamic, energizing, "becoming" aspect of human personality and of the world. Furthermore, all these provide us with "images" in terms of which we may read meaning. A more sympathetic attitude toward the function of myth, a recognition of the significance of symbol, and a readiness to employ images in the attempt to grasp the value and the deepest worth in our several approaches to reality must be accounted among the great gains of our recent decades.

All these taken together—a process metaphysic, existentialist analysis, acknowledgment of our social belonging, history as *anamnesis* or realization of the past in our present, psychological insight into the dynamics of personality, and the recognition of the inescapable necessity of and value in mythopoeic interpretation—provide the material for a natural theology, if it may be called such, which will give some sufficient base for the specifically Christian affirmations, although these affirmations of necessity must speak "from faith to faith."

II

The formulations of the significance of Christ which we have inherited from the early days of Christian theology are not to be dismissed as unimportant or irrelevant. It is true, of course, that the terminology of, say, the Definition of Chalcedon (A.D. 451) is no longer meaningful: we do not think today in a fashion which can make much use of *hypostasis, ousia, physis,* and their near-equivalents in Latin, *persona, substantia, natura.* The classical statement that in Jesus Christ there is the union of two substances, "perfect God of the substance of the Father," "perfect man of the substance of the Virgin Mary his Mother"—a union of the natures which is "indivisible, unconfused, unchanged, inseparable"—this statement, whatever may have been its importance in earlier days, now seems to say little to our thinking.

On the other hand, these formulations did have the merit of preserving, in the period when they were worked out, the basic Christian evaluation of Jesus as being both the manifest expression of the character and purpose of God and also the fulfillment of the possibilities present in manhood. Furthermore, they ruled out other interpretations of Christ which would have had the effect of reducing his significance or distorting his person by denying his true manhood or minimizing the reality of the revelation of God in him. We should be grateful, then, for the ancient Christological definitions and for their part in preserving for later ages the early

Christian awareness of the meaning of that same One who remains central for us in our Christian faith.

But this does not mean that the classical statements are viable today. The fact is that when an attempt is made to use them, in a time when the whole context of thought is changed, their own emphases are twisted and distorted. They do not fit in with the way in which we understand the world, history, human experience, or our own human development—but of course they were never intended to fit in with that kind of understanding. They were the product of, and hence they were phrased in the context provided by, an entirely different way of looking at the world, history, human experience, and human personality. The context in which any statement is made always qualifies and colors the statement. It is impossible to take one bit of ancient thought and insert it into an utterly different pattern without very seriously modifying the implications and connotations of the piece which is being inserted. This is why the not infrequent attempts at refurbishing the ancient formulations tend only to make them appear absurd or irrelevant in our own day. Nor are such attempts really loyal to the deepest intention of the great Christian thinkers who devised them in the first place. Those theologians were not concerned with *words;* they were concerned with the *facts* of experience and the *experience* of facts. They used the words which were at their disposal, of course: how could they, and how can we in our day, do otherwise? The concepts they found at hand were the ones which to them made most sense of the data to be interpreted. But the intention which was theirs was simply to state, in a form as minimal as possible, the basic reality of the Christian life as this was grounded in the whole person and achievement of Jesus: here, in this event, in the full integrity of a genuinely human life, the "nature and the name" of the supreme Reality was disclosed; and here, in this event and in this true and real man, the actuality of salvation (that is, a whole, healthy, eternally significant life) was made available to men.

To be loyal to the intention of our fathers in the faith may mean that we must depart from the concepts they employed and the statements they made. And if some complain that this will lead to failure in "orthodoxy," the response must be made that while it may involve departure from *verbal* orthodoxy it is in fact the only procedure which can retain *vital* orthodoxy. For "orthodoxy" is not so much the using of ancient language as it is the continuing participation in the reality which that language was devised to affirm, and of course to affirm in the only idiom available at the time when the affirmation was made.

In the light of our knowledge today, living as we do in a world that is in process, and aware as we are of the several other factors to which attention has already been called, any viable Christological statement must see Jesus as quite genuinely *in* and *of* this world, living as a genuine man (a genuine Jew of the first century of our era), genuinely thinking the thoughts of that period in which he lived, learning genuinely as men learn, sharing fully and completely in human experience. To speak of Jesus as if he were an intruder from some other sphere or realm, a "divine visitor" to this world, will be to make him supremely meaningless. It is precisely as one of us, as a man among men, that whatever further significance he may possess will have to be found. Furthermore, to bring into the account such notions as *enhypostasia,* in which his true "person" is not human but divine, is to remove him from his brethren and in effect to deny him any true humanity at all. All of Jesus is human—although certainly this must not be taken to mean that he is a very ordinary man; on the contrary he is, in Luther's words, "the proper Man"—and there is nothing absurd in claiming that in this instance of humanity, under its own conditions of space and time and with the factors which necessarily limit any man to his time and place, there was a bringing to special fulfillment or actualization of genuine human possibilities. He was, as we are being taught these days, "the man for others" in that his whole life was a self-giving for the neighbor; he was also, as the Gospel material makes plain, remembered especially as "the man for God" in that his whole life was a filial surrender to what he took to be the purposes of the heavenly Father to whom he gave himself utterly and completely, with no reservations and no withholdings.

In that Man, then, the early Christians saw the activity of God. Precisely because he was so open to the Father's will, he was the personal agent in whom and through whom God could work. Nor was this a matter simply of response on his side, although the reality of the human response is clear enough from the stories told about him. Much more deeply, since all human response is response to a movement from and of God to men, his openness to God was included in the divine purpose and operation. When Christians have spoken of God in Jesus, they have not intended to suggest that the divine is there by exclusion or removal of some human element proper to manhood as such; they have meant to say that in the totality of the human there was an activity of the divine. Jesus is the coincidence of God's action or agency and man's responsive action or agency, not in spite of but under the very conditions of genuinely human life—and that, Christians believe, in a degree not elsewhere known in human experience.

The way to this last assertion for us can best be taken when we recall the concept of *importance,* to which we have already referred. Some occurrence, some moment of experience, is *important* when it can be taken as throwing enormous light upon that which preceded it and so prepared for it, as being in itself a striking and notably stimulating moment or event, and as opening up for the future new and remarkable possibilities both of understanding and of action. Every man and all societies of men take (whether consciously or unconsciously) some moment, event, occurrence, conviction, disclosure, as being thus important. One can think of dozens of examples: the labors of the Founding Fathers in the American colonies and the young American republic, the granting of Magna Carta in Britain, the nailing of the theses for Lutherans, a traumatic moment in one's personal life such as falling in love or being greatly befriended when in trouble. In all these the past is illuminated, the present given point, and the future direction of a nation or a man's life opened up.

Now if the basic dynamic in the cosmos is the energizing of creative love, ceaselessly working to provide opportunity for and actualization of more widely shared good, it is not absurd to think that the event of Jesus Christ is thus *important.* For, as a matter of fact, that event did illuminate the past and make sense of the history of the Jewish people (and through them, of all other seeking for and responding to increasing good); it did, in its initial impact and in its continuing movement into the lives of those brought within its ambit, stand out as a striking and notably stimulating moment in history; it did, and it still does, open up new possibilities, opportunities, and also realizations and expressions of creative good in man's world. Furthermore, when it is taken as being thus important, it provides insight into what Professor Meland, following Whitehead, so beautifully calls the "tenderness" which is the specific quality of divinity in relation to the world and men. In other words, it is a disclosure of God, given not in theory or speculation but in concrete historical human *act*. As such, it also provides both insight and stimulus for human existence, for this can now be seen as potentially the possibility of responsive action to creative good, the expression of love such as will integrate the personality and thus establish social communication and participation which itself is a growing in love.

Finally, if one accepts the view that events in the created world make their contribution to the divine life, so that in God's "consequent nature" (as Whitehead phrased it) all the goods achieved in the world are included and play their part in providing new occasions for creative self-expression by God, one can then see that the total Christ—Jesus, with all that went before to prepare for him, with his own personal life and accomplishment, and with all that has happened through him and because of him in succeeding ages—can become, indeed has become, the element in the ongoing working-out of the divine "subjective aim" which most signally is being used to establish and augment the good—the indefatigable love—which is God's identifying characteristic in his energizing in creation.

III

It is along such lines that a Christology available for our time may be worked out. As Canon Hugh Montefiore has argued in his essay in *Soundings,* this suggests a Christology of divine and human activity, rather than a Christology of divine and human substances. It is more in accord with the total biblical perspective, with its insistence on the *living* God and his purposive self-disclosure to the world, than a formulation built upon morphological descriptive terms; that is, it is a dynamic view, like that of Scripture as a whole. Professor R. H. Fuller, in the last chapter of his *Christology,* has made the same point, and the present writer hopes that it is not immodest to mention his own book, *The Word Incarnate,* as a full-length discussion which reaches the same conclusion and seeks in consequence to follow process thought in reconceiving the meaning of Christ Jesus.

In such a Christology, one may think, the ancient notion of the divine creative Word or *Logos* can play a significant part. By the Word, the patristic writers meant to name the continuing creative revelatory activity of God in the world; they believed also that such activity is so genuinely divine that they were ready to regard it as integral to the divine in itself (hence the conception that the Word is the "second hypostasis" or "person" of the Godhead): God, in and of his very self, is creative and creatively active. In the whole world, at every point and in every time, the Word is at work; nothing comes into existence save through his energizing, and the prologue of the Fourth Gospel is an eloquent statement of this view. In human history there is an even more intensive operation of the Word; and in every human life that same Word is both the undergirding and the dynamic which is the "light that lighteneth every man." For Christian faith, the significance of Jesus is that he is the point where the Word is most signally, most intensively, most vitally and dynamically operative; in him, the Fourth Gospel says, the Word was "enfleshed"—or, as we might more readily phrase it, discovers for itself through prevenient preparation and concomitant solicitation an adequate, but genuinely human, *organon* (the word is Athanasius' own) or personal agent, decisive and crucial because it provides the *important* point for the Word's never-ending activity in the human creation.

But the creative activity which is the Word is to be characterized by the quality of "tenderness," of love. Hence we have here, in this Man, the expression in human terms and on the human level of an enormous and inexorable love, the love which is God himself. Since man, in his dynamic thrust and his identifying "subjective aim," is ever seeking fulfillment which can be found only in love and in the self-giving which *is* love, we have also the overcoming of the frustration of man as lover in response in love to the God who himself is love. In other words, man is enabled to become an integrated lover in that he is enabled to become "the man for others"; and this because he is "the man for God" who is love. So God and man are brought together in a personal unity of loving: the divine Lover acts in and through the human love of the Man of Nazareth; the love wherewith that Man loves, in his tenderness and in his courage, his humility and his boldness, is the very love "which moves the sun and the other stars."

And because that has taken place, as Christian faith proclaims it, there is released into the lives of those who respond the same power and discernment of love. "Redemption" and all the associated terms can then be seen to point to, and in their various ways describe, what it means to be caught up into the divine love, shared to others as they engage themselves in self-commitment to the way and the work of the Jesus, in whom love is thus incarnate and from whom love is thus imparted to them.

IV

There is space for but the briefest discussion of the "related questions." These, it will be recalled, had to do with "uniqueness," "finality," and "new life in Christ."

As to the first, it is obvious that the older ways of affirming uniqueness will no longer serve, for they all implied some intrusive entrance of God into a world from which he is otherwise absent —although such was not the intention of the early Christian theologians in their own formulations. For us, the uniqueness of Jesus can only be seen in his speciality, his supreme and decisive expression of that which God always and everywhere is "up to" in his world. Here a suggestion made recently in a lecture by Professor Moule of Cambridge will help. Professor Moule has noted that there are *two* kinds of uniqueness: one of exclusion and one of inclusion. Jesus is not unique, then, because of him and of him only can it be said that God is operative there; he is unique by inclusion, in that he includes, takes up into himself, and gives point to all that God is doing, has done, and will do. So once again the concept of *importance* becomes the key to his uniqueness.

Similarly with respect to "finality." If this indicates the *end*, in the sense of a terminus, it has no meaning in our ongoing processive world. But if it indicates that the clue is given, the definitive disclosure made, in that Man of Nazareth and in his achievement, the whole point of Christian faith is established. There, in Jesus and in the reception of him by those who respond in self-commitment, is the key to our understanding of God's way with men. When love of that quality—that is, when God—meets us, we *must* respond, either by acceptance or by rejection. What may happen to those who reject such love we do not know, although faith in that love would suggest that it will find other ways to reach even the most recalcitrant. But for those who accept, there is "the releasing power of a new affection," the opening of the self, the integration of the person in his relationships with others which ennobles and enriches, vitalizes and makes new. This is finality in the sense of an utterly decisive movement for those to whom the encounter comes, whether in Jesus himself or in whatever other ways may be made available to them. Nor can one think that Jesus himself would have claimed anything more than that, since *his* concern was with God and with men and not with assertions of his own importance.

Finally, new life in Christ is what we have just been talking about. It is nothing other than life in love. God *desires* men's response in love (we say this against Nygren's thesis in *Agape and Eros*); and when it comes, there is a new relationship in which God is loved *in omnibus et supra omnia,* as the ancient Latin prayer puts it, and in which men are loved in a communion that is grounded in the divine love itself. What Tillich has described as participation in the New Being is much better described as sharing in the divine-human enterprise of mutuality in love and love in community. And as St. John of the Cross once put it, "In the evening of our day, we shall be judged by our loving."

SUGGESTED READINGS

W. Norman Pittenger on Christ

Pittenger, W. Norman. "Degree or Kind? A Christological Essay," *The Canadian Journal of Theology,* 2 (1956), 189-196.

————. *The Word Incarnate: A Study of the Doctrine of the Person of Christ.* New York: Harper and Brothers, 1959.

————. *God in Process.* London: SCM Press, 1967, pp. 21-39. Paperback—Naperville, Ill.: Allenson.

———— *Light, Life, Love.* London: A. R. Mowbray, 1967.

———. *Process-Thought and Christian Faith*. New York: Macmillan, 1968, pp. 55-74.

———. *Christology Reconsidered*. London: SCM Press, 1970.

———. "The Doctrine of Christ in a Process Theology," *The Expository Times*, 82 (1970), 7-10.

On W. Norman Pittenger's Christology

Hick, John. "Christology at the Cross Roads," *Prospect for Theology: Essays in Honour of H. H. Farmer*. Edited by F. G. Healey. Welwyn Garden City: James Nisbet, 1966, pp. 139-166.

Mascall, E. L. *Theology and the Future*. New York: Morehouse-Barlow, 1968, pp. 100-126. Paperback.

McIntyre, John. *The Shape of Christology*. Philadelphia: The Westminster Press, 1966, pp. 138-141.

On Related Themes

Baillie, Donald M. *God Was in Christ*. New York: Charles Scribner's Sons, 1948.

Knox, John. *The Humanity and Divinity of Christ*. New York: Cambridge University Press, 1967. Paperback—New York: Cambridge University Press.

Thornton, Lionel. *The Incarnate Lord*. London: Longmans, Green 1928.

13 The Human Predicament

HENRY NELSON WIEMAN

The atom bomb has given the human race the option of choosing destruction or creativity. To meet the present crisis, Henry Nelson Wieman claims, man must radically re-orient himself and give priority to the creative source of good rather than to his own created goods. The following selection * draws into focus the essential elements of Wieman's process vision: the primacy of the creative source of good, which he links with God; the operation of this creative source in time, which is accessible to rational-empirical enquiry; and the uniqueness of Jesus in releasing creative power in history. Wieman sees Jesus as a catalytic agent, as if he were a neutron that started a chain reaction of creative transformation.

Henry Nelson Wieman received his doctorate from Harvard University and taught at the Divinity School of the University of Chicago from 1927 until his retirement in 1947. He was a major force in bringing Whitehead's thought to the University of Chicago and in the development of process theology. He later abandoned Whitehead's metaphysical superstructure and developed his own form of process thought, with heavy emphasis on the empirical method and the emergence of values in society.

The bomb that fell on Hiroshima cut history in two like a knife. Before and after are two different worlds. That cut is more abrupt, decisive, and revolution-

* From *The Source of Human Good* (Chicago: The University of Chicago Press, 1946; Carbondale: Southern Illinois University Press, 1964), pp. 37-46; 52-53. Reprinted with permission.

217

ary than the cut made by the star over Bethlehem. It may not be more creative of human good than the star, but it is more swiftly transformative of human existence than anything else that has ever happened. The economic and political order fitted to the age before that parachute fell becomes suicidal in the age coming after. The same breach extends into education and religion.

Men having interests in the economic and political order will vehemently deny that such a change is required of them. Men with vested interests in religion may admit that the change is demanded in the economic and political realms but will repudiate any such claim for their own special area. They will have many arguments to prove that their faith is more deeply laid, more enduring, more immune from change than affairs economic and political. Their faith may very well reach for deeper levels of existence and may seek access to a more important reality than any other human concern. But their faith is no more exempt from change in respect to the intellectual forms by which it must be lived than any other. These forms must undergo reformation as radical as any if faith meets constructively the new order of life which has been literally hurled at modern man by this coercive event.

Someone will begin at once to point to the well-known fact that cultural and social changes are never sudden. When truly significant, they require centuries for realization. Of course, this is true. The change we are now considering is the cultural shift gradually produced by modern technology. Extensive use of machinery began about 1850 and will continue for a long time to come. The release of atomic energy is merely the climax of much that has gone before. But the use of atomic bombs in war dramatizes the transition that has been occurring and may well usher in its final and consummative phase. After the age of technological consummation has been completed, the time of increasing technology may give place to a different kind of cultural achievement. Meanwhile, the bomb that fell over Hiroshima has psychological consequences that greatly accelerate the reordering and reinterpreting of human life demanded by technology grown mighty.

This bomb has become a symbol giving to all human life a new meaning with portent of dread and splendor. Not the physical impact of the bomb or the economic changes it may induce but the sudden presentation of alternative destinies for the human race

divides history into the age before and the age after the release
of atomic energy. It calls for a radical redirection of man's controlling devotion. Not the greatest good he can appreciate but the
process which creates him and all the good of life is what he must
serve. Not the goal but the source, not the highest but the deepest,
not the total unity but the creator of unity, not the universe as
known to him but the generator and recreator of every universe he
can ever know, must be his guide and master when he reaches the
peak of power.

The creative source of value must come first in man's devotion, while the specific values apprehended through the narrow slit
of human awareness must come second, if we are to find the way
of our deliverance and the way of human fulfilment. This reversal in the direction of human devotion is not new. It is, we believe, the very substance of the original Christian faith. What is
new is the need to reinterpret the creative source of human good
in such wise as to render it accessible to the service of the mighty
tools of science and technology.

We must try to demonstrate the original Christian nature of
this reversal in the direction of human devotion. Otherwise, it will
seem alien to the best in our tradition. In fact, it is not alien but
essential and intrinsic to that best. If this is true, we should be able
to see the truth of it by simply looking objectively at the events
which originated the Christian faith. No subtle logical devices or
rationalizing systems should be required. Let us, then, look at these
originative events of our traditional religion, endeavoring to see
them as naïvely and objectively as possible. The creative source
of human good operating in time and plainly accessible to rational-
empirical inquiry, yet commanding this reversal in the direction
of human devotion, should stand there in clear silhouette.

THE ORIGINATING EVENTS OF OUR FAITH

Jesus engaged in intercommunication with a little group of
disciples with such depth and potency that the organization of
their several personalities was broken down and they were re-
made. They became new men, and the thought and feeling of each
got across to the others. It was not merely the thought and feeling
of Jesus that got across. That was not the most important thing.
The important thing was that the thought and feeling of the least

and lowliest got across to the others and the others to him. Not something handed down to them from Jesus but something rising up out of their midst in creative power was the important thing. It was not something Jesus did. It was something that happened when he was present like a catalytic agent. It was as if he was a neutron that started a chain reaction of creative transformation. Something about this man Jesus broke the atomic exclusiveness of those individuals so that they were deeply and freely receptive and responsive each to the other. He split the atom of human egoism, not by psychological tricks, not by intelligent understanding, but simply by being the kind of person he was, combined with the social, psychological, and historical situation of the time and the heritage of Hebrew prophecy. Thus there arose in this group of disciples a miraculous mutual awareness and responsiveness toward the needs and interests of one another.

But this was not all; something else followed from it. The thought and feeling, let us say the meanings, thus derived by each from the other, were integrated with what each had previously acquired. Thus each was transformed, lifted to a higher level of human fulfilment. Each became more of a mind and a person, with more capacity to understand, to appreciate, to act with power and insight; for this is the way human personality is generated and magnified and life rendered more nobly human.

A third consequence followed necessarily from these first two. The appreciable world expanded round about these men, thus interacting in this fellowship. Since they could now see through the eyes of others, feel through their sensitivities, and discern the secrets of many hearts, the world was more rich and ample with meaning and quality. Also—and this might be called a fourth consequence—there was more depth and breadth of community between them as individuals with one another and between them and all other men. This followed from their enlarged capacity to get the perspectives of one another and the perspectives of all whom they might encounter. Of course, this apprehension of the other's perspective is never perfect and complete. But the disciples found themselves living in a community of men vastly deeper and wider than any before accessible to them.

Thus occurred in the fellowship about Jesus a complex, creative event, transforming the disciples as individuals, their relations with one another and with all men, and transforming also the appreciable world in which they lived.

Let us not be misunderstood. The creative transformative power was not in the man Jesus, although it could not have occurred apart from him. Rather he was in it. It required many other things besides his own solitary self. It required the Hebrew heritage, the disciples with their peculiar capacity for this kind of responsiveness, and doubtless much else of which we have little knowledge. The creative power lay in the interaction taking place between these individuals. It transformed their minds, their personalities, their appreciable world, and their community with one another and with all men. In subsequent chapters we shall try to demonstrate that this creative power is the source of all good in human existence. What happened in the group about Jesus was the lifting of this creative event to dominate their lives. What happened after the death of Jesus was the release of this creative power from constraints and limitations previously confining it; also the formation of a fellowship with an organization, ritual, symbols, and documents by which this dominance of the creative event over human concern might be perpetuated through history. Of course, there was little if any intellectual understanding of it; but intellectual understanding was not required to live under its control in the culture then and there prevailing, for men did not have our technology.

The creative event is always working in human life, but ordinarily it is ignored and excluded from human concern and the intent of devotion. Other interests usurp its place in the life of man. Salvation is found only when it is lifted from this ignored and excluded level relative to human concern and is made the dominant directive of human endeavor. What happened in the group about Jesus was this lifting of the creative event from the subterranean depths to the level of domination. We repeat: this did not mean any intellectual understanding of it by the disciples. Rather it occurred because Jesus and other factors present were of such sort as to release the power of this event to such a measure that it achieved domination over these lives.

This lifting to domination could not, however, by itself alone, accomplish the salvation of man. It had to be perpetuated in history. Otherwise, it could not reach you and me. It could not reach the atomic age, when salvation and destruction were to become more decisively than ever before the alternative destinies of man.

This domination is not perpetuated in the sense that any group of people lives continuously under the supreme control of this creative interchange, but it is rather perpetuated by ritual, myth, and Bible, so used and interpreted that people can always recover a sense of the supreme importance of the source of all good to be found in creative interaction. Hence the ritual and myth, the symbols and the Bible, become the "means of grace." The church is the historic continuity of these means by which men may recover a renewed access to that way of life in which creative interchange dominates the life of man as it did in the fellowship of Jesus. The perpetuating symbolism and ritual may become a hollow shell, transmitting nothing of importance; but, even so, the vital significance and function of it can be restored. On that account it continues to be, even when hollow and formal, the most precious heritage of man, for it is the means by which the creative event can again be lifted to dominate human devotion and command the complete self-giving of man to its saving and transformative power.

But we must continue the Christian story. We have told of the life of Jesus. The death of Jesus is equally important. Indeed, it is indispensable to our salvation. So long as Jesus lived, the creative event was bound to limits and confined by obstructions which would have prevented it from bringing salvation to man if Jesus had not been crucified. To see this clearly, let us transpose the situation to our own time and see it by way of an analogy.

The fourfold creative event which we have described as dominating the fellowship of Jesus is present in our own lives also. But it can work with us only so long as it measures up to the standards of American culture. Just so long as it creates good that is felt to be good by Americans, we may follow it and yield to its transforming power; but we may not allow it to transform us and our world in such a way as to include the needs and interests of Communists.

Now that is the way it was with the disciples before the Resurrection, when this creativity could work with them mightily but only within the confines of the hope of Israel and the perspective of their inherited culture. Jesus might be the Messiah, but, if so, he must do what the prophets said the Messiah was sent to do, namely, give to all the world the immeasurable blessings of the Hebrew heritage—even as Japan today sought to bless the world by giving all men the good of Japanese culture descended from heaven. Americans have the same noble impulse with regard to American democracy. In like manner, before the Resurrection, the disciples of Jesus were unable to undergo the transformations of creative interchange beyond the bounds of their cultural heritage.

What happened at the Resurrection was the breaking of these bounds, whence issued the "power of the Resurrection," about three days after the Crucifixion. When Jesus was crucified, his followers saw that he could never carry to fulfilment the mission of the Jewish people as they conceived it; hence there was no good in him of the sort that had led them to follow him. They had thought that he would save the world by making supreme over human existence the good as seen in the perspective of Jewish culture. Now they saw that he never could do anything of the sort. He was not the messiah they had expected, and, so far as they could see, he was no messiah at all. The depth of devotion and the glory of the vision they had possessed made their disillusionment all the more bitter and devastating. They had given up everything for him, and now he was shown to have no good in him of the sort they could understand or appreciate. They reached that depth of despair which comes when all that seems to give hope to human existence is seen to be an illusion. This was the immediate consequence of the Crucifixion.

After about the third day, however, when the numbness of the shock had worn away, something happened. The life-transforming creativity previously known only in fellowship with Jesus began again to work in the fellowship of the disciples. It was risen from the dead. Since they had never experienced it except in association with Jesus, it seemed to them that the man Jesus himself was actually present, walking and talking with them. Some thought they saw him and touched him in physical presence. But what rose from the dead was not the man Jesus; it was creative power. It was the living God that works in time. It was the Second Person of the Trinity. It was Christ the God, not Jesus the man.

OUR NEED OF SALVATION

If this account and analysis of what originated the Christian faith has in it any truth, it shows the reversal which human devotion must undergo if we are to be saved. What blocks the saving power of the creative event is the projection of human purpose as sovereign over it. While this blockage of creativity by human purpose could, in times past, hold man to a meager and dying level of existence, it could not bring on great destruction because man did not have sufficient power to be so destructive. Only now in the age of man's power does the domination of human purpose over the creative event bring us to the edge of the abyss.

How and why this false order of domination can be so destructive should be apparent enough. Suppose we imagine the very wisest and noblest and most righteous men given supreme authority. Suppose philosophers, in Plato's style, were kings. Suppose all men recognized them to be the noblest and best, as, in truth, they were. Thus they themselves could know themselves to be so and would thereby derive the confidence required for such high office. But the human mind cannot possibly fathom the vital needs and interests of others without the kind of interchange which we have called the "creative event." Therefore, if this creativity were subjected to the domination of the projected purpose of these good men, they would, inevitably, with their righteousness suppress and kill the good of the vast majority of other men—all this with the best intention in the world. But if these other men had some control over the power of modern technology, they would rebel against this deadly righteousness. Furthermore, these righteous men, being cut off from the source of creative intelligence, would rapidly decline in their power. So, even if they were given supreme power in the beginning they could not monopolize it continuously. Hence would arise opposed and conflicting groups. If they all, or any two opposing groups, had access to atomic energy, the dominant authority of human righteousness over the creative event might lead to the destruction of man.

Nothing is so deadly as the noblest and most righteous human purpose when it is made dominant over the creative event. The order of domination must be reversed in the age of atomic power. Creative interchange must dominate, whereby the needs and interests of others get across to me, transform my own mind, my own desires and felt needs, so as to include theirs and thereby vastly magnify the appreciable world for each and the depth of community among all. There is no other way of salvation; and the greater the power of man, the more imperative becomes the demand of the living Christ to take sovereignty over human purpose. The living Christ is the domination of the creative event as revealed in Christ two thousand years ago and perpetuated through history in the way already noted. . . .

THE GREAT TRANSITION

We are passing over one of the great divides of history; possibly it is the last high pass over the top mountain range before we enter the valley of abundance—the valley sought by man in all his wanderings since first he was man. Perhaps beyond the high pass, flinty and cold and narrow, is a region where men may live richly under the rule of a redirected devotion for a thousand years and more. But can we pass over? We see the tracks of other cultures and civilizations on the steep ascent up which we go— they go up with firmness, but they come down tottering. Shall we come down tottering, or shall we not come down at all, dying in the high pass?

That question will be answered not by the statesmen, not by the industrialists, not by the scientists and military men; for it can be answered only by religious leaders. There is a creativity in our midst, and if it be released to work as it will, we shall go over the high divide into the valley beyond. But it must be proclaimed and interpreted in terms that science can search and technology can serve.

The masses of men keep coming on; they have already reached the entrance of that narrow defile where death and life await them. Never before in all his long pilgrimage has man so fatefully met these two companions. After that meeting, either death or life will be master of man.

SUGGESTED READINGS

Henry Nelson Wieman on Christ

Wieman, Henry Nelson. *The Wrestle of Religion with Truth.* New York: Macmillan, 1927, pp. 54-67.

———. "Appreciating Jesus Christ," *The Christian Century,* 47 (1930), 1181-1184.

———. (With Douglas Clyde Macintosh and Max Carl Otto.) *Is There a God? A Conversation.* Chicago: Willett, Clark, 1932.

———. "Was God in Jesus?" *The Christian Century,* 51 (1934), 589-591.

———. "Some Blind Spots Removed," *The Christian Century,* 56 (1939), 116-118.

———. *The Source of Human Good.* Chicago: The University of Chicago Press, 1946, pp. 214-217; 263-293. Paperback—Carbondale: Southern Illinois University Press.

On Henry Nelson Wieman's Christology

Carnell, Edward John. "The Son of God," *The Empirical Theology of Henry Nelson Wieman.* Edited by Robert W. Bretall. New York: Macmillan, 1963, pp. 306-314. With a reply by Henry Nelson Wieman, pp. 315-318.

Horton, Walter Marshall. "God in Christ: Soteriology," *The Empirical Theology of Henry Nelson Wieman,* pp. 180-189. With a reply by Henry Nelson Wieman, pp. 190-193.

Loomer, Bernard M. "Wieman's Stature as a Contemporary Theologian," *The Empirical Theology of Henry Nelson Wieman,* pp. 392-397.

Williams, Daniel Day. *What Present-Day Theologians Are Thinking.* 3rd edition, revised. New York: Harper and Row, 1967, pp. 168-171. Paperback—New York: Harper Chapel Books.

PART FOUR

TEILHARD-EVOLUTION AND CHRISTIAN BELIEF

Theodosius Dobzhansky
Pierre Teilhard de Chardin
Henri de Lubac
N. M. Wildiers
Georges Crespy
Christopher F. Mooney

14 Teilhard de Chardin and the Orientation of Evolution: A Critical Essay

THEODOSIUS DOBZHANSKY

Teilhard's theology attempts to incorporate the findings of modern science, especially biology and pale-
ontology. At the core of both his theology and his
science is the concept of evolution. Around this concept he attempts to interpret the entire universe in
a process of becoming and to rethink the Christian
message in terms of a developing and convergent
world. Hence one side of his vision is bound up with
the on-going scientific exploration of the evidence for
evolution and its theoretical interpretation. The present selection * gives a scientist's response to Teilhard's synthesis—both sympathetic and critical—from
the standpoint of evolutionary biology.

*Theodosius Dobzhansky is one of the world's leading
geneticists and theoreticians of evolution. Born and
educated in Russia, he came to the United States in
1927. He taught at the California Institute of Technology, Columbia University, and the Rockefeller
University, and is presently at the University of
California in Davis, California. Like Teilhard, Dobzhansky has sought to develop an overview that
integrates biological evolution and humanistic values.*

Man does not live by bread alone; he has a
drive to understand himself and the uni-
verse in which he lives. There are several sources of understanding,

* From *Zygon*, 3 (1968), 242-258. Reprinted with permission.

and they are not equally congenial to different people. A powerful and articulate group holds that science is the sole and only valid source. At the opposite extreme are those who dismiss science as dealing with impersonal objects, and consequently irrelevant to problems of personal existence and selfhood. Such problems must, allegedly, be approached through personal involvement, art, poetry, mysticism, religious inspiration, and revelation. There is also a middle ground. Knowledge gained from science is as necessary as it is by itself insufficient. It must be supplemented by the insights of poets, artists, mystics, and by religious experience. Teilhard de Chardin stood firmly on this middle ground. I take my stand on this middle ground also, although my co-ordinates are not quite the same as Teilhard's.

The enterprise of science is at the same time highly individualized and socialized. Scientific facts are discovered, scientific laws are formulated, and theories are constructed by individual scientists. Even where scientific research is carried on by groups or "teams," the contributions of the participants are as a rule recognizably individual. And yet the scientific movement is a corporate venture. It has its rules of the game. The basic rule is dispassionate objectivity. This does not mean that a scientist has no personal involvement in his work and no emotional attachment to its results. Any scientist worth his salt has both. Objectivity means only that observations and conclusions are recorded irrespective of whether they do or do not please the observer. Some beginners like to describe the difficulties they had and the hard labor they invested in their work; they have to be taught that this kind of information may be of interest only for their autobiographies or obituaries, and it does not belong in scientific publications. What matters are the results, not the difficulties. Science is mostly public rather than personal knowledge. Again, this does not mean that anybody can easily verify any scientific fact or theory to his satisfaction. Most of the "public" would have no idea how to go about such verification. Competence in science requires prolonged preparation and hard work; those willing and able to struggle through, however, will master at least that particular line of scientific endeavor which they find most interesting.

The public character of science means also that the same science is valid everywhere. The talk about bourgeois science,

Communist science, Aryan science, Jewish science is rubbish. Hitler's racist "science" made as little sense in Germany as Lysenko's "michurinist science" made in Stalin's Russia, and vice versa. It is not an exaggeration to say that scientists form a subculture, international in scope, and distinguishable from the cultures and subcultures of the nations to which the scientists belong. The rules of the scientific game are not officially codified, yet are freely accepted and occasionally enforced. The scientific subculture has its specialized language and its patterns of thought. There ought to be no secret science; secrecy is incompatible with the mores of the scientific community. Because science is public rather than private or occult knowledge, it has a high degree of reliability and acceptance. It is really not a matter of personal taste, disposition, or preference whether to accept or to reject a scientific finding, a hypothesis, or a theory. After due consideration and repeated testing, the scientific community usually approaches a consensus, which becomes effectively binding to its members. This does not mean that anything in science is immune to questioning. Quite the opposite; any scientific statement is open to challenge. Yet at any given state of scientific knowledge, certain views command acceptance and others are rejected. Thus, any informed person accepts that biological evolution has taken place. This is not because the evolution theory has become a "fact." A theory is based on facts, but it can never be transformed into a fact. Anti-evolutionists are outside the pale of the scientific community; they regard this an injustice, yet there is no other way, since they are unable to produce facts or arguments against evolution which stand scrutiny. However unlikely, it is thinkable that some day such facts will be discovered; if so, a revision of the whole of biology will become necessary.

TEILHARD'S BLEND OF SCIENCE AND MYSTICISM

Teilhard de Chardin was an eminent scientist. His purely scientific writings are, however, seldom read, except by geologists and paleontologists. There is, to my knowledge, no plan afoot, to publish a complete collection of Teilhard's works, including his technical papers. Had he written only these papers, he would be remembered as a contributor to his special field of science. He was, however, more than a scientist; he was also a mystic and a poet.

This is not altogether exceptional; there were other scientists who had, with more or less success, written poetry and the products of their mystical insights. Teilhard was not content to keep his science, his mysticism, his poetry, and his religion in separate compartments. He reached for a synthesis. In so doing, he collided with the accepted mores of both communities to which he belonged—the scientific and the religious. What many members of these communities failed to see, and many of them still fail to see, is that Teilhard did not seek to deduce, or even to support, his religious convictions by his scientific findings. Teilhard's writings are not natural theology; they deal with a theology of nature. Violent, and even venomous, attacks on Teilhard have been made by some scientists. This could be understood, if not excused, if all Teilhard's books were scientific monographs. In an unguarded moment, Teilhard claimed this for his major work, *The Phenomenon of Man*. Yet it is more than that: an attempt to formulate a world view, a Weltanschauung. His world view includes science as one of the components, though one of cardinal importance.

Raw materials of science are sense data. However, these sense data are recorded and interpreted by human observers, and this is where the personality of the scientist unavoidably enters. Nevertheless, the language of science is a spectator language, not an actor or participant language. It is the opposite in the arts, poetry, mysticism, and religion. A poet aims to convey some of his personal emotions or insights by composing word patterns in which subtly allusionary and metaphorical, rather than the everyday, meanings of words are often predominant. Mystical and religious experiences are basically ineffable and can be communicated only by means of parables, symbols, paradoxes, if at all. An actor or participant language, if mistaken for a spectator language, may strike one as incoherent and even absurd. Teilhard has, in developing and presenting his synthesis, unavoidably used both spectator and participant languages. Let it also not be forgotten that poetry is notoriously difficult to translate into foreign languages, except perhaps by other poets whose perceptions are attuned to the poetry of the original. Mere knowledge of, say, English equivalents of the French words used by Teilhard is far from sufficient. Teilhard coined many of his own words and used many existing words, giving them his own special meanings; so much so that one of his French followers has published a dictionary of the Teilhardese. I have not seen this work, and it would probably be of small help to English readers.

Teilhard's failure to separate clearly his scientific generalizations from his mystical insights has been often regretted. To some extent, that is indeed unfortunate. Two things must, however, be said in this connection. First, it was his synthesis that Teilhard intended to communicate: his vision of the evolving universe, illuminated by his personal religious experience and his poetic inspiration. Second, Teilhard did not in the least try to hide his mysticism. One is liable to get a very incomplete picture of his Weltanschauung if one reads only *The Phenomenon of Man*. Though it is his chief work, it is a sequel to many previous essays in which ideas are presented that are taken almost for granted in *The Phenomenon of Man*. Teilhard's mystical vision and religious exaltation come through very clearly in, for example, *La Messe sure le monde, Le Christ dans la Matière,* and *Le Milieu divin.*

EVOLUTION—GENERAL AND PARTICULAR

There is no satisfactory or accepted definition of evolution. Evolution is change, but not all change is evolution. A most restrictive definition would recognize only biological evolution. The elementary events of which biological evolution is composed are easily specifiable—they are changes in the gene frequencies in living populations. Emergence of strains of bacteria resistant to antibiotics, or of insects resistant to insecticides, is a paradigm. Accumulation and integration of such genetic events over long periods of time lead to major biological change; it can transform an amoeba, or a primordial virus, into man or into an oak tree. Some three billion years ago life first arose on the planet earth, and possibly elsewhere in the cosmos, as a result of a complex series of changes in the inorganic nature. And perhaps some two million years ago biological evolution produced an extraordinary species, mankind, capable of abstract thought, communication by symbolic language, and endowed with self-awareness and death awareness. Radical changes must have intervened between the "Big Bang," which five to ten billion years ago started the formation of chemical elements, and the appearance of conditions which made the origin of life possible. These changes constitute the cosmic, or inorganic, evolution. Mankind became the protagonist of a history in which the biological changes are outweighed, though not abolished, by changes in the cultural heredity, transmitted by instruction and learning. History of mankind is, in the main, evolution of culture.

The inorganic, organic, and cultural evolutions are constituent parts of the one grand process of universal evolution. Teilhard thought about evolution always in this inclusive sense. The broad definition of evolution should not be construed as an underestimate of the basic differences between the prebiological, biological, and the cultural (and, in a sense, postbiological) phases. They occur in different dimensions, or on different levels, of existence. On each succeeding level, we discover laws and regularities which do not apply to preceding levels. A single example will suffice here. Some authors like to describe the origin of life from non-living nature as a result of a kind of a natural selection; the history of culture is also alleged to be governed by a natural selection of ideas, instead of genes. This is perhaps acceptable as an instructive analogy, but miscomprehension results if the analogy is mistaken for a basic similarity or identity. Natural selection is differential reproduction of the carriers of different hereditary endowments. It could not start before there were self-reproducing systems capable of undergoing mutational changes. Such systems are already living, by any reasonable definition. Rivalry of ideas is not natural selection either; ideas do not reproduce themselves, except in an allegorical sense.

Universal evolution, and also biological evolution, can be considered in two aspects, which I would like to call the particular and the general. For example, one may investigate and describe the changes which took place in the evolution of the horse family, or in the ancestry of man, or in a given solar and planetary system, or in the Greco-Roman civilization. On the other hand, one may seek a general view of the universal evolution as a whole, or of the inorganic, organic, and human evolution as wholes. The general can hardly be investigated apart from the particular, and of necessity a lion's share of evolutionary studies is concerned with particular evolutionary histories. And yet some scientists are by preference generalists, and others are specialists and particularists.

Teilhard has carried out several studies of particular histories of certain groups of fossils. What inspired him most was, however, not the particular but the general. Another characteristic of Teilhard's approach must be mentioned. Although his scientific life spanned the period when biology was making rapid advances in discovery of the causation of evolutionary changes, he had, perhaps surprisingly, little interest in or knowledge of these advances.

Chromosomes, genes, biochemical foundations of the evolutionary changes, the mechanisms of adaptation and of race and species formation, all these and many other important problems are rarely or not at all mentioned in his writings. This was, indisputably, a serious weakness; it made Teilhard the target of some not wholly unjustified criticisms by other scientists. On the other hand, it is too easy to criticize books for not being what their authors did not intend them to be. To Teilhard, only the universal evolution, considered as a whole, appeared meaningful. He viewed the evolution of the universe as a single creative process, composed of the inorganic, organic, and human phases. The particular histories are sequences of unique events; in the organic and the human histories these events are more and more individualized, and their sequences are unrepeatable. Yet when considered in the perspective of the evolution as a whole, these events cohere into a meaningful pattern. There seems to be a general direction or trend, which Teilhard found possible to discern. He went even further. If one understands what evolution has achieved from the beginning of the universe, say from the "Big Bang" to the present, then it may be possible to extrapolate and thus to predict its likely future course, from the present to eternity. This certainly was an audacity which few other evolutionists ever possessed.

CHANCE AND ANTI-CHANCE IN PARTICULAR EVOLUTIONS

The problem of directedness or directionality of evolution is an old one. It was debated by many authors before and after Teilhard. Condorcet was the first, or one of the first, to claim that the history of mankind moves in a discernible direction, through stages from primitive savagery to eventual perfection. Danilevsky, Spengler, Sorokin, and others saw the histories of civilizations moving in circles. Toynbee discerns cyclic movements as well as a general forward trend. Still others see no general direction at all. No force, agency, or general principle is, however, discernible guiding the particular events of which the history of humanity is composed.

These events are neither all good nor all evil, neither all aimed toward progress nor toward conservation, neither all guided by economic interests nor all by spiritual interests of the peoples involved.

In the biological realm, the causation of the particular evolutionary changes is at present reasonably well understood. The process of mutation yields the raw materials from which the evolutionary changes are compounded. The compounding is done by natural selection. Mutation is said to be a chance or random process. This is valid only in the sense that mutations arise regardless of whether they may be useful or harmful to a given kind of organism at a given time, or ever. In point of fact, most mutations are deleterious, and not a few are lethal. Which mutation arises in a given gene depends, however, on the structure of that gene and, consequently, is not a matter of chance alone. On the other hand, a gene can change presumably in numerous different ways, so an element of chance is introduced again.

Natural selection is, on the contrary, an anti-chance process. The selection perpetuates genetic constitutions which are adaptive in a given environment and fails to perpetuate the less well-adapted ones. The measure of the adaptedness is the reproductive performance of the carriers of a given genotype in relation to the performance of other genotypes in the same environment. The surviving "fittest" is then, contrary to the nineteenth-century views, nothing more remarkable than a parent of the most numerous viable progeny! Natural selection is a process conveying "information" about the state of the environment to the genotypes of its inhabitants.

It is nevertheless misleading to say that evolutionary changes are directed by the environment. The situation is actually more subtle. The environments present challenges to a living species—to which the latter may or may not respond by adaptive alterations—of its hereditary endowment. Successful responses mean survival, spread, and, sometimes, conquest of new opportunities for living; failure to respond, or a wrong response, may end in extinction. The environment is, however, neither static nor changing always in the same direction.

Teilhard was rather skeptical concerning the role of natural selection in biological evolution. Nevertheless, he gave a most apt characterization of the course of evolution, which can apply only to evolution by natural selection. Evolution proceeds by groping (*tâtonnement*). A living species is groping, as though in the dark, for possibilities to survive and to spread. The groping may, however, end in breakdown and extinction, as well as in survival and discovery of new modes of life. Groping is evidently the antithesis of directedness. Particular evolutionary changes, at least on the biological level, show no indication of being, in any meaningful sense, directional.

GENERAL EVOLUTION—DIRECTED OR DIRECTIONAL?

Lack of directionality in particular evolutionary changes does not preclude the possibility that it may be present in general evolution. The achievements of the evolutionary process can be described in both a spectator and a participant language. Conditions propitious for the origin of life have arisen as a result of stellar and planetary evolution, at least on earth and possibly elsewhere in the cosmos. Whether life arose on earth only once or repeatedly we do not know, but in at least one instance the newly arisen life was not snuffed out by hostile environments. On the contrary, life spread, evolved, and became marvelously diversified. There are about two million known species now living on earth, and possibly as many or even more as yet undescribed ones. Some of these forms of life appear to us strange, bizarre, almost whimsical creatures. Each and every one of them has, however, its ecological niche carved out of nature's domain. Some two million years ago, quite recently on the cosmic time scale, biological evolution transcended itself by giving rise to an extraordinary being, man. Mankind evolves not only by means of genetic changes as do all other living species, but also, and even mainly, by changes in what people learn themselves and teach to others.

Man is both an observer and an actor in the drama of evolution. Can one validly make the statement in both a spectator's and a participant's languages that evolution has been on the whole progressive? Despite numerous attempts, biologists have not succeeded in formulating a rigorous definition of what constitutes progress in biological evolution. And yet the progress is intuitively evident. As Ian Barbour put it, "By almost any standard, man represents a higher level than primeval mud." A biologist would go further: a bacterium represents a higher level than a virus, worm higher than bacterium, fish higher than worm, dog higher than fish, and man higher than dog. It must, however, be made very clear that evolutionary progress did not mean that lower organisms were in time always replaced by higher ones. Higher and lower organisms often coexist, each in its ecological niche.

Many forms of life, both low and high ones, ended in the history of the earth by becoming extinct. Extinction is the price which has to be paid for evolution by groping. If particular evolutionary histories were all directed, extinction would be inexplicable. A direction which leads to extinction is misdirection. On the contrary, extinction of some branches of the evolutionary tree is virtually certain to occur if evolution proceeds by groping, that is, by natural selection. The same applies to human societies. By almost any standard, our society represents a level higher than that of paleolithic hunters or of a band of australopithecines. Nevertheless, some primitive societies, though their days may be numbered, still exist alongside the burgeoning giant—the cosmopolitan, industrial civilization. Many societies of which historical records are available became lost, and doubtless many which left no record suffered the same fate. Nineteenth-century evolutionists might have said that the highway of progress is strewn with corpses. We are no longer so fond of such metaphors.

Teilhard's attention was firmly riveted to general evolution. His vision revealed to him that, "from the beginning stages of its evolution, the living matter which covers the earth manifests the contours of a single gigantic organism." In this planetary, or even cosmic, supraorganism he saw a process of paramount importance taking place, namely, "The grand orthogenesis of all that lives towards greater immanent spontaneity. . . . Without orthogenesis life would only spread; with orthogenesis there is the invincible ascent of life."

Teilhard at this point made no distinction between the general evolution of his planetary supra-organism and the particular evolutionary transformations. He erroneously believed that mutations "add up, and their sum grows in a predetermined direction." He thus seemed to accept, without considering them closely and critically, the orthogenetic and finalistic interpretations of evolution which were rather popular, at least in continental Europe, during the 1920's. Finalists, of whom Lecomte du Nöuy was a more recent and widely read representative, assumed a guidance of evolution by supernatural forces, or directly by God. There were several versions of orthogenesis. The assumption common to all of them was the evolutionary changes proceed in a predetermined direction, owing to forces "within" the organism. Versions bordering on finalism pòstulated a guiding agent transcending biology and physics, yet immanent in the organism itself. A more mechanistic version (that of L. S. Berg) envisaged the hereditary endowment constructed in a manner analogous to atoms of radioactive elements, which undergo predetermined changes in a fixed order. All theories of the above sorts are flagrantly inconsistent with Teilhard's own view that evolution proceeds by "groping." The inconsistency is not removed by the paradoxical assertion that "the groping is not chance alone . . . but directed chance." Yes, the groping is "directed" indeed by the anti-chance agency called "natural selection."

The evolution of the universe is directional, although not necessarily directed. There is no discernible directionality in particular evolutionary histories. This apparent contradiction is seen most clearly in biological evolution. The environment presents challenges to which the species living in its respond by genetic alterations. The alterations are usually adaptive, that is, as a rule they promote a harmonious adjustment of life to its environment. The alterations are, however, often opportunistic; they are adaptive in the environments which exist here and now and may be injurious in future environments. A species deeply specialized and committed to deal with its present environment may have lost its evolutionary plasticity. This is a consequence of "groping," and the groping often ends in extinction. And yet the three billion years of opportunistic groping have resulted, on earth, in some of the descendants of the "primeval mud" becoming marvelously contrived living systems which dominate their environments. One of these living systems has transcended biology by evolving self-awareness and death awareness. Teilhard's planetary supra-organism has risen certainly above the level of the primeval mud.

Except in man, no indications of planning, design, or conscious impulsion can be seen in evolution. Man and man alone has discovered that he is a product of an evolutionary process and that this process is still going on. Man may gain enough knowledge to direct the evolution of his own and of other species, ultimately perhaps that of the whole universe. If so, it will be man who will choose the direction and the goal, in accord with the dictates of his wisdom or unwisdom. Yet, if the evolution thus far was neither planned nor directed, how are its achievements explained? It was often progressive, despite some cases of standstill and of regressive episodes. Teilhard tried to answer this question in a poetic, participant's, rather than in a drier, spectator's language.

Things have their "insides" and their "outsides." [1] These are coextensive; the "inside" has, however, elements of consciousness and of spontaneity. Moreover, all energy is basically psychic [2] in nature. Energy "is divided into two distinct components: a tangential energy which links each element with all other elements of the same order (i.e., of the same complexity and the same 'centeredness') as itself in the universe; and a radial energy which draws towards ever greater complexity and centeredness, in other words forwards." Now, Teilhard surely does not claim to have discovered two new kinds of energy previously unknown to physicists and to physiologists. Things may, however, be observed and studied in isolation or in their interrelations with the rest of the world. One may investigate things as they are or may try to discover how they got to be what they are and what they are likely to become in the future. When phenomena are studied in their connectedness, questions arise about their meaning and value in the general scheme of things and in the personal world view of the investigator. Questions of this last sort were basic in the highly personalistic approach to the world so characteristic of Teilhard's thinking and writing.

The achievements of the evolutionary process came about, in Ian Barbour's words, "not because of divine intervention but because of laws built into its structure. It would be precisely the operation of these laws—not their violation—which has brought about the intended result, and thereby displayed the divine purpose." Modern cosmological theories disclose a kind of orthogene-

[1] In the original, "le dedans" and "le dehors," rendered in English also as "the within" and "the without."

[2] In the first English translation (*The Phenomenon of Man*, p. 64), this is mistakenly printed "physical in nature," but this has been corrected in the paperback edition.

sis (although this term is not used) in stellar evolution. There is a "main sequence" of stars, as well as its turns leading to "red giants" and "white dwarfs." A star burns its hydrogen "fuel" by means of thermonuclear reactions transforming hydrogen into helium and, further, its helium into carbon[12], oxygen[16], and neon[20] with liberation of enormous amounts of energy. The surface temperature of a star and the emission of light change with the star's age; there may supervene a gravitational collapse, a sudden explosion with rapid release of more energy, and eventual "death" when the energy supply finally falls to low levels. This evolution is, at least as described by cosmologists, more rigidly directional and hence considerably less "free" than biological evolution. There is nothing, however, to suggest individual stars being stirred on their evolutionary courses by anything other than the general laws applying to all of them.

In biological evolution there is, as stated above, no orthogenesis. The groping course introduces an element of freedom, although evidently of freedom not in human sense. There is, rather, an interesting kind of indeterminacy; evolution is a succession of unique and unrepeatable events, and the events which actually occur are drawn out of vastly greater numbers of potentially possible events, most of which are never realized. Evolutionary changes, excepting the most elementary ones like mutations which confer drug resistance on bacteria, are irreversible and unrepeatable. This is not because of any mysterious force which prevents their repetition, but simply because exact repetition has a probability close to zero.

The evolution on earth has culminated in man. It is most unlikely that anything even remotely like man has merged in the evolution of extraterrestrial life, even if such existed; it is just as unlikely that, if mankind were destroyed or destroyed itself, a new mankind would evolve again. Suppose, however, that extraterrestrial life does exist, or that the life on earth will be destroyed and will arise again. If this were so, and if the new life did not become extinct soon after its origin, then this life would be virtually certain to undergo an evolutionary development and diversification. Moreover, this evolutionary development would, despite many false starts and blind alleys, be on the whole progressive. Only a very rash or very ignorant biologist could venture predictions as to just what sort of a living world would develop, except that it would not be the same as the one which actually exists on our earth at present.

For a biological evolution to occur, two necessary and sufficient conditions must be present: heredity and mutation. A corollary of these two is natural selection. Natural selection is the anti-chance agent which makes evolution in a sense directional: at least in a short run, evolution tends to be adaptive to the environment. Heredity rests on the ability of certain molecules or molecular aggregates to reproduce themselves, that is, to induce synthesis of their true copies from materials available in the environment. Heredity is a fundamental property of life. It provides a continuity and stability of the living systems. Yet the precision of heredity falls short of perfection. The self-copying is sometimes inexact; the new, mutant entity reproduces, however, its altered structure with a fidelity of about the same order as did the original one. In other words, an absolute fidelity of the process of copying and self-reproduction would make evolution impossible, and incessant mutability would make maintenance of life unlikely. In reality, mutations occur from time to time probably in all kinds of organisms. This is not surprising; the wonder is, rather, that the self-reproduction is generally as precise as it is, not that on rare occasions some mistakes do occur.

In sum, biological evolution is not directed but is directional, in the sense that it tends generally toward maintenance or betterment of the adaptedness to the environment. This is what Teilhard's "radial energy" really means in the living world. In *Some Reflections on Progress* (1941), he wrote: ". . . the fact remains that for 300 million years life has paradoxically flourished in the improbable. Does not this suggest that its advance may be sustained by some sort of complicity on the part of the 'blind' forces of the universe—that is to say that its advance is inexorable?" Yes, indeed, life has paradoxically flourished and apparently not for three hundred million but three billion years! Let us, however, try to pinpoint where the "complicity" resides; it seems to be a consequence of the basic properties of all living matter—heredity and mutability. They make the adaptedness of evolutionary changes not exactly "inexorable" but at least very probable.

We do not know what primeval life was like. It is, however, a good guess that it was initially frail and that it could perpetuate itself only under some particularly favorable conditions, available perhaps in only a few places. Perhaps life arose repeatedly from a non-living, inert matrix. If so, most of these feeble beginners soon flickered out. At least one has, however, secured a firmer hold on its environment, multiplied, spread, and inherited the earth. We are its descendants. J. M. Thoday very perceptively pointed out that the probability of a unit of evolution having living descendants after the lapse of a long period of time is a meaningful criterion of fitness, durability, and of evolutionary progress. Primordial life had, in this sense, very low fitness, since it was at the mercy of its environment. By a lucky chance, one of its beginnings survived, however, and its descendants gradually mastered more and more environmental opportunities. The mastery of the environment has reached its climax in man. Mankind is unlikely to become extinct, except as a result of a suicidal folly of its own. It is the apex of evolutionary progress to date.

MANKIND—THE PRIVILEGED AXIS

Teilhard complained that "men's minds are reluctant to recognize that evolution has a precise orientation and a privileged axis." The orientation, the "Ariadne's thread," is toward "cerebralization," rise of consciousness, of self-awareness—in short, toward mankind. Since we are not only spectators but also participants in the evolutionary process, an anthropocentric absorption is legitimate and in fact unavoidable. To man, the limb and the twig of the evolutionary tree leading to mankind indeed compose the privileged axis. The universe without man is meaningless. Any theodicy must necessarily make sense of the evolution as a whole, not of the human part alone. For otherwise what was God doing during the eons before mankind finally appeared? These eons are, to us, inevitably preparatory for the entrance of mankind on the cosmic scene. Teilhard has forcefully and eloquently made this clear.

A complementary analysis of the evolutionary process is just as legitimate and necessary. Evolutionary progress in general, and the emergence of man in particular, were neither foreordained nor were they lucky accidents in the cosmic game of chance. Was man latently present, but hidden and undeveloped, in the "Big

Bang" at the beginning of the universe? This is trivial—a positive answer means only that man has in fact appeared. The same answer becomes misleading if it implies that some privileged axis was impelled, by its own constitution or by somebody's volition, to grow in the direction of man, regardless of its surroundings, of its environment in the widest sense of that word. Biological evolution consists, as stated above, of genetic responses of living species to the challenges of their environments. In the animal kingdom, the development of sense organs and of central nervous systems are examples of highly successful responses. In a single evolutionary line, that of mankind, there were added the crowning achievements —a capacity for symbolic thought, communication by language, and finally self-awareness and death awareness. A privileged status can objectively be claimed for this line in one sense only— that it has evolved a quite novel and highly effective form of adaptedness, transcending anything known in other animals. This, to be sure, is a great enough distinction. The evolution in the "privileged" line was, however, brought about by the same causes as in the unprivileged ones.

The finalist view, that either evolution in general, or at least that of the privileged line, was planned and piloted by some transcendental or occult forces, may be rejected as unnecessary and unenlightening as far as scientific understanding is concerned. There is, however, a debate among philosophers and theologians as to whether the past, the present, and the future are equally known to God and are simultaneously present to his view. Traditionalist religions answer this question in the positive, since God is believed to be omniscient. This amounts, however, to a denial of any genuine novelty or contingency in the cosmogenesis. The beginning and the culmination of the cosmos are equally predetermined and are exactly known to God, although not necessarily to man.

A different view is suggested by some process philosophers, especially Whitehead and Hartshorne, and by their followers among the theologians. God possesses a perfect knowledge of the past and the present, but not of the future. The future is not completely predestined because the world contains elements of freedom. Genuine alternatives do exist in cosmogenesis, and particularly in human evolution or noogenesis, to use Teilhard's term. God has voluntarily limited his omniscience and omnipotence in order to endow his creation with freedom. Freedom is a divine gift, and its range increases as evolution proceeds.

Though Teilhard was apparently unfamiliar with White-head's philosophy, he had to deal with the problem of evolutionary determinism and freedom. This problem presents itself most insistently when human evolution, noogenesis, is considered. Mankind has reached the level of reflection and self-awareness. Moreover, man has discovered the phenomenon of evolution. Neither in the biological nor in the cultural dimensions is man any longer obliged to accept the evolutionary direction of blind forces of nature. Man can choose the direction himself. Being, within certain limits, a free agent, man can make wrong as well as right choices. In Teilhard's words: "The possibility must be faced that mankind will suddenly fall out of love with its own destiny," and also, "The components of the world may refuse to serve the world, because they think. More precisely, the world may refuse itself, perceiving itself through reflexion." Yet a refusal is improbable: "My purpose is not to show the existence of a necessary and infallible line of progress, but simply that for mankind as a whole a way of progress is offered and awaits us, analogous to that which the individual cannot reject without falling into sin and damnation." Teilhard was consistently optimistic, and although he realized that "sin and damnation" are possible, he felt secure that mankind will not choose the wrong road.

Optimism is a commodity in short supply in the modern world. Teilhard's optimism is surely one of the reasons for the wide appeal of his thought. The universe is not an absurdity, it is a cosmos, an increasingly orderly system; its history is not a farce but the cosmogenesis, the Creator's enterprise. The cosmogenesis had started before mankind appeared on the scene. The billions of years of the inorganic evolution are seen in retrospect as preparatory for the appearance of life; the billions of years of organic evolution were preparatory for the appearance of man. And one hopes that the presently known two million years of human evolution (in Teilhard's days, the estimates were even shorter than our present ones) must be preparatory for some sublime and infinitely precious future. The evolution of mankind is in the main the evolution of thought, noogenesis. And, "In the direction of thought,

can the universe terminate in anything less than the measureless.
. . ?" To Teilhard, this was far more than an inference from his
scientific knowledge: "By definition and in its essence Christianity
is the religion of the Incarnation: God uniting himself with the
world which he created, to unify it and in some way to incorporate
it in himself." The ultimate goal of evolution is God-Omega.

The Omega is evidently no extrapolation, however bold, from
scientific data. It is a prophetic vision. It is derived (although,
perhaps strangely, Teilhard does not mention its source) from that
other vision recorded in the Book of Revelation: "I am the Alpha
and the Omega, the first and the last, the beginning and the end."
The question that immediately suggests itself, is on what grounds
we can be sure that the noogenesis is indeed directed toward, and
will actually culminate in, the Omega. Can we ignore the potentiality of error and evil which are implicit in the gift of freedom which
mankind received? Teilhard offers really no more than his assurance that it is simply unthinkable that the billions of years of
cosmogenesis will finally come to naught. He is sustained by his
religious faith and his mystical insight: "Let us suppose that from
this universal center, the Omega point, there constantly emanate
radiations hitherto only perceptible to those whom we call 'mystics.'
Let us further imagine that, as the sensibility or response to
mysticism of the human race increases with the planetisation, the
awareness of Omega becomes so widespread as to warm the
earth psychically while physically it is growing cold. Is it not conceivable that mankind . . . will detach itself from this planet and
join the one true irreversible essence of things, the Omega point?"

Teilhard's predictions of the direction and the goal of cosmogenesis and noogenesis do not belong to the category of verifi-
able "public" knowledge. They are not derived from scientific
data and cannot be tested by experiments, but only by following
their author along the path of his faith and his mystical experience.
It is nevertheless senseless to attempt to purge the Teilhardian
synthesis of its religious, mystical, and poetic components, as some
authors (e.g., Julian Huxley) tried to do. The value of the Teilhardian intellectual legacy lies precisely in his synthesis; the scientific and the religious components of the synthesis are not detach-
able from each other without making the whole lose its meaning.
This is not to say that the synthesis is final and needs no revision

and improvement. Such a claim would surely have been rejected by Teilhard as contrary to his convictions. No apology is therefore necessary for the present essay being in part critical.

Teilhard aimed at no less than a total integrated system of thought, which would show to modern man that he is placed on this earth not through some silly accident but that he is the vanguard of the billions of years of cosmogenesis and noogenesis. In this system of thought, science is an essential component, but only a component. The other components do not conform to the patterns of thought of the scientific community and, consequently, do not command acceptance to the same degree as do scientific theories. It is nevertheless important that these other components are also not contradictory to any scientifically established facts or to scientific theories generally considered as valid. Nothing like Teilhardian synthesis could have been attempted by anyone lacking a first-hand familiarity with science. Yet Teilhard makes it abundantly clear that his message is addressed to the whole of mankind, not to scientists alone. "No evolutionary future awaits man except in association with all other men." Teilhard let slip in his now-published correspondence some statements which show that he was far from being a democrat. He nevertheless realized that "It is mankind as a whole, collective humanity, which is called upon to perform the definitive act whereby the total force of terrestrial evolution will be released and flourish; an act in which the full consciousness of each individual man will be sustained by that of every other man, not only living but the dead." Teilhard's religion was that of a great thinker who was aware that he lived in an age of science.

SUGGESTED READINGS

On Scientific Evolution and Theology

Barbour, Ian G. *Issues in Science and Religion.* Englewood Cliffs, N.J.: Prentice-Hall, 1966.

Dobzhansky, Theodosius. *The Biology of Ultimate Concern.* New York: The New American Library, 1967. Paperback—New York: Meridian Books.

Francoeur, Robert. *Perspectives in Evolution.* Baltimore: Helicon, 1965.

————. *Evolving World, Converging Man.* New York: Holt, Rinehart and Winston, 1970.

Haselden, Kyle and Philip Hefner (eds.). *Changing Man: The Threat and the Promise: Five Scientists and Five Theologians on Christian Faith and Evolutionary Thought.* Garden City, N.Y.: Doubleday, 1968. Paperback–Garden City, N.Y.: Anchor Books.

Nogar, Raymond J., O.P. *The Wisdom of Evolution.* Garden City, N.Y.: Doubleday, 1963. Paperback–New York: Mentor-Omega.

15 My Universe

PIERRE TEILHARD DE CHARDIN

From a theological standpoint, Teilhard is concerned chiefly with Christology, specifically with the role of Christ in an evolving and convergent universe. Although Teilhard does not reject or bypass the historical Christ, he focuses his attention on the cosmic Christ. Throughout his writings one theme is paramount: that Christ is present throughout the physical universe and that he exerts a force drawing all things towards a developing and converging unity. This theme so permeates Teilhard's writings that many texts could be chosen as representative. The following passage * has the advantage of giving Teilhard's own grounding of the cosmic Christ in Scripture and his understanding of Christ as physically active throughout the universe. Although this piece was written early in his career, 1924, it expresses the essential elements of his Christology, which his later writings would develop but not alter.

Born in France in 1881, Pierre Teilhard de Chardin was a Jesuit priest and scientist. After receiving a doctorate in geology from the Sorbonne, he spent much of his life in paleontological research in China, with travel also to Southeast Asia and Africa. His last years were spent in New York City, where he died in 1955. Since his death, more than fifteen volumes of his writings have been published, along with countless studies of his thought.

* From *My Universe*, published in *Science and Christ*, trans. René Hague (New York: Harper and Row, 1968), pp. 54-60. Reprinted with permission.

A. Christ is Identical with Omega

In order to demonstrate the truth of this fundamental proposition, I need only refer to the long series of Johannine—and still more Pauline—texts in which the physical supremacy of Christ over the universe is so magnificently expressed.[1] I cannot quote them all here, but they come down to these two essential affirmations: 'In eo omnia constant' (Col. 1. 17), and 'Ipse est qui replet omnia' (Col. 2. 10, cf. Eph. 4. 9), from which it follows that 'Omnia in omnibus Christus' (Col. 3. 11)—the very definition of omega. I am very well aware that there are two loopholes by which timid minds hope to escape the awesome realism of these repeated statements. They may maintain that the cosmic attributes of the Pauline Christ belong to the Godhead alone; or they may try to weaken the force of the texts by supposing that the ties of dependence that make the world subject to Christ are juridical and moral, the rights exercised by a landowner, a father or the head of an association. As regards the first subterfuge, all I need to do is to refer to the context, which is categorical: even in Col. 1. 15 ff, St Paul quite obviously has in mind the theandric Christ; it was in the Incarnate Christ that the universe was pre-formed. As regards the weakened interpretation of the Apostle's words, I dismiss it simply because it is less in conformity with the spirit of St Paul as it animates the body of his Epistles, and less, too, in conformity with my general view of the world. However, I have given up hope of converting those who reject my version. I have, in fact, become convinced that men include two irreconcilable types of minds: the physicalists (who are 'mystics') and the juridicists. For the former, the whole beauty of life consists in being organically structured; and in consequence Christ, being preeminently attractive, must radiate physically.[2] For the latter, being

---

[1] See, in particular, St. Paul: Rom. 8. 18 sq.; 14. 7, 9; 1 Cor. 4. 22; 6. 15 sq.; 10. 16; 12. 12 sq.; 15. 23-9; 39 sq.; 2 Cor. 3. 18; 4. 11; 5. 4; 19; Gal. 3. 27, 28; Eph. 1.10, 19-23; 2. 5, 10, 13, 14; 3. 6, 18; 4. 9, 12, 13, 16; Phil. 2. 10; 3, 10, 11, 20-1; Col. 1. 15-20, 28; 2. 9, 10, 12, 19; 3. 10; 1 Thess. 4. 17; Heb. 2. 7-8. (Ed.)

[2] This reasoning, which assumes that the *Reality* of Christ is gradually *defined by the increasing requirements* of *our ideal*, is legitimate. It is not because Christ is the most beautiful being that is, absolutely, possible (does that, in any case, mean anything?), but because he is the most beautiful relatively to us (since it is he who fulfils us), that we are justified in saying:

is embarrassing as soon as it disguises something vaster and less patient of definition than our human social relationships (considered from the point of view of their artificial content). Christ, accordingly, is no more than a king or a great landowner. These (the juridicists), logically inconsistent with their theology of grace, will always understand 'mystical' (in 'mystical body') by analogy with a somewhat stronger family association or association of friends. The physicalists, however, will see in the word mystical the expression of a hyper-physical (super-substantial) relationship —stronger, and in consequence more respectful of embodied individualities, than that which operates between the cells of one and the same animate organism. The two types of mind will never understand one another, and the choice between the two attitudes must be made not by reasoning but by insight. For my own part, it has been made, irrevocably and as long as I can remember. I am a physicalist by instinct: and that is why it is impossible for me to read St Paul without seeing the universal and cosmic domination of the Incarnate Word emerging from his words with dazzling clarity.

This is the point we must bear in mind: in no case could the cosmos be conceived, and realised, without a supreme centre of spiritual consistence. It would be most unreasonable to imagine the separate creation of an atom or a group of monads, not only in view of the particular principles expressed in creative union, but simply as a matter of sound metaphysics. The goal before Creation and attained by Creation is in the first place the whole, and then, in and after the whole, all the rest. On any hypothesis, if the world is to be thinkable it must be centred. The presence, therefore, at its head, of an omega has nothing to do with the fact of its 'supernatural elevation'. What gives the world its 'gratuitous' character is precisely that the position of universal centre has not been given to any supreme intermediary between God and the uni-

---

'This is more beautiful than that: *therefore* it is this, and not that, which belongs to Christ.' The difficult problem for Christian thought (and the stimulus behind the evolution of dogma) is precisely to maintain at all times in Christ the plenitude of these three attributes: being at the same time historic, universal and ideal. To be 'ideal' is a way of being universal; it is to be capable of meeting the aspirations of mankind of all periods. One might also say, reciprocally, that Christ must be universal because our ideal demands his universality.

verse, but has been occupied by the Divinity himself—who has thus introduced us 'in et cum Mundo' into the triune heart of his immanence.

That, then, will suffice to make any theological position clear. Now to look more closely, in its physical potency, at the Mystery of Christ.

B. THE INFLUENCE OF CHRIST-OMEGA
THE UNIVERSAL ELEMENT

Having noted that the Pauline Christ (the great Christ of the mystics) coincides with the universal term, omega, adumbrated by our philosophy—the grandest and most necessary attribute we can ascribe to him is that of exerting a supreme physical influence on every cosmic reality without exception.

As we have already seen, in the light of pure reason, nothing in the universe is intelligible, living, and consistent except through an element of synthesis, in other words a spirit, or from on high. Within the cosmos all the elements are dependent upon one another ontologically, in the ascending order of their true being (which means of their consciousness); and the entire cosmos, as one complete whole, is held up, 'informed', by the powerful energy of a higher, and unique, Monad which gives to everything below itself its definitive intelligibility and its definitive power of action and reaction.

So: it is that energy, 'qua sibi omnia possit subjicere' (Phil. 3. 21), which we must unhesitatingly attribute to the Incarnate Word, if we are not to allow a world to assume greater dimensions, to overflow its limits, around the figure of Christ—a world that would be more beautiful, more majestic, more organic, and more worthy of worship than Christ. Christ would not be the God of St Paul, nor the God of my heart, if, looking at the lowliest, most material, created being, I were unable to say, 'I cannot understand this thing, I cannot grasp it, I cannot be fully in contact with it, except as a function of him who gives to the natural whole of which it is a part its full reality and its final determined form.' Since Christ is omega, the universe is physically impregnated to the very core of its matter by the influence of his super-human nature. The presence of the Incarnate Word penetrates everything, as a universal element. It shines at the common heart of things, as a centre that is infinitely intimate to them and at the same time (since it coincides with universal fulfilment) infinitely distant.

The vital, organising, influence of the universe, of which we are speaking, is essentially grace. We can see, however, from the point of view of creative union, that this wonderful reality of grace must be understood with a much greater intensity and width of meaning than is normally attributed to it. Theologians, in order to make it clear that grace does not make us cease to be ourselves, include it in the humble category of 'accidents', along with sonority, colours, or good spiritual qualities. Enslaved to their philosophical categories they make it (in contrast with the universal practice of the mystics) into something infra-substantial.[3] This, we say, is because they cannot bring themselves to accept the existence of incomplete substances, hierarchically ordered, in other words, Substances-of-Substance. We, on the other hand, take this new class of beings as the foundation of our explanation of the world, and in consequence will say that grace is no less intimate to ourselves, no less substantial, than humanity. It is, indeed, even more so. By Baptism in cosmic matter and the sacramental water we are more Christ than we are ourselves—and it is precisely in virtue of this predominance in us of Christ that we can hope one day to be fully ourselves.

So much, then, for the physical intensity of grace. As for the scope of its 'morphogenic' influence, it is boundless. In fact, since Christ is omega, he does not restrict his organising activity simply to one zone of our being—that of sacramental relationships and the 'habitus' of virtues. To enable himself to unite us to him through the highest part of our souls, he has had to undertake the task of making us win through in our entirety, even in our bodies. In consequence, his directing and informing influence runs through the whole range of human works, of material determinisms and cosmic evolutions. By convention, we call these lower processes in the universe 'natural'. In reality, by virtue of Christ's establishment as head of the cosmos, they are steeped in final purpose, in supernatural life, even to what is most palpable in their reality.

[3] While St Thomas says that grace is a quality (an 'accident') since it is the splendour of the soul, at the same time he speaks of it (and, it would seem, by preference) as a *new nature* which allows man to participate 'according to a certain likeness, in the divine nature, by a sort of generation or new creation' (S. Th. I, II, q. 110, art. 4). (Ed.)

Everything around us is physically 'Christified', and everything, as we shall see, can become progressively more fully so.

In this 'pan-Christism', it is evident, there is no false pantheism. What normally vitiates pantheism is that, by setting the universal centre below consciousness and below the monads, it is obliged to conceive 'omega' as a centre of intellectual dissociation, of fusion, of unconsciousness, of relaxation of effort. As soon as the true perspective is restored, as we have done, all these objectionable features disappear. Because our omega, Christ, is placed at the upper term of conscious spiritualisation, his universal influence far from dissociating, consolidates; far from confusing, differentiates; far from allowing the soul to wallow in a vague, supine, union, it drives it ever higher along the hard and fast paths of action. The danger of false pantheisms has been removed, and yet we retain the irreplaceable strength of the religious life that the pantheists unjustly claim as their own.

All around us, Christ is physically active in order to control all things. From the ultimate vibration of the atom to the loftiest mystical contemplation; from the lightest breeze that ruffles the air to the broadest currents of life and thought, he ceaselessly animates, without disturbing, all the earth's processes. And in return Christ gains physically from every one of them. Everything that is good in the universe (that is, everything that goes towards unification through effort) is gathered up by the Incarnate Word as a nourishment that it assimilates, transforms and divinises.[4] In the consciousness of this vast two-way movement, of ascent and descent, by which the development of the Pleroma (that is, the bringing of the universe to maturity) is being effected, the believer can find astonishing illumination and strength for the direction and maintenance of his effort. Faith in the universal Christ is inexhaustibly fruitful in the moral and mystical fields.

---

[4] In short, Christ, understood in this sense, is the milieu in which and through which the (abstract) attribute of *the divine immensity* is concretely realised for us.

SUGGESTED READINGS

Teilhard de Chardin on Christ and Evolution

Teilhard de Chardin, Pierre. *The Phenomenon of Man.* Revised English edition. New York: Harper and Row, 1965, esp. pp. 254-313. Paperback—New York: Harper Torchbook.

————. *Hymn of the Universe.* Translated by Simon Bartholomew. New York: Harper and Row, 1965. Paperback—New York: Harper.

————. *The Divine Milieu.* Revised Translation. New York: Harper and Row, 1965. Paperback—New York: Harper Torchbook.

————. *Writings in Time of War.* Translated by René Hague. New York: Harper and Row, 1968.

————. *Science and Christ.* Translated by René Hague. New York: Harper and Row, 1968.

————. *Comment je crois.* Vol. X, *Oeuvres de Teilhard de Chardin.* Paris: Seuil, 1969.

————. *How I Believe.* Translated by René Hague. New York: Harper and Row, 1969. Paperback.

Teilhard de Chardin, Pierre, and Maurice Blondel. *Pierre Teilhard de Chardin/Maurice Blondel Correspondence.* With notes and commentary by Henri de Lubac, S.J. Translated by William Whitman. New York: Herder and Herder, 1967.

16 The Cosmic Christ

HENRI DE LUBAC

How is Teilhard's concept of the cosmic Christ related to the Christian tradition? Is it found in Scripture, specifically in the writings of Paul? In the selection below,* Henri de Lubac, the distinguished
historian of Christian doctrine, outlines an answer to
this question. He claims that Teilhard's concept is
solidly grounded in Paul, since the Apostle teaches a
true action not only of the Word, but of Christ over
the cosmos. Like Paul Teilhard links the cosmic
Christ with Jesus of Nazareth. Yet Teilhard's concept has an element of newness; for in an evolving
universe, "the cosmic Christ must be interpreted as
the evolutive Christ." Although neither Paul nor
John experienced the world as evolving, Teilhard
was convinced that what they expressed in terms of
cosmos must be transposed into cosmogenesis. In so
doing, Teilhard remained, according to de Lubac,
within the spirit of Paul.

*A close friend and advisor of Teilhard, Henri de
Lubac has been his chief defender in the area of
theology. De Lubac, who is a Jesuit priest, is a leading specialist in patristic and medieval theology. His
writings on Teilhard include* The Religion of Teilhard de Chardin, Teilhard de Chardin: The Man and
His Meaning, *and* Teilhard Explained.

* From *Teilhard Explained,* trans. Anthony Buono (New York: Paulist
Press, 1968), pp. 14-21. Reprinted with permission.

257

"The blessed Reality of Christ!" It is here that Pierre Teilhard de Chardin places himself more especially in the line of St. Paul.[1]

He reads and continually rereads the Pauline Epistles. He fashions a little notebook for himself that will be his companion for many years in which he copies the Christological texts of the Apostle together with those of St. John. He has pored over them in a favorable climate during the course of his theological studies; he continues to meditate on them, wishing to understand them "without attenuation and without gloss."[2] Père Emile Rideau has drawn up a list of the texts which he utilizes in his written work:[3] though the citations are frequent, the number of texts cited is not large: some twelve or fifteen; but they are very typical, and they are not brought into his developments simply as decorative or confirmatory material. They constitute inspirational texts.

Père Teilhard does not usually go into details of philology or history, or any critical discussion regarding them—he did not profess to be an exegete; but he has pondered their essential meaning and he asks how they should be received by us today as Christians of the 20th century so as to retain their full meaning in our minds.

Thus, with the Epistles as a starting point, he will elaborate his teaching on "the cosmic Christ," or "the universal Christ," which later becomes the doctrine of "the evolutive Christ." For this, he undertakes to Christianize the new dynamic representation of the cosmos—just as Paul had to Christianize certain Stoic views.

There must be in the cosmos, he believes, "a privileged place where as in some universal boulevard everything is seen, everything is felt, everything is commanded, everything is animated, and everything is touched. Is this not a wondrous spot in which to place —or better acknowledge—Jesus? . . . He is the First and he is

[1] From whom he does not separate St. John. Cf. *Christianisme et Evolution* (Peking, 1935). *The Phenomenon of Man* (New York: Harper & Row, 1955), pp. 296-297. In a report presented to the "Colloquy of Vezelay" (1965) Père Elliot showed the points of agreement which also exist between the Christology of Père Teilhard and that of the Gospel according to St. Mark.

[2] *L'Union créatrice* (November, 1917), p. 2 (*Ecrits.* . . , p. 196).

[3] *La Pensée du Père Teilhard de Chardin* (Paris: Ed. Seuil, 1964).

the Head. In him all things have been created, and all things hold together, and all things are consummated." Thus we see him rejoice and be distended in these perspectives. Not for an instant does he doubt that they are not "in striking harmony with the fundamental texts" of St. Paul as well as St. John and the Greek Fathers.[4]

Evidently, we can ask if the work of continuation and transposition, which Père Teilhard realizes in this way, succeeds in finding its perfect expression.[5] We can also debate the question of knowing whether, for example, in his use of a word like "pleroma" he is fully in accord with his model. The answer in this case will depend on the conclusions of the exegetes, who are not agreed among themselves. Indeed, the Teilhardian use of the word is found to be authorized by the exegesis of Pierre Benoit.[6] However, this is a secondary question.

What is more important and indeed of paramount interest is the question of knowing whether the Teilhardian ideas of the cosmic Christ and the universal Christ do or do not reproduce the principal components of the Pauline idea. We believe we can give an affirmative answer to this question.

First of all, no matter what has been said, St. Paul teaches a true action not only of the Word but of Christ—and more especially of the risen Christ—over the cosmos, and this dominating action is essentially a unifying one. It began to be exercised the moment the world came into existence. This tells us immediately

[4] *Christologie et Evolution* (1933). *Quelques réflexions sur la conversion du monde* (1936).

[5] The same is true of all analogous cases. We can ask, for example, without disrespect toward St. Thomas, if the transposition he effected from the Aristotelian contemplation to Christian contemplation found in him its full fruition. Cf. Lucien-Marie de Saint-Joseph, *L'Impatience de Dieu* (1964), p. 268: "Eight of the nine reasons given by him are taken from Aristotle (*Secunda secundae,* q. 182, art. 1). Doubtless, these reasons have been baptized. Doubtless, too, their content is profoundly transformed by recourse to Scripture, etc. Still, there is no less danger in this recourse to a vocabulary taken from a contemplation which is not that of the Gospel. . . ."

[6] See the references in Henri de Lubac, *Teilhard de Chardin: The Man and His Meaning* (New York: The New American Library, 1967, A Mentor-Omega Book), p. 41. This is also the interpretation of Christopher F. Mooney, S.J. "The Body of Christ in the Writings of Teilhard de Chardin" in *Theological Studies* (1964), 25, p. 604. Cf. also a later work: *Teilhard de Chardin and the Mystery of Christ* (New York: Harper & Row, Publishers, 1964), pp. 94 ff.

the texts which Père Teilhard loves to cite: *In ipso condita sunt universa. . . . Omnia in ipso constant,* etc. [In him all things were made. . . . In him all things hold together.] [7]

Those who regard the idea of a cosmic activity of Christ as "unacceptable" either have not studied the texts of the Apostle closely, or make too little of them; neither have they to any greater extent envisaged "the cosmological role of Wisdom," whose attributes are applied to Christ by the New Testament.[8]

Further, no more for Père Teilhard de Chardin than for St. Paul is this cosmic Christ—in whatever way one might wish to understand him later—a kind of organism that would have only a more or less extrinsic relationship with the personal being whose name history knows as Jesus of Nazareth. For him as for Paul, the Person of Jesus Christ is in the words of Charles-Harold Dodd author of the work *The Meaning of Paul for Today* "intensely individual and yet wonderfully universal." [9]

It is really Jesus himself who is at the head of the whole Body and its unifying principle, and his organic influence extends throughout the universe. It is the same Word of God who was made man in the womb of the Virgin, died on Calvary and rose on the third day. *Descendit, et ascendit, ut impleret omnia* [He descended and ascended, that he might fill all things].

Once again it is a text of St. Paul that his disciple loves to cite and summarize; it is even through this same text—he once confided to Père Pierre Leroy—that he most freely expressed all his religious thought, all his mystique. This enables us to under-

[7] References will be found in *Teilhard de Chardin. . .*, pp. 35-44. See also Theodore of Mopsuestia, *Third Catechetical Homily* no. 9; Athanasius, *On the Incarnation of the World,* ch. 45. *L'Ame du Monde* (Epiphany, 1918): "Far from eclipsing Christ, the universe finds its stability only in him." (*Ecrits. . .*, pp. 227-228). Concerning Col. 1, 16 consult André Feuillet, "La création de l'univers dans le Christ," in *New Testament Studies,* 12, pp. 1-9. Cf. O. Cullmann, *La foi et le culte de l'Eglise primitive* (1963), pp. 13-15.

[8] Cf. Romano Guardini, *Le Seigneur* (Paris-Strasbourg, Alsatia, 1945), I, pp. 250-251. Paul Beauchamp, "Le salut corporel des justes et la conclusion du Livre de la Sagesse," in *Biblica* (1964), p. 496.

[9] *The Meaning of Paul for Today* (Cleveland & New York: The World Publishing Co., Meridian Books, 1957), p. 90. Compare this with the "concrete universal" notion of Maurice Blondel, *Exigences philosophiques du Christianisme,* p. 185.

stand his special devotion to the mystery of the ascension whose feast he annually celebrated with love.

By this same fact, finally, it is clear that the growth of the cosmic Christ and his fulfillment-to-come do not at all affect or in any way compromise the eternal actuality of the divine Word or the initial historical reality of the incarnate Word: [10] "The immense enchantment of the divine *milieu* owes all its value in the long run to the human-divine contact which was revealed at the Epiphany of Jesus. . . . The mystical Christ, the universal Christ of St. Paul, has neither meaning nor value in our eyes except as an expansion of the Christ who was born of Mary and who died on the cross." [11] "If our Lord Jesus Christ does not have a personal and objective reality, the entire Christian religious current vanishes— and the world is left without an Omega point.

"But we must explore the cosmic profundity of Christ." [12]

In what then does the newness consist with respect to St. Paul? In this, as we have said, that in a universe conceived of as evolving (in the complete sense of the word, no longer only tellurical or biological, but spiritual [13]), the cosmic Christ must be called the "evolutive Christ." For, if everything has been created in Christ "as in the supreme center of harmony and the cohesion which gives the world its meaning, its value, and thereby its reality," to use the words of Père Joseph Huby in his commentary on the Epistle to the Ephesians; [14] and if, in the words of Père Teil-

[10] *Teilhard de Chardin.* . . , pp. 49-54. Teilhard's formulas on this subject which have been criticized are entirely in conformity with tradition. See, for example, Theophylactius, Commentary on the Epistle to the Ephesians, in reference to chapter 1, 3: "Christ is fulfilled in all his members" (Migne, P.G., 124, 1049-1050 BC: "For Christ will be fulfilled and as if consummated through all his members in all the faithful. . . . For then will our Head Christ be fulfilled, that is, he will receive a perfect body, when all of us will be joined and welded together").

[11] *The Divine Milieu,* p. 117.

[12] Written in 1919. The ardor of his desire never knew any decline. It might be interesting to note that in 1961 at New Delhi the representatives of the young (Protestant) Afro-Asiatic Churches reproached European Protestantism for having let the cosmic dimension of Christ become obscured over the centuries: Helmut Riedlinger, "The Universal Kingship of Christ," in *Concilium,* 11 (January, 1966), p. 126, note 35.

[13] *Teilhard de Chardin.* . . , pp. 143-161.

[14] Saint-Paul, *Epîtres de la captivité* (Collection "Verbum Salutis," Paris: Beauchesne), p. 40.

hard, "the universal Christ means that Christ exerts a physical influence on all things"; then to maintain this total influence he must be conceived of as exerting himself in some manner over the evolution of the world.

On this precise point, Père Teilhard again follows St. Paul. He is more seriously faithful to St. Paul, at least in principle, than if he were merely content to repeat his formulas. The Apostle, as we have seen above, incorporated into his conception of Christ a certain number of Stoic views that had become current in his day: [15] Teilhard intends to continue Paul's process, by incorporating into the same basic Christian conception the evolutionary views characteristic of our age. Similarly, just as Paul completely transformed those views, purifying them of their original pantheism, so does Teilhard continue to do today.

With some measure of astonishment, Teilhard ascertained that "the theory of the universal Christ as taught by St. Paul"—a theory in which he saw "the very marrow of the Christian tree swollen with sap"—has yielded only little fruit until our day. Accordingly, he believed that the time is now ripe "to resume its growth." Yet in thus seeking to achieve "the synthesis of the new and the old," he regards himself in no way as an "innovator." He refuses this designation.

In his view, no modification touches upon the articles of faith as such. These (to which we will return) remain unchanged in their substance, even if they must be explained by new applications and become the principle of new syntheses. "Applied to the new turn taken by the human spirit, the moral and intellectual directives contained in Revelation are preserved without change in relationships that give the essential figure of Christ and of the Christian." [16] It is always a question of preserving and proclaiming

---

[15] Concerning St. Paul and Stoicism: J. Dupont, *Gnosis* (Louvain-Paris, 1949), pp. 431-435, etc. See *Teilhard de Chardin. . .* , pp. 176-178. It was through Léontine Zanta, author of a thesis on Stoicism in the 16th century (*le Stoïcisme au seizième siècle*), that Teilhard had discovered the meaning of Stoic pantheism: letter of April 14, 1919 (*The Making of a Mind*, p. 291).

[16] *Note sur le Christ universal* (1920); *Oeuvres*, vol. 9 (pp. 43-44). *Le sens humain* (1929). *Comment je crois* (1934). *Quelques réflexions sur la conversion du monde* (1936).

"the essential function as consummator assumed by the risen Christ as the center and peak of creation." [17]

The observation has been justly made that "neither the Gospel, nor St. John, nor St. Paul, has experienced or had any need to experience this evolutionary vision" [18] which is unfolded in the Teilhardian work. The observation is evident and in addition imposes itself on every Christian. Père Teilhard readily subscribed to it. Even more, he advanced it. "Through the Incarnation," he wrote, "God descends into nature to super-animate it and lead it back to him"; in itself, he believed, this dogma can be adapted to a good many diverse representations of the experimental world, and he ascertained that in fact Christians never incurred difficulty in considering their faith within the framework of a static universe.[19]

However, it does not follow that to preserve in our day both the fullness and the urgency of the affirmations of a St. Paul or a St. John we do not perhaps have to transpose "in terms of cosmogenesis the traditional vision expressed in terms of cosmos," [20] and consequently "to translate the idea of a mastery of Christ over the cosmos in terms of the corresponding idea of an evolutive Christ." [21]

Such at least was Père Teilhard's conviction, and we do not see that there is anything unacceptable about it a priori—rather, the contrary is evident. Doubtless, such a transposition, entailing

[17] Letter to Père J. B. Janssens, Cape Town, October 12, 1951 (*Letters from a Traveller*, pp. 42-43).

[18] *Nova et vetera* (Fribourg), 1965, p. 306.

[19] *La Mystique de la Science* (1939) (*Oeuvres,* vol. 6, pp. 220-221).

[20] January 1, 1951. It is principally in this perspective that the texts of Père Teilhard on the Eucharist should be regarded (see *Teilhard de Chardin. . . ,* part I, ch. 8, pp. 59-64). Cf. Jean Mouroux. *Le Seigneurie de Jésus-Christ:* It is "in a mysterious and sealed sign—the Eucharist—that the transfiguration of the world and human travail is inaugurated," while waiting for "the full, marvelous and definitive reality, in which are transfigured in Jesus Christ 'who fills all things' (Eph. 4, 10) mankind and the entire world." (In the Appendix to *Consolez mon peuple* by Paul Gautier: Paris: Editions du Cerf, 1965, pp. 304-305.)

[21] Cf. Piet Smulders, *The Design of Teilhard de Chardin* (Westminster: The Newman Press, 1967), pp. 58-59. After remarking that "evolver" is "the grammatical parallel of creator," the author concludes that the "great merit of Teilhard will probably lie in having grasped the necessity for a renewal and another orientation of the image of creation."

such a translation, will pose more than one problem in which the faith may find itself involved and which it does not pertain to any one man to resolve—or even to perceive in a completely distinct manner. Thus, in his view which has remained that of a man of science, Père Teilhard did not analyze nor even completely envisage the kind of distinction and the type of relation that exists between the natural history of the world, human history, and the history of salvation; these would have led him to make a good many complementary precisions concerning the role of Christ.

These are inadequacies that might be termed inevitable; nor did they entirely escape Teilhard's attention, although he did not perceive them with complete clarity. It suffices that in undertaking "to disengage dogmatically in the person of Christ the cosmic face and function which constitute him organically as the prime mover and director, the 'soul' of evolution," he remained within the logic of the Pauline thought.

This is the point that Père Joseph Maréchal had perceived at Louvain. He once wrote to Père Teilhard, after reading one of his essays *Christologie et Evolution* [*Christology and Evolution*]: "Like yourself I believe that the 'well understood' progress of natural philosophy should enrich our understanding of the mystery of the Incarnation and give a more real content to the very beautiful expressions of St. John and St. Paul which we have preserved without sufficiently 'realizing' their primary significance." [22]

Père Teilhard had himself posed the problem very well: "What must Christology become *if it is to remain itself?*" [23] A bit later, he similarly defined its purpose, specifying that for him it was a question of nothing else but to "preserve for Christ the same qualities which form the basis for his power and our adoration." [24]

Dogma does not keep itself alive in the integrity of its substance unless it retains its assimilative force in the mind of the believer. Newman wrote in a page of his *Development,* a book which Père Teilhard read very carefully and which provoked

[22] Letter to Père Teilhard, 1933; cited by Emile Rideau, *La Pensée du Père Teilhard de Chardin* (Paris: Ed. du Seuil, 1963), p. 400.

[23] Letter of December 9, 1933 (*italics added;* cited in *Teilhard de Chardin. . .*, p. 51, note 19).

[24] *Comment je crois* (1934). The italics for the word "preserve" are the author's. *Quelques réflexions . . .* (1936): "Christ grows by remaining what he is, or to put it in a better way, *in order to remain* what he was."

lengthy reflections on his part: "Was [the Christianity lived by the Fathers of the Church] unitive? Had it the power, while keeping its own identity, of absorbing its antagonists, as Aaron's rod, according to St. Jerome's illustration, devoured the rods of the sorcerers of Egypt? Did it incorporate them into itself, or was it dissolved into them?" [25]

This interrogation does not concern only primitive Christianity; it remains actual from age to age. We fully realize that the work of Père Teilhard de Chardin presents it with a new occasion to arise. But we must be persuaded of it: if there is always a danger in ourselves that the Christian faith might experience death by dissolution, there is also—something certain conservative spirits are too prone to forget and in forgetting it they thereby increase the first danger for others—another symmetrical danger, the danger of death by estrangement and separation. When truth is no longer fruitful, it is close to death. If the danger on either side were avoided, it would not be difficult to see on which side can be found the spirit of St. Paul, that is, the true missionary spirit, essential to the Christian spirit.

This has been perfectly grasped by Jacques-Albert Cuttat, who could not fail to encounter the work of Père Teilhard when he undertook to examine whether the Christian experience is capable of assuming Oriental spirituality:

Examined, weighed, and judged in the light of a theology whose Object is Someone and not Something, . . . the basic inspiration of Père Teilhard de Chardin's work—so revolutionary on the surface—reveals its profound biblical and traditional core. Have the defenders of an immobile ecclesial traditionalism, a static fidelity to the Catholic splendors of the past, given thought to the frightful "backlash shock" that threatens a Christian conscience *pretending to ignore* the fact that "we are today assisting at a changing face of nature which holds prodigies?"

Do they sufficiently realize that we need *more*—not *less*—faith in the Word through whom "all things were made. . . , and without [whom] was made nothing that has been made" (Jn.

[25] John Henry Cardinal Newman, *An Essay on the Development of Christian Doctrine* (New York: Doubleday & Company, Inc., 1960, Image Books), part II, ch. 8, p. 337; ch. 5, section 3: "An eclectic conservative, assimilating, healing moulding process, a unitive power, is of the essence, . . . of a faithful development" (p. 190).

1, 3) and in the "Father [who] works" without ceasing (Jn. 5, 17), in order to safeguard and preserve intact in the midst of the 20th century—"to conserve" while revitalizing—the conviction that "the better we know nature, the better we will be able to know God" (Etienne Gilson)?

Is there a more Catholic and more Orthodox task than the renewal of the Christocentric cosmology of St. Paul and the Greek Fathers undertaken on the level of our astronomical, geological, biological, and anthropological horizon which has become so vast since then as to appear to so many cultured minds—believers included—as incapable of being set against a personal transcendence? [26]

SUGGESTED READINGS

Henri de Lubac on Teilhard

Lubac, Henri de, S.J., *Teilhard de Chardin: The Man and His Meaning.* Translated by René Hague. New York: Hawthorn Books, 1965. Paperback—New York: Mentor-Omega.

———. *The Religion of Teilhard de Chardin.* Translated by René Hague. New York: Desclée, 1967. Paperback—New York: Paulist Press.

———. *Teilhard Explained.* Translated by Anthony Buono. New York: Paulist Press, 1968. Paperback.

On Teilhard's Christology

Bravo, Francisco. *Christ in the Thought of Teilhard de Chardin.* Translated by Cathryn B. Larme. Notre Dame: University of Notre Dame Press, 1967.

Crespy, Georges. *From Science to Theology: An Essay on Teilhard de Chardin.* Translated by George H. Shriver. Nashville: Abingdon Press, 1968, pp. 79-95.

[26] In the collective work *La Mystique et les Mystiques,* edited by André Ravier, S.J. (Paris: Desclée de Brouwer, 1965), p. 887. From the same author, *La rencontre des religions* (Paris: Aubier, 1957), p. 46: "The evolutionary Christocentrism of Teilhard de Chardin in sum only restores to Copernican heliocentrism its true spiritual significance," and it does so "by assuming in the Christian faith an eminently Oriental contemplative dimension."

Gray, Donald P. *The One and the Many: Teilhard de Chardin's Vision of Unity.* New York: Herder & Herder, 1969, pp. 95-132.

Mooney, Christopher, S.J. *Teilhard de Chardin and the Mystery of Christ.* New York: Harper and Row, 1966. Paperback—Garden City, N.Y.: Image.

Solages, Mgr. Bruno de. *Teilhard de Chardin: Témoignage et étude sur le développement de sa pensée.* Toulouse: Privat, 1967, pp. 354-362.

Van Til, Cornelius. *Pierre Teilhard de Chardin: Evolution and Christ.* Philadelphia: Presbyterian and Reformed Publishing Co., 1966. Paperback.

17 Cosmology anh Christology

N. M. WILDIERS

If one conceives the universe as evolving, what effect does this have on his understanding of Christian doctrine; and what significance does Christian doctrine have for such an understanding of the world? This is the twofold question that Teilhard's thought raises. In the present selection,* N. M. Wildiers explores this question from the standpoint of Teilhard's Christology. Since Teilhard sees the whole of evolution as an ascent to Christ, Christian doctrines must be read in developmental and convergent terms. In this context, Wildiers surveys the general outlines of Teilhard's Christology as it relates to cosmology and history. He indicates the affinity between Teilhard's position and that of Duns Scotus on the primacy of Christ in creation.

N. M. Wildiers is the author of the introductions to the volumes of the Oeuvres de Pierre Teilhard de Chardin. *A Franciscan priest, he teaches theology at the University of Louvain and the University of San Francisco. He has written what is considered by many to be the best introduction to Teilhard's thought. It is from this introduction that the following selection is taken.*

The early Fathers of the Church, and the theologians of later periods, made it their business to formulate as accurately as they could the relation be-

* *An Introduction to Teilhard de Chardin,* trans. Hubert Hoskins (New York: Harper and Row, 1968), pp. 130-141. Reprinted with permission.

tween Christ and the world and to define precisely in what way he is connected with the history of mankind, with the past and with the future. Even so, the world which they had in view was a static world, the intrinsic cohesion of which they were in no position to guess at. The question that they posed, therefore, was as to the place of Christ within the static and constricted world of their day.

For Teilhard this problem necessarily assumed another aspect, in view of the revolution that had occurred in our manner of envisaging the world. We live in an evolving world with a convergent structure; so that when the theologian is faced with the question of what place Christ occupies in the world as a whole, he is obliged to take this new world view into account. Is there any link between the God-man and this evolving world; and if there is, is it to be construed as a merely external, juridical connection, or ought we to think of it rather as a close, organic relatedness? If Teilhard's contribution was original, it is because he stated the old problem of the place of Christ in God's plan for the world in a new way.

i Earlier Conceptions

But if we are to get a good grasp of his ideas on this score, we must cast our minds back for a moment to the way in which previous ages offered to solve the problem. Strictly speaking, no clear and generally agreed solution had hitherto been found. People since the Middle Ages, meditating on the meaning of the Incarnation, had arrived at two different conceptions of it— usually referred to as the Thomist and Scotist theories—which despite a great deal that they had in common nevertheless parted company on an important point.

According to the Thomist view of the matter,[1] a rigid distinction must be drawn between the order of creation and the order of redemption. In the original plan for the world (the order of creation) no provision was made for an Incarnation of the Word. If the first human being had not sinned, the Incarnation would not have taken place. The Incarnation was "decreed" only after man had sinned, and so it derived entirely from that circumstance. To

---

[1] *Summa theologica*, III, 9. 1., art. 3: *Utrum, si homo non peccasset, Deus incarnatus fuisset* (Whether, if man had not sinned, God would have become incarnate).

restore the primal world order—blighted by sin—the Son of God was born into this world as a man in order to set the human race once more upon the path to its ultimate destiny. In this account of things the link between Christ and the world is merely accidental. No Fall, no Incarnation. The cosmos had been created by God without any connection with the God-man. Through Christ's appearing on earth, however, the world, via man, has been hallowed and redeemed. From that moment a moral and juridical bond between Christ and the world comes into being: by virtue of his hypostatic union with the Word and of his merit as Redeemer he acquires a title to kingship over the entire world.

The distinguishing mark of this interpretation is of course the fact that it kept the divine decree regarding the Incarnation outside the original plan of creation and therefore accorded the Incarnation itself no place in the concrete order of things. This makes it difficult to say specifically what place Christ has in the world. It is only within a sinful humanity that he has any function to fulfil: the function of Redeemer, from which a state of moral and juridical relatedness to the whole world ensues as a consequence. There could be no question, in that case, of a function, conceived in organic terms, within the whole of the cosmic order.

Very different from this is the Scotist interpretation, as it is called. In this view, which appeals to numerous texts in the Scriptures and numbers among its advocates such great names as those of St. Francis de Sales, Newman and Scheeben, Christ is held to be the goal and crowning-point not only of the supernatural but of the natural order. Right from the beginning—that is to say, quite independently of the Fall—the whole creation was planned with the God-man in view. Even if man had not sinned, the Word would have become man; for the truth is that Christ is the supreme revelation of God in this world and the masterpiece of God's creation. It seems hard to believe that this disclosure would only have taken place on the assumption that man would first have committed sin. The Incarnation was contained, therefore, in the original plan of creation. The Fall introduced only an accidental change in this: the God-man, who had been conceived as the goal and crown of the whole created order, would also through his sufferings and death act as the redeemer of all mankind.

Thus this interpretation ascribes to Christ a central function in the cosmos—a function, that is, not to be understood in purely moral or juridical terms. In its very existence the world is centred on Christ—and not *vice versa,* as the first interpretation avers. In the beginning it was orientated upon him, so that we are indeed right to say that he is the beginning and the end, the Alpha and Omega, of all things. Christ's place in the cosmos is an organic function: that is, the world is centred on Christ in respect of its intrinsic structure, in its actual mode of being, so that—to use St. Paul's expression—he "is in all things pre-eminent".[2] In this context also E. Schillebeeckx writes: "We may, and indeed we must, say that the One who is risen from the dead is the purport and centre of the concrete creation, even insofar as it was *not as yet* sinful: namely, in Adam." [3]

This is not the place to go more fully into the matter of these two interpretations. They both have their right to exist in Catholic theology; and both are entirely consonant with the fundamental tenets of Christianity. This is a case of an "open question", concerning which every Christian may think whatever appears to him to accord best with the evidence of Scripture and the tradition of the Church. If we have recalled these interpretations offered by traditional theology here, it is in order to demonstrate that the question of Christ's place in the created order is in no sense a new question which Teilhard has thrown up, and at the same time to show that what we have here is an issue allowing of further development.

The place accorded to this problem in most manuals of theology is only a secondary one. Often it is just treated as a kind of historical reminiscence to which only a more or less academic interest attaches—although in earlier centuries it did, of course, exert a certain influence on the spiritual temper of the two schools. In Teilhard's view, however, what is at issue here is a very relevant and very present problem; and finding the answer to it, as he believed, may well help us in no small measure to build up a spirituality attuned to the spiritual and intellectual needs of contemporary man. That is why he centred his attention on this problem in theology. The principal task of theology to-day consists, as

[2] Col. 1. 18.
[3] E. Schillebeeckx, *"De zin van het mens-zijn van Jezus, de Christus"*, in *Tijdschrift voor Theologie,* 2nd Vol., 1962, p. 168.

COSMOLOGY AND CHRISTOLOGY 273

he believed, in this: "to analyse the relationship, in the matter of existence and influence which links together Christ and the Universe" [4]; "to elucidate the very Catholic idea of Christ Alpha and Omega".[5] "The truth is, the keystone of the arch which has to be erected lies in our hands. If we want to achieve the so much needed synthesis between faith in God and faith in the world, then the best possible thing for us to do is to bring to the fore on a dogmatic basis, in the person of Christ, the cosmic aspect and the cosmic function which make him organically the principle and controlling force, the very *soul* of evolution." [6]

ii The Place of Christ in the Cosmos

The view that Teilhard developed regarding the place which accrues to Christ in the whole of cosmic history shows a great affinity with the so-called Scotist interpretation.[7] For Teilhard too the entire creation centres upon Christ as its natural crowning-point, so that the order of creation is inconceivable without him. One is struck by the fact that the scriptural passages which Teilhard adduces in support of his opinion are the very same ones as are cited by the champions of the Scotist interpretation. Yet there are also important points of difference to be stressed, which spring from a different conception of the structure of the universe. The cosmos that Teilhard envisages is obviously quite different from the picture of the world which forms the background to mediaeval theology. The whole point of the exercise, for him, is to indicate the place of Christ in a creation with an evolving and convergent character. He believes that this new world view offers a better chance of understanding Christ's place and function than was the case with the earlier one.

As he saw it, there was not really much chance of being able to indicate the place that Christ occupied in the world, so long as it was statically conceived; for such a view was bound to remain tied to purely extrinsic and juridical concepts. Men attributed a

[4] *Christianisme et Évolution*, 1945, p. 3; (also in *Oeuvres* XI).
[5] *Note sur le Christ Universel*, p. 1; (also in *Oeuvres* IX).
[6] *Christianisme et Évolution*, p. 3; (also in *Oeuvres* XI).
[7] Teilhard sometimes made explicit reference to the Scotist view of the matter; see: *Esquisse d'une dialectique de l'Esprit* in *L'Activation de l'Énergie*, p. 158. (*Oeuvres* VII); not to mention any specific further instances.

"kingship" (what an antiquated sound that metaphor has!) to Christ, a "kingship" over the created order, a "kingship" conferred upon him by the Father, and one to which he was "morally entitled" by virtue of his redeeming death. Thenceforward everything was subject, therefore, to his juridical authority. *Rex regum et dominus dominantium.* And question of an organic link between Christ and the world simply does not come into it—and indeed could hardly do so. In a world mechanistically and statically conceived there just was no really central place which one could point to as adequately representing the dignity and status of Christ.

But in the perspective of the new view of the world the situation is quite altered. Here one can indeed indicate a point which governs the whole of cosmic evolution, forms the keystone and climax of it and exerts a power of attraction giving to the whole evolutive process its intrinsic drive and orientation. This universal cosmic centre of human—and thus also of cosmic—evolution, in which everything is bound in the end to attain its unity and consummation, is signalized in the phenomenology of the universe by the term: the Omega point.

Is not this precisely the place which according to Christian doctrine is to be ascribed to Christ? Do not the characteristics of the point Omega meet all the requirements that we must lay down in this case? Is not our whole insight into the mystery of Christ hereby deepened in a fruitful and wonderful way, wholly consonant with St. Paul's teaching? "If we pursue the perspectives of science as they relate to the humanization process to their logical and final conclusion, we then discover the climax of anthropogenesis to be the existence of an ultimate centre or focus of personality and consciousness which is indispensable for the orientation of the historical growth of spirit and for its synthesis. Now this *Omega point* (as I have called it), is it not the ideal centre from which to see radiating the Christ whom we worship—a Christ whose supernatural lordship is accompanied, as we are aware, by a predominating physical power over the natural spheres of the world? *In quo omnia constant.* Marvellous coincidence, indeed, of the data of faith with the processes of reason itself! What at first appeared to be a threat instead turns out to be a splendid confirmation. Far from coming into opposition with Christian dogma, the vastly increased importance assumed by man in nature results (when considered exhaustively) in traditional Christology being given a new lease of relevance and a new vitality." [8]

For Teilhard there can be no real doubt. "Christ occupies for us, *hic et nunc,* so far as his position and *function* are concerned, the place of the point Omega." [9] To persuade ourselves of this we have only to look at the most traditional data supplied by Christianity and the most authentic utterances of Holy Writ regarding the status and function of Christ. Everything has its being in him. Everything is brought into unity by him. In him everything finds its completion, not only in the order of grace but in that of nature too.[10] In the Christian idea of things the whole of history is directed toward the building up and unifying of the entire human race into a supranatural community of which Christ is the head and all of us the members. Christianity has an essentially eschatological character. It bids us look toward the future, toward the realization of the Kingdom of God. Christianity's vision of the future is a vision of a supernatural and definitive unity, a unity built up and held together by a personal centre, the historic Christ, whose return at the end of the Age we now await. The doctrine of the Mystical Body, which St. Paul and St. John expressed under a variety of images and similes, is one of the most central data of the Christian tradition. "The essence of Christianity is nothing more or less than a belief in the world's coming to be one in God through the Incarnation." [11]

Thus when one sets the perspectives of science alongside those of faith, one simply cannot escape the impression that both are con-

---

[8] *Le Christ Évoluteur,* 1942, p. 4 (*Cahiers Pierre Teilhard de Chardin,* 5, Ed. du Seuil, Paris).

[9] *Super-humanité, Super-Christ, Super-charité,* 1943, p. 9.

[10] See Mgr. L. Cerfaux, *Le Christ dans la Théologie de Saint-Paul,* Paris, Ed. du Cerf, 1951: "Thus we notice in the Epistles of the captivity a tendency . . . to extend Christ's pleroma, that is to say the sphere within which the writ of his authority runs, to the cosmos" (p. 322).—"All things have been created by him; and they are created for him, they tend toward him, in order through him to realize their end, which is to make God manifest" (p. 323).—"Although the primary intention has been frustrated, the Christ is still he in whom all things cohere, and on whom they depend (to whom they are subject), with an intrinsic dependence; no creature can escape from his domain" (*ibid.*). (English translation, *The Church in the Theology of St. Paul,* New York, Herder and Herder, 1959).

[11] *L'Énergie Humaine,* p. 113 (*Oeuvres* VI).

276 N. M. WILDIERS

verging toward one and the same point. How could it be otherwise? If that were not the case, then we would have to conclude that Christ is no longer in the full sense of the word the world's crowning point and consummation, since there would be, beyond him, yet another climax and consummation. "It is in fact to Christ that we direct our gaze when, to whatever degree of approximation it may be, we look forward to some higher Pole of humanization and personalization." [12] For Teilhard then, Christ is the goal and crown of the natural as of the supernatural order—a position wholly compatible with the strictest orthodoxy. Of course, there is an important distinction to be made between the two perspectives. The one relates to the plane of nature, the other to that of the supernature. The one operates in the plane of creation, the other in the plane of grace. But let us not lose sight of the fact that whilst there is indeed a distinction between nature and grace, there is no separation; that they interpenetrate each other and that the distinction which we draw between various "planes" in the work of God conceals a large measure of anthropomorphism. God's work is *one* work. As the classic formula puts it, grace does not annul nature but on the contrary assumes, ennobles and exalts it. Ought we not to say, therefore, that the supernatural unification of mankind presupposes a natural unification and indeed elevates it to a supreme dignity and completion (in a higher order)? One of the things that theology has always said, surely, is that nature is ordered upon supernature, so that it is perfectly legitimate to exhibit the harmony existing between them.

It has sometimes been argued that this way of representing Christ does not have much to do with the historic Christ of the gospel. But arguments of this sort rest on a false assumption. "Against this elevation of the historic Christ to a universal physical function, against this ultimate identification of cosmogenesis with Christogenesis, it has sometimes been objected that such a conception involves the risk of causing the human reality of Jesus to fade away into the super-human or to vanish into the cosmic. Nothing would seem to me more ill founded than this misgiving. The more, in fact, one considers the fundamental laws of evolution, the more one becomes convinced that the universal Christ would not be

[12] *Super-humanité, Super-Christ, Super-charité,* p. 9.

able to appear at the end of time, unless he had previously inserted himself into the course of the world's movement *by way of birth,* in the form of an *element.* If it is really by Christ-Omega that the universe is held in movement, on the other hand, it is from his concrete source, the Man of Nazareth, that Christ-Omega (theoretically and historically) derives for our experience his whole stability." [13] In other words: without a historic Christ there could be no mystical body of Christ, no total Christ.

Certain of Teilhard's expressions and turns of phrase may on occasion strike one who is used to the traditional formulas of theology as, to begin with, rather disconcerting. If, however, we transpose his ideas into a more traditional language, it soon becomes apparent that the basic idea that he is trying to get across ties in to a large extent with one of the most ancient schools of thought in Catholic theology—always granting, of course, that he combines this theological interpretation of his with a world view which was utterly unknown to earlier centuries but now imparts a new background, a new dimension, to the traditional figure of Christ. We may sum up Teilhard's understanding of the matter in the words of Claude Cuénot: "On the one hand you have the Christ of Christian mysticism . . . described with such deep feeling by Paul. On the other you have the cosmic pole which is a postulate of modern science and is necessary in the whole new picture that we have of the world, in order to draw together at its apex, and so to unify, ascending evolution. Now Teilhard was of the opinion that between these two poles there must exist a degree of correspondence, of homogeneity and, at bottom, an ultimate identity. Only at a later stage will the fact of this coincidence, of this identity, permeate into the consciousness of men; and only at the end of time will it find its consummation in the Parousia. Then science and mysticism will fuse together. Then the two poles will reach a condition of mutual influence, so that an interchange of attributes can ensue, and Christ envelops the entire cosmos, whilst the Christified cosmos itself becomes an object of love." [14]

iii Christ as the Meaning of History

Teilhard believed, therefore, that the place which we must assign to Christ in the universe coincides with the place denoted in

[13] *Christianisme et Évolution,* p. 6; (also in *Oeuvres* XI).
[14] C. Cuénot, *op. cit.,* p. 450; English translation, p. 370.

his scheme of the world by the point Omega. But what does such an identification really mean? What does such a thesis imply?

It implies, of course, in the first place what we said earlier on: that Christ is linked, not simply in a moral or juridical context but as it were structurally and organically with the cosmos. In and with the very process of creation the world is orientated upon him. All things are created in him: *in ipso condita sunt universa*.[15]

Secondly, it implies that through Christ the world acquires its ultimate unity and cohesion. The point Omega is indeed the element that imparts to the whole of cosmic evolution its final unity —the point at which multiplicity is reduced to unity and on which all the threads of history converge. It is just such a function that we are to ascribe to Christ. He is the cornerstone in God's plan for the world. In him, as St. Paul says, all things are brought to unity: *Omnia in ipso constant*.[16]

It implies in the third instance that Christ is the very meaning of history. The point Omega gives to evolution its orientation: *de facto*, evolution is focussed upon this final term; and at the deepest level its laws are governed and regulated by this final goal. Even this property of the point Omega can be assigned to Christ. In the Christian perspective he is truly the meaning of history, in that everything is centred on him. The whole world order is to be discovered in St. Paul's words: *omnia vestra sunt, vos autem Christi, Christus autem Dei*.[17] The entire lower world is centred in man —but man is centred in Christ, and Christ in God. Transposed into Teilhard's terms, this notion may be expressed as follows: cosmogenesis eventuates through biogenesis in a noogenesis; but the noogenesis is consummated in a Christogenesis. "The Universe," wrote Henri Bergson, "is a machine for making gods." As Teilhard envisaged it, we could say that the world is an instrument for realizing the total Christ. Looked at from this standpoint, Christ really does govern and control the vast abysses of time and space. However brief the span of his earthly life—now two thousand years ago—there is nothing to prevent his constituting the axis and the apex of a universal process of maturation.[18]

[15] Col. 1. 16.
[16] Col. 1. 17.
[17] I Cor. 3. 23.
[18] *Christologie et Évolution*, 1933, p. 9; (also in *Oeuvres* XI).

Lastly, this thesis implies that Christ is the great source of power and energy which is drawing all things toward itself. From him there radiates an influence which in the final instance nothing can escape. "Being so situated [in our world view] Christ must necessarily, whatever the ultimately supernatural character of his domain, exert his radiating influence by degrees over the whole body of nature. Since, in the concrete sense, there is but one synthesizing process taking place *from top to bottom* in the universe, it follows that no element whatsoever, no movement at any level of the world, can exist outside the *informing* influence of the main centre of things. Thus, already co-extensive with space and time, Christ, by reason of his position at the world's central point, is also automatically co-extensive with the scale of values which extend from the peaks of Spirit to the depths of matter." [19]

So we can see that the various attributes which Holy Scripture ascribes to Christ, far from being even partly undermined or lessened, within the context of the new world view acquire their most comprehensive and most concrete significance. So far as essentials are concerned, such an interpretation is in every respect at one with the views which the Greek Fathers developed regarding Christ's place in the universe, and which in Byzantine art found expression in the figure of Christ *Pantokrator*.

Teilhard recapitulated this doctrine in terms which at first sight seem strange to us. He talks about "the Universal Christ", about "Christ the Evolver", about "the Super-Christ", about "the Christic". We must not allow ourselves to be put off by these unfamiliar expressions. In point of fact what they are really saying, when put back into the framework of the modern view of the world, is part and parcel of the Christian tradition and of its most authentic content. If Teilhard had had to limit his activities to the theological field, then he would perhaps have stated these things in more traditional terms and concepts. But as he was a man of science and was addressing himself to the men of today who live within these new perspectives, that circumstance was bound to affect his language and mode of expression.

The doctrine that even in the order of nature Christ is the goal and head of the whole creation is one of extraordinary richness; and we shall see in more detail to what important conclusions

[19] *Ibid.*

it can lead us. That a deeper theological treatment of it is much to
be desired can scarcely be denied, therefore. Meanwhile, Teilhard
is unquestionably right when he argues that his conception of
Christ fits perfectly with that of Holy Scripture. In particular he is
right in saying that Christians generally do not attach sufficient
importance to a doctrine which is nevertheless fundamental to
Christianity: namely, that of Christ's return at the end of the Age.
"On the horizon of the Christian world the Parousia (that is,
the return of Christ in glory at the end of time) occupies a
central place—something which, because men have awaited it over
so many centuries, is easily forgotten. In this unique and supreme
event, in which (as the Faith instructs us) the historic is to be
fused with the Transcendental, the mystery of the Incarnation
culminates and is manifested with the realism of a physical 'elucidation' of the universe." [20]

In a Christian perspective it is conceivable, therefore, that this
moment of Christ's Parousia should coincide with the moment at
which mankind will have attained its natural completion: namely,
in the moment Omega. In a sense, this natural completion would
form the condition, as it were, for the second coming of Christ at the
end of the Age. "Christ's first coming to earth was only feasible—
and nobody will dispute this—after the human species, in the setting of the general process of evolution, had been anatomically
constituted and from the social standpoint had attained in some
degree a collective consciousness. If this much be granted, why
not go a step further and ask whether in the case of his second
and last coming *also,* Christ defers his return until the human community has realized to the full its *natural* potentialities, and
thereby becomes qualified to receive through him its supernatural
consummation? Indeed, if the historical development of spirit is
bound by definite physical rules, must not this be equally the case
—*a fortiori,* even—where its further unfolding and completion are
concerned?" [21]

Theologically speaking, such a line of argument is surely
acceptable. Furthermore, the quotation is of special interest because it illustrates so very well that contrary to what some critics
have averred Teilhard distinguishes very clearly between the nat-

[20] *Trois Choses que je vois,* 1948, p. 7.
[21] *Ibid.,* pp. 8-9.

ural and the supernatural order and plainly declares that the natural completion of mankind can at most constitute a condition, and *not* a cause, of its supernatural consummation. The second coming of Christ, like the first, has the character of a free and unmerited gift.

Thus we are to understand the whole of history as an ascent of the whole world toward its consummation in the natural and supernatural order—and the two forms of completion do not in any way conflict. "And when all things have been subjected to him, then shall the Son also himself be subjected to the One who subjected all things to him, that God may be all in all." [22]

SUGGESTED READINGS

On Teilhard and the Christian Tradition

Allegra, Gabriel M., O.F.M. *My Conversations with Teilhard de Chardin on the Primacy of Christ.* Translated by Bernardino M. Bonansea, O.F.M. Chicago: Franciscan Herald Press, 1971.

Benz, Ernst. *Evolution and Christian Hope: Man's Concept of the Future from the Early Fathers to Teilhard de Chardin.* Translated by Heinz G. Frank. New York: Doubleday, 1966. Paperback—New York: Anchor.

Maloney, George, S.J. *The Cosmic Christ: From Paul to Teilhard.* New York: Sheed and Ward, 1968.

Theological Themes in the Light of Evolution

Baltazar, Eulalio, *Teilhard and the Supernatural.* Baltimore: Helicon, 1966.

————. *God Within Process.* Westminster, Md.: Newman Press, 1970.

Crespy, Georges. *From Science to Theology: An Essay on Teilhard de Chardin.* Translated by George H. Shriver. Nashville: Abingdon Press, 1968.

Hulsbosch, Ansfried, O.S.A. *God in Creation and Evolution.* New York: Sheed and Ward, 1965.

[2] I Cor. 15. 28.—See: *Introduction à la Vie Chrétienne*, 1944, p. 1; (also in *Oeuvres* XI).

North, Robert, S.J. *Teilhard and the Creation of the Soul*. Milwaukee: Bruce, 1967.

Rust, Eric C. *Evolutionary Philosophies and Contemporary Theology*. Philadelphia: Westminster Press, 1969.

Schoonenberg, Peter, S.J. *God's World in the Making*. Pittsburgh: Duquesne University Press, 1964. Paperback—Techny, Ill.: Divine World Publications.

Smulders, Piet, S.J. *The Design of Teilhard de Chardin: An Essay in Theological Reflection*. Translated by Arthur Gibson. Westminster, Md.: Newman Press, 1967.

18 The Problem of Evil in Teilhard's Thought

GEORGES CRESPY

Perhaps the most serious theological objection against Teilhard is directed to his treatment of evil. In his evolutionary perspective, the mystery of evil seems rationalized and minimized, with a consequent weakening of the doctrines of original sin and redemption. In the following selection,* Georges Crespy explores Teilhard's treatment of evil, in the light of his doctrine of creative union: God creates by gradually unifying the vast multiplicity of elements in the universe. As a by-product of this process, evil is a statistical necessity. Against this background, Crespy examines Teilhard's treatment of original sin and redemption, pointing out both the weakness and strength of Teilhard's position.

Georges Crespy is a leading Protestant interpreter of Teilhard. A member of the theology faculty of the University of Montpellier, France, Crespy was a visiting professor at the Chicago Theological Seminary in 1965, when the selection below was presented as part of a series of lectures. His writings on Teilhard include From Science to Theology: An Essay on Teilhard de Chardin *and* La pensée théologique de Teilhard de Chardin.

It is often said and repeated that Teilhard's thought in regard to the problem of evil is absolutely unsatisfactory. The remark is also made that Teilhard

* From *From Science to Theology: An Essay on Teilhard de Chardin,* trans. George H. Shriver (New York: Abingdon Press, 1968), pp. 96-113.

had more intelligence than feeling and that his vision of the world is finally an impassible and perhaps insensible one, somewhat like that of the Stoics. As proof of this, reference is made to the character of his theology of the cross as being deficient. It will be necessary for us to return to this point since (as one will already have noticed) the discussion of Teilhard's Christology passed silently by the matter of the crucifixion and the correlative doctrine of substitutionary redemption.

But even before we can examine the reproaches addressed to Teilhard and before we can find out how his problematic of evil is arranged and presented, we must give some general attention to the celebrated problem of evil itself. At various times Teilhard stated that this problem does not really exist except as it is found to be posed by the intellectual attempt to make the following items coexist—an immobile God and yet one responsible for being and a man in a state of completed being who is also responsible. In brief, it would be the fixist position of thought which would create the problem.

In effect, the problem of evil presents itself most often to us as a problem of *position*. Suppose on the one hand a God who is perfectly good and all powerful and on the other hand a world created good and now become bad—how has the positional *plus* sign been transformed into the positional *minus* sign? How does the *minus* proceed from the *plus*, or again (and in Augustinian terms this time), how can *nonbeing* be born from and develop itself until it becomes *anti-being?* Who is responsible for this change in signs? Three traditional answers have been given to this question, and not one of them appears to be satisfactory.

One answer says that this change in signs had been unforeseen by God and that man is responsible for it. If such were the case, it would be necessary for man who is "admitted as creature" to be able to draw upon something from his position as creature with which to resist a Creator who is not only all good (and consequently incapable of having made a being capable of evil) but who is also all powerful (and consequently incapable of tolerating the existence, however surprising, of a reality—evil—which does not fall under his power).

The second "solution" says that God has put evil into the world just as he has put good into the world and that our mistake is our division of reality into *good* and *evil*, because these qualifications are our own and refer only to our reactions. The wisdom of God would know that what we call evil is only disguised good. This is the Stoical position. But if this be true, then whence comes the strange possibility of *calling* evil that which we believe to be evil and good that which we believe to be good? And if we truly and universally have the experience of what we then call evil, is it necessary to make God the author of evil?

In brief, the two solutions to which we have referred invite us to choose between a God without knowledge and a God without feeling. Moreover, neither of them solves the problem in any way.

The third answer is found in the tradition of apophatic theology, and it is Berdyaev in particular who has skillfully developed it. According to this answer, evil should not be *posited* in any way (in God or in man); on the contrary, it results from uncreated liberty; it has a meonic status (this expression is composed of the Greek negation *me* and the Greek word for "being," *to on*). Its being then is to lack being. We could conceive of it as a hollow, an empty being in the midst of being, and consequently in some respects as an aspiration to be.

This third solution is interesting because it shifts the direction of the problem. In effect, it does not turn us toward the *origin* of evil (since by definition uncreated liberty does not and cannot have an *origin*), but toward its *nature*. This solution asks us not to confuse evil as social, moral, or religious reality (*transgression* and *guilt*) with evil as *ontic* reality, relative to being as such. Its weakness is correctly seen in the difficulty which it experiences in ascribing *transgression* and *guilt* (in brief, *history*, since all transgression and guilt are situated in time) to the fundamental incompleteness of being. Because of this it does not appear to answer the conditions of the problem.

But can the problem be solved? It appears that if such were the case, the problem would already have been closed and that after Spinoza, Hegel, Renouvier, and others we would no longer be troubled by this besetting question which ceaselessly haunts us.

On the contrary, it is probable that the problem of evil as such is insoluble and that it will remain even in an evolutionistic view of the world. And besides, if Teilhard often said that it was fixism which made the problem insoluble, and if he added that in the perspective of his own phenomenology "the famous problem does not exist" (*Comment je vois*), he has also strongly emphasized that "it is one thing . . . for us to explain rationally the co-possibility of evil and God and another thing to bear suffering in our flesh and in our spirit" (*ibid.*). The *explanation* of evil never gives a suitable answer to the *fact* of evil. With this point of view we can already guess that Teilhard's "solution" will show itself to be rather inadequate. But before judging it, let us try to present it, and to that end let us read that which in my opinion is a most crucial passage from *Comment je vois:*

But let us set aside imaginary speculations in order to look at the real conditions which we observed the creative act must satisfy. It follows from our analysis, that *not at all because of inability* but by virtue of *the very structure of nothingness* over which God leans, in order to create he can proceed *in only one way*. He must under his attractive influence arrange and unify little by little by utilizing the groping set of great numbers—a multiple, immense number of elements at first infinitely numerous, extremely simple, and hardly conscious and then becoming gradually more rarified, more complex, and finally endowed with reflection. But what is the inevitable counterpart of the complete success which is obtained by following a process of this type? Is it not the payment of a certain amount of waste? It involves disharmony or physical decomposition in the pre-living, suffering in the living, and sin in the domain of liberty. There is no *order in formation* which doesn't involve some *disorder* at every step. I repeat that there is nothing in this ontological condition (or more exactly ontogenical) of that-which-is-participated which does any damage to the dignity of God or limits the omnipotence of the Creator. Nor is there anything here which resembles Manicheism. In itself the purely unorganized multiple is not bad. But because it is multiple, that is, essentially subject to the law of chance in its arrangements, it absolutely cannot progress toward unity without giving rise to (free as it is) some evil here or there and that *by statistical necessity*. *Necessarium est ut adveniant Scandala*. If (as it is inevitable to admit, I think) from the standpoint of our line of reasoning there is only one possible way for God to create, that is, evolutively by way of unification, then evil is an inevitable byproduct. It appears to be a pain or affliction which is inbuilt in creation itself.

This passage which is particularly important for our purpose is also particularly obscure in appearance. What is this nothingness over which God leans? Certainly it is not that of Berdyaev and apophatic theology or the "Ungründ" of Jacob Boehme, since it is full of a more and more complex "multitude of elements." Let us note well that Teilhard posits liberty in man and nowhere else, which should be sufficient to distinguish his thought from that of Berdyaev since, as we doubtless recall, uncreated liberty is the very foundation of all being for Berdyaev. The theologian whom Teilhard most nearly approaches at this point would perhaps be St. Augustine. The Bishop of Hippo developed the idea that evil should arise from the very nothingness from which the creatures were created, that it should be in some way the nonbeing within every created being. Consequently only the Word would escape evil since the Word was born of God himself and not created (*De Civitate Dei,* Migne, PL T, XLI, col. 418).

But the difference between St. Augustine and Teilhard appears in the fact that the Augustinian universe is fixed (although the new may appear in it by virtue of the famous theory of *seminales rationes* according to which things created on the first day or at least certain ones among them contained in potentiality new things which were destined to be born at any time by reason of the power of spontaneous generation which was considered to be at work in the world in St. Augustine's time) while the universe of Teilhard is in evolution. In effect, if the world evolves and if this evolution tends toward the realization of the person, it is necessary for nonbeing to decrease. The decrease of nonbeing is correlative to the growth of being.

The growth of being itself will be expressed in Teilhard's thought through the theme of union. It is not possible within the limits of this exposition to set forth the whole Teilhardian ontology. Let us confine ourselves to pointing out that for Teilhard *esse* is identical to *unire,* because being never exists *in se* and *per se.* Being only exists "united to," and this is equally applied to the being of God since the Christian God is defined precisely as Trinity. So we can understand why "to create" is "to arrange and to unify little by little." But we can also understand at the same time why all creative activity involves *ipso facto* disorder and waste. Of necessity, to put in order and to unite is also to cut off, to suppress, and to leave aside. In order for a new species, which is better "centered" and in better alignment with the pole of evolution, to arise from the anterior "bushing out" (the vertebrates from the initial bushing out or the homo sapiens from the bushing out of the anthropoids, for example), it is necessary that numerous species not progress further from the potentialities which they have effectively realized; it is necessary that they stagnate. But to stagnate in a world in evolution is to regress. Therefore, by "statistical necessity" some disharmonies and some sufferings appear. Naturally we cannot include under the general category of "evil" everything in our experience which appears to be incomplete or unfinished. At every moment in the process of evolution there are those things which "relapse" because that which is not ascending is descending. But these relapses have allowed the growth of that which ascends—the ascent of that which ascends. Would one say that it is an "evil" when the first two stages of a rocket fall away one after the other after each has made its own strong contribution to putting the capsule in orbit? To speak this way it would be necessary to ascribe to each of these stages the *desire* to go higher and consequently the disappointment of not attaining it. In fact evil only appears as such in the context of a possible good, as the foot of a mountain appears low only when we also look at the peak, to use one of Teilhard's illustrations.

The problem of evil is therefore not posed in a world where the desire to climb higher does not exist, that is, where consciousness does not exist. That we only maintain our life to the detriment of other lives which we consume at each meal is not an *evil*, it is a *fact*. Absolute respect for life would lead us purely and simply to death. Naturally this does not mean that the dreadful waste of natural resources to which we give ourselves may be a *good;* on the contrary it may quickly appear to be an *evil*, but wholly as an *evil-for-us*.

But more precisely there is some evil, in our view, because, as Teilhard says, man "has along with the awful liberty of accepting for himself or refusing for himself in regard to the effort, the awful faculty of contending with or of censuring life." As he faces the painful labor of the effort to pursue on and the trial of going through death, man is tempted to fall back "to the depth of his prison in a grim isolation" or else to be scattered in hopeless efforts to break his chains or finally to dissolve his anguish in gratification. Thus it is that evil presents itself to the consciousness as the very aspect of the pain of life because of the movement which carries us along.

"For at least three reasons a personalizing evolution is terribly painful," Teilhard writes, because we have to undergo three "pains" which correspond to the three characteristics of evolution —the pain of *plurality* which results from the difficulty of being already fully *one,* the pain of *differentiation* because we can only rise or grow through suffering, and finally the pain of *metamorphosis* because it underscores the "only true evil of the person— death" (*Esquisse d'un univers personnel,* unpublished). Through these pains we are growing pursuant to the person, but it first appears that we are diminishing. And "what makes evil of evil is not at all the pain, but the feeling of diminishing by the pain." If we could feel that by the pain we would increase and grow, then we could accept the pain. But who can make us feel this way?

Teilhard answers—the crucified Christ!

He writes: "On the cross we are perhaps prone to see only individual suffering and simple expiation. The creative power of this death escapes us" (*apud* C. Cuénot, p. 484).[1] In reality, the Christ on the cross is, for Teilhard, "both the symbol and the reality of the immense and long-term labor of the centuries which, little by little, has raised up the created spirit in order to restore it to the depths of the divine milieu." (*Le Milieu divin.*) [2]

These burning and enigmatic words can be understood in the light of what we have just seen. The crucified Christ does not symbolize the failure of God before evil but, on the contrary, his victory through evil and also announces the possibility and the reality of a transformation of evil into good, *"omnia convertuntur in bonum,"* as Teilhard is fond of repeating with St. Paul. It is in this sense that "from the Christian standpoint the creation is consummated in the passion of Jesus." From this point of view the cross has an eminently positive meaning, and that is why for the Christian it is not a matter of swooning in the shadow of the cross but of rising up in the light of the cross."

So, evil does exist, and at the heart of and even because of evolution, but it is surmountable, and the crucified Christ has effec-

[1] See Claude Cuénot, *Teilhard de Chardin* (Baltimore: Helicon Press, 1965), p. 402.
[2] See *The Divine Milieu* (New York: Harper & Row, 1960), p. 79.

tively overcome it. Moreover, in Christian terms, it is precisely revealed to us in "the crucified death of this adored being." But this
revelation itself has for its counterpart that which Teilhard will
call "the revelation of an original fall [which gives] the reason for
certain excess in the flood of sin and suffering." [3] Though un-
usual in appearance, this theme was nevertheless expected, for
we could hardly believe that Teilhard could have dodged it even
if he had wanted to do so. There are as many people who would
prefer to give up redemption rather than to give up original sin
as there are people who would prefer to give up paradise if there
were no hell—for others.

On at least two occasions, in 1924 and in 1947, Teilhard
sketched out several reflections about original sin and proposed
them "for the criticism of the theologians." The essay of 1947 is
precisely entitled *Réflexions sur le Péché originel* and is more
complete than that of 1924. And so let us trace out the substance
of this essay.

First of all, Teilhard observes that within the last several generations our view of the world has changed because of the appearance of new "dimensions" in the field of our experience. The two
major characteristics of our new *Weltanschauung* are the *organic-
ity* of the universe—that is, the coextension of every event to the
totality of space-time; and the *atomicity* of the cosmic fabric—
that is, the fact that the world arranges itself by innumerable attempts. They do not affect the axes of Christian dogma, but it is
evident that theological thought must express itself in accord with
them so that the homogeneity and the coherence of truth may be
safeguarded. A necessary adjustment results from this, however,
which presents itself uniquely when it is a question of the theory
of original sin. In the formulation which is still current today
original sin is at the same time a difficulty and indeed a scandal
for undecided men of good will and a refuge for narrow-minded
men. Now it should be sufficient to correct a simple error in the
perspective of the usual representations so that they might stop
paralyzing the structuring of a thoroughly human Christian vision
of the world. Ordinarily original sin is considered as an event set
in a series or a chain of events *within* history. Would it not be

[3] *Ibid.*, p. 77.

better to regard it first of all as a reality of transhistorical order affecting the totality of our vision of the world?

Theologians are unanimous at one point—the "reactive" or result of original sin is death. "This is why by the use of a rigid logic the sick authors of *l'Evolution régressive* try to localize the fall before any known fossil, that is, in the Pre-cambrian." In reality, in order to get at the beginnings of death one must go well beyond this point. Indeed, what is death if not the result of the "essential disintegration of every corpuscular structure"? With this definition death appears with the atom. It is impossible to get away from the "mortal" without getting away from the world. Death affects and infects all time and space. Therefore, if there is original sin which is generative of death, of necessity it is every-where and at all times. Now it is quite proper that we are brought to this conclusion—this theological conclusion which confirms the experiential evidence—if we then extend to the very limit "the most orthodox demands of Christology."

In effect, the aim of Christian orthodoxy is brought back finally to this: "to maintain Christ as the measure and the head of creation," as immense as this may be. "But can we stress too many times the necessary corollary of this first principle?" If the fall were an event localized in the tertiary, the ruling and redemptive power of Christ "would not go beyond a short and scanty part of the universe around us." It is therefore necessary to reflect on the phenomenon of the fall "in order to see how it can be conceived and imagined not as an isolated fact but as a general condition affecting the totality of history" and therefore, anterior to history.

This line of study is not absolutely new. It has already been explored, especially by the Alexandrine school which looked at the original process (creation-fall) according to the following four stages: (1) The instantaneous creation of a perfect mankind (the first Adam) or again the "Edenic phase"; (2) the disobedi-ence of the first Adam in whatever way one wishes to conceive it; (3) the fall into the "multiple" and actually the production of the multiple as such which is the "precosmic phase of involution"; and finally (4) the redemptive reascent through progressive re-organization and reunification *toward* and *in* the second Adam which is the "cosmic, historical phase of evolution." Indeed, this scheme takes account of conditions actually posed for every theory of the fall, since it appears to us today (beyond the third state which it describes) that we are indeed caught up and involved in the movement by which the multiple moves evolutively toward unity, with death always present. Therefore this description appears to be valid. However, there are several valid reasons for correcting it. First, the initial three acts of the drama are purely imaginary and inferred. In the next place the instantaneous creation of the first Adam is understood either as an unintelligible operation or else as a word, a purely verbal declaration covering up the absence of any effort at explanation. And finally, "in the hypothesis of a *unique* and *perfect* being who is put to the test only one time, the chance of a fall is so slight that truly when it happens the Creator appears to be the most unlucky or unfortunate one in the whole affair."

For all these reasons Teilhard had been attracted for a long time by another kind of solution "with more dignity for the world and for God at the same time" which he gives to us under the heading of *evolutive creation and the statistical origin of evil*.

In the thesis of the school of Alexandria, the multiple from which evolution proceeds is a *secondary* reality and a *product* of sin at the same time. It is the fact of a broken and pulverized unity. On the contrary, let us consider the multiple as *original*. Let us represent it as this "createable-nothingness," this nonbeing which God will call into being by arranging it and unifying it. To this end we must again recover the idea that to create is to unify, and there follows from this the statement that *union creates*. If anyone should object here that union assumes preexistent matter—and therefore an anterior creation or the eternality of matter—it should be remembered that physics has demonstrated (in the case of *mass*) that experimentally the mobile is produced by movement.

Therefore, let us consider the multiple as original. As such it has no "sinfulness," but as soon as it begins the process of unification in the immensity of space-time, we see it become impregnated with pains and errors. It is statistically inevitable that in the course of the journey some local disorders will appear, and consequently there will result *collective disordered conditions* with pain in the midst of the living and sin in the midst of man.

If we accept this, the problem of original sin is solved. Indeed, the facts of science are respected since the experimental body of dogma coincides with that of evolution, but also "the (intellectual) problem of evil vanishes. Indeed, since in this perspective physical suffering and moral wrong introduce themselves *inevitably* into the world, not by virtue of some deficiency in the creative act but by the very structure of being-which-is-participated (that is, as a *statistically inevitable by-product* of the unification of the multiple), they neither contradict the power nor the goodness of God." In the last place, finally, the theology of salvation is respected and justified. Doubtless original sin ceases to be an isolated *act* and becomes a *state*. This very thing even intensifies the dogmatic characteristics of the fall and also lends itself well to the truly universal dimensions of redemption.

"On the other hand, individual baptism conserves or even augments its own *raison d'etre*. Indeed, in this perspective each new soul which is awakened to life is found completely contaminated by the totalized influences of all past, present (and future?) transgressions and errors inevitably scattered by statistical necessity within the human ensemble in the process of sanctification."

Moreover, we see how the more and more oppressive hypothesis of a *first* human *couple* is no longer evident. In brief, it is sufficient "to replace the womb of our mother Eve by a collective womb and collective heredity."

In a resumé as brief as possible, such is the Teilhardian conception of original sin. Its difficulties as well as its insufficiencies are quite apparent. It certainly does not give a truly satisfying solution to the problem of evil, which it evidently intends to give. In fact, it perhaps raises more questions than it solves.

It does not wash God entirely clean from the reproach often addressed to the Creator of all things—the accusation of also being the Creator of evil. If God is the author of the multiple which is called to unite itself through a painful process, and if the multiple as such admits of elements the arrangement of which will produce some disharmonies and some evils, how can we say that the multiple *is not* evil even though evil may in fact be produced by the operation which unites the multiple or, as Teilhard says, *creates* it? It may be true that in this view evil does not result from *created nature* but from the *creative act*. Nevertheless, God remains the *author* since he could neither make a multiple to appear which did not potentially contain future evil nor unite the multiple without allowing waste. The solution of Teilhard shipwrecks on the same beach as all the monistic-type solutions. It retains the omnipotence of God, but it includes evil in the creative act of the All-powerful. The fact of not calling this evil by the name evil but considering it as a statistically inevitable reality changes nothing in the whole question.

In addition, it is apparent that the nature of sin (original or not) is not exactly recognized. In effect, we cannot see why the necessity for creation to suffer in order to be united would call for these "redemptive compensations" to which Teilhard often makes allusion. In one way of looking at it, redemption is something other than a *compensation* because sin is something other than a statistical necessity.

We could multiply remarks of this kind, and whoever would like to show that Teilhard's theory does not furnish a satisfactory solution to the problem of evil would have an easy time of it. However, one always has an easy time of it when the destruction of the theories of evil is up for discussion. Every effort to give evil a rational status must inevitably fail (and every theory of evil is an effort of this kind) because what decisively characterizes evil is its *fundamental irrationality,* as the existentialist philosophers have correctly observed. Also, it is this very irrationality which shows that the traditional doctrine of original sin (that which we found earlier stated by Bossuet, for example) is terribly unsatisfactory. It also presents itself as a rationalization of the irrational, that is, as an undertaking which is intellectually doomed to fail. Therefore we could not place it opposite the Teilhardian solution, as one would place truth opposite error. The idea that the error of an original couple should involve all of mankind in sin is itself nothing more than a rationalization of the experience of the rupture and the misery of being which the whole Bible tells us takes its depth and its meaning from the very fact that men cannot escape from God—even when they become convinced that there *is* no God. This experience remains universal and fundamental and for this reason we will meditate about the first chapters of Genesis until the end of time. This experience can never be completely rationalized, not even in the explanations of the catechism. There is no society in which men have not experienced the misery of being. The "noble savages" have truly never existed—now or in the past. Neither has there been a society, however, which has not tried to *describe* the origin of this misery. But all these *representations* and descriptions have failed to say what they truly wanted to say. Like love, evil is inexhaustible.

Therefore, it must be understood that it is not a question of judging the Teilhardian problematic of evil from the point of view of a *correct, exact,* or *true* theory. At most we can and should ask in what way this problematic makes any progress in our necessary yet discouraging reflection in regard to evil.

It seems to me that progress is made on at least two points.

In the first place, it leads us to *situate* evil better by clearing up and freeing us from the idea that matter is evil in itself. When a lion eats a gazelle it is perhaps good for the lion (I mean for the *Weltanschauung* which the leonine species would develop, if it could philosophize). It is certainly an *evil* for the gazelle. And for the scholar it is a *fact*—one of the millions of facts which assure the biological equilibrium of the earth. It is by the projection onto this fact of information acquired in the exercise of the moral human life that one will be able to judge it as good or evil, according to whether one identifies oneself with the lion or with the gazelle. The judgment does not result from the fact; it is imposed by a demand which itself results from the *human* style of life. It is apparent that when we say that "matter" is evil we mean nothing more than this: It *appears* to be evil to our conscience. But above all it appears to be such because of the impossibility of our being able to discern the *goal* or the *end* (the *telos*) of matter. If the material processes are just without characteristics and not tending toward anything, then matter exists absurdly, and we can find it "bad." But this understanding must change at the moment when the world takes on *meaning* and *direction* for us.

When the first chapter of Genesis tells us that after each day of creation God found the creation to be "good," it only intends to say that the creation, as it has left the Creator's hands, was perfectly *fit* to realize the intention or the plan of the Creator. We have lost sight of this "goodness" because we have projected upon it the idea of an impossible moral perfection. In showing us how the world tends toward fulfillment, Teilhard helps us rediscover that the world is "good" in the sense in which the Bible speaks of its "goodness."

At the same time he helps us to rediscover that evil in the world is either not an evil but a fact or else an evil but then *our* fact—either because of our bad action or because as victims of unchained nature we experience it as bad.

In every way the statement *"the world is bad"* is stripped of meaning unless by "world" one means the *human* world. Similarly, the statement *"the world is perfect"* would also be stripped of meaning. The world is neither bad nor perfect; it is good. It is only everything that a world can and must be which, seen from our standpoint and according to our possibilities of appreciation, is in evolution and tends to realize itself through man. Evil is man's affair; not that all evil necessarily comes from man, but because all evil is evil for man.

The second point in which Teilhard's theory helps us is relative to the idea of the *origin* of evil. The hypothesis according to which a first couple was responsible for the sin of mankind by reason of the heredity of characteristics acquired through one unique act is completely unacceptable, in this form at least. Also, it is not biblical, because *Adam* in the Old as well as the New Testament is not the name of an individual but a generic term. And the idea of a heredity of sins by way of biological descendance is not a biblical idea either. On the other hand, what is biblical is the idea of the *solidarity* of the group—what Wheeler Robinson has called the idea of "corporate personality." According to this idea, the individual represents the whole group in space and in time, and reciprocally the entire group is responsible for the individual. In other words, no human act whether bad or good is the isolated act of an *individual* only. Every act involves the group and at the limit all mankind, because of the interrelationship between groups. We could expand this theme with many interesting developments (and in appearance very Teilhardian) in particular by showing how the more the world contracts, the more the influence of isolated, individual acts whether good or bad expands and strengthens itself. It is perhaps interesting to state in passing that the life and death of men today depend on the good or bad decisions made by a small number of men about whom there is no *a priori* evidence that they are necessarily the wisest or the most intelligent or better than others. But it is clear that each one of them acts as the representative of a large number of men for whom he is responsible and the spokesman. Is this not in some way "corporate personality"? And to an involved degree? The great idea of Teilhard is that men are more and more responsible for one another so that the evil which we do results in more and more evil, and the good is more and more beneficial to all.

But if such is the case today, and if such must increasingly be the case, who cannot see that what we call evil appears in the world at the same time that man appears *related* to man? But the relationship of man to man is perfectly original and basic. As Teilhard has clearly observed, it exists *before* all history since history begins with it. Evil is not an *accident* contingent upon our condition; it is a part of this very condition, or rather it is a certain coloring of our condition. It is our condition insofar as we can refuse it or, on the contrary, become "glued up" in it by refusing to believe that it could change.

Perhaps the root of evil is despair. Teilhard has very correctly observed that we always act in an evil manner when we cease to believe in the world, when we cease to believe in what we are doing, and, it should be added, when we cease to believe in what God wants us to see and do in order for the world to be "good."

But in all this it is not a question of what has come down to us from the first couple. It is rather a question of what affects the whole human race, always and everywhere, not by virtue of the heredity of an initial sin, but by virtue of an identity of the *structures* of the being-man throughout time and space. Certainly an irrationality is involved here. That which is given always and everywhere in our very structures is involved here—and without anything to render it exactly understandable! In this sense, once again the problem of evil is insoluble.

However, Teilhard is right once again when he affirms that evil is such only evolutively, that is, only relatively to future good. Evil is evil only as a consequence of a passion for the best. In other words, once again there is evil only if the world is going somewhere, if it has meaning and direction. And then evil is the *nondirection of this direction and the nonmeaning of this meaning*. It is a nonmeaning and a nondirection which can be overcome only

when he who is the very meaning and direction of the world comes
to submit himself to the law of nonmeaning and nondirection and
to give a meaning and direction to the very absurdity of his passion
and his death.

I am not sure that the last statements are very Teilhardian.
Teilhard alone could say. And he is dead, a victim also of the
apparent triumph of nonmeaning. But that we may thus prolong
the Teilhardian meditation shows clearly enough that even though
his own rationalization of evil may be unsatisfactory, Teilhard is
not a teacher of indifference and impassibility.

There remains to determine whether he has done complete
justice to good and evil considered as constant components of
human activity. In fact, this is the major problem of history.

Suggested Readings

On Teilhard and the Problem of Evil

Crespy, Georges. *La pensée théologique de Teilhard de Chardin*. Paris:
Éditions universitaires, 1961, pp. 109-133.

Gray, Donald P. *The One and the Many: Teilhard de Chardin's Vision
of Unity*. New York: Herder and Herder, 1969, pp. 52-94.

Faricy, Robert L., S.J. "Teilhard de Chardin's Theology of Redemption," *Theological Studies,* 27 (1966), 533-579.

Francoeur, Robert. *Perspectives in Evolution*. Baltimore: Helicon, 1965,
pp. 185-229.

———. *Evolving World, Converging Man*. New York: Holt, Rinehart
and Winston, 1970, pp. 124-174.

Mooney, Christopher F., S.J. *Teilhard de Chardin and the Mystery of
Christ*. New York: Harper and Row, 1966. Paperback—New York:
Image Book.

Smulders, Piet, S.J. *The Design of Teilhard de Chardin: An Essay in
Theological Reflection*. Translated by Arthur Gibson. Westminster,
Md.: Newman Press, 1967, pp. 140-195.

Whitla, William. "Sin and Redemption in Whitehead and Teilhard,"
Anglican Theological Review, 47 (1965), 81-95.

19 Teilhard de Chardin and Christian Spirituality

CHRISTOPHER F. MOONEY

Our times have witnessed a major shift in that area of life referred to as spirituality. The world and secular concerns have emerged as important for the Christian's spiritual life. In this trend Teilhard has already had a major influence and continues to provide an overview and rationale for new forms of spirituality which are emerging. In the present selection,* Christopher Mooney sees Teilhard's thought in rapport with the contemporary emphasis on the significance of matter, on self-development, and on the relativism that flows from a sense of history. Yet Teilhard balances these by finding God in matter, by integrating the Cross into personal development, and by suffusing the relativism of history with love.

Christopher F. Mooney's chief contribution to Teilhardian studies has been Teilhard de Chardin and the Mystery of Christ. *The result of his doctoral research at the Institut Catholique of Paris, this work has been accepted by critics as the major interpretation of Teilhard's Christology. A Jesuit priest, he is former chairman of the Theology Department of Fordham University and is currently President of Woodstock College, the Jesuit seminary in New York City.*

There is in the churches at present a growing awareness, especially among the young, of the inadequacy of a large segment of what has generally been called

* From *Thought*, 42 (1967), 383-402. Reprinted with permission.

Christian spirituality. I am not speaking here of practical matters, such as the amount of time given to private prayer, the mode of conducting liturgical worship, the value of this or that rule or formula, or even the emphasis today upon individual freedom and initiative. Since the Second Vatican Council the Church as a whole has been moving away from an insistence upon conformity, and it is therefore normal that we should find all around us a search for new ideas and a willingness to experiment with new modes of spiritual formation. The problem, however, is the framework within which such experimentation takes place, the mental outlook, the "view" as Newman would call it, which is the ultimate factor in anyone's style of approach to God. Over the centuries modifications in Christian living have more or less taken place within a certain fixed framework of thought, and it is precisely this fundamental Christian image of life which is now undergoing reappraisal. This is no easy matter. It is one thing to reject old styles and attitudes and quite another to get along without them or put new ones in their place. The danger, moveover, is that the new image we create may filter out completely certain balancing elements in the old image, so that our new view of life may produce in the end just as many difficulties, psychological and spiritual, as our old.

Now, without doubt the most symbolic figure in the formation of this new Christian image of the world is Pierre Teilhard de Chardin. Christians generally feel that he has given voice to much of what they experience but find difficult to articulate. "The great converters (or perverters) of man," wrote Teilhard, "have always been those who have burned most intensely with the spirit of their times." [1] What Teilhard has done is to articulate a set of positive emphases in spirituality which the modern Christian spontaneously embraces. These range over three large areas in human living and I would like to consider each of them briefly in the pages which follow. Not only are they viable for the twentieth century, but they emerge from its very core, and they are eloquent testimony that in its interaction with the world the Christian intelligence is fundamentally creative. Yet what I wish

[1] Pierre Teilhard de Chardin, *Note pour servir à l'évangelisation des temps nouveaux*, 1919, in *Ecrits du temps de la guerre, 1916-1919* (Paris: Grasset, 1965), 367.

to stress also is that, in articulating this set of emphases which are instinctively accepted by the modern Christian, Teilhard also provides a set of balances. It is these balancing affirmations which are especially necessary today lest the spirituality we are in process of developing go to extreme, and lose thereby its distinctively Christian character. The theme of this article, then, is that the spirituality found in the writings of Father Teilhard de Chardin is thoroughly modern and at the same time authentically Christian.

I

The first positive emphasis emerging in modern Christian spirituality concerns the importance of the material world in man's relationship to God. The traditional dichotomies between natural-supernatural, body-spirit, divine-human, immanent-transcendent, sacred-secular, are becoming more and more irrelevant for the modern Christian. This is not to say that he does not recognize a distinction between what is represented by these terms when such distinctions are explained to him. The point is rather that these distinctions no longer have any significance in his spiritual development. He wants to be more deeply Christian, but he resents being told that he must therefore become less secular, because deep down he suspects that anyone today less concerned for the secular is liable also to be less Christian. Nor can such an outlook be labeled an innovation, a reversal of Christian tradition. More than one theologian has pointed out that this attitude is in fact a renewal of the early Judeo-Christian sense of man's unity with matter and his relationship to God through matter. No biblical writer could ever conceive man without his body, nor could he ever disassociate man's body from God's salvific action. The "angelism" which crept into Christian spirituality toward the end of the patristic era came not from Sacred Scripture but from Augustine and Pseudo-Dionysius; and its source in both cases seems to have been the thought of Plotinus, who according to Porphyry "seemed ashamed of being in the body." [2]

---

[2] This point has been well made by Joseph Donceel, S.J., "Teilhard de Chardin and the Body-Soul Relation," THOUGHT, XL (1965), 373-374. Father Donceel adds that the realism of St. Thomas, though it had enormous influence in philosophy and theology, had practically none in the area of spirituality.

The thought of Teilhard de Chardin has given a strong impetus to this concern for the material world in one's relationship to God. Indeed, his whole evolutionary system puts such strong emphasis on the continuity of matter and spirit that he has been accused by philosophers of being a materialist and by scientists of ignoring the concrete in order to speculate about what cannot be experimentally verified. In his theological speculation he insisted again and again that theologians give serious consideration to the physical relationship between Christ and the material world. For it is precisely the physical mediation of Christ's Body-Person, he said, which gives impetus to the evolution itself, makes ultimate sense out of man's effort to build the earth, and is finally destined to bring the material world to its consummation in God-Omega. "The whole of the Church's dogmatic and sacramental economy," he wrote, "teaches us to respect matter and to value it. Christ had to assume and wanted to assume real flesh. He sanctifies human flesh by special contact and he prepares its physical resurrection. . . . Because it has been assimilated into the Body of Christ, something from matter is destined to pass into the foundations and walls of the heavenly Jerusalem." [3] The rise of "technopolis," therefore, far from being a reason for pessimistic concern, is in reality an occasion for the Christian to devote himself more completely to the world and thereby to realize in himself the full meaning of the Incarnation.

When Teilhard applied this theological speculation to Christian living, what resulted was a call to experience God in the secular world in a way that was impossible for Christians of a former age. He once complained that manuals of ascetical theology usually accepted as axiomatic that growth in spirit could only come by separating what was assumed to be the two basic components of the universe, the pure and the impure.[4] This he rejected as Manichaean. It injects one's spiritual life, he said, with a dualism which allows only partial commitment to the world, forcing the Christian in the end to lead a double life, so that he belongs neither wholly to God nor wholly to things. What was needed, he urged, was for spiritual writers to concern themselves

[3] La Vie cosmique, 1916, in Ecrits du temps de la guerre, 53.

[4] Réflexions sur deux formes universes d'esprit, 1950, in L'Activation de l'énergie (Paris: Seuil, 1963), 230, note 1.

with the material world, "to discover what there could be that is divine and predestined within the matter itself of our cosmos, our humanity and our progress." [5] The supernatural is a ferment, he wrote in another essay, not a finished organism. Its role is to transform nature, but it cannot do so apart from the matter which nature provides it with.[6]

Now as we shall see in a moment, Teilhard was well aware that such stress on the importance of the material world in one's relationship to God is not without its dangers. Not everyone today who writes on this subject, however, would seem to have such an awareness. In *The Secular City* Harvey Cox says that the Gospel is "a call to imaginative urbanity and mature secularity," and nothing more.[7] There is no concern at all in his book for any direct personal relationship between God and man. "Like his relationship to his work partner, man's relationship to God derives from the work they do together. . . . God manifests himself to us in and through secular events." [8] This is true enough, but such an "I-You" relationship, as Cox calls it, can scarcely have any Christian significance unless it is based upon a prior "I-Thou" relationship, a direct turning toward God present in the human heart. God indeed manifests Himself in the material world and in the events of our lives, but we shall never find Him there unless we have first found Him within ourselves. Significantly enough, there is no mention of prayer in *The Secular City,* no mention of converse of any kind either with Christ or with the Father. Rather the impression is conveyed that any such I-Thou relationship would be inimical to one's involvement in the human task. "God wants man to be interested not in him but in his fellow man," says Cox.[9]

Teilhard, on the other hand, was not at all content with the abstract statement that God manifests Himself to us in and through the material world. What he wanted was actually to find God, to be aware of His presence in people and things, to pos-

[5] Letter of March 15, 1916, in Henri de Lubac, S.J., *La Pensée religieuse du Père Teilhard de Chardin* (Paris: Aubier, 1962), 349.

[6] *Le Milieu divin,* 1926-1927 (Paris: Seuil, 1957), 199; Eng. trans., *The Divine Milieu* (New York: Harper and Row, revised edition, 1965), 152.

[7] Harvey Cox, *The Secular City* (New York: Macmillan, 1965), 83.

[8] *Ibid.,* 265, 266.

[9] *Ibid.,* 265.

sess Him and be possessed by Him. "The veneer of color and scene bores me to tears," he once wrote from China. "What I love is hidden. . . . Even when I am most absorbed in geology, my interest has already wandered elsewhere. It is the Other that I seek." [10] Such an attitude toward matter explains why Teilhard could look upon the world as a crystal lamp illumined from within by the light of Christ.[11] This image, mentioned first in a 1916 essay, is a graphic illustration of the idea which will impregnate all his writings, even the most philosophical and scientific, namely, that there is a creative presence of Christ in everyone and everything everywhere, a universal and cosmic "diaphany," as he calls it, which began with His historical epiphany. This presence is therefore a human as well as a divine presence, founded upon the physical relationship of Christ's Body-Person through whom the creative action of God is channeled.

Like those translucent materials which can be wholly illumined by a light enclosed within them, the world manifests itself to the Christian mystic as bathed in an inward light. . . . This light . . . is the tranquil, mighty radiance born of the synthesis in Jesus of all the elements of the world. The more completely the beings thus illumined attain their natural fulfillment, the closer and more perceptible this radiance will be.[12]

Or consider the following text:

Lord God, grant that the light of your countenance may shine forth for me in other men. . . . Grant me to see you . . . above all in the most inward, most perfect, most remote levels of the souls of my brothers. The gift you ask of me for these brothers of mine . . . is not the overflowing tenderness of those special, preferential loves which you implant in our lives, but something less tender, though just as real and even more strong. Your will is that, with the help of your Eucharist, there should be revealed between me and my brother-men that basic attraction . . . which mystically transforms the myriads of rational creatures into a single monad, as it were, in you, Christ Jesus.[13]

[10] *Lettres de voyage* (Paris: Grasset, 1961), 87, 105; Eng. trans., *Letters From a Traveller* (New York: Harper and Row, 1962), 123, 140.
[11] *Le Christ dans la matière*, 1916, in *Ecrits du temps de la guerre*, 98-100.
[12] *Le Milieu divin*, 162; Eng. trans., 130-131.
[13] *Ibid.*, 185; Eng. trans., 145.

This overreaching desire of Teilhard to see through the world of people and things and find God is the reason why he is at such pains to show that material evolution is ultimately oriented toward growth of the spiritual. Thus the function he assigns to his law of complexity-consciousness is that of allowing the "within" of things to emerge, to promote growth in "consciousness," by the interplay of radial and tangential energy. Unlike many physical scientists, Teilhard refused to see in the law of entropy a gloomy prediction that the universe will one day run down completely and stop. Such a law, he felt, told us only about the "without" of things and left untouched the world of spirit "within." "The whole movement of material growth in the universe," he wrote, "is ultimately directed toward spirit, and the whole movement of spiritual growth is ultimately directed toward Christz." [14] Hence he could pray: "By virtue of your suffering Incarnation, disclose to us the spiritual power of matter, and then teach us to harness it jealously for you." [15]

Gabriel Vahanian has written that there is no reason why secularity, by which he means involvement in the world for the sake of God's glory, should ever slip into secularism, or what he calls an immanentist religiosity.[16] This may indeed be true, but only if the person involved is ultimately seeking to possess God through this involvement. He will find God in people and things only if he wants to find Him there. This is why Teilhard, while rejecting a spirituality based exclusively upon the pure intention, puts such emphasis himself upon the virtue of purity in his own spirituality. This he defines, interestingly enough, as "the rectitude and impulse introduced into our lives by the love of God sought in and above everything." The intensity of this purity in men increases and is measured by the "degree of attraction that draws them to the divine Center." The sanctification of human effort depends then, he continues, "upon the initial and fundamental role of one's intention, which is indeed . . . the golden key which unlocks our interior world to the presence of God. . . . It is God and God alone whom [the Christian] pursues through the reality of

[14] *Mon Univers*, 1924, in *Science et Christ* (Paris: Seuil, 1965), 96.
[15] *Le Milieu divin*, 123; Eng. trans., 82.
[16] Gabriel Vahanian, *Wait Without Idols* (New York: Braziller, 1964), 235.

created things. His interest lies truly in things but in absolute dependence upon God's presence in them." [17]

These texts of Teilhard are sufficient, I think, to underline the point I am making. Christian spirituality is undergoing a long overdue change of style, and one of the elements in this change is the growing emphasis upon the importance of the material world. Teilhard has encouraged this emphasis, has to some degree even been responsible for it, in so far as he insists upon the relationship of Christ to the universe and the consequent significance of human work as a cooperation in the creative action of God. Yet this thoroughly modern emphasis has a tendency to overlook what Teilhard never overlooked, namely, that building the earth can have no Christian significance except in so far as individual men give it that significance; and this they do by their personal union with Christ and their desire above all else to seek and to find Him in every earthly task to which they commit themselves. Only then will they have a right to say with Teilhard that nothing here below is profane for those who know how to see.[18] For such "seeing" is a gift of God and is given only to those who desire it. This is the first of the balances which Teilhard brings to his spirituality of human conquest, and it keeps this spirituality authentically Christian. We might summarize it in a final text in which Teilhard speaks once more of purity:

To be pure of heart means to love God above all things and at the same time to see him everywhere in all things. Whether the just man is rising above and beyond all creatures to an almost immediate awareness of Godhead or throwing himself upon the world to conquer it and bring it to perfection, as it is every man's duty to do, he will have eyes only for God. . . . The pure heart is the heart which, surmounting the multiple and disruptive pull of created things, fortifies its unity, that is to say, matures its spirituality, in the fire of the divine simplicity.[19]

II

There is a second emphasis emerging strongly today in Christian spirituality. This is the emphasis upon self-fulfillment in man's

[17] Le Milieu divin, 166, 39, 66; Eng. trans., 133, 23, 42.
[18] Ibid., 56; Eng. trans., 66.
[19] La Lutte contre la multitude, 1917, in Ecrits du temps de la guerre, 126.

relationship with God. Here again, what we are experiencing is a reaction against a certain anti-humanist tendency in spiritual teaching. Frequently the test of one's union with God was one's willingness to embrace an ideal that was very often in opposition to one's development as a man. Hence the importance placed on certain ascetical practices, the performance of fixed penances, and the over-all suspicion of any purely spontaneous natural inclination. The rigidity of obedience was a natural offshoot of this: the spiritual ideal was never to do one's own will, always the will of another. Other things being equal, the work one was engaged in was presumed to have more value in so far as one did not really enjoy it. Many of the agonizing problems of conscience today in regard to sexual morality have their ultimate roots in the belief that even though sex was not evil in itself, it could hardly be more than tolerated in someone aspiring to lead a full Christian life. The emphasis upon the deleterious effects of original sin, upon the passion and death of Christ rather than upon His Resurrection and glory, upon the sacrificial aspects of charity rather than upon the joy of community living, upon resignation in defeat rather than battle for victory, all this set a style to Christian spirituality against which there are now open resentment and rejection.

This should come as no surprise to anyone. We are living in the era of the person. The value of the human person in all his uniqueness and freedom is perhaps the single most influential discovery of modern man. From it has come the new stress on personal initiative, responsibility and freedom. Christian spirituality must offer fulfillment to the person, and it must offer it to him now, not in some future life with which the present life has seemingly little connection. The ideal which the modern Christian wants is the ideal of the fully human. Far from being a desire to have things easy, such an ideal in fact inspires the greatest generosity, and involves a readiness to endure almost any inconvenience and hardship to help the underprivileged and to further the great social movements of our day. Witness the present response to the civil rights movement and to the call of the Peace Corps. Witness the uncompromising intellectual honesty of young people, their repudiation of violence and hypocrisy, their desire to be close to others in community. Such an outlook, moreover, has been strongly seconded by the Second Vatican Council in its *Pastoral*

Constitution on the Church in the Modern World. Its emphasis upon the humanizing influence of Christ is a clear departure in tone for Church documents. Christ is He who "fully reveals man to man himself" and "whoever follows after Christ, the perfect man, becomes himself more of a man." For it is Christ who "animates, purifies, and strengthens those noble longings too by which the human family strives to make its life more human and to render the whole earth submissive to this goal." Indeed, it is precisely the plan of God that the Church "contribute greatly toward making the family of man and its history more human." [20]

This relationship between Christianity and self-fulfillment worried Teilhard all his life. "How is one to be more fully a Christian than anyone," he asked early in life, "and at the same time more fully a man?" For what he feared was precisely that he might "remain uncommitted among my fellow men, and because of my religion they will regard me as a deserter who is only half a man. . . . It is absolutely necessary that Christ be as large as my life, my whole life. I must have an awareness of growing in him, not only by asceticism and the painful wrench of suffering . . . but also by whatever positive effort I am capable of, whatever is naturally perfective in my human achievement. I must have this awareness, I say, otherwise Christianity would be robbing me of the courage to act." [21] At another time he asked, "To be a Christian must I really give up trying to be human, human in the widest and deepest sense of the word, totally and passionately human?" [22] Five years before his death he admits that all during his life he had been "compelled by an inner constraint to leave the well beaten track of a certain traditional type of asceticism not fully human, in order to search out a way to heaven along which the whole dynamism of matter and flesh can pass by way of synthesis into the birth of spirit. . . . To reach heaven by bringing earth to perfection. To Christify matter. That is the whole adventure of my life, a great and magnificent adventure, during which I am still often afraid, but to which it was impossible not to have committed myself." [23]

[20] *Pastoral Constitution on the Church in the Modern World,* in *The Documents of Vatican II* (New York: Guild Press, 1966), 220, 240, 236, 239.
[21] Letter of December 12, 1919, in *Archives de Philosophie,* XXIV (1961), 138.
[22] *La Vie cosmique,* 1916 in *Ecrits du temps de la guerre,* 7.
[23] *Le Coeur de la Matière,* 1950, 23, 25. An unpublished essay.

This last text implies what Teilhard said explicitly more than once, namely, that certain risks are involved in leaving "the beaten track of a certain traditional type of asceticism not fully human." Hence his concern to integrate into his ideal of the fully human a set of balances. These he summarized briefly in a 1943 essay on human happiness: "To be fully human and fully alive, a man must first be centered on himself, then centered away from himself in others, and finally centered beyond himself in Someone greater than he." [24] It is possible today, by emphasizing self-fulfillment, to lose sight of the corresponding need in our relationship with God of the second two experiences which Teilhard stresses here, namely, that of decentering or detachment, and that of purification, or what he calls a "surcentering" upon God. He believed, first of all, that any man truly devoted to the human, though outwardly he might be immersed in the concerns of earth, must become a man of great detachment. Detachment for him is in fact inseparable from true possession. "To create or organize material energy, or truth, or beauty, brings with it inner torment which prevents those who face its hazards from sinking into the quiet and closed-in life wherein grows the vice of self-regard and attachment. . . . Over and over again he must go beyond himself, leaving behind him his most cherished beginnings." [25] Especially is this true of the Christian, for he knows that his function is to divinize the world in Jesus Christ, and consequently in him that detachment through action should reach its maximum.

The Christian, who is by right the first and most human of men, is more subject than others to the psychological reversal whereby, in the case of intelligent creatures, joy in action imperceptibly melts into desire for submission, and the exaltation of becoming one's own self into the zeal to die in another. Having been perhaps primarily alive to the attractions of union with God through action, he begins to conceive and then to desire a complementary aspect, an ulterior phase, in his communion: one in which he would not develop himself so much as lose himself in God.[26]

This mention of losing oneself in God brings us to the second

[24] *Réflexions sur le bonheur*, 1943, in *Cahiers Pierre Teilhard de Chardin*, II (Paris: Seuil, 1960), 61.
[25] *Le Milieu divin*, 64; Eng. trans., 71.
[26] *Ibid.*, 71; Eng. trans., 74.

balance never far from Teilhard's mind, and also indicates how closely the two balances are linked together. For in every Christian life detachment must lead to purification and there is no purification without pain. This is why there is in Teilhard a constant awareness of the harsh realities of life, above all the reality of death. The experience of death was in fact a primordial experience for him, and its theme appears again and again in his writings.[27] For this experience of human self-fulfillment cut short and of hopes shattered is one that no man can avoid. What is the use of an emphasis on self-fulfillment if it can all be swept aside in a moment by death, or by war, or by the greed and stupidity of men? And how is self-fulfillment to be integrated into the feelings of futility which come with sickness, human misunderstandings, or the inevitable failures which must somehow be part of every effort to take part in the creative activity of God? Teilhard would be quite disturbed were he to hear what is not infrequently said today, that modern man looks upon life as a set of problems, not an unfathomable mystery, that he consequently spends little time thinking about the so-called ultimate questions. Teilhard's reaction might well be that whoever this modern man is, he is not Christian man. For the real world for the Christian is the world where Christ was crucified, and if the Cross means anything it must mean that all men, even those who labor to improve the world and fulfill themselves as men, must expect and accept suffering before achievement, self-renunciation before self-fulfillment, and death before true life.

It is very significant that a man so committed to human fulfillment could write to a close friend in 1934: "What we have to learn is to preserve a real appetite for life and action while at the same time renouncing once and for all any desire to be happy just for ourselves. There is the secret—and not the illusion—of living in the divine Milieu." [28] He meant this, too, for he wrote another friend that we must "cherish, along with the fulfillments in

---

[27] For a full treatment of this large subject, see Christopher F. Mooney, S.J., *Teilhard de Chardin and the Mystery of Christ* (New York: Harper and Row, 1966), 106-121.

[28] Undated letter of 1934, quoted in *Lettres de voyage*, 180; Eng. trans., 206. The phrase "divine Milieu" was almost always used by Teilhard as a proper name for Christ, to indicate His physical omnipresence in the world. See on this point, *op. cit.*, 80 ff.

our life everything that diminishes us, that is to say, all the passive purifications which Christ has planned for us in order to transform into himself those elements of our personality which we seek to develop for him." [29] It is perfectly true that Teilhard was most concerned with the positive meaning of the Cross, the support given by Christ's sufferings and death to the pain of human endeavor and to the upward movement of man in the noosphere. Yet he has put no less emphasis than St. John of the Cross upon those passive purifications in the spiritual life which, as far as we can see, do nothing at all for our human endeavor. In these cases, he says, human wisdom is altogether out of its depth. "At every moment we see diminishments, both in us and around us, which do not seem to be compensated by advantages on any perceptible plane, premature deaths, stupid accidents, weaknesses affecting the highest reaches of our being. Under blows such as these man does not move upward in any direction that we can perceive; he disappears or remains grievously diminished." [30] How then, he asks, can such diminishments, which are altogether without compensation, wherein we see death at its most deathly, become for us a good?

His answer is that of John of the Cross: faith. "As a result of [God's] omnipotence impinging on our faith, events which show themselves experimentally in our lives as pure loss will become an immediate factor in the union we dream of establishing with him. Uniting oneself means, in every case, migrating, and dying partially in what one loves. . . . We can therefore set no limits to the tearing up of roots that is involved in our journey to God. . . . God must in some way or other make room for himself, hollowing us out and emptying us, if he is finally to penetrate into us. And in order to assimilate us in him, he must break the molecules of our being so as to re-cast and re-model us. . . . And the more threatening and irreducible reality appears, the more firmly and desperately we must believe." [31] This emphasis upon the role

---

[29] Letter of December 12, 1919, in *Archives de Philosophie*, 140.

[30] *Le Milieu Divin*, 92; Eng. trans., 87.

[31] *Ibid.*, 92-93, 173; Eng. trans., 88, 137. Teilhard especially tries to inculcate this attitude regarding moral evil, for he was fully aware of the paralyzing effect that concentration on one's sins or the world's sins had on the people he knew. Hence he speaks of the *felix culpa* of personal sin, because

of pure diminishment in the spiritual life, and upon the corresponding need of faith to support such diminishment, is, I submit, an important balance which must be inserted into the modern Christian emphasis on self-fulfillment. For the danger is precisely that when such self-fulfillment is halted, or diminished or even destroyed, we shall not have the resources to react as we must in faith, if the plan of God for our lives is to be accomplished. "We believers," wrote Teilhard, "have the strength and glory of having a faith in God more profound than our faith in the world; and that faith in God re-emerges and persists even when our faith in the world should be crushed by the impact of events." [32] There is need to remind ourselves of this today, for it will insure that our instinctive desire for self-fulfillment in our relations with God and our fellow men will remain an authentically Christian desire purified in the end of selfishness and pride.

III

There is a third emphasis which characterizes the Christian's relationship with God today, and it may be described quite simply as relativism. Its origin is the thoroughly modern experience of rapid change at all levels of human life. An ever-growing sense of history has removed the cloak of stability which institutions of all types, as well as procedures and modes of thought, have inevitably sought to throw around themselves. Whatever is labeled "traditional" is by this very fact subject to suspicion and loss of confidence, unless the needs of the present and especially the experience of the present can be appealed to for its support. On the cognitive level the problem is whether one can be absolutely certain about anything any more. Hence the extreme difficulty of total commitment to any one tradition, doctrine or way of life. In a world

"though not everything is immediately good to those who seek God, everything is capable of becoming good." Cf. *Ibid.*, 88-94; Eng. trans., 85-89. Nevertheless, while this spiritual attitude is most important for our times, the theology of sin which Teilhard used to support it lacks that sense of serious sin as a rupture of one's personal relationship with God. Cf. Mooney, *op. cit.*, 133-142.

[32] Letter of April 9, 1916, in *Genèse d'une pensée* (Paris: Grasset, 1961), 124; Eng. trans., *The Making of a Mind* (New York: Harper and Row, 1965), 98-99.

where pluralism is widespread in religion, philosophy and general human culture, it is no longer an easy thing to accept the Church as something unique, its official pronouncements as more than directives, its authority in matters other than revelation as more than provisional. In the area of spirituality this means that the Church is looked upon more as a society in process than as a finished community, and that universal and fixed patterns are no longer seen as essential to one's spiritual life.

Although it is seldom adverted to, the relativism we have just described has a fairly broad and generally positive psychological base. This is the contemporary orientation toward the future. In a brilliant essay a number of years ago, Robert Johann put his finger on the nerve center of this all-pervading expectancy of modern man, who sees the fragments of the present chiefly as building blocks for tomorrow. Such an outlook leaves room for very few absolutes, and one's life as a consequence becomes crowded with relatives. Each succeeding day becomes merely a springboard to the next, a foothold in reality where one cannot rest, and from which one must constantly project himself into what has not yet come to be. Such an orientation is capable of engendering great enthusiasm for the work at hand, a desire to build a world that will be better both for oneself and for the community. On the negative side, however, the danger is frequently enough dissatisfaction and restlessness, tension and anxiety. The "now" of one's life becomes a mere point of transition, a dot on the horizontal line of becoming, a scene glimpsed from the window of a rushing train whose only meaning is to mark the stages of one's journey. The tendency then is a readiness to work without tranquility and to hope without possession. Since the peace and happiness one craves are in such cases forever eluding one's grasp, "progress" inevitably becomes a wheel to which one is chained, inexorably moving forward yet never coming to rest.[33]

There is no need to elaborate here on the impetus which Teilhard's evolutionary system has given to this orientation of modern man toward the future. "The world holds no interest for me unless I look forward," he told a good friend, "but when my

[33] See Robert O. Johann, S.J., "Charity and Time," *Cross Currents*, IX (1959), 140-149.

eyes are on the future it is full of excitement." [34] And again: "The past has revealed to me how the future is built, and preoccupation with the future tends to sweep everything else aside." [35] Hope, he wrote in a 1941 essay on progress, must spring to life spontaneously in every generous spirit faced with the task that awaits us. Hope for the future is that which enables us to work in the present. "It is the essential *impulse* without which nothing can be done. A passionate longing to grow, to be, is what we need. . . . Life is ceaseless discovery. Life is movement." [36] Nor did Teilhard hesitate to rebuke the Christians he knew for failing to integrate their human hope in man into their supernatural hope in God, for in Teilhard's system the object of the world's development as well as the source of this development is the Person of Christ. "O you of little faith, why fear or hold aloof from the onward march of the world? Why foolishly multiply your prophesies of woe. On the contrary, we must try everything for Christ; we must hope everything for Christ. *Nihil intentatum,* that is the true Christian attitude. . . . We can never know all that the Incarnation still asks of the world's potentialities. We can never hope for too much from the growing unity of mankind." [37] In the epilogue to *The Divine Milieu* he again reproaches the Christian for his unconcern in uniting his hope in Christ with his hope in man, for his failure to do so is in large measure responsible for the fact that the world's expectation is today no longer Christian. The well-known passage is worth citing at length:

Expectation—anxious, collective and operative expectation of an end of the world, that is to say of an outcome for the world—that is perhaps the supreme Christian function and the most distinctive characteristic of our religion. . . . The Israelites were constantly expectant, and the first Christians too. . . . Successors to Israel we Christians have been charged with keeping the flame of desire ever alive in the world. Only twenty centuries have passed since the ascension. What have we made of our expectancy? . . . How many of us are genuinely moved in the depths of our hearts by the wild

[34] Letter of October 23, 1923, in *Lettres de Voyage*, 64; Eng. trans., 104.
[35] Letter of September 8, 1935, in *Ibid.*, 186; Eng. trans., 207.
[36] *Réflexions sur le progrès*, 1941, in *L'Avenir de l'homme* (Paris: Seuil, 1959), 96; Eng. trans., *The Future of Man* (New York, Harper and Row, 1964), 72.
[37] *Le Milieu divin*, 201; Eng. trans., 154.

hope that our earth will be recast? . . . Where is the Catholic as passionately vowed (by conviction and not by convention) to spreading the hopes of the Incarnation as many humanitarians are to spreading the dream of the new city? We persist in saying that we keep vigil in expectation of the Master. But in reality we should have to admit, if we were sincere, that we no longer expect anything.[38]

Nevertheless, there is risk in stressing this element of dynamic change in all human life and institutions, and it comes from not anchoring such change in the changeless. The risk is especially great today, for in religious circles we are in full reaction against what can only be called an enthusiasm to absolutize the relative. This has produced the inevitable predisposition not to recognize any absolutes at all. Teilhard himself did not have this problem. His psychological need for some absolute was itself something of an absolute for him. "As far back as I go into my childhood, nothing appears to me more characteristic or familiar in my interior make-up than the taste or irresistible need for something all sufficient and all necessary. To be really satisfied and completely happy meant for me knowing that something 'essential' exists, of which all else is merely addition and ornament." [39] His evolutionary system was an extension of this psychological need, an effort to endow cosmogenesis with a stability it could not otherwise have had, by demanding for its very existence a real attraction from a real supreme personal Being. In order to understand the dynamism of the process itself, we are thus forced to recognize the primacy of being over becoming and of act over potency. His absolute was thus outside the process, present both at its beginning and at its end, and it provided that assurance of ultimate success which was alone capable of assuaging the anxiety of modern man.

Yet Teilhard was not unaware of the risk we have mentioned in so far as it manifests itself on the psychological level. For man has to feel that the present is more than a moment in a process; though essentially changing it must somehow transcend change. Hence Teilhard's insistence upon a balance, namely, the dimension given to human hopes and aspirations by Christian charity. It is not necessary at this point to recall the decisive role played

[38] *Ibid.*, 196-198; Eng. trans., 152.
[39] *Le Coeur de la matière*, 1950, 2. An unpublished essay.

by love energy in his system of thought. This analysis has been made elsewhere.[40] It is sufficient here simply to underline once more Teilhard's conviction that love changes in a man's outlook on life. The central deficiency in all naturalistic humanisms is, he felt, that they ignore the power of love, and this is why the enthusiasm and zeal they engender eventually dry up and become cold, joyless and hard. For a Christian, on the other hand,

. . . the real is charged with a divine presence in the entirety of its tangible layers. As the mystics knew and felt, everything becomes physically and literally lovable in God; and, conversely, God can be possessed and loved in everything around us. . . . What can this mean except that every action, as soon as it is oriented towards him, takes on, without any change in itself, the psychic character of a center to center relationship, that is to say, of an act of love.[41]

Through charity, then, man can unite himself to the terminus of all human progress, even while dedicating himself to the onward movement at any particular moment in time. The union accomplished in loving and being loved by God transcends the whole order of becoming, and thereby balances expectation with possession, and surrounds the relative with an all-embracing absolute. This is why the creative presence of God in the world is so central a theme in Teilhard's thought. He sees the whole movement of evolution as a mode by which the divine presence is mediated to the world, and it is precisely by charity that we enter into this presence. To the extent that one's commitment to an endless series of relatives is impregnated with charity, it becomes an element in one's union with God and therefore of absolute significance. It becomes a force for promoting that peace and capacity to rest which so many have lost in the turmoil of our technological age.

Teilhard, however, was not content simply to emphasize the importance of charity as a balance to the danger of relativism. He was much more concerned with locating its source. This he found through what may well be one of his most original contributions to theology, namely, his insight into the Church as a phylum of

[40] See Mooney, op. cit., 52-54, 123-128.
[41] Super-humanité, super-Christ, super-charité, 1943, in Science et Christ, 213, 215.

love inserted by God into the evolutionary process to guarantee that the human phylum reach the fullness of its natural and supernatural development. The individual Christian's daily life is therefore related to an absolute not simply because it is motivated subjectively by charity, but much more so because it takes place within an objective, corporate, and highly organized phylum, whose function in God's plan is to act as the source of love energy in the world.[42]

This concept is of no small importance today. For alongside the relativism in the modern Christian's outlook, there is likewise a keen and ever-growing awareness that community based on love is absolutely essential to human life, and *a fortiori* to Christian life. The problem is that for many today traditional forms of Christian life and even religious life do not sufficiently mediate charity as a felt experience. This is not the time to discuss the reasons for this. The point I wish to make is that Teilhard had this same experience long before most of today's Christians were born. For my own part, I hope never to have to go through what he went through in his dealings with religious and ecclesiastical authority.[43] Yet however hemmed in he was by authoritarianism in the Church of his day, his reverence and respect for the Church's authority remained profound. The reason was precisely his need of an absolute. "Only in the Roman 'trunk'," he wrote as late as 1950, "do I see the biological support sufficiently vast and differentiated to carry out the enduring transformation of humanity which we await." [44] What Teilhard is telling us, perhaps, is that every man has need not only to possess an absolute among all the relatives of his life, but that he has need also to incarnate the absolute, to locate it. In other words there has to be an objective absolute for every man as well as a subjective absolute. The Church was this for Teilhard, not in its mere external organization or its changing attitudes, not in its human aspects, therefore, but in that which is divine. St. Paul called the Church Christ's Body, the Bride of Christ; the

[42] For a fuller development, see Mooney, *op. cit.*, 154-163.

[43] See René d'Ouince, S.J., "L'Epreuve de l'obéissance dans la vie du Père Teilhard de Chardin," in *L'Homme devant Dieu*, III (Paris: Aubier, 1964), 331-346.

[44] Letter of October 10, 1950, in Henri de Lubac, *La Pensée religieuse du Père Teilhard de Chardin* (Paris: Aubier, 1962), 340, note 4.

Fathers called her *Mater Ecclesia*. Teilhard was grasping for the same reality when he spoke of her as the phylum of love. It would not be out of place for the modern Christian to ask what she means to him. We live during one of those times in history when it is imperative that all her defects be clearly evident to the world as well as the contingency of much of what she says and does. But she does contain within herself an absolute, and it is this absolute which we are in desperate need of today to balance our equally desperate need to emphasize the relative in our spiritual life.

IV

The theme of this article has been that the thought of Teilhard de Chardin supports to the full what is most characteristic today in Christian spirituality, namely, the emphases upon the material, the personal and the relative. His instinctive spiritual sense, however, has enabled him to maintain as balances the three corresponding emphases upon finding God in the material, integrating the Cross into personal development, and impregnating the relatives of human life with love. It is these emphases and these balances which make his own spirituality both thoroughly modern and authentically Christian. We might note, moreover, before we close, the growing importance of Teilhard's overriding concern for what he calls quite simply "the world." This constitutes, I think, his single most significant contribution to modern Christian spirituality. For since spirituality in its broadest sense is a style of approach to God, an attitude toward life, each era must have its own, with its own set of images and its own motivations corresponding to the Christian needs of a given time. Thus, in the apostolic era it was the Parousia which fired the Christian imagination, in a later era the blood of the martyrs; still later the quarrels between Protestant and Catholic; and in recent centuries, the intense missionary activity of Christians. Today what motivates people is "the world." Christians want to feel they can reach God through the world, through the whole scientific, technological, humanistic enterprise. But not until Teilhard appeared on the scene has anyone succeeded in showing them how. He is the only one who has given this vivid image of modern man a completely Christian explanation.

"For a long time," he once wrote, "my chief interest in life has been a general attempt to find God more easily in the world. It's an all consuming effort, but it's the only vocation I know as my own, and nothing can turn me from it." [45] We are witnessing today in Christian spirituality the fruits of this "all consuming" effort of Teilhard's life. What he has given is a coherent focus for thé modern Christian imagination, a focus open to every new experience, yet supported by the deepest insights of the past. His image of the world uniting men to Christ has reopened the possibility of unity once more in Christian living. His vision of Christ not only as the model of a fully human life but the source and direction of history has strengthened hope in God and added besides an all-encompassing hope in man. He has shown to Christians the seriousness of the world, and to non-Christians he has carried the message that the world does not exclude God, that adoration is an essential part of the human life, and that union with Christ means also union with the world.

SUGGESTED READINGS

On Teilhard's Spirituality

Cren, Pierre R., O.P. "The Christian and the World According to Teilhard de Chardin," *Concilium*. Vol. XIX. New York: Paulist Press, 1966, 73-87.

Faricy, Robert L., S.J. *Teilhard de Chardin's Theology of the Christian in the World*. New York: Sheed and Ward, 1967.

Gray, Donald P. *The One and the Many*. New York: Herder and Herder, 1969, pp. 133-155.

Kessler, Marvin, S.J., and Bernard Brown, S.J. (eds.). *Dimensions of the Future: The Spirituality of Teilhard de Chardin*. Washington: Corpus Books, 1968.

Lepp, Ignace. *The Faith of Men: Meditations Inspired by Teilhard de Chardin*. Translated by Bernard Murchland. New York: Macmillan, 1967.

[45] Letter of January 21, 1936, in *Lettres de voyage*, 197; Eng. trans., 219.

Martin, Sr. Maria Gratia, I.H.M. *The Spirituality of Teilhard de Chardin.* Westminster, Md.: Newman Press, 1968.

Rideau, Émile, S.J. *The Thought of Teilhard de Chardin.* Translated by René Hague. New York: Harper and Row, 1967, pp. 192-236.

Wildiers, N. M., O.F.M., Cap. "The New Christian of Teilhard de Chardin," *Thought,* 43 (1968), 523-538.

TEILHARD AND WHITEHEAD

Ian G. Barbour

Teilhard's Process Metaphysics

Ian G. Barbour

How similar is Teilhard's thought to that of Whitehead? In the following selection,* Ian G. Barbour
studies the positions of the two thinkers in seven major areas: reality as temporal process, the "within,"
freedom and determinism, continuing creation, God
and time, the problem of evil, and the future of the
world. Barbour contends that Teilhard has a process
metaphysics similar to Whitehead's, although it is not
systematically worked out. Both Teilhard and Whitehead adopt a radically temporalistic rather than a
static viewpoint. Both affirm relatedness, continuity
and the "within." They have similar notions on continuing creation and of the interaction of God and
the world. However, Whitehead underscores plurality, while Teilhard emphasizes unity. Barbour points
out how their differing positions within process
thought situate them in varying degrees of continuity
with the Biblical tradition.

*Ian G. Barbour has a doctorate in physics from the
University of Chicago and has studied theology at the
Yale Divinity School. He is chairman of the depart-
ment of religion and professor of physics at Carleton
College, Northfield, Minnesota. His book* Issues in
Science and Religion *is a major contribution to the
dialogue of science and theology.*

* From *The Journal of Religion,* 49 (1969), 136-159. Reprinted with
permission.

The writings of Teilhard de Chardin [1] can be read in a variety of ways: as evolutionary science, as poetry and mysticism, as natural theology, and as Christian theology. There is, however, one aspect of his thought to which little attention has been given, namely, his undeveloped *process metaphysics,* which, I have suggested, plays a crucial role in his synthesis of scientific and religious ideas.[2] In this paper I will explore some of Teilhard's metaphysical categories which reflect both evolutionary and biblical assumptions. Successive sections will be devoted to: (1) reality as temporal process, (2) the "within," (3) freedom and determinism, (4) continuing creation, (5) God and time, (6) the problem of evil, and (7) the future of the world.

Teilhard's thought can be illuminated by comparing it with that of Alfred North Whitehead, the most systematic exponent of a philosophy of process. The striking similiarities may help to show the character of Teilhard's ideas. The significant differences may make more evident the points at which his contribution is distinctive, or in some cases may suggest ambiguities or limitations in his approach. I will not deal directly with his Christology, which is a major point of divergence from Whitehead; but by showing the influence of Teilhard's temporalistic metaphysics on his interpretation of a number of biblical themes, I hope to point the way to a subsequent study of his *process theology.* By concentrating on his conceptual thought, I will of course be neglecting many aspects of his complex personality, including the profound

[1] The works of Teilhard most frequently cited below (all published in New York by Harper & Row) are abbreviated as follows: *AM, The Appearance of Man* (1965); *DM, The Divine Milieu* (1960); *FM, The Future of Man* (1964); *MPN, Man's Place in Nature* (1966); *PM, The Phenomenon of Man* (1959); and *VP, The Vision of the Past* (1966). The Whitehead works cited (all published in New York by the Macmillan Co.) include *AI, Adventures of Ideas* (1933); *MT, Modes of Thought* (1938); *PR, Process and Reality* (1929); *RM, Religion in the Making* (1926); and *SMW, Science and the Modern World* (1925).

[2] Ian G. Barbour, "Five Ways of Reading Teilhard," *Soundings,* Vol. II, No. 2 (Summer, 1968), reprinted in *The Teilhard Review,* Vol. III, No. 1 (Summer, 1968). In Section V of "Five Ways" I discuss the treatment of Teilhard's metaphysics by several of his recent interpreters.

spirituality and mysticism which were his most impressive characteristics.

Teilhard's style is very different from Whitehead's. He was not a philosopher; he used vivid analogies and poetic images where Whitehead used carefully defined philosophical abstractions. Yet their underlying insights were often very similar. I will not dwell on the historical reasons for these parallels. Neither man was familiar with the work of the other, but both acknowledge great indebtedness to Henri Bergson.[3] Both were deeply impressed by the status of time in modern science—primarily in evolutionary biology in Teilhard's case and in relativity and quantum physics in Whitehead's. Our task, however, will be to examine the content rather than the genesis of their ideas. Let us start from their reflections on the general structure of the world.

I. Reality as Temporal Process

Teilhard and Whitehead both adopt a radically temporalistic outlook in place of the static viewpoint which has dominated most of Western thought. For Teilhard, "the universe is no longer a State but a Process." [4] "Taken at this degree of generalisation (in other words where all experimental reality in the universe forms part of a *process,* that is to say, is *born*) evolution has long ago ceased to be a hypothesis and become a *general condition of knowledge* (an additional *dimension*) which henceforth all hypotheses must satisfy." [5] Teilhard asserts, in a variety of contexts, that "this new perception of time" alters all our ways of looking at things. We live in "a world that is *being born* instead of a world that *is*." [6] Ours is an embryonic and incomplete universe; change and development are its pervasive features.

Teilhard suggests that we have usually thought of *time* as a kind of neutral container in which self-sufficient objects could be rearranged without being affected, "a sort of vast vessel in which

[3] See M. Barthelemy-Maudale, *Bergson et Teilhard de Chardin* (Paris: Editions du Seuil, 1963). Cuénot says that in 1945 Teilhard "songe á lire Whitehead, *La science et le monde moderne"*—which may mean that he actually read it; see Claude Cuénot, *Pierre Teilhard de Chardin* (Paris: Libraire Plon, 1958), p. 292.

[4] *FM,* p. 261.

[5] *AM,* p. 211, n. 1; cf. *VP,* p. 246.

[6] *FM,* p. 88.

things were suspended side by side." [7] But now one must acknowledge that "duration permeates the essence of every being." Reality does not consist of inert objects moving through successive instants, but of processes having temporal extension. "Every particle of reality, instead of constituting an approximate point in itself, extends from the previous fragment to the next in an invisible thread running back to infinity." [8] For Whitehead also the world is made up of events and processes. He rejects both the scholastic view of unchanging substances with changing attributes and the Newtonian picture of unchanging particles which are rearranged but never altered in themselves. Whitehead and Teilhard both employ categories of becoming and activity rather than of being and substance.[9]

Teilhard refers frequently to the organic interdependence of all entities. The world is not a collection of self-contained objects related only externally to each other, but a network of mutual influences spread through time and space. Every entity is constituted by its relationships; "every element of the cosmos is woven from all others." "However narrowly the 'heart' of an atom is circumscribed, its realm is coextensive at least potentially with that of every other atom." [10] The "web of life" is a fabric of interactions, "a single process without interruption." A close parallel is Whitehead's rejection of "Simple Location," the mechanistic assumption that independent particles can be completely described "apart from any essential reference of the relations of that bit of matter to other regions of space and to other durations of time." [11] Whitehead proposes "a social view of reality" as a community of interacting temporal events.

Despite this emphasis on interdependence, neither author ends with a *monism* in which the parts are less real then the total process. Every entity is a center of spontaneity and self-creation contributing distinctively to the future. But in Whitehead this *pluralism*, which counterbalances the idea of unity, is carried much further. He starts from a plurality of beings whose individual-

[7] *VP*, p. 128; cf. *FM*, p. 59.
[8] *FM*, p. 84; cf. *VP*, p. 129.
[9] *SMW*, pp. 71-77, 157 ff., 188-89; *PR*, pp. 122-23, 317-22.
[10] *PM*, p. 41; cf. *FM*, p. 85.
[11] *SMW*, p. 84.

ity and integrity are always preserved. Whitehead wants us to look at the world from the point of view of each entity itself—considered as a moment of experience which inherits its data from previous events, yet is radically on its own during the moment it responds. Each occasion or "concrescence" is a unique synthesis of the influences on it, a new unity formed from diversity. Only as it perishes does it influence other events.[12] Whitehead thus envisages not a continuous process but an interconnected series of discrete events. Continuity is accounted for by the succession of individual units of becoming, each of which is completed and then superseded by other units.[13] There is no agency except that of a multiplicity of actual occasions, including God. Whitehead has none of Teilhard's "temporal threads running back to infinity," but only a network of threads connecting each event with its immediate predecessors. This greater pluralism in Whitehead's scheme has repercussions which we will note in his treatment of mind and matter, freedom and determinism, and God's relation to the world.

In Teilhard, the balance between pluralism and monism is tipped in the opposite direction. "Everything forms a single whole," an integral cosmic process.[14] We will find that in some passages the whole of cosmic history seems to have a unified structure not unlike that of a single Whiteheadian concrescence; Teilhard predicts the "convergence," "centration," and "involution" of the universe. Where Whitehead is concerned to give a generalized account of the growth of all particular entities, Teilhard tries to delineate the patterns of universal history. While these two tasks overlap considerably, they tend to encourage differing emphases. At a later point, we will see that Teilhard's belief in the unity of creation was strengthened by his own mystical sense of experienced oneness and by the biblical hope of a single eschatological goal of history.

Both authors portray *continuity* as well as *discontinuity* between the levels of reality, but Teilhard puts somewhat greater stress on continuity. There are no sharp lines between the non-living and the living, or between life and mind. Each level has its

[12] *PR*, pp. 95, 188.
[13] *PR*, p. 53.
[14] *DM*, p. 30.

roots in earlier levels and represents the flowering of what was potentially present all along, though these roots are "lost in darkness as we trace them back." The higher was already present in the lower in rudimentary form: *"In the world, nothing could ever burst forth as final across the different thresholds successively traversed by evolution (however critical they be) which had not already existed in an obscure and primordial way. . . .* Everything, in some extremely attenuated version of itself, has existed from the very first." [15] Yet within this continuity there were thresholds and critical points. These "crises" were not gaps or absolute discontinuities, but each marked a major breakthrough. There was real novelty at each level (life, thought, society), even though each was anticipated in previous levels. Teilhard gives the analogy of a gradually heated liquid which reaches a critical temperature, a boiling point at which a change of state suddenly occurs.[16] He uses the words "metamorphosis" and "transformation" to describe these changes in which new properties emerged.[17]

Whitehead shares Teilhard's assumptions concerning the historical continuity of the past, though his attention is directed to the ontological similarities among differing types of entities today. For him also the higher is present in the lower in rudimentary form. Since he takes metaphysics to be the search for interpretive categories of the widest generality, these categories must be applicable to all entities. Yet the modes in which they are exemplified may vary widely; "there are gradations of importance and diversities of function." Whitehead makes greater allowance than Teilhard for the diversity of events which occur at different levels of reality.[18] Let us look in particular at their views of mental life.

II. THE "WITHIN"

In Teilhard's philosophy every entity has a "within." Even among atoms there was a tendency to build up molecules and then cells of more highly centered complexity; he attributes this to a "radial energy" which produced and maintained very improbable systems in violation of the law of entropy. Next there was an

[15] *PM*, pp. 71, 78.
[16] *PM*, pp. 78, 168; *VP*, p. 180.
[17] *PM*, pp. 79, 88.
[18] *PR*, pp. 127-67.

elementary responsiveness which was a forerunner of mental life. He does not, of course, ascribe self-awareness or reflection to simple organisms; their "psychic life" was infinitesimal, a rudimentary beginning of perception, anticipation, and spontaneity "in extremely attenuated versions." [19]

We have seen that Teilhard mentions "critical points" at which novel phenomena occurred for the first time; there were "metamorphoses" of the "within" to new forms, which were "quite different." But his terminology tends to blur any such distinctions. With the exception of reflective thought (which is imputed to man alone), Teilhard's various terms are used interchangeably all the way down the scale from man to cell: the "within," interiority, psychic life, mentality, consciousness, etc. He sometimes says that in simple organisms these are all *potentially* present (though he provides no specific analysis of the concept of potentiality). More often he says they are *actually* present in infinitesimal degree. At higher levels, consciousness is said to be proportional to the development of the nervous system and brain; at lower levels, it is said to be proportional to complexity, even in the total absence of a nervous system.[20]

Whitehead's "subjective pole" resembles Teilhard's "within." In general, every entity takes account of previous events, responds to them, and makes a creative selection from alternative potentialities. But Whitehead's basic categories characterizing all events have very diverse exemplifications. A stone has no organization beyond the physical cohesion of its parts and hence it has no "subjective pole" at all; it is a "corpuscular society" which is not the locus of any unified events. A cell has only an incipient psychism, which is so vanishingly small that for all practical purposes it may be considered absent; its response to changing stimuli testifies at most to an exceedingly attenuated form of aim or purpose. Only with animals is there a single "dominant occasion" of awareness. Whitehead holds that there is *no* consciousness, even in a rudimentary form, in lower animate beings, much less in inanimate ones.[21]

Clearly, both Teilhard and Whitehead do use human experi-

[19] *VP*, p. 235; *PM*, pp. 54 ff.
[20] *PM*, pp. 53-66, 71, 88, 149-52; *VP*, pp. 227-28; *MPN*, pp. 32-33.
[21] *PR*, pp. 164-67; *MT*, p. 38; *AI*, p. 164.

ence, with various qualifications, as a model for the interpretation of other entities. Why do they make this generalization from man? Their reasons appear to be similar:

1. *The unity of man with nature.*—Man is part of nature; he is a product of the evolutionary process. "The roots of our being," says Teilhard, "are in the first cell." Human experience is a fact within nature. We cannot be content with a physical description "which leaves out thought, the most remarkable phenomenon which nature has produced." "The apparent restriction of the phenomenon of consciousness to the higher forms of life has long served science as an excuse for eliminating it from its models of the universe. A queer exception, an aberrant function, an epiphenomenon—thought was classed under one or other of these heads in order to get rid of it." [22] Whitehead likewise defends man's unity with nature and shows the inadequacy of accounts which omit the most distinctive features of human experience. A world of particles-in-motion would be a world to which man's purposes and feelings would be totally alien.[23] We must not ignore the part of the universe we know most directly—our own experience.

2. *The continuity of the world.*—We have seen that in spite of the occurrence of thresholds Teilhard traces a continuous evolutionary development. There was an unbroken spectrum of complexity from cell to man; one can set no absolute limits at which the basic features of human experience may have been present. Nature is an integral process: "Since the stuff of the universe has an inner aspect at one point of itself, there is necessarily *a double aspect to its structure,* that is to say in every region of space and time. . . . *In a coherent perspective of the world, life inevitably assumes a 'pre-life' for as far back before it as the eye can see.*" [24] Teilhard gives another analogy: Just as we assume (in relativity theory) that a change-in-mass too small to detect occurs in objects moving at low velocity, since a detectable change-in-mass is found at high velocities, so also can we assume a "within" in beings of low complexity, since its effects are noticeable in those

[22] *PM*, p. 55; cf. *VP*, p. 162.
[23] *SMW*, pp. 78 ff.
[24] *PM*, pp. 56-57.

of high complexity.[25] The force of the analogy depends on the assumption that the "within" is, despite its "metamorphoses" into differing forms, a single continuous function of complexity. Whitehead likewise defends the continuity of historical development, but we have noted that he gives greater prominence to the emergence of genuinely new phenomena at higher levels of organization.

3. *The coherence of interpretive categories.*—The search for a coherent metaphysics presupposes the unity of the world, but it directs attention to the consistency and generality of one's conceptual system. Whitehead holds that metaphysical categories should be applicable to all events, including our awareness as experiencing subjects; human experience is taken to exhibit the generic features of all experience. "An occasion of experience which includes a human mentality is an extreme instance, at one end of the scale, of those happenings which constitute nature." [26] In order to give a unified account of the world, he seems in effect to employ concepts most appropriate to a "middle range" of organisms; these concepts can in very attenuated form be applied to lower entities, and yet they are capable of further development when applied to human experience. A similar concern for intellectual coherence in our understanding of the world seems to have been one of Teilhard's motives.

4. *The inadequacy of mind-matter dualism.*—Both authors want to overcome the dualism which has been prominent in Western thought since Descartes. They seek a unitary ontology, not by reducing mind to matter (materialism) or matter to mind (idealism), but by making organic process primary. "Mind" and "matter" are not two distinct substances, but two aspects of a single complex process. Whitehead finds them inseparably interwoven in human experience—for instance, in the bodily reference of feeling and perception. Teilhard reacts not only against the mind-matter dualism, but against the dichotomy of matter and spirit which Christian thinkers have supported. Here he adopts a biblical view of the unity of man as a whole being and rejects the assumption that matter and spirit are separate substances or antagonistic principles.

[25] *PM*, pp. 54, 301.
[26] *AI*, p. 237.

The two authors differ considerably, however, in their representations of the relationship between the "within" and the "without." In Whitehead's system, subjectivity and objectivity occur in *distinct phases* of the concrescence of an event. Every momentary subject first inherits objective data from its past. It is then on its own in subjective immediacy, appropriating this data from its unique perspective, selecting among alternative possibilities, and producing a novel synthesis. The resulting outcome is then available as objective data to be appropriated by subsequent moments of experience. Efficient causality characterizes the transition between such events, while final causality dominates the internal growth within the concrescence as it actualizes its own synthesis. Teilhard pictures no such successive phases; for him every entity is *simultaneously* subjective and objective.[27] He stresses the continuity of experience, whereas Whitehead stresses its fragmentary character.

This difference has a significant methodological consequence. Whitehead claims that the scientist, relying on sense perception, can deal directly only with the outcome of a past event; the isolated moment of present subjectivity is inaccessible to him: "Science can find no individual enjoyment in nature; science can find mere rules of succession. These negations are true of natural science; they are inherent in its methodology." [28] Teilhard agrees that the "within" of another being is not itself directly observable; but he seems to think that its effects are among the "phenomena" which a more open-minded science will in the future be able to analyze. But he has perhaps given insufficient consideration to the epistemological problem of how an inherently private mental life expresses itself in the public world.

III. FREEDOM AND DETERMINISM

For Teilhard, then, all beings are temporal, interdependent, and characterized by a "within." But is their activity free or determined? In many contexts, Teilhard seems to reject determination by either natural laws or divine omnipotence. In discussing evolution he repeatedly mentions "random mutations," "blind

---

[27] Cf. Richard Overman, *Evolution and the Christian Doctrine of Creation* (Philadelphia: Westminster Press, 1967), p. 227.
[28] *MT,* p. 221.

chance," and "billionfold trial and error." Particular combinations of atoms or configurations of species were "accidental," "fortuitous," and "unrepeatable." "Even if there were only one solution to the main physical and physiological problem of life on earth, that general solution would necessarily leave undecided a host of accidental and particular questions, and it does not seem thinkable that they would have been decided *twice in the same way*. . . . The genesis of life on earth belongs to the category of absolutely *unique* events that, once happened, are never repeated." [29] Whereas the scholastics interpreted the actualization of potentiality as the unfolding of what was there all along, Teilhard speaks of *alternative potentialities* not all of which are actualized. He gives the example of a molecule which could exist in either of two forms (mirror images of each other); it is today found in all living organisms in only one of these forms—which presumably represents the way in which the atoms happened to collide in the primeval molecule from which all the samples today are descended. The present world "exhausts *only a part of what might have been.*" [30]

With the advent of simple organisms there was novelty and spontaneity, according to Teilhard. With reflective consciousness came moral choice and responsibility. Man's destiny is now in his own hands; he can "grasp the tiller of evolution" and steer his own course. Teilhard makes frequent reference to the "choices," "options," and "crossroads" which we face. His political philosophy indorses individual freedom and diversity despite the need for collectivization and global unity.[31] He grants that in the future, man's free decisions may thwart the progress of the universe toward union; final success "is not necessary, inevitable or certain." Some men may fail to co-operate, for man has the power to refuse to love.[32]

On the other hand, many of Teilhard's statements sound completely deterministic. Various stages of past evolution were "inevitable," "inexorable," or "necessary." The future convergence of the cosmos is "inescapable." There is an "over-riding super-

[29] *PM*, p. 100; cf. *PM*, pp. 74, 307.
[30] *PM*, p. 95; cf. *FM*, p. 220.
[31] *FM*, pp. 194, 241.
[32] *PM*, pp. 288, 306; *FM*, p. 232.

determinism which irresistibly impels Mankind to converge upon itself." [33] He even suggests that it would be futile for anyone to try to oppose global socialization, since it is inevitable. The total process is one of "sure ascent" and "irreversible movement." How can one reconcile Teilhard's apparently contradictory declarations of freedom and determinism? There seem to be three ways in which he attempts a reconciliation:

1. *The law of large numbers.*—Events such as the tossing of a coin can be individually random yet statistically lawful; the individual case is unpredictable but the group can be accurately predicted. Teilhard applies this principle to chance in evolution and extends it to human freedom. He holds that each person considered separately may fail, but "by a sort of 'infallibility of large numbers,' Mankind, the present crest of the evolutionary wave, cannot fail." [34] "It is statistically necessary that in any large number of letters there will regularly be mistakes: stamps forgotten, addresses incompleted, etc. Yet each sender is free not to make mistakes." [35] Teilhard makes the rather dubious assumption that chance and freedom are subject to the same kind of statistical consideration. There are, he says, "two uncertainties related to the double play—the chance at the bottom and freedom at the top. Let me add, however, that in the case of very large numbers (such, for instance, as the human population) the process tends to 'infallibilise' itself, inasmuch as the likelihood of success grows on the lower side (chance) while that of rejection and error diminishes on the other side (freedom) with the multiplication of the elements engaged." [36]

2. *The Universe as a unified power.*—Teilhard sometimes speaks of the cosmos as a single agency which will prevail in its purposes regardless of the vagaries of individuals. In the past, evolution has won over all obstacles and found a way out of all impasses; it would be absurd for it to abort now after it has gotten this far. The subject of the following propositions is "the world": "To bring us into existence it has from the beginning juggled

[33] *FM*, p. 128; cf. *FM*, p. 71.
[34] *FM*, p. 237.
[35] See Christopher Mooney, *Teilhard and the Mystery of Christ* (New York: Harper & Row, 1966), p. 127.
[36] *PM*, p. 307.

miraculously with too many improbabilities for there to be any risk whatever in committing ourselves further and following it right to the end. If it undertook the task, it is because it can finish it, following the same methods and with the same infallibility with which it began." [37] Teilhard's confidence undoubtedly rests ultimately in the power of God, but he often writes as if the cosmic process is itself a trustworthy and purposeful agency which will determine the outcome:

No doubt it is true that up to a point we are free as *individuals* to resist the trends and demands of Life. But does this mean (it is a very different matter) that we can escape collectively from the fundamental set of the tide? . . . The earth is more likely to stop turning than is Mankind, as a whole, likely to stop organising and unifying itself. For if this interior movement were to stop, it is the Universe itself, embodied in Man, that would fail to curve inwards and achieve totalisation. And nothing, as it seems, can prevent the Universe from succeeding—nothing, not even our human liberties, whose essential tendency to union may fail in detail but cannot (without "cosmic" contradiction) err "statistically." [38]

3. *God's control of the world.*—Teilhard's conviction of the inevitable convergence of the world rests finally on his Christian belief in the omnipotence of God. "Only Omega can guarantee the outcome." To the Christian, "the eventual biological success of Man on Earth is not merely a probability but a certainty, since Christ (and in Him virtually the World) is already risen." [39] In later sections we will examine Teilhard's views of evil, progress, and eschatology. At the moment, we may note that in his doctrine of providence he faces the difficulty with which so many theologians of the past wrestled: How can one consistently believe in both human freedom and divine determination? On this problem he throws little new light.

Whitehead, by contrast, is specific in rejecting all forms of determinism. He holds that the existence of genuinely alternative potentialities is incompatible with predestination. God radically qualifies but does not determine the action of each actual entity.

[37] *PM*, p. 232; cf. *PM*, p. 276.
[38] *FM*, p. 152.
[39] *FM*, p. 237.

"It derives from God its basic conceptual aim, relevant to its actual world, yet with indeterminations awaiting its own decisions." [40] God provides a cosmic order within which there is self-determination by each being. Whitehead attacks the idea of a predetermined and fixed divine plan; God has unchanging general purposes, but his goals for particular events are modified as individual entities take their own actions in response to his initiative. Whitehead thus departs further than Teilhard from the traditional doctrine of divine omnipotence.

Teilhard has been accused of adopting pantheism, which in the past has often taken deterministic forms. But the accusation is unjust. Teilhard is critical of the Eastern "mysticism of identification," in which the individual seeks absorption in the All, hoping to merge "like a drop in the ocean." He adheres to the Western "mysticism of union," in which individuality and personality are not lost.[41] Convergence will be achieved "not by identification (God becoming all) but by the differentiating and communicating action of love (God all *in everyone*)." [42] Ultimate reality is neither an undifferentiated unity nor an impersonal structure, but a supreme person. Nevertheless the reader may easily forget, amid Teilhard's frequent references to "the All" and "the whole," that God is to be distinguished from the cosmos. In Whitehead's writing, on the other hand, it is always clear that God is one among a plurality of entities. Each occasion retains its individuality and self-determination, even in relation to God.[43]

IV. CONTINUING CREATION

For Teilhard, as for Whitehead, the understanding of the world as temporal process outlined in the preceding sections has important implications for the representation of God's relation to the world. God is not the external fabricator of an essentially static system but a creative influence immanent in an evolutionary development. Teilhard urges us to think of creation not "as an

[40] *PR*, p. 343.
[41] *DM*, p. 94.
[42] *PM*, p. 308; cf. *PM*, p. 262, and *FM*, p. 207. See Henri de Lubac, *The Religion of Teilhard de Chardin* (New York: Desclee, 1967), pp. 143-60.
[43] See William Christian, *An Interpretation of Whitehead's Metaphysics* (New Haven, Conn.: Yale University Press, 1959), pp. 403-9.

instantaneous act, but in the manner of a process or synthesizing action." [44] "Creation has never ceased. Its act is a great continuous movement spread out over the totality of time. It is still going on." [45]

Teilhard proposes that creation consists in *the unification of the multiple*. Whereas Bergson conceived of an original unity which differentiates and diverges into multiplicity, Teilhard assumes a primeval multiplicity which converges toward a final unity. In several of his early writings, he speaks of creation as "a struggle against the many," but he maintains that in its disunity "the many" represents only a potentiality for being rather than an independent reality over against God.[46] In an essay written in 1948, he imagines four "moments" in which the world originated. Initially there was only a self-sufficient First Being. Second, according to revelation, there was a movement of internal diversity and union in the divine life understood as "trinitization" rather than static unity. I quote in full his speculation concerning the third and fourth "moments," since it is controversial and not yet published:

By the very fact that he unifies himself interiorly, the First Being *ipso facto* causes another type of opposition to arise, not within himself but at his antipodes (and here we have our third moment). At the pole of being there is self-subsistent Unity, and all around at the periphery, as a necessary consequence, there is multiplicity: *pure* multiplicity, be it understood, a "creatable void" which is simply nothing—yet which, because of its passive potency for arrangement (i.e. for union), constitutes a possibility, an appeal for being. Now everything takes place as if God had not been able to resist this appeal, for at such depths our intelligence can no longer distinguish at all between supreme necessity and supreme freedom.

In classical philosophy or theology, creation or participation (which constitutes our fourth moment) always tends to be presented as an almost arbitrary gesture on the part of the First

[44] "Christologie et évolution" (1933), scheduled for publication in *Oeuvres*, Vol. XI; quoted in Robert L. Faricy, "Teilhard de Chardin on Creation and the Christian Life," *Theology Today*, Jan. 1967, p. 510.

[45] "Le milieu mystique," in *Écrits du temps de la guerre (1916-19)* (Paris: Éditions Bernard Grasset, 1965), p. 149.

[46] "L'union créatrice," "Les noms de la mattière," and "La lutte contre la multitude," in *Écrits du temps de la guerre;* also, "Mon univers," in *Oeuvres*, (Paris: Éditions du Seuil), Vol. IX.

Cause, executed by a causality analogous to "efficient" and according to a mechanism that is completely indeterminate: truly an "act of God" in the pejorative sense. In a metaphysics of union, on the contrary—although the self-sufficiency and self-determination of the Absolute Being remain inviolate (since pure, antipodal multiplicity, is, I insist, nothing but pure passivity and potentiality)—in such a metaphysics, I say, the creative act takes on a very well defined significance and structure. . . . To create is to unite.[47]

This idea of "creative union" is not in itself incompatible with the idea of "creation out of nothing." Teilhard says that God is "self-sufficing" and initially "stood alone." He denies the need for a "preexisting substratum" on which God operated and holds that matter is not eternal. As North points out,[48] the multiple is little more than potential-for-being; union is equated with being and disunion with non-being. De Lubac argues that Teilhard's "creative union" takes place moment by moment *within* the process and that one can still consider the *whole* process as created *ex nihilo*.[49] But Teilhard does treat the ongoing process (the fourth moment) rather than an instantaneous beginning as the really creative stage of God's work. In effect he seems to assume that the cosmic process has a convergent and unifying character; therefore he extrapolates to a primeval state of "pure multiplicity," whose relation to the prior unity of God remains problematical.[50]

Whitehead shares Teilhard's themes of continuing creation

[47] "Comment je vois" (1948), scheduled for publication in *Oeuvres*, Vol. X; quoted in Mooney, *op. cit.*, pp. 172-73. Alternative renditions in Robert Faricy, *op. cit.*, p. 510-11, and Piet Smulders, *The Design of Teilhard de Chardin* (Westminster, Md.: Newman Press, 1967), pp. 79-81. A letter from Teilhard to my father accompanying a copy of this essay and commenting on it is given in George B. Barbour, *In the Field with Teilhard de Chardin* (New York: Herder & Herder, 1965), pp. 125-26.
[48] Robert North, *Teilhard and the Creation of the Soul* (Milwaukee, Wis.: Bruce Publishing Co., 1967), pp. 88-91.
[49] De Lubac, *op. cit.*, pp. 195-200. See also Smulders, *op. cit.*, pp. 77-85.
[50] North, *op. cit.*, p. 116, claims that, without intending to, Teilhard adopts an implicit emanationism in which the world is made from the substance of God. North argues that if there is a temporal symmetry between Alpha and Omega, and if Omega involves "absorption in divinity," then creation must have arisen "by a sort of sifting out of divinity." However, he never shows that Teilhard's thought entails such an assumption of symmetry. See also Robert North, "Teilhard and the Problem of Creation," *Theological Studies*, XXIV (1963), 577-601.

and unification, but he explicitly rejects "creation out of nothing." He holds that time is infinite. There was no first day, no initial act of origination, but only a continuing bringing-into-being in which past, present, and future are structurally similar. God has a priority in ontological status but no temporal priority over the world. God "is not *before* all creation but *with* all creation." [51] However, no ready-made materials were given to God from some other source, and nothing can exist apart from him; he is the ground of order as well as novelty in the world. As Cobb suggests, Whitehead attributes to God a fundamental role in the birth of each new event, though there is no event which he alone determines absolutely.[52]

I would submit that even though Whitehead rejects and Teilhard qualifies the idea of "creation out of nothing," both men share the *motives* which led the church fathers to the formulation of the traditional doctrine. The formula is not of course itself scriptural; Genesis does not open with "nothing" but with the primeval chaos of a watery deep prior to God's acts of creation. *Ex nihilo* was first propounded in the intertestamental period and was later elaborated by such theologians as Irenaeus and Augustine, in order to exclude the Hellenistic idea that matter on which God imposed form existed independently of him and constituted the source of evil in the world.[53] But Teilhard and Whitehead are as insistent as the church fathers that matter is in itself basically good rather than evil.[54] An additional motive in the *ex nihilo* doctrine was the assertion of the total sovereignty and freedom of God. Teilhard and Whitehead do limit God's omnipotence, but neither of them adopts an ultimate dualism or imagines a Platonic demiurge struggling to introduce order into recalcitrant matter; this is no cosmic carpenter who must use the materials on hand. Even Whitehead agrees that nothing has ever existed in independence of God.

[51] *PR,* p. 531.
[52] John B. Cobb, *A Christian Natural Theology* (Philadelphia: Westminster Press, 1965), pp. 211-12.
[53] Langdon Gilkey, *Maker of Heaven and Earth* (Garden City, N.Y.: Doubleday & Co., 1959), chap. iii; Bernhard W. Anderson, *Creation versus Chaos* (New York: Association Press, 1967).
[54] For example, *DM,* pp. 81-84.

In regard to creation as a continuing process, it is not altogether clear how Teilhard thinks of divine activity in relation to the order of nature. He avoids claims of God's intervention at specific points; he advocates "a creation of evolutionary type (*God making things make themselves*)." [55] Such passages would be consistent with the assumption that evolution is in principle scientifically explicable in terms of natural forces. In such a framework God's functions would be (1) to design and effect a set of natural laws which would of themselves gradually produce the foreordained cosmic progression and (2) to preserve and sustain this natural system in operation and concur in its results. If this is Teilhard's view, it would be essentially the scholastic notion that God as *primary cause* works through the operation of lawabiding *secondary causes*.

However, Teilhard's terminology frequently suggests that God's role is more active than this. He says that God "animates" and "vivifies" the world, "controls" and "leads" it to fulfilment. There are passages in which God is invoked to explain phenomena held to be scientifically inexplicable: "In Omega we have in the first place the principle we needed to explain both the persistent march of things toward greater consciousness, and the paradoxical solidity of what is most fragile." [56] God's action is not simply that of an Aristotelian "final cause" which is built into the functioning of all beings as they follow their inherent natures. Teilhard seems to believe that the "within" is a more effective vehicle of divine influence than the "without," but he does not clarify the modes of causality involved.

Whitehead, on the other hand, does assign to his equivalent of the "within" the crucial role in God's action on the world. He gives a detailed analysis of causation which includes the influence of past causes, present initiative, and divine purpose in the coming-to-be of each event. [57] Briefly stated, every new event is in part the product of the *efficient causation* of previous events, which in large measure—though never completely—determine it. There is always an element of *self-causation* or self-creation as an entity

[55] *VP*, p. 154.

[56] *PM*, p. 271.

[57] See, for example, Ivor Leclerc, *Whitehead's Metaphysics* (New York: Macmillan Co., 1958), pp. 170-74.

appropriates and responds to its past in its own way. In the creative selection from among alternatives in terms of goals and aims, there is *final causation*. By structuring these potentialities, God is the ground of both order and novelty, but the final decision is always made by the entity itself; at the human level this means that man is free to reject the ideals which God holds up to him. Whitehead thus works out in much greater detail than Teilhard a set of categories which allow for lawfulness, spontaneity, and divine influence in the "continuous creation" of the world.

V. GOD AND TIME

Teilhard, like Whitehead, holds that there is reciprocal interaction between God and the world. Both men criticize traditional thought for making creation too arbitrary and the world too "useless" and "ontologically superfluous" to God.[58] In place of what he calls the "paternalism" of the classical view, Teilhard substitutes "a functional completing of the One and the Multiple." [59] He maintains that the idea of the complete self-sufficiency of God makes him seem indifferent and leads to a deprecation of the value of the world and human endeavor in it. "Truly it is not the notion of the contingency of the created but the sense of the mutual completion of God and the world that makes Christianity live. . . . God, the eternal being in himself, is everywhere, we might say, in process of formation for us." [60]

Does Teilhard imply that God experiences change? There are a number of texts which speak of "the fulfilment of God," who "consummates himself only in uniting." "God is entirely self-sufficient, and nevertheless creation brings to him something vitally necessary." [61]

In the world viewed as the object of "creation," classical metaphysics accustoms us to see a sort of extrinsic production, issuing

[58] For example, "Contingence de l'univers et goût humain de survivre" (1954), scheduled for publication in *Oeuvres*, Vol. XI. Whitehead uses almost identical terms, e.g., *AI*, pp. 231 ff.

[59] "L'étoffe de l'univers," in *Oeuvres*, VII, 405.

[60] "Contingence de l'univers. . ."; "Trois contes comme Benson," in *Écrits du temps de la guerre*.

[61] "Comment je vois," quoted in Smulders, *op. cit.*, p. 276; "Christianisme et évolution" (1945), scheduled for publication in *Oeuvres*, Vol. XI.

from the supreme *efficiency* of God through an overflow of benevolence. *Invincibly*—and *precisely* in order to be able to act and to love fully at one and the same time—I am now led to see therein (in conformity with the spirit of St. Paul) a mysterious product of completion and fulfillment for the Absolute Being Himself.[62]

Teilhard has received considerable criticism for this idea. Thus, Tresmontant comments:

In order to avoid the Charybdis of a universe created in a purely contingent and arbitrary way, Teilhard falls into the Scylla of a well-known mythology. According to it, God fulfills Himself in creating the world. God engages in a struggle with the Many (the ancient chaos) in order to find Himself again, richer and pacified, at the terminus of this world. This is an old gnostic idea which is found in Boehme, Hegel and Schelling.[63]

Mooney suggests that Teilhard's statements are less objectionable if one notes that God's "need of the world" and "dependence on man" are the results of his own sovereign decision and free self-limitation rather than of a necessity imposed on him. He also points out that some of the statements about the world as "completing" God can be interpreted as referring to man's co-operation in building up the Body of Christ in the world. I would submit, however, that Teilhard's ideas do entail a revision of the traditional understanding of God's relation to temporality.

Whitehead goes further than Teilhard in modifying the classical assertion that God is timeless and immutable. God's purposes and character are eternal, but his knowledge of events changes as those events take place in their own spontaneity; he cannot know the future if his creatures have genuine freedom. God contributes to the world and is in turn affected by it (Whitehead calls

---

[62] "Le coeur de la matière" (1950), scheduled for publication in *Oeuvres*, Vol. X; quoted in Claude Tresmontant, *Pierre Teilhard De Chardin: His Thought* (Baltimore: Helicon Press, 1959), p. 93. On p. 30 of the mimeographed version given by Teilhard to George Barbour, the phrase "a mysterious product of *completion* and *fulfilment* for the Absolute Being Himself" is replaced by "a mysterious product of *satisfaction* for the Absolute Being Himself" (italics added). Smulders, *op. cit.*, p. 276, n. 17, mentions this difference between the two versions of the essay and considers the latter "less shocking."

[63] Tresmontant, *op. cit.*, p. 94. For Mooney's comments, see n. 35 above.

this the "consequent nature" of God). Yet in his "primordial nature" he is independent of events, unchanging in character and aim; his timeless envisagement of pure possibilities is unaffected by the world. Of all actual entities, he alone is everlasting, without perishing, without beginning or end. He is omniscient in that he knows all that is to be known, all ideal potentialities, and a past which is preserved without loss.[64]

Whitehead's idea of God's "primordial nature," like Teilhard's Alpha, refers to God's eternal purposes for the world; the "consequent nature," like Teilhard's Omega, includes the world's contribution to God. For Teilhard, however, Omega is primarily in the future, though it exerts an attraction on the present. For Whitehead, the two aspects represent two continuing roles of God which are abstractions from his unity:

But God, as well as being primordial, is also consequent. He is the beginning and the end. He is not the beginning in the sense of being in the past of all members. He is the presupposed actuality of conceptual operation, in unison of becoming with every other creative act. Thus by reason of the relativity of all things, there is a reaction of the world on God. . . . God's conceptual nature is unchanged, by reason of its final completeness. But the derivative nature is consequent upon the creative advance of the world.[65]

Whitehead holds that there is successiveness and becoming within God, since he prehends worldly events which come into being successively. But God is a non-temporal single occasion who does not perish and lose immediacy as every temporal entity does. Thus, creatures in the world are *temporal,* and God's "primordial nature" is *eternal* (unaffected by time), but his "consequent nature" is neither temporal nor eternal but *everlasting,* in Whitehead's terminology. One wonders whether Teilhard might not have found such a formulation acceptable.

VI. THE PROBLEM OF EVIL

Let us consider next Teilhard's assertion that evil is an inevitable by-product of an evolutionary process. There can be "no order in process of formation that does not, at all its stages,

[64] See Christian, *op. cit.,* pp. 364-403.
[65] *PR,* pp. 523-24.

involve disorder." [66] The pain of growth and the presence of failure and death are structural concomitants of evolutive development; in any advance, much must be left behind. Ours is "a particular type of cosmos in which evil appears necessarily and as abundantly as you like in the course of evolution—not by accident (which would not matter) but through the very structure of the system." "Pure unorganized multiplicity is not bad in itself; but because it is multiple, i.e. essentially subject in its arrangement to the play of chance, it is absolutely impossible for it to progress towards unity without producing evil in its wake through statistical necessity." [67]

Teilhard is particularly concerned to show that suffering is an integral part of any evolutionary system. "The world is an immense groping, an immense attack; it can only progress at the cost of many failures and much pain." [68] Suffering and death are not in themselves products of human sin or means to its expiation:

Following the classical view, suffering is above all a punishment, an expiation; it is efficacious as a sacrifice; it originates from sin and makes reparation for sin. Suffering is good as a means of self-mastery, self-conquest, self-liberation. In contrast, following the ideas and tendencies of a truly cosmic outlook, suffering is above all the consequence and price of a labor of development. It is efficacious as effort. Physical and moral evil originate from a process of becoming; everything which evolves experiences suffering and moral failure. . . . The Cross is the symbol of the pain and toil of evolution, rather than the symbol of expiation.[69]

In answer to the charge that his interpretation limits God's power, Teilhard replies that a world in evolution and a world without disorder are simply contradictory concepts:

We often represent God to ourselves as being able to draw a world out of nothingness without pain, defects, risks, without "breakage." This is conceptual fantasy which makes the problem of evil un-

[66] "Le Christ évoluteur" (1942), in *Cahiers* (Paris: Éditions du Seuil, 1965); scheduled for republication in *Oeuvres*, Vol. XI; cf. *DM*, p. 58, n. 1.

[67] "Comment je vois," quoted in Mooney, *op. cit.*, p. 108.

[68] "La signification et la valeur de la suffrance," in *Oeuvres*, VI, 63.

[69] "La vie cosmique," in *Écrits du temps de la guerre.*

solvable. No, it is necessary instead to say that God, despite His power, *cannot* obtain a creature united to Him without necessarily entering into struggle with some evil; because evil appears *inevitably* with the first atom. . . . Nobody has ever been astonished because God could not make a square circle or set aside an evil act. Why restrict the domain of impossible contradiction to these single cases? [70]

Teilhard holds that evil is intrinsic to an evolutionary cosmos as it would not be in an instantaneously produced one; like Whitehead, he claims that this insight exonerates God from responsibility for evil. He points out also that the failure and death of individuals contribute to the advance of the total process. God can make use of patterns which entail evil; he "transfigures them by integrating them into a better plan." [71] Sin is one more form of a universal and inevitable imperfection. Original sin is a result of structural conditions, not of an accidental act on the part of Adam and Eve. I cannot at this point discuss the theological adequacy of this view of sin; it is considered here only as a form of the wider phenomenon of evil—concerning which, his position is summed up in the following sentence: "Evil, in all its forms— injustice, inequality, suffering, death itself—ceases theoretically to be outrageous from the moment when, *Evolution becoming a Genesis,* the immense travail of the world displays itself as the inevitable reverse side—or better, the condition—or better still, the price—of an immense triumph." [72]

For Whitehead, too, evil is an inescapable concomitant of temporal process. "The nature of evil is that the characters of things are mutually obstructive." [73] But he sees evil as arising not simply from the incompatibility of alternative potentialities or the unavoidable conflict among a multiplicity of beings; it also stems from the choice of less valuable alternatives by individual beings. Whitehead's stress on the freedom of each creature in choosing evil seems more compatible with the traditional idea of sin than Teilhard's ideas of statistical necessity. But has White-

[70] "Note sur les modes de l'action divine dans l'univers" (1920), quoted in Tresmontant, *op. cit.,* p. 96.
[71] *DM,* p. 27.
[72] *FM,* p. 90.
[73] *PR,* p. 517; cf. *AI,* pp. 333 ff.

346 IAN G. BARBOUR

head exonerated God from responsibility for evil at the cost of leaving him powerless to do anything about it? Whitehead's God cannot insure that what is chosen will be the ideal or even the best of the options open, but he can hold out the higher option as a possibility, and he can achieve some positive value from every event. He shows how evil can be turned to good account by integration into a wider pattern of harmony which is everlastingly preserved in his memory. He "loses nothing that can be saved." [74]

Here again Whitehead limits God's power more drastically than Teilhard. Both men object to the idea of arbitrary divine acts. But Whitehead reacts more vehemently to the image of the "absolute monarch" which he sees in much Christian thinking.[75] His assumption of a pluralism of actual occasions leads him to a greater emphasis on the world's freedom. "The divine element in the world is to be conceived as a persuasive and not a coercive agency." [76] God lures every being toward co-operation in the production of value; he is a transforming influence in the world without determining it omnipotently. But he is ultimately in control through the power of a love which respects the integrity and freedom of his creatures; like human love, it influences by the response it evokes. Even more than in Teilhard's writing, the future actualization of the divine ideal is understood to be dependent on the world's activity.

VII. THE FUTURE OF THE WORLD

Consider, finally, Teilhard's expectations of the future. Evolution continues; its next stage will be the convergence of mankind into an interthinking network, the "noosphere." The new level of planetary consciousness will require global unification and the interpenetration of cultures.[77] Teilhard is confident that such a "social organism" will not submerge individuality and diversity in totalitarian uniformity. He seems to base this vision of the future on three kinds of assumptions:

1. *Extrapolation from the convergent past.*—He projects into the future the previous trend toward greater complexity, con-

[74] PR, p. 525.
[75] PR, pp. 146, 519; RM, pp. 55, 74-75; SMW, p. 266.
[76] AI, p. 213.
[77] FM, pp. 119, 167, 228 et passim.

sciousness, and personalization. This trend will now continue at the level of culture, which is the extension of biology; man's past is today transmitted by education more than by genes. Man has not followed the pattern of most creatures, namely, divergence into separate species. Moreover, convergence is now aided by the "planetary compression" imposed by the globe's limited surface and by improved intercommunication. Teilhard also introduces a more pragmatic argument: Faith in a convergent future and in human solidarity is a condition of mankind's continued survival. Teilhard's apologetic interest in addressing the unbeliever leads him to seek grounds for hope independent of revelation, even though it would appear that his own optimism had primarily Christian roots.

2. *The unity of the world process.*—Teilhard's belief in interdependence and unity is expressed in his portrayal of a convergent cosmos. Whitehead, by contrast, visualizes *each* event as converging from multiplicity toward a new unity, which serves in turn as part of the multiple data inherited by its successors. Teilhard sees the *whole* cosmic process as one slowly culminating event with a single goal. Here, as elsewhere, the monistic elements in his thought predominate over pluralistic ones, whereas in Whitehead the relative balance is reversed. (If space permitted, we could explore how their differing assumptions concerning pluralism are reflected in their political philosophies—e.g., their views of the relation between the individual and the collective.)

3. *The unity of all things in Christ.*—Teilhard's idea of the "cosmic Christ" combines his conviction of the organic interdependence of the world and his biblical belief in the centrality of Christ. Redemption is not the rescue of individuals from the world but the fulfilment of the world's potentialities; the corporate salvation of the cosmos is integral with the activity of continuing creation. The world converges to a spiritual union with God in Christ, whose relation to the world is organic and not merely juridical and extrinsic. The incarnation reveals God's participation in matter and his universal involvement in cosmic history. The mystical side of Teilhard is expressed in his extension of the imagery of the Mass; the sacramental transformation of matter which occurs in the Eucharist is the paradigm of the universal "Christification" of matter. In a prayer written in Asia on an occa-

sion when he had neither bread nor wine, he offers the whole creation as "the all-embracing Host." [78]

Teilhard's vision of the culmination of cosmic history in the Parousia shows once more the influence of his process thought on his reinterpretation of biblical doctrines. One change, of course, is the time scale; no imminent end is expected, and Teilhard speculates that we may have "millions of years" ahead of us. Again, he is more concerned about the salvation of individuals considered separately. In Teilhard's eschatology, moreover, the Kingdom will be a transformation of our present world, not the substitution of a new world. It will not come by an arbitrary intervention of God but by the consummation of a universe already prepared for it. The actualization of the potentialities of creation is a necessary condition for the final advent of the Kingdom, even though the *eschaton* is a gift from God and not simply the world's own achievement. Man and nature collaborate with God in bringing the cosmos to completion:

We continue from force of habit to think of the Parousia, whereby the Kingdom of God is to be consummated on Earth, as an event of a purely catastrophic nature—that is to say, liable to come about at any moment in history, irrespective of any definite state of Mankind. But why should we not assume, in accordance with the latest scientific view of Mankind in a state of anthropogenesis, that the parousiac spark can, of physical and organic necessity, only be kindled between Heaven and a Mankind which has biologically reached a certain critical evolutionary point of collective maturity? [79]

Whitehead agrees that there will be a long future which will involve quite new types of orders. To this novel future both man and God will contribute. "Man's true destiny as cocreator in the universe is his dignity and his grandeur." For Whitehead also, God is primarily fulfiller of the world and only derivatively its judge. But Whitehead differs greatly from Teilhard in expecting no integrated cosmic convergence and no final consummation of history. He departs from classical Christianity in his assumption that time is infinite. Moreover he disavows any detailed fixed divine plan.

[78] See *Hymn of the Universe* (New York: Harper & Row, 1965); *DM*, pp. 102 ff.; *PM*, p. 297.
[79] *FM*, p. 267; cf. *FM*, p. 22, *DM*, pp. 133-38, "Comment je vois," etc.

God has an unchanging general purpose, the maximum actualization of value and harmony; but he does not determine the world's free activity, and much that happens is contrary to his will. Within an over-all teleology, God envisages a plurality of goals which he continually revises in the light of the world's response to his initiative. Whitehead speculates that there may be various "cosmic epochs," some having types of orders unlike those with which we are familiar.[80] His vision of God does not guarantee any final victory of good in the world. But it does assure us that God is concerned for the world, that the future is not the product of human effort alone, and that God will not be finally defeated. Moreover, it does provide the confidence that whatever is of value will be preserved everlastingly in the divine memory. The only permanence lies in the world's contribution to God's consequent nature—which treasures without loss all that has been achieved, even while it remains open to further enrichment.[81]

In summary, Teilhard's process metaphysics, though not systematically developed, shows striking similarities with Whitehead's, especially in his views of temporality, interdependence, continuity, and the "within." There are close parallels in their presentations of continuing creation, interaction between God and the world, and the idea that the world's maturation is a condition for the fulfilment of God's purposes. However, Whitehead's ontology is fundamentally pluralistic, whereas Teilhard has stronger monistic tendencies which are particularly evident in his deterministic statements and in his expectation of cosmic convergence. Teilhard's beliefs in a beginning and end to history are closer to traditional representations of creation and eschatology, and his qualification of divine omnipotence is less extreme than Whitehead's. On some issues, however, Teilhard's monistic leanings seem to take him further from the biblical tradition—in his treatment of freedom, evil, and sin, for example, or in his apparent exaggeration of the unity and continuity of the world, or in his terminology concerning "the whole" and "the All," which often sound pantheistic despite his intentions. I hope to explore in another paper Teilhard's process theology in which is reflected the influence of his

[80] Cf. *PR*, pp. 139, 148, 171, 442; *MT*, pp. 78, 212. See last paragraph of *RM*.

[81] Cf. Cobb, *op. cit.*, pp. 218-23.

process metaphysics on his interpretation of such biblical themes as the integral nature of man, the significance of secular life, the unity of creation and redemption, and above all the idea of "the cosmic Christ."

SUGGESTED READINGS

On Teilhard and Process Thought

Barbour, Ian G. "Five Ways of Reading Teilhard," *Soundings,* 51 (1968), 115-145. Reprinted in *The Teilhard Review,* 3 (1968), 3-20.

———. "The Significance of Teilhard," *Christian Century,* 84 (1967), 1098-1102. Reprinted in *Changing Man: The Threat and the Promise.* Edited by Kyle Haselden and Philip Hefner. Garden City, N.Y.: Doubleday, 1968, pp. 130-141. Paperback—New York: Anchor Books.

Barthélemy-Madaule, Madeleine. *Bergson et Teilhard de Chardin.* Paris: Seuil, 1963.

Overman, Richard H. *Evolution and the Christian Doctrine of Creation: A Whiteheadian Interpretation.* Philadelphia: Westminster Press, 1967, pp. 225-229.

Rust, Eric C. *Evolutionary Philosophies and Contemporary Theology.* Philadelphia: Westminster Press, 1969.

Whitla, William. "Sin and Redemption in Whitehead and Teilhard," *Anglican Theological Review,* 47 (1965), 81-95.

Bibliography of Process Theology

The following bibliography is limited to writings by or on the authors of selections appearing in this anthology. Selections by other authors on themes in process theology can be found in the lists of suggested readings at the end of individual selections.

Although this bibliography does not intend to be complete, it seeks to provide rather extensive guidance into an author's writings relevant to process theology. Further bibliographical material and articles by other authors can be found in the journal Process Studies, *and in* Process Philosophy and Christian Thought, *edited by Delwin Brown, Ralph E. James, Jr., and Gene Reeves (Indianapolis: Bobbs-Merrill, 1971). Extensive listings on Teilhard de Chardin can be found in* Claude Cuénot, Teilhard de Chardin: A Biographical Study, *trans.* Vincent Colimore (Baltimore: Helicon, 1965, pp. 409-485; and in *Romano S. Almagno, O.F.M., A Basic Teilhard Bibliography: 1955-April, 1970 (New York: American Teilhard de Chardin Association, 1970).*

JOHN B. COBB, JR.

Books

Living Options in Protestant Theology: A Survey of Methods. Philadelphia: Westminster Press, 1962.

A Christian Natural Theology: Based on the Thought of Alfred North Whitehead. Philadelphia: Westminster Press, 1965.

The Structure of Christian Existence. Philadelphia: Westminster Press, 1967.

God and the World. Philadelphia: Westminster Press, 1969. Paperback —Philadelphia: Westminster Press.

Articles and Chapters in Books

"The Philosophical Grounds of Moral Responsibility: A Comment on Matson and Niebuhr," *The Journal of Philosophy,* 56 (1959), 619-621.

"Some Thoughts on the Meaning of Christ's Death," *Religion in Life*, 28 (1959), 212-222.

"Nihilism, Existentialism, and Whitehead," *Religion in Life*, 30 (1961), 521-533.

"Perfection Exists: A Critique of Charles Hartshorne," *Religion in Life*, 32 (1963), 294-304.

"Whitehead's Philosophy and a Christian Doctrine of Man," *The Journal of Bible and Religion*, 32 (1964), 209-220.

"From Crisis Theology to the Post-Modern World," *The Centennial Review*, 8 (1964), 174-188.

"Ontology, History, and Christian Faith," *Religion in Life*, 34 (1965), 270-287.

"Christian Natural Theology and Christian Existence," *The Christian Century*, 82 (1965), 265-267.

"Christianity and Myth," *The Journal of Bible and Religion*, 33 (1965), 314-320.

"The Finality of Christ in a Whiteheadian Perspective," *The Finality of Christ*. Edited by Dow Kirkpatrick. Nashville: Abingdon Press, 1966, pp. 122-154.

"Speaking About God," *Religion in Life*, 36 (1967), 28-39.

"The Possibility of Theism Today," *The Idea of God: Philosophical Perspectives*. Edited by Edward H. Madden, Rollo Handy, and Marvin Farber. Springfield, Ill.: Charles C. Thomas, 1968, pp. 98-123.

"What is Alive and What is Dead in Empirical Theology," *The Future of Empirical Theology*. Edited by Bernard E. Meland. Chicago: The University of Chicago Press, 1969, pp. 89-101.

"Freedom in Whitehead's Philosophy: A Response to Edward Pols," *The Southern Journal of Philosophy*, 7 (1969-70), 409-413.

"A Process Systematic Theology" [Review of *The Spirit and the Forms of Love*, by Daniel Day Williams], *The Journal of Religion*, 50 (1970), 199-206.

"A Whiteheadian Christology," *Process Philosophy and Christian Thought*. Edited by Delwin Brown, Ralph E. James, Jr., and Gene Reeves. Indianapolis: Bobbs-Merrill, 1971, pp. 382-398. Paperback—Indianapolis: Bobbs-Merrill.

ABOUT JOHN B. COBB, JR.

Gilkey, Langdon. Review of *A Christian Natural Theology, Theology Today,* 22 (1966), 530-545. Reply by Cobb: "Can Natural Theology be Christian?" *Theology Today,* 23 (1966), 140-142.

Guy, Fritz. "Comments on a Recent Whiteheadian Doctrine of God," *Andrews University Seminary Studies,* 4 (1966), 107-134.

Ogden, Schubert. "A Review of John B. Cobb's New Book: *A Christian Natural Theology,*" *Christian Advocate,* 9 (September 23, 1965), 11-12.

Ross, James F. "God and the World," *Journal of the American Academy of Religion,* 28 (1970), 310-315.

CHARLES HARTSHORNE

BOOKS

Beyond Humanism: Essays in the New Philosophy of Nature. Chicago: Willet, Clark & Company, 1937. Paperback—Lincoln, Neb.: University of Nebraska Press.

Man's Vision of God and the Logic of Theism. Chicago: Willet, Clark & Company, 1941; Hamden, Conn.: Archon Books, 1964.

The Divine Relativity: A Social Conception of God. New Haven: Yale University Press, 1948. Paperback—New Haven: Yale University Press.

Reality as Social Process: Studies in Metaphysics and Religion. Boston: The Beacon Press, 1953.

Philosophers Speak of God (with William L. Reese). Chicago: The University of Chicago Press, 1953. Paperback—Chicago: The University of Chicago Press.

The Logic of Perfection and Other Essays in Neoclassical Metaphysics. LaSalle, Ill.: Open Court, 1962. Paperback—LaSalle, Ill.: Open Court.

Anselm's Discovery. LaSalle, Ill.: Open Court, 1965. Paperback—LaSalle, Ill.: Open Court.

A Natural Theology for Our Time. LaSalle, Ill.: Open Court, 1967. Paperback—LaSalle, Ill.: Open Court.

Creative Synthesis and Philosophic Method. LaSalle, Ill.: Open Court, 1970.

ARTICLES AND CHAPTERS IN BOOKS

"Whitehead's Idea of God," in *The Philosophy of Alfred North Whitehead.* Edited by Paul A. Schilpp. Evanston and Chicago: Northwestern University, 1941, pp. 513-559.

"Is Whitehead's God the God of Religion?," *Ethics,* 53 (1943), 219-227.

"God and Man Not Rivals," *The Journal of Liberal Religion,* 6 (1944), 9-13.

"A New Philosophic Conception of the Universe," *The Hibbert Journal,* 44 (1945), 14-21.

"God as Absolute, Yet Related to All," *The Review of Metaphysics,* 1 (1947), 24-51.

"Whitehead's Metaphysics," *Whitehead and the Modern World: Science, Metaphysics, and Civilization, Three Essays on the Thought of Alfred North Whitehead,* by Victor Lowe, Charles Hartshorne, and A. H. Johnson. Boston: Beacon Press, 1950, pp. 25-41.

"The Immortality of the Past: Critique of a Prevalent Misinterpretation," *The Review of Metaphysics,* 7 (1953), 98-112.

"The Idea of God—Literal or Analogical?," *The Christian Scholar,* 39 (1956), 131-136.

"Whitehead and Berdyaev: Is There Tragedy in God?," *The Journal of Religion,* 37 (1957), 71-84.

"The Philosophy of Creative Synthesis," *The Journal of Philosophy,* 55 (1958), 944-953.

"A Philosopher's Assessment of Christianity," *Religion and Culture: Essays in Honor of Paul Tillich.* Edited by Walter Leibrecht. New York: Harper, 1959, pp. 167-180.

"The Buddhist-Whiteheadian View of the Self and the Religious Traditions," *Proceedings of the IXth International Congress for the History of Religions.* Tokyo, 1960, pp. 298-302.

"Whitehead and Contemporary Philosophy," *The Relevance of Whitehead: Philosophical Essays in Commemoration of the Centenary of the Birth of Alfred North Whitehead.* Edited by Ivor Leclerc, London: Allen and Unwin, 1961, pp. 21-43.

"God's Existence: A Conceptual Problem," No. 26 in *Religious Experience and Truth: A Symposium.* Edited by Sidney Hook. New York: New York University Press, 1961, pp. 211-219.

"Tillich and the Other Great Tradition," *Anglican Theological Review,* 43 (1961), 245-259.

"The Modern World and a Modern View of God," *The Crane Review,* 4 (1962), 73-85.

"Religion and Creative Experience," *The Unitarian Register and the Universalist Leader,* 141 (1962), 9-11.

"Whitehead's Novel Intuition," *Alfred North Whitehead: Essays on His Philosophy.* Edited by George L. Kline. Englewood Cliffs, N.J.: Prentice-Hall, 1963, pp. 18-26.

"Abstract and Concrete in God: A Reply," *The Review of Metaphysics,* 17 (1963), 289-295.

"Abstract and Concrete Approaches to Deity," *Union Seminary Quarterly Review,* 20 (1965), 265-270.

"The Development of Process Philosophy," *Introduction to Philosophers of Process.* Edited by Douglas Browning. New York: Random House, 1965, pp. v-xxii.

"Tillich and the Nontheological Meanings of Theological Terms," *Religion in Life,* 35 (1966), 674-685.

"Religion in Process Philosophy," *Religion in Philosophical and Cultural Perspective.* Edited by J. Clayton Feaver and William Horosz. Princeton: D. Van Nostrand, 1967, pp. 246-268.

"Pantheism," *The Encyclopaedia Britannica* (1967), pp. 233-234.

"The Dipolar Conception of Deity," *The Review of Metaphysics,* 21 (1967), 273-289.

"Divine Absoluteness and Divine Relativity," *Transcendence.* Edited by Herbert W. Richardson and Donald R. Cutler. Boston: Beacon Press, 1969.

"The God of Religion and the God of Philosophy," *Talk of God: Royal Institute of Philosophy Lectures,* II, 1967-1968. London: Macmillan, 1969.

"Necessity," *The Review of Metaphysics,* 21 (1967), 290-296.
"Process Philosophy as a Resource for Christian Thought," *Philosophi-*

cal Resources for Christian Thought. Edited by Perry LeFevre. Nashville: Abingdon, 1968, pp. 44-66.

About Charles Hartshorne

Diamond, Malcolm. "Contemporary Analysis: The Metaphysical Target and the Theological Victim," *The Journal of Religion,* 47 (1967), 210-232. Reprinted in *Process Philosophy and Christian Thought.* Edited by Delwin Brown, Ralph E. James, Jr., and Gene Reeves. Indianapolis: Bobbs-Merrill, 1971, pp. 143-170. Paperback—Indianapolis: Bobbs-Merrill.

James, Ralph E., Jr. *The Concrete God: A New Beginning for Theology —The Thought of Charles Hartshorne.* Indianapolis: Bobbs-Merrill, 1967.

Peters, Eugene H., *The Creative Advance: An Introduction to Process Philosophy as a Context for Christian Faith.* St. Louis: The Bethany Press, 1966, esp. pp. 77-104. Paperback—St. Louis: The Bethany Press.
———. *Hartshorne and Neoclassical Metaphysics: An Interpretation.* Lincoln: University of Nebraska Press, 1970.

Reese, William L. and Eugene Freeman (ed.). *Process and Divinity: The Hartshorne Festschrift.* LaSalle, Ill.: Open Court, 1964, esp. pp. 471-527; 533-560. Paperback—LaSalle, Ill.: Open Court.

Ogden, Schubert M. "Theology and Philosophy: A New Phase of the Discussion," *The Journal of Religion,* 44 (1964), 1-16.

Ogletree, Thomas W., "A Christological Assessment of Dipolar Theism," *The Journal of Religion.* 47 (1967), 87-99. Reprinted in *Process Philosophy and Christian Thought.* Edited by Delwin Brown, Ralph E. James, Jr., and Gene Reeves. Indianapolis: Bobbs-Merrill, 1971, pp. 331-346.

Charles Hartshorne Bibliography

Hartshorne, Mrs. Charles. "Published Writings of Charles Hartshorne," *Process and Divinity: The Hartshorne Festschrift.* Edited by William L. Reese and Eugene Freeman. LaSalle, Ill.: Open Court, 1964, pp. 579-91. Paperback—LaSalle, Ill.: Open Court.

James, Ralph E., Jr. "The Published Writings of Charles Hartshorne from 1929 to 1967" plus recent published works treating Hartshorne's thought, *The Concrete God.* Indianapolis: Bobbs-Merrill, 1967, pp. 195-217.

BERNARD M. LOOMER

ARTICLES AND CHAPTERS IN BOOKS

"Ely on Whitehead's God," *The Journal of Religion,* 24 (1944), 162-179. Reprinted in *Process Philosophy and Christian Thought.* Edited by Delwin Brown, Ralph E. James, Jr., and Gene Reeves. Indianapolis: Bobbs-Merrill, 1971, pp. 264-286. Paperback—Indianapolis: Bobbs-Merrill.

"Neo-Naturalism and Neo-Orthodoxy," *The Journal of Religion,* 28 (1948), pp. 79-91.

"Christian Faith and Process Philosophy," *The Journal of Religion,* 29 (1949), 181-203. Reprinted in *Process Philosophy and Christian Thought.* Edited by Delwin Brown, Ralph E. James, Jr., and Gene Reeves. Indianapolis: Bobbs-Merrill, 1971, pp. 70-98. Paperback—Indianapolis: Bobbs-Merrill.

"Empirical Theology Within Process Thought," *The Future of Empirical Theology.* Edited by Bernard E. Meland. Chicago: The University of Chicago Press, 1969, pp. 149-173.

BERNARD E. MELAND

BOOKS

Seeds of Redemption. New York: Macmillan, 1947.

The Reawakening of Christian Faith. New York: Macmillan, 1949.

Faith and Culture. New York: Oxford University Press, 1953.

Higher Education and the Human Spirit. Chicago: The University of Chicago Press, 1953. Especially Chapter V: "The Appreciative Consciousness," pp. 48-78. Paperback—Chicago: Seminary Co-operative Bookstore.

The Realities of Faith: The Revolution in Cultural Forms. New York: Oxford University Press, 1962. Paperback—Chicago: Seminary Co-operative Bookstore.

The Secularization of Modern Cultures. New York: Oxford University Press, 1966.

ARTICLES AND CHAPTERS IN BOOKS

"Interpreting the Christian Faith Within a Philosophical Framework," *The Journal of Religion,* 33 (1953), 87-102.

"From Darwin to Whitehead: A Study in the Shift in Ethos and Perspective Underlying Religious Thought," *The Journal of Religion,*
40 (1960), 229-245. Reprinted in *The Realities of Faith,* pp. 109-
136, and in *Process Philosophy and Christian Thought.* Edited by
Delwin Brown, Ralph E. James, Jr., and Gene Reeves. Indianapolis: Bobbs-Merrill, 1971, pp. 411-430. Paperback—Indianapolis: Bobbs-Merrill.

"New Perspectives on Nature and Grace," *The Scope of Grace: Essays
on Nature and Grace in Honor of Joseph Sittler.* Edited by Philip
Hefner. Philadelphia: Fortress Press, 1964, pp. 143-161.

"How is Culture a Source for Theology?" *Criterion,* 3 (1964), 10-21.

"The Structure of Christian Faith," *Religion in Life,* 37 (1968), 551-
562.

"The Empirical Tradition in Theology at Chicago," *The Future of Empirical Theology.* Edited by Bernard E. Meland. Chicago: The
University of Chicago Press, 1969, pp. 1-62.

"Can Empirical Theology Learn Something from Phenomenology?"
The Future of Empirical Theology. Edited by Bernard E. Meland.
Chicago: The University of Chicago Press, 1969, pp. 283-305.

ABOUT BERNARD E. MELAND

Spiegler, Gerhard. "Ground—Task—End of Theology in the Thought of
Bernard E. Meland," *Criterion,* 3 (1964), 34-38.

Williams, Daniel Day. "The Theology of Bernard E. Meland," *Criterion,*
3 (1964), 3-9.

———. "Some Queries to Professor Meland on His Paper 'How is
Culture a Source of Theology?' " *Criterion,* 3 (1964), 28-33.

Williamson, Clark M. " 'The Road to Realism': A Report on the Spring
Conference," *Criterion,* 3 (1964), 22-24.

BERNARD E. MELAND BIBLIOGRAPHY

Denham, Robert D. "A Bibliography of the Works of Bernard Meland"
[from 1928-1964], *Quest,* 8 (1964), 76-90.

SCHUBERT M. OGDEN

BOOKS

*Christ Without Myth: A Study Based on the Theology of Rudolf Bult-
mann.* New York: Harper and Brothers, 1961.

The Reality of God and Other Essays. New York: Harper and Row, 1966.

ARTICLES AND CHAPTERS IN BOOKS

"Beyond Supernaturalism," *Religion in Life,* 33 (1963-64), 7-18.

"Bultmann's Demythologizing and Hartshorne's Dipolar Theism," *Process and Divinity: The Hartshorne Festschrift.* Edited by William L. Reese and Eugene Freeman. LaSalle, Ill.: Open Court, 1964, pp. 493-513. Paperback—LaSalle, Ill.: Open Court.

"Theology and Philosophy: A New Phase of the Discussion," *The Journal of Religion,* 44 (1964), 1-16.

"The Possibility and Task of Philosophical Theology," *Union Seminary Quarterly Review,* 20 (1965), 271-279.

"Faith and Truth," *The Christian Century,* 82 (1965), 1057-1060.

"A Review of John B. Cobb's New Book: *A Christian Natural Theology,*" *Christian Advocate,* 9 (September 23, 1965), 11-12.

"The Challenge to Protestant Thought," *Continuum,* 6 (1968), 236-240.

"Present Prospects for Empirical Theology," *The Future of Empirical Theology.* Edited by Bernard E. Meland. Chicago: The University of Chicago Press, 1969, pp. 65-88.

"Toward a New Theism," *Process Philosophy and Christian Thought.* Edited by Delwin Brown, Ralph E. James, Jr., and Gene Reeves. Indianapolis: Bobbs-Merrill, 1971, pp. 173-187. Paperback—Indianapolis: Bobbs-Merrill. Previously printed in booklet by Muskingum College, New Concord, Ohio: *Theology in Crisis: A Colloquium on the Credibility of 'God',* March 20-21, 1967, pp. 3-18.

"Lonergan and the Subjectivist Principle," *The Journal of Religion,* 51 (1971), 155-172.

ABOUT SCHUBERT OGDEN

Brown, Delwin. "God's Reality and Life's Meaning: A Critique of Schubert Odgen," *Encounter,* 28 (1967), 256-262.

Gilkey, Langdon. "A Theology in Process: Schubert Ogden's Developing Theology," *Interpretation,* 21 (1967), 447-459.

Griffin, David. "Schubert Ogden's Christology and the Possibilities of Process Philosophy," *The Christian Scholar,* 50 (1967), 290-303. Reprinted in *Process Philosophy and Christian Thought.* Edited by Delwin Brown, Ralph E. James, Jr., and Gene Reeves. Indianapolis: Bobbs-Merrill, 1971, pp. 347-361. Paperback—Indianapolis: Bobbs-Merrill.

Neville, Robert. "Neoclassical Metaphysics and Christianity: A Critical Study of Ogden's *Reality of God," International Philosophical Quarterly,* 9 (1969), 605-624.

Robertson, John C., Jr. "Rahner and Ogden: Man's Knowledge of God," *Harvard Theological Review,* 63 (1970), 377-407.

W. NORMAN PITTENGER

BOOKS

The Word Incarnate: A Study of the Doctrine of the Person of Christ. New York: Harper and Brothers, 1959.

God in Process. London: SCM Press, 1967. Paperback—Naperville, Ill.: Allenson.

Light, Life, Love. London: A. R. Mowbray & Co., Ltd., 1967.

Process-Thought and Christian Faith. New York: Macmillan, 1968.

Alfred North Whitehead. Richmond: John Knox Press, 1969. Paperback.

Christology Reconsidered. London: SCM Press, 1970.

'The Last Things' in a Process Perspective. London: Epworth Press, 1970.

ARTICLES AND CHAPTERS IN BOOKS

"The Christian Philosophy of John Scotus Erigena," *The Journal of Religion,* 24 (1944), 246-257.

"Degree or Kind? A Christological Essay," *The Canadian Journal of Theology,* 2 (1956), 189-196.

"A Contemporary Trend in North American Theology: Process-Thought and Christian Faith," *The Expository Times,* 76 (1965), 268-73.

"Some Implications, Philosophical and Theological, in John Knox's Writing," *Christian History and Interpretation: Studies Presented to John Knox.* Edited by W. R. Farmer *et al.* Cambridge: The University Press, 1967, pp. 3-16.

"Toward a More Christian Theology," *Religion in Life,* 36 (1967), 498-505.

"Bernard E. Meland, Process Thought and the Significance of Christ," *Religion in Life,* 37 (1968), 540-550.

"Reconceptions of Christian Faith in Light of Process Thought," *Princeton Seminary Bulletin,* 61 (1968), 29-37.

"A Fresh Look at Christian Moral Theology, *Religion in Life,* 38 (1969), 548-554.

"The Attributes of God in the Light of Process Thought," *The Expository Times,* 81 (1969), 21-23.

"Christian Theology After the 'Death of God'," *The Church Quarterly,* 1 (1969), 306-314.

"The Doctrine of Christ in a Process Theology," *The Expository Times,* 82 (1970), 7-10.

"Process Theology Revisited," *Theology Today,* 27 (1970), 212-220.

ABOUT W. NORMAN PITTENGER

Hick, John. "Christology at the Cross Roads," *Prospect for Theology: Essays in Honor of H. H. Farmer.* Edited by F. G. Healey. Welwyn Garden City: James Nisbet, 1966, pp. 139-166.

Mascall, E. L. *Theology and the Future.* New York: Morehouse-Barlow, 1968, pp. 100-126. Paperback.

McIntyre, John. *The Shape of Christology.* Philadelphia: The Westminster Press, 1966, pp. 138-141.

W. NORMAN PITTENGER BIBLIOGRAPHY

McDonald, Durstan R. "W. Norman Pittenger—A Bibliography: 1931-1964," *Lux in Lumine: Essays to Honor W. Norman Pittenger.* Edited by R. A. Norris, Jr. New York: Seabury Press, 1966, pp. 158-167.

WALTER E. STOKES

ARTICLES

"Whitehead's Prolegomena to Any Future Metaphysics," *Heythrop Journal,* 3 (1962), 42-50.

"A Select and Annotated Bibliography of Alfred North Whitehead," *The Modern Schoolman,* 3 (1962), 135-153.

"Recent Interpretations of Whitehead's Creativity," *The Modern Schoolman,* 39 (1962), 309-333.

"Freedom as Perfection: Whitehead, Thomas and Augustine," *Proceedings of the American Catholic Philosophical Association,* 36 (1962), 134-142.

"Whitehead's Challenge to Theistic Realism," *The New Scholasticism,* 38 (1964), 1-21.

"Is God Really Related to This World?" *Proceedings of the American Catholic Philosophical Association,* 39 (1965), 145-151.

"God for Today and Tomorrow," *The New Scholasticism,* 43 (1969), 351-378. Reprinted in *Process Philosophy and Christian Thought.* Edited by Delwin Brown, Ralph E. James, Jr., and Gene Reeves. Indianapolis: Bobbs-Merrill, 1971, pp. 244-263. Paperback— Indianapolis: Bobbs-Merrill.

"Truth, History, and Dialectic," *Proceedings of the American Catholic Philosophical Association,* 43 (1969), 85-90.

PIERRE TEILHARD DE CHARDIN

WRITINGS OF PIERRE TEILHARD DE CHARDIN

Oeuvres de Pierre Teilhard de Chardin, 10 volumes. Paris: Seuil, 1955-1969.

The Phenomenon of Man. Revised English Edition. New York: Harper and Row, 1965. Paperback—New York: Harper Torchbook.

The Divine Milieu. New York: Harper and Row, 1965. Paperback— New York: Harper Torchbook.

The Future of Man. Translated by Norman Denny. New York: Harper and Row, 1964. Paperback—New York: Harper Torchbook.

Hymn of the Universe. Translated by Simon Bartholomew. New York: Harper and Row, 1965. Paperback—New York: Harper.

Pierre Teilhard de Chardin/Maurice Blondel Correspondence. With notes and commentary by Henri de Lubac, S.J. Translated by William Whitman. New York: Herder and Herder, 1967.

Writings in Time of War. Translated by René Hague. New York: Harper and Row, 1968.

Science and Christ. Translated by René Hague. New York: Harper and Row, 1968.

How I Believe. Translated by René Hague. New York: Harper and Row, 1969. Paperback.

BIOGRAPHY

Cuénot, Claude. *Teilhard de Chardin: A Bibliographical Study.* Translated by Vincent Colimore. Baltimore: Helicon, 1965.

Speaight, Robert. *The Life of Teilhard de Chardin.* New York: Harper and Row, 1967.

Introductory Works and General Studies

Francoeur, Robert T. *The World of Teilhard de Chardin*. Baltimore: Helicon, 1961.

Hefner, Philip. *The Promise of Teilhard: The Meaning of the Twentieth Century in Christian Perspective*. Philadelphia: Lippincott, 1970. Paperback—Philadelphia: Lippincott.

Kopp, Joseph V. *Teilhard de Chardin: A New Synthesis of Evolution*. New York: Paulist Press, Deus Books, 1964. Paperback.

Murray, Michael H. *The Thought of Teilhard de Chardin: An Introduction*. New York: Seabury Press, 1966.

Towers, Bernard. *Teilhard de Chardin*. Richmond, Virginia: John Knox Press, 1966. Paperback.

Tresmontant, Claude. *Pierre Teilhard de Chardin: His Thought*. Baltimore: Helicon Press, 1959.

Theological and Philosophical Studies

Baltazar, Eulalio R. *Teilhard and the Supernatural*. Baltimore: Helicon, 1966.

Barthélemy-Madaule, Madeleine. *Bergson et Teilhard de Chardin*. Paris: Seuil, 1963.

Benz, Ernst. *Evolution and Christian Hope. Man's Concept of the Future from the Early Fathers to Teilhard de Chardin*. Translated by Heinz G. Frank. New York: Doubleday, 1966. Paperback—New York: Anchor Books.

Bravo, Francisco. *Christ in the Thought of Teilhard de Chardin*. Translated by Cathryn B. Larme. Notre Dame: Notre Dame University Press, 1967.

Chauchard, Paul. *Man and Cosmos: Scientific Phenomenology in Teilhard de Chardin*. Translated by George Courtright. New York: Herder and Herder, 1965.

Crespy, Georges. *La pensée théologique de Teilhard de Chardin*. Paris: Éditions Universitaires, 1961.

———. *From Science to Theology: An Essay on Teilhard de Chardin*. Translated by George H. Shriver. Nashville: Abingdon Press, 1968.

Delfgaauw, Bernard. *Evolution, the Theory of Teilhard de Chardin*. Translated by Hubert Hoskins. New York: Harper and Row, 1969.

Faricy, Robert L., S.J. *Teilhard de Chardin's Theology of the Christian in the World.* New York: Sheed and Ward, 1967.

Francoeur, Robert T. *Perspectives in Evolution.* Baltimore: Helicon, 1965.

Gray, Donald P. *The One and the Many: Teilhard de Chardin's Vision of Unity.* New York: Herder and Herder, 1969.

Hulsbosch, Ansfried. *God in Creation and Evolution.* New York: Sheed and Ward, 1965.

Lubac, Henri de, S.J. *Teilhard de Chardin: The Man and His Meaning.* Translated by René Hague. New York: Hawthorn Books, 1965. Paperback—New York: Mentor-Omega.

———. *Teilhard Explained.* Translated by Anthony Buono. New York: Paulist Press, Deus Books, 1968. Paperback.

———. *The Religion of Teilhard de Chardin.* Translated by René Hague. New York: Desclee, 1967. Paperback—New York: Paulist Press, Deus Books.

Maloney, George A., S.J. *The Cosmic Christ: From Paul to Teilhard.* New York: Sheed and Ward, 1968.

Martin, Sister Maria Gratia, I.H.M. *The Spirituality of Teilhard de Chardin.* Westminster, Md.: Newman Press, 1968.

Mooney, Christopher F., S.J. *Teilhard de Chardin and the Mystery of Christ.* New York: Harper and Row, 1966. Paperback—Garden City, N.Y.: Image Books.

North, Robert, S.J. *Teilhard and the Creation of the Soul.* Milwaukee: Bruce, 1967.

Philippe de la Trinité, O.C.D. *Pour et Contre Teilhard de Chardin.* Paris: Édition Saint-Michel, 1970.

Philippe de la Trinité, O.C.D. *Rome et Teilhard de Chardin.* Paris: Fayard, 1964.

Philippe de la Trinité, O.C.D. *Teilhard de Chardin Etude Critique.* Paris: La Table Ronde, 1968.

Rabut, Olivier, O.P. *Teilhard de Chardin: A Critical Study.* New York: Sheed and Ward, 1961.

Rideau, Emile, S.J. *The Thought of Teilhard de Chardin.* Translated by René Hague. New York: Harper and Row, 1967.

Smulders, Piet, S.J. *The Design of Teilhard de Chardin.* Translated by Arthur Gibson. Westminster, Md.: Newman Press, 1967.

Van Til, Cornelius. *Pierre Teilhard de Chardin—Evolution and Christ.* Philadelphia: Presbyterian and Reformed Pub. Co., 1966. Paperback.

Wildiers, Norbert Max, O.F.M. Cap. *An Introduction to Teilhard de Chardin.* Translated by Hubert Hoskins. New York: Harper and Row, 1968.

Zaehner, R. C. *Matter and the Spirit: Their Convergence in Eastern Religions, Marx and Teilhard de Chardin.* New York: Harper and Row, 1963.

PIERRE TEILHARD DE CHARDIN BIBLIOGRAPHY

Almagno, Romano, O.F.M. *A Basic Teilhard Bibliography.* New York: American Teilhard de Chardin Association, 1970.

Archivum Historicum Societatis Jesu. Rome (Via dei Penitenzieri, 20). A complete bibliography of all works, in all languages, which are published each year on Teilhard since 1956 appears annually in the July-December issue.

Cuénot, Claude. "Bibliography of the Works of Teilhard de Chardin," in *Teilhard de Chardin: A Biographical Study.* Translated by Vincent Colimore. Baltimore: Helicon, 1965, pp. 409-485.

ALFRED NORTH WHITEHEAD

BOOKS

Science and the Modern World. New York: Macmillan, 1925. Paperback—New York: Free Press.

Religion in the Making. New York: Macmillan, 1926. Paperback—New York: Meridian Books.

Symbolism: Its Meaning and Effect. New York: Macmillan, 1927. Paperback—New York: Capricorn.

Process and Reality: An Essay in Cosmology. New York: Macmillan, 1929. Paperback—New York: Free Press.

The Function of Reason. Princeton: Princeton University Press, 1929. Paperback—Boston: Beacon Press.

The Aims of Education and Other Essays. New York: Macmillan, 1929. Paperback—New York: Free Press.

Adventures of Ideas. New York: Macmillan, 1933. Paperback—New York: Free Press.

Modes of Thought. New York: Macmillan, 1938. Paperback: New

York: Free Press.

Essays in Science and Philosophy. New York: Philosophical Library, 1947; Westport, Conn.: Greenwood Press, 1968.

Dialogues of Alfred North Whitehead. As recorded by Lucian Price. Boston: Little, Brown, 1954. Paperback—New York: New American Library.

ARTICLES AND CHAPTERS IN BOOKS

"Immortality," *The Philosophy of Alfred North Whitehead.* Edited by Paul A. Schilpp. Evanston and Chicago: Northwestern University, 1941, pp. 682-700.

"Autobiographical Notes," *The Philosophy of Alfred North Whitehead.* Edited by Paul A. Schilpp. Evanston and Chicago: Northwestern University, 1941, pp. 3-14.

ON ALFRED NORTH WHITEHEAD'S PHILOSOPHY

Christian, William A. *An Interpretation of Whitehead's Metaphysics.* New Haven: Yale University Press, 1959. Paperback—New Haven: Yale University Press.

Emmet, Dorothy M. *Whitehead's Philosophy of Organism.* London: Macmillan, 1932; New York: St. Martin's, 1966.

Hartshorne, Charles, A. H. Johnson and Victor Lowe. *Whitehead and the Modern World.* Boston: Beacon Press, 1950.

Jordan, Martin. *New Shapes of Reality: Aspects of A. N. Whitehead's Philosophy.* London: George Allen and Unwin, 1968; New York: Humanities Press, 1968.

Kline, George L. (ed.) *Alfred North Whitehead: Essays on His Philosophy.* Englewood Cliffs, N.J.: Prentice Hall, 1963.

Lawrence, Nathaniel. *Whitehead's Philosophical Development.* Berkeley: University of California Press, 1956; New York: Greenwood Press, 1968.

Leclerc, Ivor (ed.) *The Relevance of Whitehead: Philosophical Essays in Commemoration of the Centenary of the Birth of Alfred North Whitehead.* New York: Macmillan, 1961.

———. *Whitehead's Metaphysics: An Introductory Exposition.* New York: Macmillan, 1958.

Lowe, Victor. *Understanding Whitehead.* Baltimore: The Johns Hopkins Press, 1962. Paperback—Baltimore: The Johns Hopkins Press.

Reese, William L. and Eugene Freeman (ed.) *Process and Divinity: The Hartshorne Festschrift*. LaSalle, Ill.: Open Court, 1964, pp. 51-268. Paperback: LaSalle, Ill.: Open Court.

Sherburne, Donald W. *A Key to Whitehead's Process and Reality*. New York: Macmillan, 1966.

Schilpp, Paul A. (ed.). *The Philosophy of Alfred North Whitehead*. Evanston and Chicago: Northwestern University, 1941.

ALFRED NORTH WHITEHEAD BIBLIOGRAPHY

Lowe, Victor and Robert C. Baldwin. "Bibliography of the Writings of Alfred North Whitehead to November, Published through January 3, 1951 (With Selected Reviews)," *The Philosophy of Alfred North Whitehead*. Edited by Paul A. Schilpp. New York: Tudor, 1951, pp. 745-778.

Parmentier, Alix. *La philosophie de Whitehead et le problème de Dieu*. Paris: Beauchesne, 1968, pp. 587-635. Contains English and foreign language entries relevant to Whitehead to 1967.

HENRY NELSON WIEMAN

BOOKS

Religious Experience and Scientific Method. New York: Macmillan, 1926; Westport, Conn.: Greenwood Press, 1968.

The Wrestle of Religion with Truth. New York: Macmillan, 1927.

(With Douglas Clyde Macintosh and Max Carl Otto) *Is There a God? A Conversation*. Chicago: Willett, Clark, 1932.

(With Bernard E. Meland) *American Philosophies of Religion*. Chicago: Willett, Clark, 1936.

(With Walter Marshall Horton) *The Growth of Religion*. Chicago: Willett, Clark, 1936.

The Source of Human Good. Chicago: The University of Chicago Press, 1946. Paperback—Carbondale: Southern Illinois University Press, 1964.

Man's Ultimate Commitment. Carbondale: Southern Illinois University Press, 1958. Paperback—Carbondale: Southern Illinois University Press.

Intellectual Foundations of Faith. New York: Philosophical Library, 1961.

Religious Inquiry: Some Explorations. Boston: Beacon Press, 1968.

ARTICLES AND CHAPTERS IN BOOKS

"Appreciating Jesus Christ," *The Christian Century,* 47 (1930), 1181-1184.

"Was God in Jesus?" *The Christian Century,* 51 (1934), 589-591.

"Some Blind Spots Removed," *The Christian Century,* 56 (1939), 116-118.

"Power and Goodness of God," *The Journal of Religion,* 23 (1943), 266-275.

"The Promise of Protestantism—Whither and Whether," *The Protestant Credo.* Edited by Vergilius Ferm. New York: *Philosophical Library,* 1953, pp. 163-187.

"A Waste We Cannot Afford," *Unitarian Universalist Register-Leader,* 143 (November, 1962), 11-13.

"Time and Man's Ultimate Commitment," *The Journal of Religion* 34 (1954), 173-186.

ABOUT HENRY NELSON WIEMAN

Bretall, Robert W. (ed.) *The Empirical Theology of Henry Nelson Wieman.* New York: Macmillan, 1963. Paperback—Carbondale: Southern Illinois University Press.

Hartshorne, Charles and William L. Reese. *Philosophers Speak of God.* Chicago: The University of Chicago Press, 1953, pp. 395-408. Paperback—Chicago: University of Chicago Press.

HENRY NELSON WIEMAN BIBLIOGRAPHY

"Bibliography of the Works of Henry Nelson Wieman to 1961," *The Empirical Theology of Henry Nelson Wieman.* Edited by Robert W. Bretall. New York: Macmillan, 1963, pp. 399-414. Paperback—Carbondale: Southern Illinois University Press.

DANIEL DAY WILLIAMS

BOOKS

God's Grace and Man's Hope. New York: Harper and Brothers, 1949.

What Present-Day Theologians Are Thinking. 3rd edition, revised. New York: Harper and Row, 1967, pp. 72 ff. Paperback—New York: Harper and Row.

The Spirit and the Forms of Love. New York: Harper and Row, 1968.

ARTICLES AND CHAPTERS IN BOOKS

"Christianity and Naturalism: An Informal Statement," *Union Seminary Quarterly Review,* 12 (May, 1957), 47-53.

"Moral Obligation in Process Philosophy," *The Journal of Philosophy,* 56 (1959), 263-270. Reprinted in *Alfred North Whitehead: Essays on His Philosophy.* Edited by George L. Kline. Englewood Cliffs, N.J.: Prentice Hall, 1963, pp. 189-195.

"God and Time," *The South East Asia Journal of Theology,* 2 (January, 1961), 7-19.

"Deity, Monarchy, and Metaphysics: Whitehead's Critique of the Theological Tradition," *The Relevance of Whitehead.* Edited by Ivor Leclerc. New York: Macmillan, 1961, pp. 353-372.

"How Does God Act?: An Essay in Whitehead's Metaphysics," *Process and Divinity.* Edited by William L. Reese and Eugene Freeman. LaSalle, Ill.: Open Court, 1964, pp. 161-180. Paperback—LaSalle, Ill.: Open Court.

"The Theology of Bernard E. Meland," *Criterion,* 3 (1964), 3-9.

"Some Queries to Professor Meland on His Paper 'How is Culture a Source of Theology?' " *Criterion,* 3 (1964), 28-33.

"The New Theological Situation," *Theology Today,* 24 (1968), 444-463.

"Suffering and Being in Empirical Theology," *The Future of Empirical Theology.* Edited by Bernard E. Meland. Chicago: The University of Chicago Press, 1969, pp. 175-194.

ABOUT DANIEL DAY WILLIAMS

Cobb, John B., Jr. "A Process Systematic Theology" [Review of *The Spirit and the Forms of Love*], *The Journal of Religion,* 50 (1970), 199-206.

Subject and Author Index

371